Praise for *The Boy Crisis*

"Original, thoughtful, and filled with gems of practical wisdom to understand and support the future of boys."
—Jack Canfield, coauthor of the #1 *New York Times* bestselling Chicken Soup for the Soul® series

"As an activist in the women's movement, I'm proud of expanding life choices for our daughters. But no one did the same for our sons—until now. Dr. Warren Farrell shines his searchlight on the 'boy problem with no name' in this totally absorbing, astonishing, and masterful book. Best of all, he offers parents and educators straightforward solutions with a heart full of compassion."
—Gail Sheehy, author of *Passages* and *Understanding Men's Passages*

"*The Boy Crisis* is the most important book of the 21st century. Farrell and Gray are absolutely brilliant. Their decades of experience addressing gender issues, and meticulous research, shines light on why our sons are failing, and why we live in a world of increasing violence. More important, they offer solutions that we can all unite behind. If you care about the very survival of humankind, you must read this book."
—Jed Diamond, PhD, author of *The Irritable Male Syndrome*

"A must-read for anyone who cares about our boys, our schools, our culture, and the future of our country."
—Helen Smith, PhD, author of *Men on Strike*

"*The Boy Crisis* is a groundbreaking and exhaustively researched book about one of the most vital and disastrous yet underreported topics in America by one of the most thoughtful writers of our time. As the wife of a dad-deprived man, and the mother of a dad-enriched son, I can personally vouch for its deep significance."
—Suzanne Venker, Fox News contributor and author of *The War on Men*

"In the last fifty years, nobody in the world has written more searchingly about men and women than Warren Farrell and John Gray. Finding these two brilliant minds joined in *The Boy Crisis* is like witnessing a pair of searchlights merging and focusing on the most important social question of our age: What is to become of the boys of today, the men of tomorrow?"
—**Neil Lyndon, author of *No More Sex War***

"*The Boy Crisis* is a heroic, compassionate book with clear analyses and accessible solutions. As a boy who grew up in crisis myself, I recognize how Drs. Farrell and Gray give us the roadmap to a better future for our boys, our families, and our country."
—**Thabiti Boone, former President Obama White House Fatherhood and Mentoring Initiative champion, who chose raising his daughter over an NBA career**

"Reading *The Boy Crisis* is disturbing and disquieting. The deprivation, alienation, and loneliness I experienced with my father I imitated to a large degree with my own sons. With this exceptional book, Warren Farrell shows us a clear path to how we, as men, and as families, can break this cycle."
—**David Meggyesy, former NFL linebacker and regional director of the NFL Players' Association and author of *Out of Their League***

"I now have two young great-grandsons and *The Boy Crisis* will my bible."
—**Erin Pizzey, founder of the world's first domestic violence shelters for women**

"A very important, powerful book, backed by incontrovertible research to allow each parent and professional to positively reshape boys' lives."
—**Michael Gurian, author of *The Wonder of Boys* and *Saving Our Sons***

"With the compassionate wisdom of a wise cultural warrior, Dr. Farrell emerges as a counselor not only to *The Boy Crisis*, but to society itself as he identifies the underlying conditions faced by our sons, from the 'Hero

Paradox' to male-style depression, and ways to rectify our sons' mental, physical, economic, and educational health."
—**Barbara Marx Hubbard, Foundation for Conscious Evolution**

"*The Boy Crisis* is a goldmine. As a foster parent to hundreds of male teens at a group center, I know that had their parents been able to read The Boy Crisis, they would have avoided being taken from their homes, and experienced more effective and loving parenting."
—**Dr. Vanessa Dahn, executive director,**
Safe Landing Group Center

"A must-read for any parent of a boy. You will find guidance in every area from physical health to mental health to creating stability for your son. Not only does it explain how, but the book provides reasons why, so you understand the full picture."
—**Rachel Alexander, contributor, *Townhall***

"As a therapist for thirty-plus years, I have witnessed firsthand the quiet yet lethal crisis Drs. Farrell and Gray have identified by a socialization which prepares young men more effectively for death than life. With depth and urgency, Farrell and Gray give ever-penetrating attention to its amelioration."
—**Lori D. Galperin, LCSW, cofounder,**
Castlewood Treatment Centers

"Farrell and Gray present an insightful, candid, and eye-opening view of the problems facing millions of boys and young men."
—**Dr. Linda Neilson, professor of education, Wake Forest University;**
author of *Father–Daughter Relationships*

"Any help given to boys is often seen as taking away from helping girls. Warren Farrell helps us to understand why, if boys lose, girls lose as well. But what boys need to flourish is different from what girls need to flourish. Warren Farrell gets this. As the father of a daughter, I believe we all can benefit from reading *The Boy Crisis*."
—**Leonard Sax, MD, PhD, *New York Times*–bestselling author**
of *Boys Adrift* and *Why Gender Matters*

"*The Boy Crisis* is a game-changing book. If you love your son, brother, husband, boyfriend, or any other man, it will change your life and theirs. It is filled with insight, compassion, and a powerful vision of the evolution of love. A must-read."
 —Dr. Marc Gafni, president, Center for Integral Wisdom

"Poignant, inspiring, and information-packed."
 —Troy Kemp, executive director,
 National Center for the Development of Boys

THE
BOY
CRISIS

THE
BOY
CRISIS

Why Our Boys Are Struggling and
What We Can Do About It

WARREN FARRELL, PhD
and
JOHN GRAY, PhD

BenBella Books, Inc.
Dallas, TX

BenBella Books, Inc.
10440 N. Central Expressway, Suite 800
Dallas, TX 75231
www.benbellabooks.com
Send feedback to feedback@benbellabooks.com

Printed in the United States of America
10 9 8 7 6 5 4 3 2 1

Library of Congress Cataloging in Publication Control Number: 2017056217.

ISBN 9781942952718 (trade cloth)
ISBN 9781942952725 (electronic)

Editing by Leah Wilson
Copyediting by Miki Alexandra Caputo
Proofreading by Sarah Vostok and Cape Cod Compositors, Inc.
Indexing by WordCo Indexing Services
Text design by Publishers' Design and Production Services, Inc.
Text composition by Aaron Edmiston
Cover design by Connie Gabbert
Jacket design by Sarah Avinger
Printed by Lake Book Manufacturing

Distributed to the trade by Two Rivers Distribution, an Ingram brand
www.tworiversdistribution.com

Special discounts for bulk sales (minimum of 25 copies) are available. Please contact Aida Herrera at aida@benbellabooks.com.

To my wife, Liz; sister, Gail; daughters, Alex and Erin; son-in-law, Hutch; and grandson, Finley
—Warren

To my wife, Bonnie
—John

Contents

PART IV: Dad-Deprived Boys Versus Dad-Enriched Boys

PART V: Heroic Intelligence Versus Health Intelligence

PART VI: ADHD: Treatment With or Without Medication

Is There Really a
Boy Crisis?

I am sorry for being a man.

—David Cunliffe, New Zealand Leader
of the Labour Party, 2014

In the middle of an invigorating dinner conversation involving a former governor, a minister, an owner of a PR firm, two authors, and a UC Berkeley professor (three men and three women, two strong feminists), one of the hosts, author Sam Keen, asks, "If you were born today, which would you rather be—a boy or a girl?"

Every man answered, "A girl." As did two of the three women.

At another dinner party, Melissa, the daughter of close friends, told my wife, Liz, and I that she was pregnant. I asked her husband, Andy, what he looked forward to if their child were a boy. Andy's eyes lit up. "When he's a baby, I look forward to lifting him real high, and rolling around with him. I guess I mostly think about him being a little older, and us roughhousing, and playing ball. And I can't wait to teach him how to fish. And to play soccer. I remember when my dad pretended to let me kick a ball past him and score a goal, the first thing I yelled to Mom when we got home was how I beat Dad. I want to do that for him."

Later that evening, I asked Andy, "If you had to choose, which would you prefer—a boy or girl?" After a second's hesitation, he said in a serious tone, "A girl. Today . . . today, a girl." When I asked why, he was matter-of-fact. "Girls today can be whatever they want to be; guys can't. And I'm more afraid a boy would screw up in school or get buried in video games . . . stuff like that."

Of course, girls still face cultural biases, both external and internal. But I was struck that despite Andy's powerful fantasy of playing with a son, his desire for his child to have the best possible life trumped his fantasy of what he could contribute to it, and thus a daughter became his choice.

In the past, most dads wanted their first child to be a son. No longer. Andy's deeper "fatherhood instinct"—wanting what is best for his child over what he wants for himself—is in sync with most dads today: **dads-to-be are almost twice as likely to prefer a daughter to a son**.

As for moms-to-be, they are 24 percent more likely to prefer their firstborn child to be a daughter.

In the past, most of us would have imagined that daughters would be more likely to move back in with their parents as adults than sons. Because that was reality. No longer. Today, **young men between twenty-five and thirty-one are 66 percent more likely than their female counterparts to be living with their parents.**

For the first time in recent history, young men are more likely to live with their parents than with a partner. In contrast, women are more likely to live with a partner.

Kevin's dad, William, told me, "When Kevin moved back in to his childhood room shortly after we gave him a wonderful thirtieth birthday party, I can remember thinking to myself, 'This is "proof" I've failed as a dad.' I never said this to Kevin, but it still haunts me."

Kevin nevertheless picked up on his dad's shame. And yet something bothered Kevin even more: "This girl and I were flirting something fierce at a party. I wanted to ask her to leave with me, but I couldn't invite her back to my parents' home, so I just kept flirting. Finally, she says it: 'It's so noisy in here. Should we go somewhere else?' So I suggest a bar. She looks at me like something's wrong with me. Then her eyes become seductive, and she runs her finger over the buttons on my shirt, and says, 'Maybe your place? . . . You live near here?'

"I said I did, but that I lived with my parents. I wanted to ask if she had a place we could go to, but I saw how the second I said I lived with my parents, her body language froze. She excused herself 'to go to the ladies' room,' and when she came out, she walked over to a girlfriend, and they both started sneaking glances over at me and laughing. I don't ever remember feeling more humiliated."

On the opposite end of the productivity spectrum is the boy who is highly motivated. What do he and Kevin have in common? Sensitivity. And shame. Amid an atmosphere of Bill Cosbys, Harvey Weinsteins, and other fallen icons, each newly revealed sexual harasser, rapist, and serial killer leaves a sensitive boy feeling ashamed that he is male. You can feel the shame Royce Mann has absorbed by age fifteen, as expressed in this excerpt of his 2017 prose poem performed for HATCH, a global community designed to "hatch" creativity.

> . . . recently I became a man. It happened the first time a woman avoided me on the sidewalk . . . when the woman ten feet in front of me glanced back . . . She changed direction, crossing the street like Moses did the Red Sea . . . Her footsteps taught me the danger of my own hands. Taught me what it truly means to be a man, though I may never know what it means to fear one. You know, in that moment, I finally understood Peter Pan. You see, I wanted to stay a boy, not become a man, because a man, as I now knew, was a mix between a father, brother, and attacker, mostly the latter.

The shame Royce has already absorbed teaches him "the danger of my own hands." His primary view of male identity is someone who is feared. His conclusion: "I wanted to stay a boy"—a Peter Pan—because a man is "mostly" an "attacker." You can just feel the shame—and this from a brilliant boy.

The good news: Royce is unlikely to be a sexual harasser. But in no part of Royce's talk did he discuss the healthy aspects of masculinity that he looked forward to contributing to his family and the world. Feeling like he is programmed to increasingly become an attacker will limit his contributions to those motivated by guilt.

Whether a Kevin or a Royce, your son is growing up at a time when an article in *The Atlantic* titled "The End of Men" so resonated with *The Atlantic*'s thoughtful readers that the author was asked to make it into a book, also to be called *The End of Men*. Imagine your daughter growing up at a time that predicted "The End of Women." No boy or girl has ever before grown up in a time that predicted the end of their gender. **Anticipating "the end of men" is not exactly an inspiration for your son's life journey.**

But can our sons' situation really be labeled a crisis? Or is it just that our daughters are doing better and our sons are remaining the same? As the chapters on the evidence make clear, boys are declining in a dramatic way in virtually every key metric. And this worldwide decline among our sons will also hurt our daughters, their marriages, and their children's emotional and global security.

Yet we are largely blind to the problem. A Google search on September 16, 2017, for "boy crisis" reveals a first page half-devoted to a band called Boy Crisis. Among results related to a cultural boy crisis, about half the articles dismiss it as a myth.

Understanding the depth and international scope of the boy crisis has deep psychological benefits. If your son is experiencing a failure to launch it is tempting to feel, like William did when Kevin moved back home, that *you* failed to launch as a parent. But when you witness the degree to which this is happening with boys in all developed nations, you realize it is not your fault. Yet there is a lot you can do both to prevent your son from being absorbed by the crisis and to help him turn the crisis into an opportunity. And that's what *The Boy Crisis* is about.

My Personal Journey into *The Boy Crisis*

It was 1970, and the leaders of the women's movement were being labeled "bra burners," "ugly," "dykes," and "man-haters." I asked some of my students at Rutgers to role-play—or "walk a mile in the moccasins"—of these women's movement leaders. I then organized the remaining students to play either the silent majority or the name-calling minorities. They played their roles passionately. I responded by asking them to do the unforgivable: reverse roles.

My students' passion for my passion to have them understand women's issues inspired me to change my PhD dissertation to focus on the messages of the women's movement. The National Organization for Women (NOW) in New York City got wind of my verve and asked me to form "men's consciousness-raising groups"—support groups with a feminist filter. Before I knew it, I was elected to NOW's board of directors, speaking around the world on behalf of feminism and, after each engagement, forming hundreds of both men's and women's support groups in Johnny Appleseed–type fashion.

As NOW and the perspective of feminists went mainstream, especially in the universities, my speaking career boomed. I was delighted that the expansion of opportunities for women had begun to exceed my expectations.

Later in the seventies, as I began to witness a sharp increase in divorces, I also noticed that many of the children were living primarily with their moms. The cultural meme about dads was focused on dad's money, not on his involvement. So when dads did not pay child support, we labeled them "deadbeats." I accepted that meme. Until I also listened to these dads in my men's groups.

Once I listened, I was struck by how much the dads cared. When they vented their anger about discrimination against them in family court, they sounded legalistic, angry, and bitter. But when I asked them about their children, tears flowed down their cheeks. Their anger was but a mask for vulnerability—the powerlessness they felt as words like "visitation" and "custody" made them feel like second-class citizens, and how being able to see their children only every other weekend made them feel that anything they had to contribute would be washed away between visits.

I watched some of the dads spiral downward into depression, and others desperately try to finance court fights to be equally involved dads. Some of the dads couldn't afford the legal fight. Other dads tried to earn enough money, only to feel they then didn't have the time to be equally involved dads.

As this was transpiring, my sister, Gail, an elementary school teacher in Allendale, New Jersey, called to my attention how a few of her students whose productivity and attitude had uncharacteristically deteriorated ultimately shared with her that their parents were in the throes of a divorce.

When *Why Men Are the Way They Are* was published in 1986, the subsequent foreign translations led to dads worldwide sharing with me similar frustration, depression, and anger. Back in the US, the children of early seventies divorces were becoming high schoolers. After my presentations parents would share with me, disappointment flooding their eyes, their sadness at the challenges their children were experiencing. Yet as a researcher and feminist I wondered whether the children's problems were due more to the emotional stressors of divorce, to being deprived of their dads, or to other factors. This inspired the research that ultimately resulted in my book *Father and Child Reunion* in 2001. In that research, dad deprivation surfaced as the leading cause of more than twenty-five social, psychological, academic, and physical health problems that overwhelmed these children.

The research available back then made it clear that both boys and girls without dads suffered. But by the time I was writing *The Boy Crisis*, it was apparent that dad deprivation had an even more negative impact on boys. And that the damage to the boys was also longer lasting.

The question was why. A leading cause was that the women's movement had done a brilliant job preparing girls for the divorces that developed countries had gained the luxury to permit, yet no one was doing the same for our sons. So our daughters were experiencing expanded senses of purpose (raise children, raise money, or some combination of the two), while our sons were experiencing a "purpose void." As I discovered more about boys' purpose void, I could see why those without the guidance of a dad to fill that void were falling so far behind boys who were enriched by their dads' involvement.

In brief, I saw how "dad deprivation" and the purpose void had a compounding effect.

Worse, I increasingly saw how boys' historical sense of purpose required encouraging boys to develop a "heroic intelligence" that is at odds with their "health intelligence"—with both their physical and mental health. I watched parents, peers, and cheerleaders yelling, in essence, "First and ten, do it again!" without realizing they were encouraging the boy to risk a concussion. Then when he was injured, they would send him get-well cards so he could "get back in the game" and face yet another concussion.

As I was beginning to make these connections, my wife Liz and I moved to Mill Valley, California. There we met John Gray, the author of *Men Are from Mars, Women Are from Venus*, and John and I took the first of what is now about four hundred hikes together amid the redwoods and streams of Mill Valley. I was surprised to discover that while John is famous for helping men and women develop compassion for their differences, John had also spent the last decade doing pioneering research on nonmedical solutions to ADHD—solutions that addressed its underlying causes. Since one of the most common faces of our sons' vulnerability is ADHD, I asked John to share with you what he had shared with me.

He went well beyond that. In part VI John offers parents and educators a way out of a core dilemma: their acceptance of prescription drugs as a quick fix that may create new problems, to be fixed with more drugs.

During this period, in April of 2009, I got an unexpected call from the White House. President Obama had just created the White House Council on Women and Girls. I was asked, given my background with NOW, if I would be an adviser. I responded enthusiastically, and added that there was also a need for a White House Council on Boys and Men— to work synergistically with the Council on Women and Girls—to alert the nation to the challenges our sons are facing.

When I was told that would require a separate proposal, I invited a multipartisan coalition of thirty-two of the country's leading authors and practitioners to work with me to draw up that proposal. It took us eighteen months of debating and listening to integrate the best of our thinking. And although neither presidents Obama nor Trump have created a council on boys and men, our debates exposed me to some of the best thinking on boys' and men's issues.

In the nine years of research that followed, my understanding deepened considerably, and I shifted my focus from what the federal government can do to what parents, teachers, and local communities can do. And another shift occurred. When I was working on the multipartisan proposal, I had to consider everyone's feelings. With *The Boy Crisis*, I am trusting that when being straightforward conflicts with being politically correct, you would prefer that I be straightforward. By the end of *The Boy Crisis* I want you to walk away with a picture that reflects your family and son's reality. Some of that may be hard to hear, but solutions that are not grounded in reality soon crumble, and are replaced by a deeper hopelessness.

For each problem in *The Boy Crisis* I try to offer multiple solutions that you can tailor to your family. But with the much greater complexities today's families face in raising children who have flexible choices rather than prescribed roles, I have found that the most important single tool you can give your son is a once- or twice-weekly "family dinner night."

However, family dinner night can easily become "family dinner nightmare" if not conducted well. For example, striking the right balance between empathizing with your son and expecting him to empathize with you and his siblings is both an art and a discipline. So both the art and discipline are outlined in Appendix A's family dinner night guidelines.

And throughout the book, as we encounter areas in which your son is likely to repress feelings, I will call these to your attention as possible family dinner night topics.

When I Write "Your Son" in This Book: Who *The Boy Crisis* Is For

In *The Boy Crisis* I often use the phrase "your son." That's because I am asking that each reader take this journey through the eyes of a boy who might be your son.

Two caveats. First, the *you* implied in "your son" is *not* code for moms. *You* emphatically includes dads. Second, the *son* in "your son" is not your son alone. It is all our sons. If you are a teacher, "your son" is each male student. If you lead a faith-based community, "your son" means each boy in your community.

Do men read "self-help" books? Yes. They are called "business books"—self-help books for dads to do better in their business so their families can do better in life. Today, as more moms work, for the first time in history more dads are able to focus more directly on the "business" of their families. Now that the boy crisis is his business, *The Boy Crisis* is his business book.

As for parents with daughters, well, John and I have five daughters between us. And while the focus of *The Boy Crisis* is on boys, we are always mindful of the impact the boy crisis has not just on our daughters, but on all girls and women. Men and women may be from different planets, but we are all rowing the same family boat. Between the sexes, there is no such thing as "winning." **Whenever only one sex wins, both sexes lose**.

You'll also discover in *The Boy Crisis* that even if you never have a child, you are working every day to pay taxes to compensate for the boy crisis. For example, we'll see how ISIS recruits have in common a purpose void from dad deprivation that is vulnerable to exploitation. ISIS's growth alone has meant the need for more spending on homeland security, cyber-warfare, defense, and taking care of new veterans. And that's in addition to the more direct costs of crimes and prisons, plus the costs incurred when the government's welfare programs serve as a "substitute husband." When we add the tax income never received from unemployed men, just in the United States we're paying in excess of a *trillion* dollars *per year*.

Of course, these direct costs ignore the psychological costs. The fear of our children's school being the next victim of a school shooting, which we'll see is more likely among dad-deprived boys. Or the anxiety that our son's yearning for a father may make him more vulnerable to a sexual predator.

In brief, *The Boy Crisis* is written for everyone.

In a Book About Boys, Why Discuss Men?

We cannot solve the boy crisis by looking only at boys. Seeing my dad forfeit promotions so he could have more time with my sister, brother, mom, and me gave me a role model in my dad that was more than a financial womb—more than a success object.

I discuss men in a book about boys because men are the role models who either offer your son structure and inspiration, or leave him rudderless and depressed. Especially with his dad, the boy tends to become what he sees in the men around him: "like father, like son," "he's a chip off the old block." Or they are the role models who leave your son scared as to how to pursue life—his divorced dad prevented from seeing him, living in a small apartment, and turning to drink. If he cannot articulate what scares him, he may withdraw into video games and video porn and develop a virtual life to mask his depression. What is past is prologue.

Similarly, even if your son does live with both his dad and mom, if he sees his dad doing work that is meaningless to him because he needs to support the family, it can dampen your son's inspiration to work hard, marry, and have children himself. He may experience a "failure to launch." Especially if your son is bright and sensitive, this can emanate not from laziness or ignorance, but from his unconscious wisdom.

The Great Law of the Iroquois is that our most sacred duty is to think seven generations ahead in making any decision—to be aware of whether the decisions we make today will benefit not just ourselves and our children, but our children's children several generations into the future. *The Boy Crisis* takes this multigenerational view as we look at our heritage of heroic intelligence and see how it affects our sons' and grandsons' health intelligence.

Grandpa, Take Note

When grandpa was a dad, no research documented why a dad's typical style of hands-on parenting, such as roughhousing, or his expectation that his children serve rather than be served, was so crucial to his children's development. *The Boy Crisis* makes that clear so grandpa can both understand his value to his grandson, and share that with grandma.

But there is one change that requires grandpa's attention: When grandpa grew up, masculinity came with a built-in sense of purpose of being the provider-protector (e.g., warrior; sole breadwinner). Today, there is a purpose void. *The Boy Crisis* can help grandparents understand the purpose void, as well as how to help inspire their grandson with new senses of purpose. A grandpa I knew, for example, told me he used to whisper in his grandson's ear how playing with him makes him happier than any work he'd done. His grandson, although successful at work, has refused promotions that would have required him to travel so, he says, "I can do what I love most—be with my precious kids and wife."

The Goal of *The Boy Crisis*

A generation ago, a boy who was a "geek" in school was subjected to derision. So his parents might have tried to get him to lift weights or join the wrestling team—trying to protect him from derision, but perhaps unwittingly signaling to him the unacceptability of his nature. However, had a book catalyzed a national discussion that helped his parents foresee how technology would allow geeks to be among the respected leaders and multimillionaires of the future, they could have helped their son feel optimistic about his future and inspired to cultivate his gifts rather than lift weights in shame.

While no vision of the future can be perfect, the goal of *The Boy Crisis* is to integrate the half century of national discussion about the challenges faced by girls and women with an equally nuanced national discussion about those facing boys and men. *The Boy Crisis* explores the major causes of that crisis, plus hundreds of solutions every parent, teacher, and policymaker can employ.

Since every boy is different, read this book first, then listen to your son to determine whether what John or I write applies to him. Since "a prophet is never a prophet close to home," you may wish to give the book directly to your son so he may discover himself, as well as directly to your daughter so she may love with knowledge and lead with empathy.

Warren Farrell, PhD
Mill Valley, California
November 1, 2017
www.warrenfarrell.com

PART I

Is There Really a Boy Crisis?

CHAPTER I

The Crisis of Our Sons' Mental Health

Murder and Suicide

When a boy drives down the serpentine road of mental health, feeling depressed and isolated because he feels no one who knows the real him loves him, no one needs him, and there's no hope of that changing, he may one day find a cliff and drive off. That choice may be direct, as with suicide, or it may be indirect, as in a school shooting. School shootings are homicides that are also suicides—even if the boy doesn't end his own life literally, for all practical purposes, his life is still ended.

The rate of mass shootings has tripled since 2011.[1] We blame guns, violence in the media, violence in video games, and poor family values. Each is a plausible player. But our daughters live in the same homes, with the same access to the same guns, video games, and media, and are raised with the same family values. Our daughters are not killing. Our sons are.

The murder-suicide combination of school and other mass shootings is largely young white boys' way of driving off the cliff at the end of mental health's tortuous road. Consider three of the most notorious white male shooters: Adam Lanza (Sandy Hook), Elliott Rodgers (UC Santa Barbara), and Dylann Roof (Emanuel African Methodist Episcopal Church in Charleston).

The National Academy of Sciences reports that **the increase in suicide among white males led to as many white males' lives lost to suicide as have been lost to AIDS.**[2] (Only Native Americans commit suicide at rates similar to whites; Hispanics and Asian Americans commit suicide at about one-third the rate of whites—about the same rate as the African American population.[3])

African American males, by contrast, stick with murder and being murdered. Thus, while only 6 percent of the overall population, black males make up 43 percent of murder victims.[4] More black boys between ten and twenty are killed by homicide than by the next *nine* leading causes of death *combined*.[5]

Suicides increase as the pressures of the male role and hormones increase. Before puberty, the suicide rates among males and females are about equal. However, between ten and fourteen, boys commit suicide at almost twice the rate of girls.

Between fifteen and nineteen, boys commit suicide at four times the rate of girls; and between twenty and twenty-four, the rate of male suicide is between five and six times that of females.[6]

The Connection Between Masculinity and Suicide

Before age 9   Age 10–14   Age 15–19   Age 20–24

Source: Centers for Disease Control and Prevention (CDC) and Web-based Injury Statistics Query and Reporting System (WISQARS)[7]

You have probably seen pictures of men in the Great Depression jumping from tall buildings, falling faster than the stock market, only to be spread out on the sidewalk below, lost to their world and loved ones. **Worth less, men considered themselves worthless.** Thus, at the height of the Depression, 154 men committed suicide for each 100 women.[8]

Yet by 2015, in good economic times, boys and men were committing suicide *three and a half* times more often than women.[9]

Is this because females are inherently better at handling stress? Perhaps not. When men and women are exposed to similar pressures to perform, as among men and women in the military, the female suicide rate soars almost as high as the male rate.[10] But men, like Brad, are prone to doing it differently.

In 2016 Brad returned from his third tour of duty in Afghanistan with a reasonable amount of economic security. But he felt like a stranger to both his wife and himself, and quickly alienated his children with his temper. His PTSD and the tension at home left him feeling like a burden. One day, after losing his temper again, Brad bought his wife her favorite flowers and their children the newest PlayStation, gave his wife and kids especially long and loving hugs and kisses, and took out the older of the family cars. He said he was going shopping; instead, he sped quickly down a curved road and "skidded" off a cliff.

Looking back, Brad's widow "knew" he had committed suicide— "After he'd 'lose it' he'd always say he was worth more as an insurance policy than a husband and dad." But because he had faked it as a car accident so the family could get the insurance, he wasn't counted as a suicide.

Since both young and old men are often more motivated to commit suicide when they feel their loved ones will benefit more from their money than themselves, they have a need to cover it up so that insurance will pay. So although more veterans commit suicide each year than were killed in the wars in Iraq and Afghanistan,[11] even that staggering number is probably a vast underestimation of the true suicide rate of male veterans, as well as older men, who are also, as we'll see in part V, more prone to feel they are worth more to their family dead.

The Incarceration Nation Versus the Prevention Nation

There is probably no better evidence of the increase of the boy crisis as a mental health problem than the fact that the US jail and prison population increased by more than 700 percent between 1973 and 2013.[12] Of that population, 93 percent are male and are disproportionately young.[13]

700% Increase in Prison Population (93% Male), 1972–2013

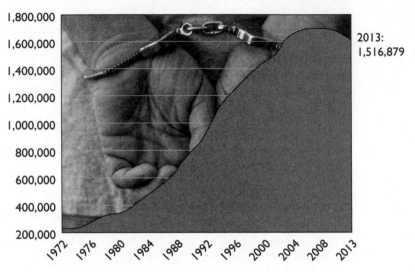

2013:
1,516,879

Source: Bureau of Justice Statistics Prisoners Series[14]

The American Psychological Association (APA) calls the United States "incarceration nation."[15] Why? We are 5 percent of the world's population with almost 25 percent of the world's prisoners.[16] The APA estimates half of those prisoners have mental health problems.

We often allow that the disproportionate percentage of young black men in prison may reflect our racism, but rarely contemplate whether, since the other half of "black men" is "men," that it may *also* reflect our sexism. Might the 700 percent increase in the 93 percent male prison population in the last half century mean that the way we our raising our sons in the last half century is leading to a deterioration in their mental health? Addressing that question would be preventive. **To date, our prison debate has focused on rehabilitation versus incarceration, rather than prevention versus imprisonment.** And just as this hurts African Americans more than any other race, it hurts our young men more than our young women.

Less Boy Crisis, Less Budget Crisis: Mental Health *Pays* the Taxes

Can we afford to focus on preventing imprisonment? We can't afford *not* to. **Prison spending has increased at five times the rate of spending per grade school student.**[17] Even in progressive California, twenty-three new prisons have been built for every one new college since 1980.[18]

In addition to the immeasurable grief and self-blame among family and friends, suicide has an estimated economic cost to the United States of $44 billion *a year.*[19] And suicide is only the tip of the mental health iceberg. For *childhood* mental disorders alone—predominantly affecting our sons—the United States now spends a quarter *trillion* dollars annually.[20]

We pay taxes to rebuild what mentally unhealthy boys destroy. Prevention cultivates mentally healthy sons who pay taxes. The less our boy crisis, the less our budget crisis. Investing in turning our "incarceration nation" into a prevention nation will cost us less—in every way.

CHAPTER 2

The Crisis of Our Sons' Physical Health

Being male is now the single largest demographic factor for early death.

—Randolph Nesse, Director of the Center for Evolution and Medicine at Arizona State University[1]

In Nesse's summary assessment of a study of premature deaths in twenty countries, in which he found that "being male is now the single largest demographic factor for early death," the word "now" is important. It is only *now* that boys and men under fifty are *twice* as likely to die as girls and women the same age. That is a greater life-expectancy gap than at any time since World War II.[2]

Your son's increased vulnerability can also be detected in the change in his sperm count. Boys today have sperm counts less than half of what their grandfathers had at the same age.[3] And the problem is getting worse. The average sperm count in the United States continues to drop 1.5 percent every year.[4]

"May You Live Until 120" . . . or Not

When Jews traditionally wish for others to live to 120 (inspired by the Torah, in which Moses was said to live to 120), their wish includes their sons. But your son's reality makes that much less likely for him than for your daughter.

Our sons, husbands, and fathers die at a younger age from fourteen out of fifteen leading causes of death.

Rank	Cause of Death	M–F age-adjusted death ratio
1	Diseases of heart	1.6
2	Malignant neoplasms (cancers)	1.4
3	Lower respiratory (lung) diseases	1.2
4	Accidents (unintentional injuries)	2.0
5	Cerebrovascular disease (stroke)	1.0
6	Alzheimer's disease	0.7
7	Diabetes mellitus	1.5
8	Influenza (respiratory) and pneumonia	1.3
9	Nephritis (kidney inflammation)	1.4
10	Intentional self-harm (suicide)	3.7
11	Septicemia (blood poisoning)	1.2
12	Chronic liver disease and cirrhosis	2.0
13	Essential hypertension and hypertensive renal (kidney) disease	1.1
14	Parkinson's disease	2.3
15	Pneumonitis (lung inflammation)	1.8

Source: Adapted from National Center for Health Statistics' *National Vital Statistics Reports*[5]

The disease that gives your son a predictably shorter life is the outcome. Our expectations for him as a male contribute to the cause.

The "Death Professions": Your Son's "Glass Cellar"

Every day, 150 workers die from hazardous working conditions.[6] And 92 percent of them are male.[7]

The less formal education and more children your son has, the more likely he is to feel he'll help his family live a better life by risking his own life working in what might be called "the death professions."[8]

Why? To receive the "death professions bonus." Jobs like crab fishing in Alaska (think *Deadliest Catch*), working on an oil rig, in a coal mine, as a lumberjack, long-distance driver of a semi (or eighteen wheeler), as a welder a hundred feet above a bridge, as a cab driver at night in an inner city, as a pilot of a small plane dropping pesticides, as a roofer, or a construction worker—they all pay more money than safer, similarly low-education jobs. In exchange for this "death professions bonus," millions of dads with less education risk their lives to give their children options they don't have. And tens of thousands of single young men try to save up enough to make themselves attractive as a future dad.

Most of us take for granted how the home we live in was created at the risk of the lives of young men. For example, the wood in your home likely began its journey with young lumberjacks risking their lives as loggers. The trees they felled were then hauled by long-distance truckers (another hazardous profession) to a site near to what would become your home. On their way, the truckers repeatedly stopped for fuel extracted by other men who had risked their lives on oil rigs (as in *Deepwater Horizon*). And the wood was ultimately used by construction workers and roofers—who, in the United States, die at the rate of one per working hour.

A friend of mine was a firefighter. He and his wife, both Mormon, had eight children. One day, when my friend was in his early fifties, his wife, in tears, called to tell me he had died of lung cancer from the chemical-laden fumes he had ingested over the years. Few parents realize, as they proudly watch their son don a firefighter's uniform, that in hazardous professions, death *after* the job takes *twelve* times as many of our sons' lives as death on the job.[9] Hazardous occupations on the job are merely the smoke; occupation-remnant diseases—such as black lung disease among miners—are the fire.

In aggregate, these jobs might be thought of as "glass cellar" jobs—all-male, because it is almost exclusively our sons who are willing to risk death so their family will have a better life.

"Bigorexia" and Obesity

While your daughter may suffer from anorexia or bulimia, your son is more prone to respond to the pressures he feels with bigorexia or obesity.

Jonathan was a freshman when his older brother, a junior, was making a name for himself as their high school's lead wrestler. After his brother introduced him to a teammate, his brother casually revealed that the teammate had later laughed that he and his brother were like the two guys in the movie *Twins*—his brother like the Arnold Schwarznegger character, and him more like Danny DeVito.

The reference haunted Jonathan. He knew he couldn't bridge the height gap, but he set out to make sure no one ever saw him as the short weakling again. He began lifting weights, ultimately working out obsessively and taking massive quantities of supplements. Proud of his progress, but still feeling unable to match his brother, he began taking steroids. He was soon abusing them.

Jonathan suffered from *bigorexia*, the body dysmorphia that occurs when a young man like Jonathan continues working on his physical strength, often temporarily magnifying it with steroids, in the hope that it will fill the black hole of his psychic wound. Just as the cultural ideal of thinness blinds many friends and parents of anorexic girls to their suffering and need for help, so our respect for male muscle blinded Jonathan's friends and parents to his suffering and need for help.

And bigorexia has further complications: if your son is preoccupied with body image, he is also more vulnerable to binge-drinking and overuse of drugs.[10]

While Jonathan's psychological struggle was marked by muscle mass and motivation, the struggle of Jonathan's friend Austin was marked more by fat mass and lack of motivation. When Jonathan's motivation stepped up, Austin couldn't keep up and just gave up. Taking refuge in video games and eating, for Austin the presence of online friends couldn't compensate for his feelings of exclusion by real-life friends, and led to obesity and depression.

While the rate of obesity among adolescent girls has stabilized, the rate for our sons is increasing.[11] Aside from their physical health, this damages both our sons' psychological security, and our nation's global security: a third of young men are not fit for military service owing to obesity and other physical and mental problems.[12] And this problem extends to other professions on which our security depends: 70 percent of firefighters and 80 percent of police officers are also obese or overweight.[13] The US has the highest rate of overweight males among all major countries.[14]

Whether through bigorexia or choosing the death professions, our sons, like our daughters, are often responding to what they feel will give them more approval and respect. For example, in the same way that many guys are attracted to quasi-anorexic girls, so many of our daughters find themselves attracted to firefighters, marines in dress uniform, football players in padded uniforms, and winners in other sports that put our sons' lives at risk.

The Crisis of Our Sons' Economic Health

The challenge for your son's grandpa was grandpa's job going nowhere; the challenge for your son is his job going elsewhere. Your son is more likely to seek a job in a sector that is being increasingly outsourced overseas—as with computer technology and manufacturing, as well as online jobs. Your daughter is more likely to hold jobs in stable sectors that are more recession proof, like health and education, both of which are 75 percent women.[1]

Half the 6.5 million US jobs *lost* since the 2009 recession were in manufacturing and construction.[2] In contrast, personal care and home health aides are projected to be the fastest-growing occupations, and women are predicted to fill the majority of these new jobs.[3]

In addition to outsourcing, something else has changed since grandpa's day. If grandpa wasn't educated, he probably supported his family with his muscle. But **your son will enter an economy that has made a transition from muscle to mental—or from muscle to microchip.** For example, many of the nation's approximately 1.7 million truck drivers are predicted to be largely replaced by trucks that drive themselves, such as those currently being tested by Uber-owned Otto.[4]

The implications for your son? **Over the last forty years, the median annual earnings of a boy with just a high school diploma dropped 26 percent.**[5] Without that diploma, his chance of being unemployed during his prime working years (twenty-five to fifty-four) is 20 percent, almost 400 percent greater than the average.[6]

If your son plans to live in an urban area, he'll likely live in one of the 147 US cities in which young women under thirty haven't just caught up to their male peers, but now outearn them (by an average of 8 percent). In only three cities do young men earn as much or more.[7] And single women are now buying their own homes at two and a half times the rate of single men.[8]

If your son is heterosexual, these transitions lead to a bigger problem, one which may be tough to hear. But I promised you I would be straightforward so that our solutions can be built on your son's real vulnerabilities.

Every Kiss Begins with Kay . . . Still

You've heard the ad for Kay Jewelers, "Every kiss begins with Kay." Translation: a diamond for a kiss. Or, every kiss begins with *pay*.

Is this still true today? Yes. On a survey on splitting the bill on a first date, 72 percent of women responded that the man should pay the full bill.[9] Moreover, 82 percent of the men agreed.[10]

If your son and a woman who wants children take a liking to each other and make a mutual decision to have dinner, he may fear that if he asks for "equal pay for equal pleasure" when it comes to paying the check, he increases his likelihood of being rejected as a cheapskate. The message he hears is "no money, no honey."

And if your son is unemployed? Three out of four women say they would not date an unemployed man.[11] In contrast, for two-thirds of men, dating an unemployed woman is a nonissue.[12]

If your son is heterosexual, then he discovers **the harder it is to find a job, the harder it is to find a woman**. Especially if that woman has children—or wants them. If your son is unemployed, a future mom may assume he'll just be one more child she needs to support.

This is neither women's nor men's fault. Historically, women whose children survived had found men who provided—both for them and their children. Nature programmed men to be willing to die without complaining by programming women to reproduce with alpha men, not whining men. That is our genetic heritage. The process led to our survival in the past, but is not needed for our future. But since we can't change evolution overnight, let's help your son through the transition.

If your son is tall and good looking, he may appeal to the one out of four women who would date him if he is unemployed. But although your handsome unemployed son may be accepted by her for a date and possibly sex, few young women will fantasize about *falling in love* with your son reading *The Boy Crisis* in an unemployment line! So unemployment means his good looks will ultimately only increase your son's likelihood of being rejected for love.

We'll see later why your son is so much more vulnerable to the loss of love than virtually anyone would imagine. And why it is doubtless part of the reason a man who is unemployed is twice as likely to commit suicide as an employed man.[13]

Suppose your son *is* employed, but trying to save for a down payment on a home, or graduate school, and hopes to split the dinner bill. Should he go on a dinner date with a woman? As we saw, 72 percent of women feel the man should pay the full bill on the first date.[14] While he doesn't know the statistic per se, his life experience validates it. And he is probably part of the 82 percent of men who agree. So while just talking with a woman he hopes to ask out can catalyze his fears of rejection and being unworthy—he may fear looking like a fool for taking a nice conversation to a romantic level—the thought of not being able to pay the full bill magnifies those fears.[15]

In these ways, your son's economic health can dictate his ability to be loved, which makes his economic health inseparable from his mental health, and therefore his physical health. And few things affect his economic health more than his education.

CHAPTER 4

The Crisis of Our Sons' Education

Worldwide, reading and writing skills are the two biggest predictors of success.[1] These are also the two areas in which boys fall the most behind girls. **In the United States, by eighth grade, 41 percent of girls are at least "proficient" in writing, while only 20 percent of boys are.**[2]

Many boys used to "turn around" in about their junior or senior year of high school. Anticipating the need to become sole breadwinner, and therefore gain familial pride, peer respect, and female love, they got their act together. The expectation of becoming sole breadwinner became his purpose. No longer. In one generation, young men have gone from 61 percent of college degree recipients to a projected 39 percent; young women, from 39 percent to a projected 61 percent.

The number of boys who said they didn't like school has increased by 71 percent since 1980.[3] Boys are also expelled from school three times as often as girls.[4]

Why? In a study of boys and girls in the United States at the primary level, when it comes to standardized tests versus grades, "Boys who perform equally as well as girls on reading, math, and science tests are graded less favorably by their teachers."[5] Interestingly, the boys who behaved in the classroom in ways the study identified as more commonly associated with girls—for example, by being attentive and eager—did receive grades equal to girls who scored equally in standardized tests. Boys may

Percentage of College Degrees Received by Gender

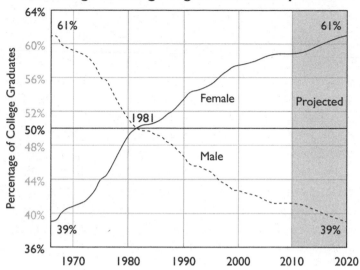

*(Includes Associate's, Bachelor's, Master's, First-professional and Doctor's degrees)

Source: Digest of Education Statistics, 2016[6]

feel teachers are discriminating against their "boy-style" behavior, which understandably leads them to like school less.

(In the chapter *"Why* Are Dads So Important?" we'll also discover the many ways the massive increase in dad-deprived children has had a powerful impact on boys' lack of motivation, which obviously decreases attentiveness.)

The Infinite Consequences of Uneducated Boys

While boys who are motivated can become many of society's most constructive forces—becoming inventors and implementers of what they invent (the Amazons, Apples, Facebooks, Microsofts, and Googles)—boys whose energies are poorly channeled can become society's most destructive forces—our serial killers and prisoners.

Ironically, as our sons become less educated, our daughters increasingly desire partners who are *more* educated. In 1939 women ranked education as only the *eleventh* most important attribute in a husband. Recently, women rank education as the *fourth* most important.[7]

And with less education leading boys to the unemployment line, it creates what I call the drop-out, left-out cycle:

The Drop-Out, Left-Out Cycle

1. In neighborhoods where marriage is scarce, fathers are scarce, and more than *half* of boys don't finish *high school*.[8] The boy drops out.
2. The less education a young man has, the more likely he is to be unemployed or underemployed. He's left out of the workplace.
3. Women who desire children think of an uneducated young man as undesirable, and an unemployed man as "another child"—hardly marriage material. He's left out of marriage and fathering.
4. Some of the women with whom he nonetheless has sex become pregnant, and raise children without him. Thus, we're back to step one: the left-out dad and the drop-out son.

The Implication for Global Leadership

Our sons receiving only about 40 percent of college degrees also damages American global leadership. Why? When we do not simultaneously explore our sons' full potential as dads, this leads to an inability to make use of our daughters' full potential at work. So women receiving about 60 percent of college degrees does not translate into women becoming 60 percent of CEOs of start-ups and corporations or 60 percent of inventors or political leaders.

Why? In part this is because a relatively small percentage of women wish to live out-of-balance lives and neglect their families for a career-only life. That is, women are more likely to opt for a balanced life, which is usually a happier life. But the second part is that families have not learned to make use of your son as a full-time dad, which might allow his wife to be a CEO with a happy marriage and well-raised children.

What can our schools do? Integrate curriculum on the future of the family into the school curriculum. Help our daughters and sons free themselves from the rigid roles of the past toward more flexible roles for their future. As we'll increasingly see, for any country to be a global leader with citizens who are fulfilled, it will have to recruit executives and parents based on motivation and talent, not biology as destiny.

How Schools Can Help Boys Make a Transition from Muscle to Mental

In the future, much of the muscle in manufacturing and construction will be replaced by the mental: robots and artificial intelligence. If your son wants a good job as a welder, he will also need physics and chemistry. If he wishes to make a living with computers, he will need to know how to code, program, and develop software. Grandpa and dad may have worked on appliances like cars, refrigerators, and thermostats; your son will need to master how these appliances collect and exchange data using embedded sensors. That is, he will need to understand the "internet of things." The common denominator? His mind. His mind educated in boy-friendly ways.

What's a boy-friendly way for a nonacademically inclined boy to use his mind? Having a concrete goal. If a boy has a concrete goal of being a welder, that catalyzes motivation to study the physics and chemistry necessary to become a high-paid welder.

How might a school encourage this? By increasing vocational education. Instead, most schools have been decreasing vocational education.

Japan has vastly increased its vocational education programs, with 23 percent of Japan's high school graduates studying at vocational schools. The result: **99.6 percent of Japanese vocational students received jobs upon graduation.**[9] The psychological and economic implications of that difference are infinite. (Incidentally, some Japanese schools are actively recruiting foreign students.)[10]

Our schools are perpetuating the boy crisis in a second way. Girls learn emotional intelligence as part of the socialization to be female. For boys there is an ever-widening gap between the heroic intelligence that it took our sons to be respected as men in the past and the emotional intelligence needed for your son's future. Yet few schools are teaching communication skills and empathy training to help boys make that transition.

Here's why I predict emotional intelligence will be paramount for your son's future: **the more sophisticated artificial intelligence becomes, the more we will yearn for humans to fill the emotional intelligence void.** The more caring professions (e.g., health care, home care—professions currently dominated by women) will thrive even as the traditional male careers shrink.

Can't artificial intelligence mimic emotional intelligence, as illustrated in the movie *Her*? To a degree, yes, but within the span of your son's career, it will not replace the nuances of emotional intelligence needed by a dad, male partner, or health care or home care worker—for example, the ability to respond sensitively to body language, tones of voice, hesitation patterns, and eye contact. Or knowing when to listen, when to talk, when to be proactive, and when to create space. These are the voids AI will create, for which we will increasingly value (and pay) those most able to fill them.

Can your son learn empathy and emotional intelligence, or is this something that girls and women are just better at? Studies reveal that when observing casually, women pick up more accurately what others are feeling. But here's what's fascinating: **when both sexes are offered *pay* should they assess the feelings of others accurately, the empathy gender gap disappears!**[11] The implication? The capacity for empathy and emotional intelligence is latent inside boys and men; we just have to let guys know we'll value them for focusing on it.

Even when emotional intelligence is so undeveloped that hate becomes an unchecked bonding mechanism, as among hard-core white supremacists, Life After Hate groups have successfully reversed the hatred of thousands and replaced it with empathy, love, and self-forgiveness.[12] There are, then, ways emotional intelligence and empathy can be learned even by those we might assume are hopeless.

There is a second application of training for emotional intelligence and empathy. If the haters can learn empathy, maybe we can learn empathy toward the haters. When our only response to haters is to hate, we increase our brain's training to hate and decrease its training to empathize. We become a bit of the enemy we hate.

How can our schools help? Currently our schools are funded to stop bullying. However, **both bullies and the bullied have three things in common: both come from negative family, school, and community environments; both have low self-esteem; and both have poor social skills.**[13] That is, both the bullied and the bully are similarly vulnerable, and teaching the skills that will help both simultaneously is a positive-sum strategy. Since empathy and emotional intelligence can be taught, and these skills are key to preparing our sons for the professions that will be in the greatest demand, we need to integrate this curriculum into our schools in the formative years. (We'll see more about how that can be done in part V, "Heroic Intelligence Versus Health Intelligence.")

Exacerbating the Education Crisis: Caring Less

It's 2016. I receive an email from UCLA (an alma mater) promoting the PhD dissertation presentations of ten of their leading young political scientists. I notice something: all ten are women. I call the political science department and inquire as to why there are no men. The response? "Oh, yes, you're right. I didn't notice that."

We don't notice the norm. In the fifties, the normal was few women in MBA and MD programs. It took the women's movement to help us notice. Today, boys' absence from lists of achievers in education has become the new normal.

It's easier to notice when we care. Friends of mine recently attended their daughter's graduation. Their daughter was co-valedictorian with another girl, and a member of the honor society, which had but a sprinkling of boys. Their son was a junior in the same school. He and his male friends had as many Ds and Fs as As and Bs.

His parents cared, so they noticed. It didn't surprise them to hear that nationwide girls make up 70 percent of valedictorians,[14] while boys get 70 percent of Ds and Fs.[15] In fact, it made them feel less disappointed in their son.

My friends grew up in the era in which girls were doing badly in math and science. They recalled how we concluded the trouble was with the schools. They also saw how now that boys are doing badly in almost every subject, we say the trouble is with the boys.

Solving the boy crisis, in education and in the other areas we've discussed, starts with noticing it's happening—not just here in the United States, but worldwide.

CHAPTER 5

The Crisis of Our Sons Worldwide

Item. "More men in the UK have died by suicide in the past year than all British soldiers fighting in all wars since 1945."[1]

Item. Boys scored lower than girls in the sixty-three largest developed nations in which the PISA, a set of international standardized tests, was given.[2]

Developed nations each have unique colloquial terms to describe their boy crisis: In China, they say *yin sheng, yang shuai*, which means the female (yin) is on the way up, while the male (yang) is on the way down[3]—a gender stock market. In Japan, they use the derisive expression *soshoku danshi* ("herbivores")[4] and *hikikomori* ("socially isolated") to describe the new generation of boys.[5] In European countries, the acronym *NEET* describes young men who are "not in education, employment, or training."[6]

Worldwide, boys are 50 percent more likely than girls to fail to meet basic proficiency in *any* of the three core subjects of reading, math, and science.[7] Among these core subjects, the UN finds that reading is the skill that best predicts future success worldwide—and reading is the core skill in which our sons are doing the worst.[8]

Grades translate into expectations about one's future. Internationally, girls now have higher expectations for their future careers than boys.[9]

Boys' lower expectations can translate into depression, including one of its major symptoms, obesity. Obesity among boys and men is increasing worldwide. Roughly a quarter of Australian, British, Canadian, German, Polish, and Spanish boys and men are obese.[10]

A large study from the UK finds that **boys' IQs have dropped about 15 points since the 1980s.**[11] Researchers are discovering many environmental reasons for this.[12] One is less time spent with fathers. In part IV I document how time spent with fathers prior to age eleven increases children's IQ.[13] Yet in the UK, as in the US, father-child bonding has plummeted to such a degree that one in three children in both countries grow up without a dad.[14]

Male Life Expectancy and Suicide: The New Final Solution

When evolutionary biologist Randolph Nesse looked at the results of the twenty-country study of premature deaths among men referenced earlier, he concluded, "If you could make male mortality rates the same as female rates, you would do more good than curing cancer."[15] The average global life expectancy for girls is about 7 percent greater than for boys.[16]

One of the biggest contributors to this life expectancy gap is suicide. Suicide is one area where our sons and fathers are taking the lead not just in the US but worldwide: by a ratio of four to one.

Suicide now takes "more lives than war, murder, and natural disasters combined, stealing more than 36 million years of healthy life" around the world.[17] In many countries the *rate* of increase in suicides is growing much faster for men than for women. For example, **the rate of increase in male suicide in India is growing at more than *nine* times that of female suicide** (37 percent versus 4 percent since 2000).[18]

We can see, then, why a dad-to-be might not want his next child to be a boy—to face the life a boy today faces. Or, perhaps, to face a life like his.

CHAPTER 6

Why Are We So Blind to the Boy Crisis?

When a police officer shoots a black boy, we protest, "Black lives matter." Good. These protests catalyze an important examination of our underlying biases. But the other half of "black boy" is "boy." The police are twenty-four times more likely to shoot a male than a female.[1] The boy is shot both because he's black, *and* because he's a boy.

So why are we blind to the "boy" in "black boy"? Because for much of our history, blindness to boys' deaths is the way we, as a society, have survived. When our very survival is dependent on our sons' willingness to die, **sensitivity to the death and suffering of boys and men is *in competition* with our survival instinct.**

To win wars, we had to train our sons to be disposable. We honored boys if they died so we could live. We called them heroes.

Because of the potential deaths of our sons, we could not psychologically afford to attach ourselves emotionally to our sons in the way we could with our daughters. And to prepare our sons to fight and potentially die, we had to train our sons to repress their feelings. And the more a boy represses his feelings and puts armor around his heart, the harder it is to open our hearts to him.

This detachment creates what I call the "gender empathy gap": caring less about a boy dying than a girl. So much so that it would not even occur to a reporter to do the research that would uncover that the police are twenty-four times more likely to shoot someone male than someone female.

But while this gender empathy gap is part of what enables our blindness to the boy crisis, we have been blind to that sexism throughout human history, and there has not previously been a boy crisis. So why are we suddenly dealing with a worldwide boy crisis now?

The answer will allow you to know why your son's crisis is not your fault and, once you know what creates the crisis, how to both fortify your son against it and prepare him to take advantage of the new opportunities it presents.

PART II

Why the Boy Crisis
Isn't Your Fault

CHAPTER 7

The Boy Crisis: A Problem Created by a Solution

When William (see introduction) concluded, "This is 'proof' that I've failed as a dad" after Kevin moved back home at thirty, his assessment was the end of a long road of guilt and denial that his own son was a "failure to launch."

Kevin's parents, William and Anastasia, had tried medications to help Kevin with his ADHD and lethargic behavior; now they were afraid of depression and occasionally feared suicide. They had set up playdates and activities to help him move from video game isolation to social connection, but to no avail. When Kevin lost interest in his classes, they hired tutors and sent Kevin to a private school, but his grades just got worse. They had tried to interest him in sports, but the soccer lessons, baseball glove, and even the basketball hoop in their driveway went unused.

When Kevin wanted to move back home, William and Anastasia felt caught between their fear of being enablers and their fear of Kevin feeling deserted in a time of need.

If your son is a Kevin, it is natural to blame yourself. But since, as we've seen, the boy crisis is a problem in all sixty-three of the largest developed nations, chances are it's not your fault! Rather, it is the "fault" of problems that have infiltrated millions of families in developed countries—problems created, ironically, by a good thing: easier access to the means of survival.

Access to the means of survival has progressed exponentially since the industrial revolution in the eighteenth and nineteenth centuries, with revolutions in science, technology, and information exchange (i.e., the digital revolution) allowing for developed countries to increasingly shift their focus from ensuring survival to increasing individual freedoms.

But new freedoms create new problems. By bringing to the conscious level problems often created by these new freedoms, you have more choice as to which solutions are applicable to your family.

The good news is that within each new problem's solution is the opportunity for your son to make advances parallel to those our daughters have already made, as well as to facilitate the next stage of advancement by our daughters. I'll give teasers toward these solutions here, but the angels are in the details (and, yes, the details are the rest of the book!).

1. Marriage and Divorce

Survival-based mandate. The social stigma against divorce gave children the benefit of both parents, thus enhancing their potential for survival.

Freedom. Easier access to the means of survival allowed for the luxury of divorce. The women's movement, in combination with other forces (e.g., the pill) created an "era of multi-option women" for our daughters. The women who were freest to take advantage of these new options were the ones married to men who earned the most money.

Problem. The qualities the traditional husband needed to succeed at work (e.g., repressing rather than expressing his feelings) often led to failure in love. But these men's wives now had more freedom to translate their disappointment into divorce. Divorces put father involvement at risk, creating dad deprivation. A woman's greater financial freedom to choose whether to marry her child's father in the first place led to millions of children being raised by single mothers. Dad deprivation led to problems for both girls and boys, but boys proved even more vulnerable.

Solutions and new opportunities. Socializing our sons to be involved dads. Universal communication training in primary school to make quality relationships "natural," so fewer couples will want divorces. When parents do divorce, both biological parents are equally involved.

2. Sense of Purpose

Survival-based mandate. Each sex was assigned a role designed to enhance survival (e.g., females: risk life in childbirth, raise children; males: risk life in war, raise money). These became each sex's sense of purpose.

Freedom. Women gained the freedom to work outside the home, which also freed men from the mandate to be the sole breadwinner. The need for fewer soldiers allowed military service to become an option for boys rather than an expectation or requirement.

Problem. Boys' two senses of purpose—sole breadwinner and warrior—were diminished. Dad-deprived boys had less guidance for alternative senses of purpose. Many boys experienced a "purpose void."

Solutions and new opportunities. Supporting boys, individually and socially, to find new senses of purpose suited to their individual personalities and values. Fostering the discipline needed to achieve those new senses of purpose. As much social support for boys as future dads as for girls as future executives.

3. Heroic Intelligence Versus Health Intelligence

Survival-based mandate. Societies that survived enemy attacks used "social bribes" such as honoring boys as heroes and giving them greater access to sex, love, marriage, children, and respect (if they survived) to persuade them to risk death in war. "Heroic intelligence"—socialization for risking one's life—was emphasized over "health intelligence"—socialization for a long physical life and a healthy emotional life.

Freedom. With a need for fewer soldiers post–World War II, and fewer heroes-as-role-models, boys were freer to pursue safer careers.

Problem. The social bribes designed to prepare boys to be heroes (e.g., "big boys don't cry" and "when the going gets tough, the tough get going"—but not to a therapist) remain. Without support systems to develop physical and emotional health intelligence, boys externalize and "act out" their fear of not measuring up with drugs, drinking, and delinquency, or by emotionally withdrawing. The damage to self and others from acting out distracts parents and teachers from the underlying depression, and boys' emotional withdrawal inhibits emotional support.

Solutions and new opportunities. Educating boys that heroic intelligence is socialization for a short life, while "health intelligence" is socialization for a long life. Redefining masculinity as the courage to think for oneself rather than cave in to social pressure in order to avoid being called "chicken." Teaching your son how to feel feelings, when to express what he feels, how to be assertive but not aggressive, the power of listening, and that health intelligence is not a facade of strength but the strength to not have a facade.

4. ADHD

Survival-based mandate. A "spare the rod, spoil the child" attitude toward discipline ensured children learned to do what they had to do before doing what they wanted to do. This developed the ability to postpone gratification that survival required. Fathers were expected to apply this discipline ("Wait till daddy comes home"), especially to sons. Physical labor (e.g., farming) was required to survive even as it allowed for boys to apprentice with their dads.

Freedom. With less fear of starving in middle-class and wealthier homes, parents felt freer to allow their children to do what they wanted to do rather than focus on what they had to do. Parents increasingly nurtured their sons' unique personalities and adapted to their needs and desires.

Problem. Especially in dad-deprived homes, less boundary enforcement further allowed children to do what they wanted to do rather than focus on what they had to do. This led to less postponed gratification and an ever-shortening attention span. This problem was intensified as boys' greater need for physical activity was more likely to be neglected in favor of video games and online friendships. Pesticides, fungicides, and nutrition-depleting preservatives compounded boys' problems further, and medications that temporarily reduced boys' symptoms often damaged their brains and bodies. Cumulatively, boys' deficit of attention often became a disorder.

Solutions and new opportunities. Consistent exercise and a healthy diet. Postponed gratification as a core discipline. Family dinner nights to cultivate a boy's emotional intelligence, health intelligence, and sense of purpose. Then, if ADHD still remains a problem, John Gray's myriad natural and creative solutions—from art classes to hot water therapies.

These are not the only forces driving the boy crisis. In future books I'll dive deeper into others: how our attitudes toward sex have become differently destructive than in the past, and the hazards this creates for your son; issues around schools (see the bibliography for Michael Gurian and Leonard Sax's contributions); the gap between the adaptation of careers and the adaptation of our sons (see bibliography for Marty Nemko); the impact on our sons' unconscious of the negative images of men; and solutions to video game addiction.

But in *The Boy Crisis* I address what a decade of research has led me to identify as the most foundational issues: the purpose void, dad-deprived boys, and how heroic intelligence undermines health intelligence. Let's start with the purpose void.

PART III

The Purpose Void

CHAPTER 8

The Path-to-Purpose
Generation Gap

The Power of Purpose

The Japanese call it *ikigai*, or "a reason for being."

Japanese men with ikigai are less likely to die of heart disease. And both sexes with ikigai live longer.[1] Whether we call it ikigai or sense of purpose, when we pursue what we believe gives life meaning, it gives us life.

Historically, a boy's journey to prove himself is what gave him that sense of purpose. Most cultures, to survive, assigned each sex Mars/Venus-type roles that were "sold" to each sex as its purpose in life. The underlying goals of both parents' roles-as-purpose were to optimize their children's chance of survival and make their children's lives better than theirs.

But as we saw in part II, as developed countries had the luxury to permit divorce, they responded by creating the "era of the multi-option woman" (raise children, raise money, or some combination of both) while continuing the historic "era of the no-option man." That is, a dad's "three options" were still raise money, raise money, or raise money. However, with women often sharing the breadwinner role, a young man could no longer find his purpose as a man by being a "sole breadwinner." And, as fewer warriors were needed, boys began experiencing a "purpose void." Dad-deprived boys, without the guidance of dads in finding alternative senses of purpose, were hit the hardest.

But today, even when dad is involved, son and dad often encounter a "path-to-purpose generation gap" on a boy's journey to manhood. If dad's mantra is "I exist, therefore I serve," he may feel dismayed at a culture that seems to be emphasizing "I exist, therefore I *deserve*." He may feel your son is being sucked into the black hole of entitlement. Your son may feel you are depriving him of his "right" to the pursuit of happiness.

How do you bridge the gap? For starters, by exploring with your son ways he can serve by *finding a purpose larger than himself*. The alternative is a purpose void, often triggering a "failure to launch," and its collateral damage: depression and self-disgust.

Helping your son develop his sense of purpose requires beginning at a very different place than his dad—or granddad. His dad or granddad was *told* his sense of purpose. Your job is to help your son *find* his sense of purpose. Your dad's sense of purpose began with *giving up* what created the glint in his eye, whereas your son's sense of purpose must begin with *finding* the glint in his eye.

Since understanding the path-to-purpose generation gap is central to guiding your son to his sense of purpose, I want to share an experience I facilitate in my workshops that has proved life-changing for its participants both understanding their dad's sense of purpose and helping their sons find theirs. Pretend you are in that workshop and I am asking you to . . .

"Recall a Time When Your Dad Had a Glint in His Eye . . ."

Try to recall a moment in your dad's life when he had a glint in his eye—an excited sparkle without worry, preoccupation, or thought of criticism, of either you or himself.

Maybe you saw the glint when he was roughhousing, playing tag or soccer, or tossing a ball with you or your children—laughing unselfconsciously with an I've-lived-for-this-moment delight. Or maybe you detected the glint on a camping, swimming, or fishing trip. Perhaps it was when he came in from the garage after building something useful or fun, or when he was singing in a band or choir, acting in a play, watching his team win a championship game, or telling a story that always elicited laughter or respect.

If you didn't know your dad, or he left when you were young, what's your best guess as to what might have created that glint? (Remember, we all have a relationship with our dads, even if based only on who we imagine him to be and whatever we imagine that he felt about us.)

Your Dad's Sense of Purpose: Glint Versus Job

Recall what your dad did for a living. Then pretend your dad and mom, just before you were born, tried to figure out which of these two things—his glint or his job—would create more *dependable* income that would allow you to live where you lived and have the opportunities you had.

That is, if your parents did the math, would they have concluded your dad should do what created the glint in his eye (take you fishing one day, and acting, drawing, making music, or writing the next), versus doing what he actually did for a living?

Chances are your dad quietly "got it": **if he followed *his* bliss, it's the money *you*'d miss.** While his "glint" may have been writing, art, music, or time with you, he understood that being an engineer would catch more fish to feed you than fishing with you. He may have wanted to leave for work later, or get home earlier, but felt the more he earned, the more he could give you a life that was more fulfilling than his.

In brief, if your dad was a "good" dad, though he would never have said it, he quietly understood that **the road to high pay is a toll road**.[2] He understood that more fulfilling occupations pay less. Why? The more fulfilling the occupation, such as being an artist, the more people want to do it, especially in comparison to the number of people wishing to be, say, a garbage collector. Yet you probably need your garbage collected more than you need to add to your art collection. Since the supply of aspiring artists is greater than the demand, the pay doesn't have to be much—hence the trope of the starving artist. (Yes, a *few* artists earn a living through their art, but they are the exception, not the rule.) Therefore, few of our dads enter the "fulfillment professions."

Why was your dad willing to forfeit the glint in his eye? Well, he didn't, exactly. He *traded in* his glint for his "sense of purpose": the hope of making life better for you than for himself. The hope that a new glint would replace the old glint—the glint that would appear when *you* graduated,[3] got married, had children, were happy.

Fatherhood was about your dad trading in the old glint in his eye—what *he* loved to do—for the new glint in his eye: his love for you.

"My Father's Glint Was His Career—He Always Did Just What He Wanted."

After performing this visualization, a woman in one of my audiences declared, "My father's career was the exact same as the glint in his eye. My father always did what he wanted to do." Her resentment was palpable.

Since her father was still alive, I asked the woman to ask her dad what the glint in his eye was *before he met her mom* and *before he chose a college major*. I gave her my business card. Some months later, she called.

"Well, I did what you suggested. Dad said that when he was in high school he loved being in plays and telling jokes. But that he couldn't afford to spend years in Hollywood or New York to find out if he could 'make it.' He said he chose a science major in college because his parents said that was more practical than theater. Turns out he didn't like science that much."

I could tell something had happened, because she was now referring to her dad as "Dad," not as "my father":

Before Dad met Mom, he said he got into flying small planes. He got in all the hours and made enough money to be able to fly by himself. When he met Mom, he took her for a sunset flight, and even though she was nervous, she always told us kids how Dad had waxed poetic about drifting into the sunset, and how that was when their first kiss happened and all that.

Dad's a pilot, so I figured that was what you call the glint in his eye. But he said being a pilot is about FAA regulations and responsibility, not freedom and poetry and first kisses. So that made me understand what you meant about the difference between "glint" and a profession.

But that wasn't the big news! I always resented that Dad never took *me* flying. That I wasn't part of the glint in his eye. So I got up the nerve to ask him about that. He told me that Mom absolutely prohibited him taking us kids, including my brother, flying in the small plane, because small planes were so dangerous. And he said Mom and he agreed she wouldn't go with him again after she became pregnant, until we kids got older.

So, I guess what I'm saying, Dr. Farrell, is that this was the most important discussion I ever had with my dad. It makes me feel a lot better about him, especially knowing that the reason I never went with him in the small plane is that I meant so much to him, not that I didn't mean enough to him. Thanks a lot.

Oh, just one more thing. I feel kinda bad that since my dad has been putting me and my brother through college that he's pretty much given up his small plane flying. Do you think I should encourage him to get back into it?

I told her, "Ask him how he feels about it now. But more important, just tell your dad how much you appreciate him giving up the glint in his eye for you, and for your mom and brother. Once you let him know that, the hope he had for you being the new glint in his eye will be restored. When he feels appreciated by you, and by your brother and mom, his life's purpose will be fulfilled."

"I Never Thought You Cared Enough to Ask."

As I was working on a previous book in the Pannikin café in Encinitas, California, a young man looked me over a couple of times, then hesitantly approached me.

"You're Warren Farrell, aren't you?"

When I affirmed with a welcoming smile, he started:

I attended one of your workshops where you did that thing with our dads. I just want to share with you what happened for me.

On Father's Day, I figured I'd ask my dad that question you asked about what created the glint in his eye. He didn't seem to quite get the "glint" bit, so I gave him some of the examples you gave—fishing, hobbies, that type of thing. He said, "Jimmy, is this some type of question you got from one of your airy-fairy workshops? You realize life is not about glints, it's about responsibilities. When you learn that, you'll be a man."

At first, I was furious at you for setting me up like that. But then I told my dad, "Dad, the workshop made me realize I was so focused on myself and everything that isn't just perfect, that I realized I'd never asked you about who you are, and what were your hopes and dreams when you were younger. And that's not OK."

Warren, just as I was finishing, I noticed my dad was tearing up. This was amazing, 'cause the only time I had ever seen him cry was at his dad's funeral.

I said, "Dad, what's the matter?"

He assured me that it was OK. Then he paused and said, "I just never thought anyone would ever care enough to ask." Then his tears really flowed. He hugged me in a way he had never held me before.

"In a way that said, 'Now I feel complete'?" I asked him.

"Yes. Yes, that's it . . . In a way that said, 'Now I feel complete.'"

"I never really knew my dad."

At my next workshop, I mentioned this incident while introducing the visualization. After the exercise, a guy stood up and offered,

I never really knew my dad—he left when I was four. I haven't seen him in years. But I know he had an alcohol problem and an anger problem.

I don't for sure know what the answer is to the glint-in-his-eye question, but I know that before he had me, he used to win some trophies surfing. I don't know that I'm right, but just thinking about him not being able to handle the change in life from surfing to wiping my rear, and giving up what probably made him sane . . . Well, it makes me think it probably wasn't me he left, that his drinking and anger was probably about him losing himself.

Realizing that, I'm feeling better about him, and that's making me feel better about myself. This is cool.

This young man did not think he had a relationship with his dad. But **whether or not we know our dad, we have a relationship with him. The relationship in our mind *is* our relationship**. As we look at either of our parents' worlds through their eyes, our relationship with them changes. It changes from a focus on the hurts we experienced to a compassion for the hurts they experienced. It changes from being all about us to being more about them. And that changes our relationship with them, and with ourselves.

How Does This "Glint Versus Job" Exercise Help You Guide Your Son to His Sense of Purpose?

As your son feels the power of his dad giving up one glint in his eye for the glint that emerges when he sees his family is fulfilled, your son feels good about how much he is loved and what his family means to his dad. If you are divorced, it helps him see that his dad's love for him survived what otherwise appeared broken.

It is from that place of greater security that your son is able to see how focusing on something larger than himself can create fulfillment and purpose. As he sees his dad as a "winner" who does not resent him for what he "gave up," dad becomes his inspiration—whether he chooses to have children himself, or chooses to contribute to something larger than himself in a different way. Dad becomes his role model, whether he pursues the traditional male role as purpose or a different role as purpose. You will have built the bridge over "the path-to-purpose generation gap."

Your Son's Unconscious Wisdom

If your son is bright and sensitive, then guiding your son to discover himself also means opening yourself to his unconscious wisdom that there's something about the traditional male role that isn't all it's cracked up to be. He'll hear phrases like "male power" and "male privilege," and while he may get that when he looks at all the presidents and CEOs, **your son may simultaneously feel that the male role is pressuring him to feel obligated to earn money someone else spends while he dies sooner.** That may feel to him like neither power nor privilege. Here is some of what he may be absorbing that can contribute to his purpose void, for which he will need your help to create constructive alternatives . . .

No American boy born after 1960 has had a role model of a US president whose primary identity was as a military hero. With fewer great wars, there are fewer great warriors.

As the warrior role diminished, men shifted from killing in war to "making a killing" on Wall Street. But these men are now portrayed less as their family's saviors and more as corporate sexists—as in the retrospective look at the straw men of *Mad Men*. And as modern-day bankers are labeled "banksters," and big pharma, big auto, big tobacco, big soda, and big oil are seen as crony capitalists who put profit before people, many boys who might otherwise contemplate the corporate climb to manhood now view it as a Faustian deal.

As for making the world a better place through politics, well, if your son is a bright and sensitive conservative, President Trump may fall short of role model status; if he's a liberal straight white male, he may be put off by a culture personified by the DNC's (Democratic National Committee) 2017 email seeking eight new positions on their Technology Team, but saying explicitly that straight white males need not apply. Not for any of them. Regardless of qualifications.[4]

While your son may see heroes in the Jobses, Gateses, and Zuckerbergs of the world, or in the founders of Oracle (Larry Ellison), Dell (Michael Dell), Twitter (Evan Williams), or Whole Foods (John Mackey), every one of them dropped out of school. **Your son's heroes didn't climb traditional ladders—they built their own.**

This purpose void is not confined to American boys. In Japan fathers put in so many hours in the corporate world that their stress and exhaustion led to the creation of the Japanese word *karoshi*, variously translated as "death from overwork" and "death at the desk."

Today's Japanese boys' mounting contempt for a lifestyle of karoshi can be seen in the popularity of the video game *Karoshi, in which the "winner" is the first to "off" oneself!*[5]

Yes, you read that right. In essence, **the Japanese boys' unconscious wisdom is: their dad as winner is really their dad as loser**. He "wins" the game of life—gaining money and power—by losing in the reality of life. And often losing his life. To what end? Japanese boys become clear, too, that marriage is not about intimacy as they hear common Japanese sayings such as "a good husband is healthy but absent."[6]

Boys in Korea and China hear words equivalent to karoshi. In Korea, death from overwork is called *gwarosa*; in China, *guolaosi*. Worldwide, the collective unconscious wisdom of bright boys who in their dad's generation would have climbed the corporate ladder to karoshi, gwarosa, or guolaosi, is that if this is male power, well, no thank you.[7]

For the most observant boys, the image of a "successful" man in the *Mad Men* mode is best represented in the prelude to each episode by the silhouette of the man jumping out of his skyscraper's office to his death. The so-called powerful executives' compulsive drinking reflects their feelings of powerlessness.

Your Son and Draft Registration: From Purpose to Purpose Void

Notice in the following three posters from three different eras in the United States **the evolution of the attitude toward the men we ask to die: from inspiration, to obligation, to contempt.**

Early 20th century   Late 20th century   Today

In the early twentieth century, great-great-grandpa's sense of purpose was inspired by being told he was wanted and needed.

In the late twentieth century, inspiration was replaced with **obligation**: "A Man's Gotta Do What a Man's Gotta Do."

Today, the obligation is still there, but that expectation to fulfill his obligation comes hand-in-hand with contempt: It's so easy, even you can do it. Note that each instruction in the current message maxes out at two words: "Read it." "Fill it." "Mail it." Or more precisely, just one word he hasn't already read: "Read," "Fill," "Mail."

As with Japanese boys, your son does not hear gratitude for the way these men risked their lives—and often died early—for their families. He hears it called sexism. And he may sense—but be unable to articulate—that the sexism that kept women out of work was the same sexism that kept the men overworking.

This is the wisdom some of our sons are unconsciously contemplating: **if Don Draper *ended up* at Esalen in a state of introspection about what it means to be a man, maybe that's where he should start.**

For those boys who join the military, the brightest are often the ones most likely to become disenchanted with what they perceive as the purposelessness of their mission, and to feel the most disposable thanks to the way they are treated upon returning by the very government for which they willingly risked their lives. For example, Corporal Clay Hunt was a sniper for the marines. In 2009, after his second tour, he sought treatment for depression and PTSD. Though he fought tirelessly to get the VA's attention, he felt thwarted by delays and inadequate treatment. Finally, he shot himself, ending his life at age twenty-eight.

Jake Wood, a friend of Hunt's, explains the experience of a returning veteran: "We came home from war unprepared for peace . . . There is so much isolation and lack of purpose."[8]

When our sons worldwide see senses of purpose that end in suicide, or pathways to a sense of purpose disappearing and creating a "purpose void," their unconscious wisdom tells them there must be something more than climbing a ladder to nowhere.

FAMILY DINNER NIGHT
How Social Bribes for Male Disposability Have Evolved

Here is a question worthy of class discussion or family dinner night: Do these posters' evolution reflect a journey over the last century from man as needed, to man as obligated, to man as needed for potential death but condescended to in life? If so, why?

Discussion starter: As we need fewer men to be disposable in war, or in first-responder capacity, do we show less and less respect for men?

Now deepen the discussion. Is there any parallel between the male-only military registration obligation and the history of slavery in the United States, an institution in which we plundered (rather than honored) black persons' bodies and minds? Or is the gap between a legal obligation created by a free person in charge of

making the law, versus slavery, so great as to make the two circumstances incomparable?

    Too controversial? Your son is more likely to be turned off by
boredom than controversy. And you will create exciting enough
conversations to make your son glad he didn't bring his iPhone to
the table!

From Myth to Abyss: Boys' "Purpose Void"

The more your son sees the hopelessness of his dad's life, and fears that
could be him someday, the deeper his emotional abyss—the deeper his
purpose void.

The cultural shifts that have led to the purpose void are perhaps best
illustrated by Japan. Japan made a transition from Axis power to virtually
no offense or defense after World War II. Japan's defense was being "parented" by the United States. In one generation, boys and men went from
being expected to be killer-protectors to being protected from killing.
The sense of purpose a Japanese boy could previously feel by becoming
a warrior evaporated.

This, combined with the fear of being programmed for death from
overwork (*karoshi*) that prevented boys from finding purpose in corporate
work, spawned a large number of Japanese boys who are derisively called
"herbivores" (*soshokukei danshi*).

Herbivores spend almost as much on cosmetics and clothes as women.
One company alone (WishRoom) has sold more than five thousand *bras*
to these boys. Herbivores, also called "parasite singles" (*parasaito shin-
guru*), are typically apathetic about careers, dating, sex, and marriage.
The herbivore typically lives with his parents. He is especially close to
his mom.

This trend of maternal closeness and dependency is increasingly common throughout Western Europe. In Germany boys may be derided as
nest-sitters (*Nesthocker*) for living at "Hotel Mama"; in Italy boys increasingly return home at their mother's encouragement, even as they (and
sisters who accompany them) may be mocked as *bamboccioni* (big babies).
In Greece and Spain, the youth unemployment rate exceeds 50 percent

(versus 12 percent for US youth), replacing millions of young men's traditional sense of purpose with a sense of dependency.

This is not a historical first. During Japan's longest period of peace (the Tokugawa period, 1603–1868), with no need for men as warriors, men played women and women dressed as men for the theater, while erotic art celebrated bisexualism and transgender role-playing.

Then and now, the good news is that fewer boys define their purpose as a man as becoming heroes in war or at work—and risking their health and lives to do so. The bad news is that no one is filling boys' purpose void with viable alternatives.

But are there viable alternatives that your son can pursue and still be respected? Yes. But it starts with thinking a bit out-of-the-box about career.

The women's movement warned every girl how marriage can seduce her to make a sacrifice *of* her career. But no one warned every boy how marriage can seduce him to make a sacrifice *in* his career.

I had a powerful, perhaps life-altering, experience in 1976 that catalyzed my understanding of exactly what is being sacrificed *in* a career . . .

Can a "Real Man" Transition from Provider–Protector to Nurturer–Connector?

I had recently returned from my first book's paperback book tour. I was at a large party with other writers for *Ms.* magazine celebrating *Ms.*'s success. As I was making eye contact with Gloria Steinem to ascertain that our earlier "Let's talk at the party" promise became reality, a man interrupted.

"You Warren Farrell?"

"Yes," I responded, still distracted.

"I joined a men's group you formed, but never met you 'cause the guys said you form a lot of groups and leave as soon as they get underway."

As I nodded, he teased, "A 'love 'em and leave 'em guy,' eh?"

I began to explain, then caught the twinkle in his eye.

"Well, I just wanted to tell you the group had a real impact on my life. It led to my decision to raise my son full-time."

"Full-time?" Now he had my attention. "Had you been working?"

He smiled. "Yeah. 24-7. That's why I had neglected my first son and lost my wife. I got remarried, but I'm still working 24-7."

Knowing that "24-7" usually denoted success, and that many a new mom's desire to have a more involved dad was not accompanied by a desire for her husband to quit a successful day job, I asked, "Was your wife OK with that?"

"Her support was everything. Hers, and the men's group."

"How did the group help?"

"One of the exercises you had taught the group to do was to go around and have each of the guys discuss 'The biggest hole in my heart is . . .' Well, one of the things that blurted out of my mouth was 'neglecting my son because of my career.'"

"What triggered that, do you think?"

"Probably my wife having recently told me she was pregnant, and our just finding out it's a boy! Anyway, the group then asked me another one of your fantasy questions, 'What would you do if you could do anything you wanted, without having to worry about money?'"

"I gave them this fantasy: 'Take off a few years and raise my kid.'"

"Then the guys asked me if I had asked my wife if she would be OK with that. I gave a number of reasons why I thought it was impractical, but they got me to give them a commitment to at least ask her. And I did."

"And she said yes?"

"Yeah, we had a lot of discussions, and she was very supportive every step of the way."

"Fantastic. How long have you been doing this for?"

"He's a year-and-a-half now."

"Is it going well? Are you glad you're doing this?"

"Warren, raising my son is by far the best decision I've ever made in my life."

"How so?"

"It's like I discovered a whole different type of love. I didn't even know that type of love existed. Here and there I had had little glimpses of that with my first son, but never knew what would unfold until I immersed myself."

"For example?"

"Stuff that I thought would be meaningless—being able to turn his crying into a smile; getting his arm through a sleeve; listening for his first 'daddy' and 'mommy'—it all became everything because he was everything.

"You know, Warren, until then I had talked about love, but never really knew what it meant to totally immerse myself in someone else's well-being with no expectation of getting anything back. Everything follows from that. I never knew what I was missing."

The framework from which he looked at raising a child launched us into such an inspired conversation that I forgot about Gloria. After an hour or so, though, one young man broke our invisible energetic barrier.

"Can I have your autograph?"

I had just returned from a book tour in which I had done a lot of TV, so I reached up for the paper and pen he offered.

He seemed uncomfortable.

"Is something the matter?" I asked.

"Um, no. Yes, I'd love your autograph, too, sure. But I actually came for John's . . ."

As I suffered something between embarrassment and humiliation for my assumption that he meant me, my new friend reached up. The quickness with which he signed the paper signaled that it had not been his first time.

"Wow. Sorry for assuming he meant me. I rarely watch TV. May I ask who are you?"

"I actually preferred it the way it was! I'm John."

"John. It's been a great conversation. John who?"

"John . . . Lennon."

Being TV-deprived, I was, er, "proud" of myself for being able to ask the next question: "You're with a singing group, aren't you?"

With a bemused smile, he nodded.

"Forgive me," I said, "but what's the name of the group again?"

"The Beatles."

This ignorant I was not. I felt every cell in my body blush in harmony. I realized I shared his happiness about my ignorance and felt blessed by John's wisdom to avoid mentioning the Beatles, Yoko, or anything that might have clued me in and triggered my self-consciousness.

To me, John's decision to be a full-time dad destroyed the myth that "men who can, do; men who can't, become full-time dads." Here is a man who had one of the most enviable and successful careers in history, yet swore the best decision of his life was to forfeit his career for half a decade to raise his son.

As I reflected on John's decision, I had two powerful realizations:

1. What John Lennon had discovered was the hidden John Lennon. The John Lennon who *earned* love discovered the John Lennon who could *be* love.
2. **Had John attended to his first son, Julian, the way he attended to Sean, we would never have heard of John Lennon.**

It might seem like it was easier for John to leave his career to become a full-time dad because he had money. But that money and success came with its own tangled web of obstacles. John educated me on the levels of legal complexities—and the minefield of egos—required to clean out the emotional and monetary expectations of the other band members and their loved ones, plus a myriad of managers, accountants, and lawyers. And then there was the emotional dependencies of a billion fans, and, yes, his own emotional dependency *on* his fans.

John realized he had slid far down the slippery slope of "what you own, owns you." Yet he had enough fame to know the limits of fame, and enough internal security to not be confined by the need for fame. He understood the limits *in* a career.

John had five additional ingredients that made his decision possible:

- a wife who cared more about him than money;
- a pushy men's group;
- a hole in his heart;
- the ability to imagine; and
- the courage to execute.

You can give your son the opportunity to be a pioneer in this evolutionary shift to find within himself the hidden man who can *be* love, rather than feel he has no option but to earn love by being away from the ones he loves—the father's catch-22.

Creating alternatives for your son does not just mean opening your son's mind to being a full-time dad, but also opening his mind to growth professions of the future that will most allow him to value himself. I'll discuss these in chapters 10 and 11. But before your son can discern which professions will allow him to value himself, he must understand the social bribes he will unconsciously confront as a boy to value himself by not valuing himself. He must understand the "hero paradox."

CHAPTER 9

The "Hero Paradox": Value Yourself by Not Valuing Yourself

A Hero with a Thousand Faces

How many roads must a man walk down before they call him a man? . . . The answer is blowin' in the wind.

—Bob Dylan, "Blowin' in the Wind"

To become a "real man," no matter which road a boy chooses—whether a samurai, knight, mafia don, Navy SEAL, CEO, entrepreneur, or fireman—he had to be *prepared* to slay any "dragon" that might threaten his family, village, or country. But to graduate from being a "real man" to a "hero," the dragon had to appear, and he had to be a "first responder" among those who defeated it.

What is a hero? **The word *hero* derives from the root **ser-*, from which we also get the word "servant"** (think "public servant"), as well as slave, and protector.[1] In Japan and China, the word *samurai* also derives from the word for servant, *saburai*. Billions of boys throughout history have embraced the opportunity to serve and to protect in the hope of being labeled a hero or samurai. Though the fiercer the enemy, the greater their chance of death, boys were willing to exchange their lives for the label. They were, in a sense, slaves to the potential honor they might receive if they served and protected their families, villages, or countries.

The reason boys needed to be sold on this was the same reason girls needed to be sold on risking their lives in childbirth: survival. Survival was threatened in so many ways that the hero could have, in Joseph Campbell's terms, a thousand faces.

Who sold this to boys? Parents, grandparents, schools, churches . . . everyone. How? Via a complex web of what I call a "chorus of social bribes"—or the "Sirens" of social bribes. Since our survival was dependent upon young men and women attracting each other, let's start there . . .

The Sirens of Social Bribes

Social Bribes: Females

My brother, Wayne, and a female friend at the University of Utah, went cross-country skiing in the Grand Tetons. It was April, and as the weather warmed, the snows had begun slipping from the mountains. One pass seemed especially vulnerable to avalanches. Trained in survival skills, Wayne doubtless assessed that venturing forward together would give each the opportunity to save the other, but also place them both in jeopardy.

Wayne went forward alone. An avalanche tumbled its thousands of frozen pounds over my brother. Days later, dynamite allowed his body to be found, buried under forty feet of snow.

Wayne would have been twenty-one. I doubt he would ever have questioned making the choice to protect his female friend—being her "unpaid body guard." Of course, when his friend recounted the story to me at Wayne's funeral, neither of us put it that way. Both Wayne's choice to go first, and his friend's choice to let him, were doubtless unconscious.

How deeply are these choices—to protect and to reward that protection—embedded in our unconscious?

When male vervet monkeys fight in their wars with other groups of monkeys to protect their territory or to get food, female monkeys reward the best surviving "warriors" by grooming them. The social status of these warrior monkeys goes up, and therefore more female vervet monkeys want to mate with them. In contrast, the female monkeys ignore and "snap" at the male monkeys who abstain from battle.[2]

Do the female monkeys' social bribes work? Yes. By the next battle, the monkeys who participate most vigorously are the ones rewarded with offers of sex and the ones who abstain are "punished" by being ignored and snapped at.[3] Lysistrata's flip side.

The roots of female social bribes for males to risk their lives to receive female love run as deep as the roots of warfare. It is part of our genetic heritage.

Fast forward to today. As we'll see in our analysis of current films like *Star Wars* and *Hunger Games*, your son still sees women falling in love with the *Officer and a Gentleman*, not the *Private and the Pacifist*. Both our sons and daughters also hear songs like Bonnie Tyler's "Holding Out for a Hero," a classic because its sentiment endures:

He's gotta be strong
And he's gotta be fast
And he's gotta be fresh from the fight!

We are able to sell boys the "hero" status in exchange for dying so others may live as a boy's sense of purpose because our sons, like our daughters, are social animals—and therefore vulnerable to social bribes. As Margaret Mead put it, though, the female role is more natural; the male role is more socially prescribed. Which makes your son more vulnerable than your daughter to defining a social bribe as his sense of purpose.

However, your son's vulnerability to social bribes begins way before he is interested—or not interested—in girls.

Part of the pain of our sons' purpose void is that even as the role for traditional male heroes is shrinking, few parents are aware of how many of the messages that we send to our son may unconsciously communicate to him that we'll love him more if he is a traditional hero. Here's the way Jack saw it . . .

Social Bribes: Dad

Jack recalled:

One of my first memories was watching my dad and his buddies cheer for some college quarterback completing a pass with a dislocated shoulder. When the commentator admired the quarterback's "courage," I could see my dad and all his buddies nod and say "yeah"—sort of like a "choir of admiration."

I most remember wondering if I could ever do anything to be admired like that by my dad.

Maybe it was a year or two later—I think I was in first grade—that my dad told me that I was eligible for Pop Warner football. My dad said that if I played, he'd coach. I jumped at the chance. I became pretty good. My dad was a proud coach.

But when I was in high school, my dad's alma mater, Notre Dame, was having a great season. Maybe around 2012. Dad lived for the next game, when "we" would beat Michigan, or whatever. Dad's hero was Brian Kelly. I wanted to be like Brian, and I had a good throwing arm, but not a great throwing arm. As my dad put it, "You're a Jack of all trades."

The more Dad boasted about Brian—as if Brian were "his"— the more I felt Dad wished I was like Brian. I know Dad didn't mean that, but I felt like such a disappointment to him.

Preparing his son to be a football hero was Jack's dad's unconscious way of preparing Jack for manhood by preparing him to sacrifice his body in exchange for the social bribes of being praised and valued. The expectation of a father to sacrifice his son is deeply rooted in the Hebrew Bible, in which God commands Abraham to sacrifice his son Isaac. And, as in the Hebrew Bible, every dad hopes that in the final analysis his son will be spared.

But why is it that your son will risk his life for love or praise? Or go for a touchdown even though he knows that each time he catches the football in his hands he increases his risk of a concussion in his brain?

There is a core hub of your son's brain (the rostral cingulate zone, or RCZ) that is responsive to social approval—especially when your son is a teenager.[4] This hub can be responsive enough to the social bribes of cheering, praise, respect, approval, prayer, and music (e.g., drum and bugle corps) to inspire your son to sacrifice his life. Each social bribe stimulates dopamine, motivating him to do more of whatever garnered the praise.

Social bribes and the RCZ facilitate the unity that inspired our sons to die so we might live free of Hitler. And to risk their lives as lumberjacks and construction workers to build our homes, and in coal mines and on oil rigs to warm those homes. But they've also led millions of young men to end their lives early so we could live our lives comfortably.

Social Bribes: Mom, Men, the Media, the Military

After 9/11, our first responders were on a pedestal.[5] Of those emergency workers who lost their lives, 99 percent were male, and if your son was watching the news, it might have been the first time he saw men as a praiseworthy gender.

The message? The more survival is at stake, the more boys are valued to risk death so others might live. **Your son learns the "hero paradox": to value himself by not valuing himself.**

Until recently, any call to serve one's country was heeded—as my classmate Al Zimmerman did back in the sixties. Al and I did battle on the Midland Park High School track team in New Jersey virtually every spring school day. A tenth of a second made one of us a winner, the other a loser. The competition created a bond. Al was an honor society student who carried himself like a young Dwight Eisenhower. He could easily have gone to college and avoided the war in Vietnam with a 2-S student deferment. But he felt he needed to serve—to protect his country.

On Christmas break of my freshman year of college, I called Al. When his mom answered, she choked up. She passed the phone to his dad. "Warren," his dad told me, "Al was killed in Vietnam."

Al was not required by law to give his life to protect his country—just as my brother, Wayne, was not required to give his life to protect his friend. But they had both, in different ways, internalized the social bribes of being a man.

I miss them both.

And I especially miss Wayne.

Today the military remains appealing as a sense of purpose, and a way of learning discipline to achieve one's purpose, especially to those of our sons who are not as academically inclined. Like Ryan . . .

Ryan's dad was a marine. The happiest day of his dad's life was the day Ryan was born. The proudest day was when Ryan announced he wanted to become a marine, too. The day Ryan left on his first tour of duty, Ryan's dad shed tears of pride; Ryan's mom shed tears of fear. But just under the surface, Ryan's dad's tears were mixed with fear, and Ryan's mom's tears were mixed with pride.

Billions of parents have experienced this tug-of-war between their desire for their son to be safe, and their pride in their son for risking his life. This World War I–era poster honors the sentiment:

Sheet music cover for "America Here's My Boy," words by Andrew B. Sterling, music by Arthur Lange.

What's obvious in war is less obvious in peace. We saw above the number of "death professionals" it took to build your home. We appreciate our home, and like to be appreciated for having it, but rarely appreciate how the lumberjack, roofer, and cross-country truck drivers risked their lives to build it.

Eric got his first hint of this when he was fourteen, when he invited his friend Sam to dinner for the first time. When Sam ate healthy portions of everything but politely passed over the fish, Eric's father, Robert, queried, "Are you a vegetarian?" When Sam said yes, Robert asked him to share what inspired that decision. Sam explained that he personally felt that killing fish or animals was immoral, but understood that not everyone saw it that way. Robert praised Sam both for his concern for what was moral and the courage of his convictions. This led to a lively discussion on the morality of killing fish and animals for humans to eat.

Now, here's the rub. No one—including Sam—thought to even consider whether it was moral that our demand for fish or crabs also leads to many *men* being killed or paralyzed each year in the process of catching them. **In the *Deadliest Catch*, the death the men face is the source of entertainment, but not of concern.** Our concern is with the fish. We've heard people plead "Save the Whales," but not "Save the Males." Thus, neither Sam nor Eric's family thought to say, "I don't eat crabs because I don't want to be paying men to die."

As Eric's family and Sam disposed of their garbage, nor did anyone think about the morality of virtually every garbage collector being male—men whose alarms would awaken them at three in the morning, sending them into the darkness and black ice hiding under the frozen snow of a Wisconsin winter, using their backs to absorb the weight of hundreds of garbage cans, and their lungs to absorb toxic fumes.

Is the social bribe, then, the sense of purpose your son may experience if he makes enough money to make his children's lives better than his?

Yes. But the social bribes that create the hero paradox of your son valuing himself by not valuing himself are so deeply embedded in his psyche that he will forfeit his life even when there is no pay. Thus, 76 percent of American firefighters receive neither bonus nor pay. They are *volunteers*. Almost 100 percent men.

The pay of the volunteer fireman? Praise. Respect. Purpose. The potential to graduate to hero if he kills the fire-breathing dragon and saves someone else's life. The knowledge that if, in the process, he loses his own, his status as a hero only increases.

These are the social bribes that, if your son absorbs them before the point where he is old enough and mature enough to understand their purpose, can make your son a slave to the safety of others with little regard for the safety of himself. And in our collective unconscious we know that the more our sons "buy into" these social bribes, the more our homes and our homeland are protected. We have developed an unconscious investment in social bribes that put our sons in jeopardy so we may live. Or live better.

Male-Only Draft Registration: When Social Bribe Becomes Legal Mandate

Male-only draft registration is more than meets the eye. The pressure on your son to take physical risks as part of his male identity does not stop with social bribes. It is solidified with legal mandates.

In school, your son learns that the Fourteenth Amendment guarantees equal protection for both sexes, but when he turns eighteen, only he and other boys will be required by law to register for the draft.

Even a Houdini cannot escape the US law of male-only draft registration. If your son fails to register, he's subject to up to five years in prison and a quarter-million dollar fine.[6] Worse, his name is referred to the Department of Justice for possible investigation and further prosecution.[7]

Even if he serves five years and you pay the quarter million, and he avoids further prosecution, his failure to register will quickly close other doors. It starts on the federal level: He'll be denied federal student loans or grants (e.g., Pell Grants), and even be prohibited from participating in federal vocational training programs or getting a job in the US Post Office or any part of the executive branch of government.[8]

On the state level, forty states add further penalties, such as **revoking the privilege to a driver's license**.[9] Other states prevent your son from holding a state job or attending a college that receives state-funded higher education benefits.

The Catch-22 of Your Son-as-Hero

The catch-22 of your son as hero is that the more he becomes a hero as killer, the less likely he is to become a hero as husband. As we'll see in the chapter on heroic intelligence versus health intelligence, many of the qualities your son develops to kill in war—or be a hero at work—undermine the qualities it takes to love at home. In brief, what he does to be loved often divorces him from love.

Those social bribes are, as Bob Dylan sings, what's "blowin' in the wind." But also blowin' in the wind are other unseen forces, ones that destroyed the marriage of Ethan's parents and are jeopardizing Ethan's future . . .

CHAPTER 10

Why Do More Marriages Fail in Countries That Succeed?

Ethan's Story

Who will be my role model, now that my role model is gone?

—Paul Simon, "You Can Call Me Al"

Ethan was eight. His mom and dad had just gotten divorced. He yearned to see his dad—to roughhouse and play catch, to chase him and be chased, to go camping and kayaking. But his mom had gotten a better job in another state, and moved him and his sister to what she felt would be a better school district. Ethan's dad was living in a small apartment and could only afford to fly out and see him for a couple of days a month. When he pressed his dad as to why, his dad finally explained that he was going to court to ask the judge if he could see him more, but he didn't have enough money to hire a good lawyer.

When Ethan began acting up at school, the school assigned him a therapist. When she asked Ethan to draw some pictures of his family, Ethan drew a picture of a small box on the left side of the page. He drew his dad alone in the box. On the right side, he drew a picture of a house, with his mom looking away from his dad's small box, but he and his sister looking out the windows toward his dad in the box. Between his house and his dad's little box was a fence so big it was taller than the house.

When the therapist asked Ethan to explain the picture, he said the little box was like the apartment his dad lived in. "I know my dad wants to be with us—he's looking out the windows to see us. And we're looking out our windows, but with that big fence we can't see him."

When asked if he would like to be a dad someday, Ethan hesitated. "Maybe not." Then only his eyes spoke, with sadness. When the therapist asked why he was sad, Ethan said, "I would want to have children, but I'd want to see them, and they'd probably be too far away and they couldn't get over the big fence to see me."

Ethan saw his future in his dad, and it wasn't a future he wanted. The more he let himself absorb being a dad as a sense of purpose, the sadder he became. His fear of ending up like his dad created his purpose void.

What are the dynamics that lead to so many Ethans?

Marriage: Breaking the Success-Freedom-Divorce-Fatherlessness Cycle

The reasons often cited for initiating divorce—affairs, money, drinking, children, abuse—have been with us for centuries. Then why are more marriages ending recently, in countries that succeed? Why, in the United States, are 69 percent of those divorces initiated by women?[1] Especially women with a college education?

As we've seen, the women with the most options were often successful themselves, and almost always married to men who were even more successful. This allowed the women to go to psychologists, be introspective, and raise expectations about their marriage.

Their successful husbands had learned that earning money led to love. Why? Because it did. However, earning money didn't *sustain* love. As women were becoming more in touch with and sharing what was bothering them, their husbands were often burying their heads in the sand, hoping the bullets would miss. The more successful they were, the more they learned to repress their feelings, not express their feelings. Ironically, then, many of **the women who were best able to grow spiritually and psychologically had married men who were the least able to grow.**

Kamala saw how powerful Kenneth was outside the home but was clueless as to how powerless he felt inside the home—especially when she was critical or complained. Nor did Kamala realize that Kenneth making partner in his prestigious accounting firm was not fulfilling his dreams, but conflicting with his dream—his dream of being a novelist. But Kenneth had mentioned that only as a fantasy, and Kamala couldn't hear what Ken didn't say.[2]

Once Kenneth became a partner, he traveled more, and Kamala felt more disconnected. Her work with her therapists and discussions with women friends helped her make a transition from "stage I" expectations of being a role mate, to the stage II expectations of being a soul mate. Kenneth wasn't keeping up. When Kamala met a man in one of her group counseling sessions, her affair with him made palpable the emptiness in her marriage. A year later, she filed for divorce.

FAMILY DINNER NIGHT
Role Mate or Soul Mate

Using the table below on family dinner nights to discuss with your son the gap between stage I roles and stage II goals can help him identify his goals, choose a partner based on those goals, and then negotiate their optimal path to soul mate.

Role Mate to Soul Mate

STAGE I ROLES	STAGE II GOALS*
Marriage	**Marriage (or Long-Term Relationship)**
Survival	*Fulfillment*
Role mates: Women and men married to create a "whole"	**Soul mates**: "Whole" persons partner to create synergy
Division of roles	Flexibility of roles
Woman raises children; man raises money	Both sexes raise children; both sexes raise money
Children obligatory	Children a choice
Mom expected to risk life in childbirth; dad expected to risk life in war, or to protect family	Childbirth rarely life-threatening; war a choice; both sexes check out the burglar

STAGE I ROLES	STAGE II GOALS*
Sex for procreation, and/or to meet husband's needs	Sex for mutual fulfillment
Neither party can end contract	Either party can end contract
Women as property; men expected to die before "property" was hurt	Sexes equally responsible for self and other
Both sexes subservient to needs of family	Both sexes balance needs of family with needs of self
Love emanates from mutual dependence	Love emanates from a compatibility of soul and values
Love **less conditional** (till death do us part)	Love **more conditional** (e.g., no abuse; *expectations* of happiness; mutual respect)
Choice of Partners	*Choice of Partners*
Parental influence is primary	Parental influence is secondary
Women expected to marry their source of income ("marry up")	Neither sex expected to provide more than half the income
Pre-Marital Conditions	*Pre-Marital Conditions*
Men addicted to female sex and beauty, then deprived of "fix" until they supply security	Neither sex more addicted or deprived than the other

* The word **goals** in "stage II goals" implies that many, if not most, have **not** yet been achieved.

Source: Updated from *The Myth of Male Power* by Warren Farrell, PhD

Women in the early seventies who were married to successful men were the first large group in human history with, first, stage II marital expectations in a stage I marital reality, and, second, the money to afford divorce.

The journey to a stage II soul mate reality was most likely to be interrupted by two unconscious forces once couples had children: the father's catch-22 and personality adaptation. Nick and Brittany are examples. . .

The Father's Catch-22

When Brittany became pregnant, Nick went along with Brittany's desire to cut back on work so she could focus on their daughter-to-be. But they both also felt a larger home located in a good school district would be better for the two or three children they anticipated. They agreed that Nick, who was a teacher, could make much more money in real estate. And they were right.

Too right. Nick soon had western US responsibility for Coldwell Banker. Which led to him often being on the road for three or four days at a time. And when he *was* at home in San Rafael, California, he had to leave home early for his hour-plus traffic commute to his San Francisco office. He'd often get home late. And even when he was physically at home, he was mentally still at work.

Nick yearned for his children—his kids and Brittany meant everything to him. But **Nick was experiencing the father's catch-22: loving his family by being away from the love of his family.**

Being away created another problem. As Brittany's world became their daughter, Charlene, Brittany became increasingly protective of Charlene, and Nick increasingly sensed that his parenting style created more criticism and conflict. Brittany feared that Nick was well intentioned but that she had to walk on eggshells to inform him of what he was doing wrong. They were unwittingly experiencing personality adaptations that would make them less able to recognize the person they had married.

Personality Adaptation

So why didn't Nick and Brittany discuss their feelings with each other? Nick saw that Brittany admired his success, and they both loved the educational advantages the school system offered their now three children. So though being a teacher tapped into the glint in Nick's eye and he could feel himself losing that, he said nothing, and drank to relieve the stress from both the pressure of his work and his lack of fulfillment.

Nick's personality was unconsciously adopting traits that would help him succeed at work, but fail at home. And Brittany, feeling less connected to Nick, immersed herself more in the children, friends, exercise, spiritual, and alone time. Eventually, yearning for the same care that had originally made her fall in love with Nick, she met a teacher at the gym and began a passionate affair. Nick, spending lonely nights on the road, feeling the lack of his and Brittany's prechildren passion, and having less time than Brittany with children and intimate friends, also found himself with a sex and intimacy void. His occasional affairs were momentarily satisfying, but left him with an even greater yearning for the intimacy with Brittany he was missing.

Nick felt a self-loathing for his personality adaptation. And Brittany felt Nick had become someone she no longer knew.

The Nick-Brittany dynamic is most notable for Nick's personality adaptation. When success requires supporting five people, as in Nick's case, then the qualities it takes to succeed at work are in tension with the qualities it takes to succeed in love. Nick was becoming less lovable even as he yearned more for love.

Brittany felt she had "lost" Nick. This feeling contributes to the reason women initiate 69 percent of divorces. From the woman's perspective, she really isn't filing for divorce from the man she married. She is filing for divorce from a different man.

For your son, this is a cautionary tale about the potential outcome of a male-as-sole-breadwinner-marriage-with-children. While he may initially feel he has found his soul mate, to support five people, he and his wife become role mates. And he experiences both the father's catch-22 and personality adaptation.

The Era of the Multi-Option Mom and the No-Option Dad

It's easy to see how Nick and Brittany's choice of traditional roles—mom, raise children; dad, raise money—decreased their passion and increased their disconnect even as it gave them reason to stay together. Nick and Brittany stayed legally married, but felt psychologically divorced—in a minimum-security-prison marriage.

Nick and Brittany felt they had other choices for Brittany, but not for Nick. Because Brittany was married and Nick was working, Brittany saw three options for a sense of purpose:

- Children full-time
- Work full-time
- Some combination of both

Brittany was part of the the "era of the multi-option mom." However, neither Brittany nor Nick saw the potential for a multipurpose dad. Nick saw three "slightly" different options for a sense of purpose:

- Work full-time
- Work full-time
- Work full-time

Nick and Brittany could have reversed roles. But Nick had significant earning potential; stay-at-home dads are more likely to be dads by default—dads who have lost their job, or dads whose wives earn considerably more than they do. And although the children usually do extremely well with dad as the primary parent, if the mom does not see the light at the end of the tunnel of his unemployment, she often loses respect for him. Moreover, he feels that loss of respect both from her and from within himself. This makes him even less appealing to her, which increases his insecurity, and the marriage becomes vulnerable to divorce.

That said, dad can exercise the full-time dad option to the benefit of everyone (as we'll see in part IV on dad-deprived boys versus dad-enriched boys) without endangering the marriage if these five conditions are met:

The Five Conditions for Successful Marriage with a Full-Time Dad

1. The dad is internally secure.
2. The dad understands and articulates to the mom the nature of his value to the children.
3. The mom fully values his stay-at-home dad role and never shames him for earning less.
4. The mom finds enormous purpose in her career, and also carves out time for the children.
5. The mom does not feel resentful of the children's deeper connection to the dad.

If the dad is also either making a reasonable income from home, or developing something they both feel will eventually succeed, that enhances the probability of mom maintaining respect for dad.

Since meeting these five conditions is more the exception than the rule, the stay-at-home dad with a happy marriage is more the exception than the rule. Communicating about these conditions can help your son and his partner be an exception.

Why might your son not feel that a working wife frees him to engage in more fulfilling work that pays less? Because he may not see his wife as interested in a husband who is paid less. He may fear that more-fulfilling work that pays less will leave him without love. **And without love, your son's purpose has no purpose.**

Simultaneously, our sons' other traditional sense of purpose—being a warrior—is also evaporating. Since the warrior class draws disproportionately from the poor and less educated, joining the military traditionally filled three voids: an economic security void, an education void, and a purpose void. The good news is that fewer of our sons are dying. The bad news is that if your son experiences these voids, he may see no way of filling them.

If your son is feeling a purpose void but unable to articulate what he is feeling, and simultaneously hearing in school and on the news that he has all the power and privilege and is the reason women were held back, he may withdraw into the video games and video porn that can distract him from his frustration and alienation. As he sees single moms by choice and single moms by divorce, and women who choose not to marry at all, he may intuitively sense he is living in an era of the multi-option woman and the no-option man but never be able to articulate it.

Without purpose, a boy often feels unneeded; if he feels ashamed to admit that he feels unneeded—or doesn't know that's what he's feeling—he may also feel unheard and unseen. These feelings were common among the working-class males who supported Trump in the United States, and Brexit in the United Kingdom. The fact that polls predicted neither victory gives us a sense of exactly how unseen these men are, as well as how afraid they are to speak their feelings.

The good news is gender roles within your son's lifetime have the potential for a greater liberation from rigid roles for your son as well as your daughter. The bad news is that the transition this gender liberation requires has yet to include your son. You can begin to encourage his inclusion as you acknowledge him for the validity of his unconscious wisdom.

How Did Our Daughters Avoid the Purpose Void?

Women are not immune to the purpose void. Even when women's primary purpose was clearly defined as caring for the home and children, women who had neither children nor the need to struggle to survive could experience just such a purpose void. The novelist Flaubert gave us a picture of such a woman in the 1830s, *Madame Bovary*. Emma Bovary was smart, beautiful, and among the freest of women. **Emma Bovary had everything, and therefore nothing.** Devoid of purpose, she found her life going astray until her loss of self-respect culminated in her tragic suicide.

With our sons' options currently about a half-century behind our daughters', a quick glance at women's journey of the last half century can offer some hints as to how we can best support our sons' futures.

The era of the multipurpose woman, catalyzed by the women's movement, educated parents, teachers, and counselors to proactively introduce young women to the advantages of entering occupations they traditionally avoided such as the STEM (science, technology, engineering, and math) professions. If one of these was a "match," she was exposed to the potential support of thousands of corporate and government grants and scholarships offered to women only. To deal with the barriers women encountered being the sole woman among men, every profession developed special groups for women; every corporation had human resource divisions focused on women's special needs—from flexible time and maternity leave to sexual harassment and affirmative action. And a myriad of women-focused conferences dealt with women's issues from women's perspectives.

As women's concerns developed consensus, they were enacted in law. Affirmative action left fewer women as the sole woman in her law firm. Title IX addressed women's sports and concerns such as sexual harassment. Virtually every school trained teachers to understand how girls learn, and professional conferences helped them change their teaching methods accordingly. Seven federal offices of women's health addressed women's specific health concerns. And a White House Council on Women and Girls was buttressed by multiple White House conferences and special White House initiatives (e.g., Girls Rising; #62MillionGirls). As someone who was on the board of the National Organization for Women in New York City, and as author of *The Liberated Man*, I immersed myself in many of these efforts.

The problem? There has been no parallel effort to help our sons become multipurpose men. The female-only scholarships and affirmative action for our daughters to enter the STEM professions is not matched by male-only scholarships and affirmative action for our sons to enter the "caring professions"—elementary school teachers, social workers, nurses, dental hygienists, marriage and family therapists, or becoming a full-time dad. Despite the Gurian Institute's success in training teachers in how boys' brains learn differently, only about 5 percent of schools offer that or similar training to their teachers.[3] There are few professional and corporate conferences focused on boys' and men's issues. There is no White House Council on Men and Boys, and no federal offices of boys or men's health. There are few laws addressing concerns your son may experience, such as being deprived of equal access to his children should he get divorced, or being deprived of due process if he is falsely accused of sexual harassment or date rape.[4] There's no male birth control pill, no affirmative action for the hiring of elementary school teachers or any caring professional, no . . . well, you get the point.

A half century of developing multipurpose women and no-purpose men has taken a toll that is both all around us and rarely seen: a cultural shift met by a cultural shrug. Why? This Superbowl ad delivers a powerful answer . . .

"Sorry, It's a Boy"

A 2015 Superbowl ad for T-Mobile zeroed in on three women talking with each other: one from her mansion, another from her in-home petting zoo (yes, you read that right!), and the third from her in-home underground delivery room. As the third woman is delivering an infant to its mom, she apologizes, "Sorry, it's a boy."[5]

Yet in rural China we might hear, "Sorry, it's a girl." Why? The more survival is at stake, the more boys are needed: to plow fields, build homes, and fight enemies. It is no coincidence that the T-Mobile ad's women characters were super wealthy and entitled. Without fear of starvation, deprivation, or outside attack, an in-home petting zoo is worth bragging about, a boy worth apologizing for.

The more survival is at stake, the more we say, "Sorry, it's a girl." The more luxury we feel, the more we can say, "Sorry, it's a boy." Today, fertility doctors report that 80 percent of aspiring parents would prefer a girl.[6] Adoptive parents put their money where their mouth is, paying an average of $16,000 more (in finalization costs) for a girl than a boy.[7]

Along with African American babies, boys are least likely to be adopted.[8] The anti-boy bias is even greater among single moms-to-be and same-sex couples.[9]

As technology allows for gender selection to go from about $5,000 per year to affordable for most parents who desire it,[10] a Google search predicts the future: *four* times as many searches for "foods to eat to conceive a girl" than "foods to eat to conceive a boy."

It is ironic that it is largely men playing the male role that created the industrialization and technology that freed both sexes to have the luxury to value our sons less. But valuing either sex less is unacceptable. So the next challenge is how to both retain technology's gifts and also guide our sons toward new senses of purpose in which they may be valued for something other than heroic disposability.

CHAPTER 11

How Raising Our Sons Successfully in the Past Differs from Raising Our Sons Successfully for Their Future

The Old Family Boat Versus the New Family Boat

Imagine the family as being in one "family boat." Before the women's movement, children would see their moms rowing from only the right side of the family boat (raising children); their dads, only from the left (raising money). The women's movement helped girls become women who could row from both sides, but without a parallel force for boys, boys became men who had still learned to row only from the left.

The problem? If a mom tries to exercise her newfound ability to row from the left, and the dad can still row only from the left, the boat spins in circles.

A family boat that spins in circles is more vulnerable to the sharp rocks of recession—especially to dad being unemployed. An unemployed dad who isn't prepared to be a fully involved dad means mom is having to row on both sides while dad rows on neither. The result? A family boat with three holes: first, neglected children; second, a dad with a purpose void; and third, a stressed and overwhelmed mom. In addition to the overwhelmed mom, this is not good for the father, son, or holey boat.

Repairing the holey boat requires some unfinished work in women's development as well. In the past half century, we have done a good job socializing men to be proud of wives and daughters with full-time careers; we have done a poor job socializing women to be proud of husbands and sons who are full-time dads. And that's a problem.

Why? As the research of renowned couples therapist John Gottman finds, one of the strongest predictors of a happy marriage is a happy wife.[1] As the old adage goes, "Happy wife, happy life." A wife who thinks of her full-time-dad husband as "my unemployed husband" is an unhappy wife—and leaves her husband feeling shame at a primal level for not fulfilling what he thinks of as his primary way of being valued. It is like a husband saying "my unattractive wife."

How can a dad be happy if he is feeling shamed for being a loser? By articulating to the mom what a devoted dad contributes to the raising of children that will help make his children winners. And therefore make him and mom winners. (A dad's unique contributions are discussed in part IV, "Dad-Deprived Boys Versus Dad-Enriched Boys.")

Now, back to our sons . . .

The Future Is Not Role Mate Versus Soul Mate, But . . .

The future is not role mate *versus* soul mate, but role mate *and* soul mate. **Women who have the option of being economically self-sustaining will increasingly want your son to also have emotional and relationship intelligence.** Your son will need these not as a tool that he can eventually fetch from the clutter of his mental garage to repair the damage of a fierce argument but as an instinctive reflex that comes as naturally as tying his shoes.

As part V on the tension between heroic and health intelligence clarifies, there are multiple skill sets that boys learn reflexively that discourage the emotional and relationship intelligence his potential soul mate will desire, and a partner who is self-sustaining will require. The most important is knowing how to handle criticism without becoming defensive. Since few schools address these issues, family dinner nights are the single most important preparation for helping your son internalize emotional intelligence.

For your son, the qualities it takes for him to become successful at work will often undermine what it takes for him to be successful in love. But that's just the starter challenge.

While your son may—or may not—learn in school skill sets that will prepare him to earn money, he doubtless will absorb his generation's inspiration to "make a difference." What most schools fail to do, though, is prepare your son for why making money is so often at odds with "making a difference"—for understanding why, in the real world, that **should your son follow his bliss, it's most likely the money he'll miss.** Nor will his school teach him how to bridge the gap between the two.

Making Money Versus Making a Difference

As we saw when I shared my conversation with John Lennon, "making a difference" comes at a cost—if John had prepared himself to be a full-time dad to his first son, Julian, we likely would never have heard of John Lennon. Making a bigger contribution to the world often means making a smaller contribution at home. Which can be at odds with a happy partner and children, and ultimately dig a hole in your son's heart.

While I spent an entire book, *Why Men Earn More: The Startling Truth Behind the Pay Gap—and What Women Can Do About It*, on the trade-offs men and women encounter as their pay goes up, I've included a list below of starter themes to frame a discussion on the hierarchy of happiness and purpose to guide your son to strike the right balance between making money versus making a difference.

- Being **employed, or being the primary parent** if your son and his partner both view it as employment. (See "The Five Conditions for Successful Marriage with a Full-Time Dad" in chapter 10.) Unemployment is highly correlated with vulnerability to disease,[2] suicide,[3] and divorce.[4]
- Making *enough* **money for his family's necessities.**
- Having a sense of **purpose**, either by seeing that the next layer of money is creating a better life for his family (e.g., better home in a better school district) or because his work is itself inherently fulfilling and meaningful (e.g., art, or writing books like this!).
- Having a sense of **mission** (e.g., being an inventor who is creating something no one else has created, an entrepreneur creating

a unique business that will save peoples' lives, or a pioneer in a movement that helps people).

Your son may be the exception, but the research finds that the foundation of happiness is built by preparing your son for being employed. A mission can greatly enhance a sense of purpose, but if it is not channeled into employment before having children, it can also be a powerful relationship destroyer. How to strike the right balance depends on your son's personality and abilities.

How to Guide Different Boys Toward Different Senses of Purpose

Whether or not your son is academically inclined may affect what paths to purpose you encourage him to explore, and which he eventually chooses.

Boys Who Are Academically Inclined

We saw that a contributor to the boy crisis is the transition from muscle to mental—or from muscle to microchip—that has led to many traditionally male-dominated jobs (e.g., manufacturer, miner, and farmer) declining while female-dominated jobs (e.g., dental hygienist, physician's assistant, nurse, pharmacist) are both on the upswing and more recession resistant. Nevertheless, few parents consider suggesting these "women's professions" to their sons.

If your son is academically inclined, disciplines like education, nursing, and pharmacy provide a variety of potentially high-paying opportunities. For example, the average salary of a nurse anesthetist is $175,000 per year; of a pharmacist, $120,000. If your son's interest is in education, some charter schools (e.g., in New Orleans and Orlando) pay high school principals in excess of $200,000 per year.[5]

However, encouraging boys into currently female-dominated professions is not the goal. The goal is expanding options. And finding a match between personality and options. It is the process that is paramount. As with Aiden and Trish . . .

A few days before Thanksgiving, Aiden and his wife were delighted to learn they were expecting. Aiden recalled to me, somewhat bemused, "When Trish announced her pregnancy to our families over Thanksgiving dinner, we spent much of the rest of the evening talking about whether Trish wanted to continue being an accountant full-time, cut back to part time, or focus on raising our child." Aiden smiled. "Sort of like what you write about."

Taking that as a hint to broach what had been left out, I asked, "Aiden, would *you* like to be a dentist full-time, or cut back to part-time, or focus on raising your child?"

He laughed. "Hah . . . actually, I never applied those options to myself!"

"What do you guess that you learned as a kid that led to your never thinking of that?" I followed up.

"I don't know, it just never came up . . . Let me think about it."

Later in the evening, Aiden volunteered,

> I've been thinking about your question. The first thing that comes to mind is when I was maybe a fifteen-year-old, back in Minneapolis. I recall loving kids, and even my mom complimenting me about how good I was with them. But when our neighbors needed a babysitter, they asked my mom about my sisters—even my younger sister—but never about me. And apparently my mom never said, "Aiden is great with kids; I could ask *him*."
>
> In high school, I was good with science, and when my dentist complimented me on that, and suggested I become a dentist, my parents gave me a lot more support for that than they had when I had talked about becoming a science teacher. So I became a dentist. Which I found, er . . . boring.

The seeds that Aiden's family had planted—which grew into a career in which Aiden made about twice as much money as he would have as a science teacher—ironically made it much harder for anyone in the family to even think about him becoming a full-time parent while Trish remained a full-time accountant.

What, then, could Trish and Aiden do to allow each other—and, in the future, their child—to create carefully considered options rather than reflexive roles? For starters . . .

- **Exploring all the options.** Trish asking Aiden—or Aiden speaking up—about his desires could expand Trish's three mom options to six or more. For example, Trish and Aiden can both work part-time or one can work full-time, the other part-time.

- **Rotating roles.** Trish can parent full-time the first year, Aiden the second year.
- **Raising children with different expectations.** If Trish and Aiden have a son, they can proactively raise him to take responsibility for younger children, and then recommend him as a babysitter. If they have a daughter, they can prepare her to share the breadwinning role by, for example, starting a website she monetizes.[6]
- **Raising children with emotional intelligence.** If Trish and Aiden have a son, they can help him develop his emotional intelligence so he doesn't feel he has to pay for women to be worthy of their company.
- **Discussing trade-offs.** Trish and Aiden can generate options—to solve both actual and hypothetical problems—at family dinner nights—not as right-or-wrong solutions, but to assess the trade-offs.

The purpose of all of this? To try on different costumes in front of the mirror before wearing them for the first time on the stage of life.

Boys Who Are Not Academically Inclined

If your son is not academically inclined, he is especially vulnerable to his job being outsourced. The health care field has many professions that are not prone to outsourcing, do not require a lot of education, and are male friendly, such as emergency medical technicians and radiographers.

There are many other traditionally female-dominated health professions that cannot be outsourced, require little education, and pay well. Three I recommend investigating with your son are dental hygienist, massage therapist, and physician's assistant. Dental hygienists average $72,000 per year, twice that of a dental assistant. Caveat: there is discrimination against males as dental hygienists, since some patients—both female and male—prefer a woman over a man putting fingers in their mouths. The same discrimination applies to male massage therapists, but if your son is physically strong, the demand for deep-tissue massage will give him an advantage. While massage therapists average $48,000 per year, many independent massage therapists can command $80 an hour and create flexible schedules. If your son chooses a wealthier community, his clientele will be able to pay him even more. Last, a male physician's assistant does not face the discrimination issue, and averages in excess of $100,000 per year.

Boys who are not interested in school almost always have an interest that can be catalyzed into future employment if it is pursued via hands-on experience. For example, Adam and school were like oil and water. But Adam's parents noted that Adam loved caring for a disabled neighbor. When they learned that the home health care industry was projected to grow at almost 40 percent per year, they felt that its current low pay would soon go up.[7] So they took Adam to visit a friend in a nearby community with senior citizens. When Adam felt how he was adored by some of the elderly for his gentle manner, he felt needed. He had a spark in his eye that had been a long time coming.

Nothing hurts our nonacademic sons more than our massive neglect of vocational education. To many families, cutting vocational education leads to feeling that the needs of these boys—and hence, these boys themselves—are disposable. We have seen Japan's success with providing vocational education to its students, with 99.6 percent of the vocational education graduates finding employment.

Where schools are failing, individual teachers can help. Teachers who inform themselves of where the opportunities are can also use that to help fill a boy's purpose void. Brandon remembered, "I wasn't much for school, but everyone said I was great with people. Then one of my teachers, Ms. Kaplan, just happened to mention in class one day how much men were needed as elementary school teachers and social workers. On my way out of class, she singled me out and said she had me in mind when she made that comment. Her singling me out pumped me up enough that, after a long process, I eventually went to college after all, and got an elementary school certificate."

This is exactly why we need affirmative action, grants, and scholarships facilitating the entrance of boys like Adam and Brandon into traditionally women's professions. Affirmative action is more than opportunity, and scholarships are more than money. Such affirmative action and scholarships are social cues, translated as, "Boys and men, we need you in social work. We need you in elementary schools." Instead of "Uncle Sam Needs Your Body," the social cue your son would hear is "Our Children—Our Society—Need Your Mind."

Introducing Your Son to His Sense of Purpose in Everyday Life

Andreas and Anna Merkel introduced their kids, Lukas and Marianna, to their sense of purpose via a favorite game the family played on road trips.

Each family member took turns naming either something they saw, like a skyscraper, or something they spotted someone doing, like pumping gas. They would then name some job or profession related to what they saw. For the skyscraper, it might be an executive in an office in the skyscraper or a welder in the building's construction.

When either Lukas or Marianna came up with something that interested them, they would all give their impressions of what life might be like if they had that job.

Andreas recalled,

As the kids discussed their fantasy of life in different jobs and professions, Lukas at first said he wanted to be a window washer: "Just the top floors of all the skyscrapers." Eventually, we took our imaginations inside the skyscraper. Lukas told us, "I think I wanna be an executive who flies all over the world . . . make big deals and get to see the world for free."

I asked Lukas if he would like to be away from home when he was a dad. That stopped him in his tracks. But just for a minute. "I'll take my wife and my kids with me." Before we knew it, we were discussing whether he wanted to be single, or married to someone who worked outside the home or who parented full-time and could travel with him and the kids. This just naturally introduced them to the whole idea of trade-offs.

"Did you and Anna also play?" I asked.

"Yes. And when we'd say, for example, why we didn't want to be traveling executives once the kids were born, it gave them a sense of their importance to us—and a sense of our values, without it sounding like a lecture."

When I asked Anna and Andreas about the biggest impact the game had, Anna assessed, "It's made both Lukas and Marianna so much more curious. Last week, Lukas asked how the traffic light got there, who makes it . . . And they have both gotten so much more thoughtful about their future than any of their friends."

Our Sons' New Sense of Purpose: The Hero's Journey to Emotional Intelligence

In part V I bring to a conscious level the many unconscious ways we send our sons mixed messages: messages that support health intelligence (emotional and physical), or socialization for a long life, versus messages that support for heroic intelligence, usually socialization for a short life. Helping your son discover a sense of purpose will only confuse him if our messages are directing him down different roads.

The traditional hero's journey is not about being in balance. It is about being out of balance. Take, for example, courage versus fearlessness. Most dads wouldn't question their son wearing a "No Fear" T-shirt. And if his son was the star in a school championship in ice hockey, football, wrestling, or boxing, most dads and many a mom would be reinforcing his fearlessness as they cheer him on.

That fearlessness, though, is in tension with his emotional intelligence. **A key measure of emotional intelligence is knowing that every virtue taken to its extreme becomes a vice.** Fearlessness is courage taken to its extreme.

Similarly, we want our son to have integrity, but if he turns himself into the police because he went 59 in a 55 mph zone, well . . . We want him to be assertive, but not aggressive; to be empathetic, but not naive; to be "a doer," but also introspective; to be perseverant, but not stubborn; to be prepared, but not obsessive; to help people, but not enable them . . .

As you are helping your son define his purpose, it's pivotal to ask him for examples of situations in which his ideal or ambition might be a virtue taken to its extreme. When he is routinely asked by you to answer that question himself, seeking balance becomes internalized. But note that's a very different process than cutting down his idea before he has a chance to discover for himself whether it can blossom.

You'll likely find it easy to start practicing the balance-seeking process, as your son is exposed almost daily to "dream the impossible dream" fantasies. As soon as your son tunes in to Walt Disney, he'll see, "If you can dream it, you can do it."

Aaron took that to heart. He dreamed of being an astronaut. But he wasn't good at math, and didn't like engineering or science. And when he gave up his dream, he thought of himself as a failure. When someone has a strong sense of purpose that goes unrealized, research shows that it can be life depleting.[8]

Barry's inspiration to dream the impossible dream—in his case, becoming a professional basketball player—were two potent social bribes. Barry was the third most valuable player on his high school basketball team:

> In my freshman year I also had almost all As. But my parents were divorced and the only time I saw them both together was at every game. They were so proud.
>
> In the meantime, I had my eye on this gorgeous cheerleader. She only noticed me as part of the collective team—until I told her I had my eyes set on the NBA. She told the other cheerleaders, and suddenly she was competing with them for me! I didn't want to fail, so I practiced all year. My grades slipped big time. I only got a small basketball scholarship to a college that was still too expensive, and I ended up going to a community college until I pulled my grades back up, instead.
>
> If I had to do it over, I would have focused on my grades.

If your son's dream is a poor match for his abilities, what's the best way to handle that? For sure, use his dream to teach him how to stretch beyond self-imposed limits. But simultaneously encourage him to examine his gifts and his goals, as well as the trade-offs of pursuing a goal that is not in alignment with his gifts.

That said, don't stop cheering. When your son sees you cheering for him, he receives three extremely positive messages: "Mom and Dad care"; "What I do matters"; and "I'll be rewarded for not giving up." And praising success is a positive even when it translates into a certain amount of pressure.

How do you avoid your son feeling seriously disheartened if his goal goes unmet? The solution is clarity from dad that his dad loves him for who he is, not what he does. (Boys rarely worry that their mom's love is conditional upon their winning.)

It is rare that either a dad's or mom's love is in fact conditional on their son winning or achieving a goal. Nevertheless, it can still feel that way to your son. Dad, check out these two litmus tests:

- Is the sport or goal your son is pursuing your primary source of excitement—as Notre Dame football was for Jack's dad?
- Do you engage in "son-dropping"—as with Kyle's dad?

Son-Dropping

Kyle recalled,

> When I reached up for my first two passes, I knew Dad was watching; I was so nervous that I missed both passes—both catchable passes. But the third one I caught, and then evaded two tacklers.
>
> After that game, the first thing my dad said was, "I'm so proud of you. I told everyone around us, 'That's *my son* there—who just caught that pass.'" He didn't need to tell me that he claimed being my dad when I caught the pass, and not either time that I had missed it! But to this day, it's like his pride in me when I caught the pass is carved into the stone of my psyche.
>
> My younger brother was there, too, and I relished being a great role model for him. But years later my brother told me how *invisible* he felt. And how the better I got, the more he felt like he was "Dad's disappointment." When we had our first heart-to-heart talk and I held him in my arms, he burst into tears, crying, "When you messed up your back, I felt so guilty, but once I thought, 'Now maybe Dad will notice me.'"

Kyle's dad's "son-dropping"—or dropping his son's name to make sure his son's newfound glory also reflected on his parenting—is not a problem *per se*. However . . .

- Be aware of the power of son-dropping—and what it is empowering. In this case, it was Kyle's discipline, confidence, and mastery of a skill . . . as well as the risk of concussions and what would become Kyle's "messed-up back."

- Be aware of leaving brothers and sisters feeling invisible at best, and at worst, feeling less loved than the son whose name you are "dropping." Are you paying equal attention to his siblings' strengths, especially their character strengths, like kindness, or their emotional intelligence?

Kyle and his brother are now parents, and Kyle has a son, Owen. Kyle recounts:

When Owen was playing Ping-Pong with his friend in our basement, his friend hit a shot that may or may not have touched the end of the table. Owen called it in his *friend's* favor, and his friend won the game. That was a long time coming for him! I complimented Owen in front of his friend, and again later at our dinner with his mom. And then, when I led our Thanksgiving grace, I included, "Thank you, Lord, for giving me a son who can call a point in his friend's favor even when it was too close to call." The family all picked up on that, telling stories about how much more mature he is than they had been at his age—or even now! And his uncle added, "You lost the game and won a friend." Owen was beaming with pride.

Kyle had learned how to use son-dropping to reinforce his son's emotional intelligence. In this case, although Owen's brother and sister were at the family table, the open acknowledgment was not a problem because what he was praising—calling a close shot in favor of an opponent—was also within their ability to master.

CHAPTER 12

Raising a Balanced Son in an Out-of-Balance World

We interview people who are extraordinary successes, so they are visible. We ignore people who create a balanced life, so they are invisible. That is, we rarely interview and make visible those who spend the amount of alone time, spiritual time, family time, friend time, and share-the-housework time that takes away from their success at work but adds to their love at home.

In a world where celebrity is an international passport, your son's optimal heroic journey is to be internally secure enough to evolve a life in which he *becomes* love as he gives love rather than becoming dependent on approval via social bribes, whether from dad, the "in-group" in high school, or the adulation of strangers. This "becoming love" is what John Lennon told me he experienced as he took out five years to raise Sean— "the best decision of my life."

In contrast, the black hole of addiction to adulation creates a pressure to perform from which the psyche needs to escape, whether directly by suicide (e.g., Ernest Hemingway and Robin Williams) or indirectly via an addiction to drugs (e.g., Marilyn Monroe, Michael Jackson, Jim Morrison, Janis Joplin, Jimi Hendrix, Prince, and Whitney Houston).

While your son's internal security is most likely to be enhanced by the hands-on involvement of both parents, even one conscious parent can lead the way.

What Happened to Pickup Team Sports?

Perhaps the most-likely-to-succeed single vehicle for leading your son toward internal security is sports. The Centers for Disease Control and Prevention finds that **exercise helps build the muscle of a child's brain** *even more effectively than studying.*[1] Organized team sports also hone your son's social skills, and the team and leadership skills needed for the workplace. Individual sports train him to work independently. A blend of both creates flexibility. But there are still two steps missing before sports can become an accessible liberal art for your son (or daughter) . . .

First, while all children need sports, varsity and junior varsity sports permit only a small percentage to get competitively involved. Schools make their varsity sports so visible and their intramural sports so invisible that your son may receive virtually no support for participating in a combination of multiple intramural team and individual sports. You may need to take the lead to get his school to develop a broader intramural program that gets him involved for his good, not for the school's good. And if you take that lead, have your son *work with you.* The experience of creating change is as important as the change itself.

Second, there's the big hole in what your son may be missing from sports: pickup games. **Pickup sports are excellent preparation for entrepreneurship.** For example, pickup games encourage entrepreneurship by giving your children practice in

- creating something from nothing;
- recruiting and organizing;
- creating their own rules rather than just following the rules of others;
- integrating friends with strangers without favoring friends (or losing because one favored friends);
- negotiating boundaries that give everyone an equal chance—or ones that give one's team, with their skills, a competitive advantage; and
- creating consequences for rule breakers, and deciding when to enforce them.

When your son participates in individual sports, plus both organized and pickup team sports, he will be experiencing sports as a

boy-friendly liberal art. Instead of manhood's "rite of passage" being varsity visibility, it becomes his ability to develop a broad skill set, and implement it both in a team and by himself.

However, using sports to develop a balanced boy involves more than a balanced sports curriculum. It requires your guidance in how he plays the sports. The siren song he will hear is "When the going gets tough, the tough get going." But what he needs is to develop an internal radar that helps him tune into himself to know when to tough it out and when to get out.

Helping Your Son Find His "Edge"

Why do we tell our sons to "tough it out" right after we've said "be careful"? Because in battle we needed boys to ignore injuries to continue fighting the enemy. Ignoring the injury meant his testosterone would increase as he increasingly felt he was making a contribution to defeating the enemy.[2] But the increase in testosterone also weakened his immune system, and increased his adrenaline (or epinephrine), which made him vulnerable to blood clotting, and therefore to heart failure.[3]

When we cared more about developing warrior boys—even if the boys died—this was functional. But since you care about your son living, it is dysfunctional. If your son is seduced only by the need to prove himself by "toughing it out" and ignoring pain, his body's built-in capacity to tune in to pain becomes dormant.

Conversely, if he is taught only to "get out" of the game, his body's ability to help him discover his "edge," and thereby maximize his potential, becomes dormant.

Your deeper challenge, then, is to help your son understand that his mind and body are most powerful when he uses all the resources it has evolved for millions of years. Rather than his motto being "When the going gets tough, the tough get going," **the motto for the evolved boy is "When the going gets tough, *tune in* to know *when* to tough it out."**

You'll be teaching him how to tap into the gift of his entire genetic inheritance. We might think of it as preparing your son to get a couple of steps ahead of evolution's curve.

Maslow's Hierarchy Versus Your Son's Hierarchy

When you hear the term "self-actualized" you may think of Maslow's pyramid of the hierarchy of needs, which many of us were introduced to in school. At the pyramid's pinnacle was self-actualization.

Maslow's Hierarchy of Needs

Source: Saul McLeod, *Simply Psychology*[4]

Look at where the most basic, primal needs appear here: food, water, and safety.

Now compare their placement on Maslow's hierarchy to where they fall on a hierarchy of a pyramid neither you nor your son have seen (because I've only just created it), my pyramid of the traditional male hero's values:

Farrell's Hierarchy of the Traditional Male Hero's Values

Safety, warmth
and rest

Being a dominant,
revered, kind and wise force

Being a dominant, feared force

Survival (but not safety), food, water

Belongingness and Love Needs: Winning the
hand of a beautiful woman in marriage by protecting and
providing for her and the children

Respect and Approval Needs: Trying to get society's respect
by fulfilling what society expects of him, even if that means being
killed in war or dying from stress from overwork

Note the differences:

- For the traditional male hero, self-actualization is nowhere. **The traditional male hero is about self-sacrifice, not self-actualization**.
- What Maslow describes as the most basic needs—food, water, safety—are needs the male hero only allows himself as a means to an end: to have the strength to kill the dragon. Whether he is a marine, Navy SEAL, or firefighter, the hero only allows himself to indulge in safety, warmth, and rest for his own personal comfort *after* his missions are accomplished. Thus, safety, warmth, and rest are missing from the bottom of the hero's pyramid, and appear only at the tip of his pyramid, like frosting on the cake of his life.
- **In the traditional male hero's hierarchy of needs, self-actualization is nowhere to be found—because the more he values himself, the less he is willing to sacrifice himself.**

Should we just replace the traditional model of male hero with a model of self-actualization? No. That's throwing out the boy with the bathwater—it will dispose of our son by disposing of the best of what creates his purpose. The traditional boy's journey to self-sacrifice incorporated service to others, and required responsibility, loyalty, honor, and accountability. It created his mission. And his mission created his character.

If we go from teaching our sons "I exist, therefore I serve" to "I exist, therefore I deserve," we repeat the tendency of new freedoms to create new problems. To illustrate the dangers of replacing heroism with simple self-satisfaction, I've also constructed the "Hierarchy of the *Self-Satisfied* Nontraditional Male's Values":

Farrell's Hierarchy of the Self-Satisfied Nontraditional Male's Values

To be re-
spected, loved
and revered for
whatever is fulfilling
and comes naturally

Receiving immediate gratification
with friends' and family's respect

Receiving immediate
gratification with friends

Receiving immediate gratification
in whatever form that takes

Warmth and rest provided without effort

Survival: food, water, safety provided without effort

This "I exist, therefore I deserve" model facilitates a boy's immediate gratification by allowing him to focus on what he wants to do when he wants to do it (e.g., have his dessert first). So he never develops the ability to postpone gratification (e.g., eat his peas before his ice cream). The result is a deficit of attention to what he needs to do—a setup for attention deficit disorder and ADHD.

The discipline of postponing gratification is the single most important discipline your son needs. Postponing gratification stretches the psychic muscles required to make his dreams today more than disappointments tomorrow. If he doesn't develop it, repeated disappointments make him afraid to dream. He becomes a boy without purpose. A failure to launch. Your disappointment in him pales in comparison to his shame and disappointment in himself.

The solution—raising a balanced male—requires blending the best of the traditional male with the self-actualized male. His hierarchy:

Farrell's Hierarchy of the Self-Actualized Nontraditional Male

Self-actualization and contributing-to-others as purpose

Esteem needs met by weighing his assessment of parental, societal and "his own" evolving issues

Belongingness and love need met by family and/or a supportive community

Pursues learning of academic, career and emotion skills

Basic needs provided for as he strives to be self-sustaining

Supporting your son toward becoming a self-actualized nontraditional male involves:

- Loving your son for who he is—in fact, helping him discover his "different drummer" or "unique self"[5]—and how it might contribute to his sense of purpose.
- Helping him distinguish between the value of listening to others and being enslaved by the need for the approval of others.
- Exposing him to careers most likely to create both economic and emotional well-being, given his gifts, interests, and personality.

- Helping him understand why both sexes fall in love with members of the other sex least likely to be able to provide them with a long life of love—and what he can do about it.

These discoveries can be catalyzed by family discussions. We saw how the Merkels used their road trips to imagine potential future careers. A skyscraper, for example, triggered an image of an executive or window washer, which in turn jump-started a discussion of what a life doing that might be like.

Tom and Lydia Johnson used family dinner nights to play a game they called "Who's most popular [at school] now?" When the kids chose someone, they asked them for their best speculation as to why and then asked, "Would you like to be more like, or less like, that person?" The kids loved that question, and the next one: "What do you think you might like and dislike about her or him twenty years from now?"

Tom said,

As our son, Spencer, started dating, we morphed the game into "Who are you dating—or would like to be dating—now?" Playing the "most popular" game for years seemed to make it easier for Spencer to cough up his romantic interests—I know a lot of boys his age don't like talking to their parents about that.

The first answer to the next question, the "why" question, was usually a simple, "She's one of the prettiest girls in the school—or at least the prettiest one who isn't 'taken'!" So we had to follow that up with a "What *else* do you like about her?"

And then came the big question: asking Spencer to choose the girl in his school who he thought would make the best wife and mother. He'd start out saying "Her," but when we pushed him to really think, he'd usually choose someone else altogether. And that got the most useful discussions started—about who we fall in love with versus who we might have the best life with.

Lydia and I learned a lot, and Janine, Spencer's younger sister, really got into it, too—both kids were both so curious, and sad, about how Spencer was attracted to the girl who wouldn't usually be his best life partner. The game got them to be conscious about that, and I could see Spencer's choices begin to change a little.

By the time Janine started taking an interest in boys, she was asking herself that love versus life question from the start. Janine was attracted to the tight end on the football team, but as she thought about the type of long-term partner the tight end might make, she ultimately switched over to the forward on the basketball team. Ahh, it's what a parent lives for!

Filling Your Son's Purpose Void: Your Son as Hero

Preparing our sons for senses of purpose for their futures that are not dependent on our need for them to be disposable requires an evolutionary shift in both parenting and schooling. We need warriors, just like we need young women to bear children, so our kids need to see role models of both. Yet we also have the luxury to guide our kids toward choosing their role on life's stage.

As you use family trips and family dinner nights to facilitate your son discovering himself and his purpose, he will learn how to take what he learned under your care and adjust it to those stages of his life when he is under his own care. What will be common to each stage, though, is your gift of encouraging him to be a human being first, and enough of a human being to support being that better human being. You will give him the gifts to perfect himself without killing himself.

The best gift we can give a boy, to help him become self-actualized enough to feel free to choose to be either traditional or nontraditional, is a mom and dad devoted to the art and discipline of raising children together, even if that means living in separate, but nearby, homes. Once a family of four hits an income threshold where they can afford necessities—usually $50,000 to $80,000—the rest is, as we've seen, about the time, not the dime. Few children tell their psychologists, "I would have felt so much more loved by my dad if he had gotten more promotions."

We will see in part IV exactly why having the checks and balances of both mom and dad is most likely to create the security a son needs to succeed in more than fifty areas—including becoming secure enough to respect himself, secure enough to incorporate the best of others, and *secure enough to empathize with the pain that creates the worst in others.*

The boy crisis cannot be solved, then, without addressing the most important single crisis in developed countries: dad-deprived children, and especially dad-deprived boys.

PART IV

Dad-Deprived Boys Versus Dad-Enriched Boys

The boy crisis' primary cause is dad-deprived boys. Dad deprivation stems primarily from the lack of father involvement, and secondarily from devaluing what a father contributes when he *is* involved. Whether our children become financially rich or poor—or emotionally rich or poor—depends increasingly on whether they grow up dad-rich or dad-poor.

When the medical community discovers a new disease, one of their first steps toward conquering it is to name it. We can legitimately say that our children are being raised in the Era of the Dad Deprived, especially the Era of the Dad-Deprived Boy. A first step toward bringing that era to a close is to acknowledge the generations from millennials on as the generations of the dad-deprived.

The need to end the era of the dad-deprived is not a crisis about which the sexes are divided. When asked, 93 percent of moms agree there is a crisis of father absence in the US today.[1] And our dads and children concur.

The damage of dad-deprivation starts early—in our children's genes ...

CHAPTER 13

Dad-Deprived Boys

Depriving a child of his or her dad is depriving a child of part of her or his life. That is, findings published in *Pediatrics* in 2017 concluded that "at 9 years of age, children with father loss have significantly shorter telomeres."[1] Telomeres in our cells are what keep our genes from being deleted as our cells divide. As the National Academy of Sciences reports, "Telomere length in early life predicts lifespan."[2]

How much damage to life expectancy is created by dad-deprivation? Children with father loss already have by age nine telomeres that are 14 percent shorter.[3] However, when compared to girls, the telomere damage from father loss is "40% greater for boys."[4]

Dads—like moms, air, and water—are essential to our lives. But we've tried to live without dads. We haven't tried to live without moms, air, or water.

Why is it that in a generation producing some outstanding young men, whether a boy is in crisis or leading us out of a crisis is significantly influenced by whether he is dad deprived or dad enriched? Dad-enriched boys tend to fill the purpose void with constructive new senses of purpose; dad-deprived boys are more likely to either drown in their purpose void, or fill it with destructive senses of purpose.

Our daughters are also either damaged by dad deprivation,[5] or empowered by dad involvement on many more measures than lifespan alone.[6] But the impact on boys is proving considerably greater—not only during their childhood and teenage years, but through their lives. This is true not only of boys' economic future, but also of boys' emotional intelligence and marital potential—all of which are inextricably connected.[7] Whether because of the slower maturation of boys' brains[8] or poorer social skill socialization, our sons are more vulnerable than our daughters.

And when boys are hurt, they hurt us—physically, psychologically, and economically.

Boys Who Hurt, Hurt Us

> **Item.** A study of ISIS fighters concluded that almost all had in common "some type of an 'absent father' syndrome."[9]

If fighters in ISIS (aka ISIL or Daesh) have in common "some type of an 'absent father' syndrome,"[10] the implications extend to our national security policy: replace drones with dads.

When a boy sees little of his own dad, he hurts. Boys who hurt, hurt us. Not only in the Middle East, but also in the United States . . .

At age nineteen, Anthony Sims' participation in a gun battle led to him slaying a young mother in Oakland, California. Anthony's final Facebook post before his arrest was "I wish I had a father . . ."[11]

Dad deprivation is the main hole in the heart common to boys vulnerable to gangs[12] and to boys targeted by sexual predators. It was also common to boys recruited by Hitler for Hitler Youth.[13] And boys too alienated to be recruited by others may recruit themselves—as, for example, lone school shooters.

The Lost Boys: Mass Shooters

My TEDx talk on the boy crisis in 2015[14] illustrates the connection between dad-deprived boys and the school and other mass shootings by Adam Lanza (Sandy Hook), Elliott Rodgers (UC Santa Barbara), and Dylann Roof (Charleston church).[15]

Yes, these shooters committed multiple homicides. But, either directly or indirectly, each committed suicide. Living in homes without dads is more correlated with suicide among teenagers than any other factor.[16]

Note that these boys—and many other school shooters such as Karl Pierson, the Arapahoe High School shooter, and Michael Brandon Hill, the

Discovery Learning Academy shooter[17]—are not poor black or Hispanic inner-city youth with dozens of other probable deprivations as causes. They are usually Caucasian boys, often suburban and dad deprived.

With the frequent background of dad deprivation, perhaps school shootings are a Caucasian boy's way of acting out his anger at the school that couldn't adequately replace his dad, and at the peers who rejected him for his lack of social and emotional intelligence.

ISIS: A Gang of Dad-Deprived Boys?

Studies of recruits of ISIS (a.k.a., ISIL or Daesh),[18] and reports by faith-inspired leaders working directly with Muslim youth and their imams both draw the same conclusion: what ISIS recruits most have in common is that they are boys—and some girls—with absent dads.

Fiyaz Mughal, a radicalization prevention specialist who works with the Faith Matters Network, discovered that faith does not matter when working with dad-deprived boys. "All of those kids, they have an absent father . . . The kids fought police, fought at school, rebelled against every power structure at every opportunity."[19]

Some reports about ISIS find that it is less akin to a religion and more akin to a gang.[20] Why? ISIS fills many of the parameters sought by boys without dads: purpose, excitement, and identity. For some, religion may represent but one more authority to distrust. But for others, religion offers a structure that strengthens their sense of purpose and mission. For these boys, the need for purpose, excitement, and identity are met more through ISIS's requirements to sacrifice, serve, and represent a mission they feel has a higher morality than is represented by the "immorality" of the United States. Above all, these boys are looking to represent something larger than themselves.

When a boy harbors a void of identity and is seduced by the siren song of ISIS promising to fill that void, some boys cannot resist, even if it means destroying themselves and others in the process.

Hitler Youth: Filling the Dad Void

Source: National Archives and Records Administration

Many of the children recruited by Hitler Youth were fatherless boys.[21] *History Place* reported that these boys, once recruited, were isolated in camps where weakness was despised.[22] They were trained "without any counterbalancing influences from a normal home life . . . The youngest and most vulnerable boys were bullied, humiliated . . . including repeated sexual abuse."[23]

Reports from British and Canadian soldiers fighting in World War II noted that, in battle, these boys "sprang like wolves against tanks." Even if encircled, they fought until the last boy was killed. "Young boys, years away from their first shave, had to be shot dead by Allied soldiers old enough, in some cases, to be their fathers."[24]

Dad deprivation still leaves boys vulnerable to Nazis—these days, neo-Nazi groups. Former neo-Nazi T. J. Leyden, who joined the skinheads after his parents divorced, reported that the neo-Nazis look for "young, angry kids who need a family"—which, in practical terms, usually means that they need a dad.[25]

Jeff Weise's dad killed himself when he was thirty-two, while Jeff was a young teenager in Minnesota. Jeff soon began posting on neo-Nazi

(National Socialist) websites. At age sixteen, Jeff became a mass-murderer, leaving ten dead victims.[26]

These examples reflect a pattern: After divorce or loss of a father, both girls and boys experience unhappiness, but especially with divorce, girls' grief eases within a year or two, while boys' does not.[27] Similarly, among children with unmarried teen mothers, it is the boys who experience "alarmingly high levels of pathology": substance abuse, criminal activity, and prison time. These problems persist beyond their teen years: boys with teen mothers also have far more problems than girls as adults.[28]

Boys who hurt, hurt us. But they are also vulnerable to being hurt. Particularly by being exploited sexually.

Fathers Lost, Fathers' Prey: The Dad-Deprived Boy

The film *Spotlight* helped the world see how the 6 percent of Catholic priests who molested children homed in on dad-deprived boys.[29] It was as if the priests could smell these boys' desperation for a father's attention, love, and guidance.

While the film exposed the church's cover-up, what went unexposed is what made the priests so desperate: Celibacy? Their own dad-deprivation? Or something else?

If we wish to stop boys who hurt hurting us, it helps to start with how the adults who hurt were themselves hurt so the entire cycle can be broken. Those adults include women.

Female Rehabilitators' Prey: The Dad-Deprived Boy

Juvenile detention centers are filled with dad-deprived boys. A US Department of Justice report found that 7.7 percent of boys in these centers reported being sexually abused by adult staff.[30] However, there were two major distinctions between this abuse and the male Catholic priest sexual exploitation:

- 89 percent of the juvenile detention staff perpetrators were *female*; and
- once uncovered, the systemic sexual abuse by male priests was a worldwide scandal; in contrast, the systemic sexual abuse by the

female staff—although uncovered by the Department of Justice—is still ignored.

Our collectively turning a blind eye to women who abuse creates a double jeopardy: First, we leave the boys who are abused feeling isolated, and if they get up the courage to report their abusers, we leave them having to fight for credibility—the same problems female victims face. Second, stopping the cycle of abuse by female detention center employees must, as with male Catholic priests, include putting a spotlight on the vulnerabilities of the abusers themselves. When we turn a blind eye to the abuse, we are unable to consider how these women themselves were hurt, which would open the door to breaking the entire cycle—whether in detention centers or places we have yet to discover.

In brief, whether our spotlight is on ISIS, gangs, Hitler Youth, neo-Nazis, the church, or in facilities designed to rehabilitate boys, boys who are dad deprived today are the boys who are tomorrow's prey.

Fortunately, the seeds of dad involvement are easily germinated. Until recently, even as men were discovering outer space, they were missing a discovery in their inner space: their dad brain.

Bio Dad: The Discovery of the Dad Brain

Perhaps your son feels that monogamy is monotony and changing partners is more fun than changing diapers. It may help your son to know that being an *involved* dad creates a "dad brain" that replaces his single-man desires. He'll experience a decrease in the testosterone previously used in the hunt for sex and recovery after rejection, and an increase in oxytocin emanating from the joys of loving and being loved by an infant who needs him. Here's how this happens . . .

When a man becomes a hands-on dad he activates his "dad brain"—a nest of neurons that would otherwise remain dormant. This dad brain is very similar—although not identical to—the circuits triggered in expect-ant moms.[31]

A hands-on dad also experiences fundamental hormonal changes.[32] First, he will begin producing more oxytocin, a hormone that stimulates nurturing, trust, and affection, and therefore encourages bonding. He'll also produce more estrogen, as well as prolactin, the hormone that in women helps produce breast milk. Finally, just as your son's testosterone level drops if he is in a committed relationship, it will drop even more if he becomes an active dad.

In a dad's brain, an increase in oxytocin activates a greater facility to connect with his children. It does this by enhancing his brain's centers of social cognition, something that is called "parent-child synchrony."[33]

But while the changes in a dad's brain do resemble those in a mom's, the dad brain also drives contributions that are different from mom's. For mom, it's baby talk and staring into the baby's eyes; for dad, it's playful touching and behavior, physically moving the baby, and introducing the baby to new objects.[34]

When does a dad's brain and hormone adaptation occur most fully? When there is no mother in the picture. Among male same-sex couples who are both primary caregivers, their adaptation is slightly different. Both partners' neural activity mirrors that typical of mothers.[35]

When a dad is hands-on, then his neurological and hormonal systems adapt to his new role. We have long theorized that women's brains and hormones, and particularly the adaptations that occur during pregnancy, combine to create a maternal instinct. We now see that a hands-on dad also fairly quickly develops both a dad brain and paternal hormones, or a paternal instinct.

We know a hands-on dad is good for the children. But what can you tell your son about whether these changes will be good for him? The research of Yale psychiatrist and parenting expert Kyle Pruett finds that as the involved dad's health improves, so do his relationships, his warmth, and even his job satisfaction.[36] As one dad put it, "Once you have held your sleeping child night after night or walked for years with their hand in yours, you are a changed person."[37]

When Margaret Mead said that a woman's role is more biologically determined, whereas a man's is more socially determined, she was mostly right. What she missed was that the social decision catalyzes a biological adaptation.

It is often quipped, "When women marry, they hope to change the man; when men marry, they hope the woman will remain the same. Both are disappointed." Your son's future spouse no longer has to prepare for disappointment: your son can, in fact, change.

When it comes to parenting, it's like everyone is given an iPhone at birth, but new dads need permission to turn theirs on. But do dads *want* to turn on their dad brain?

Do Dads Really *Want* to Turn on their Dad Brain?

Until recently, no one asked. When asked, 70 percent of dads have said they'd prefer more time with the family even if that meant earning less.[38] But more astonishing, in a recent Pew Research Center survey, even full-time working dads were expressing a *preference* for being home with their children rather than at work without their children. That is, half of working dads said, "I'd prefer to be home with my children, but I need the income so I need to work."[39]

If your son chooses to be a primary parent when his children are young, will he feel weird? It depends on how he sees things. On the one hand, there has been a *ninefold* increase since 1960 in the percentage of households with minor children headed by a single dad.[40] If we add dads who are primary caretakers while also working outside the home, some estimates are up to seven million.[41] On the other hand, if he wishes to stay at home full-time and not work at all outside the home, that nine-fold statistic is nine times what was only a tiny fraction in 1960. Here's a macro view...

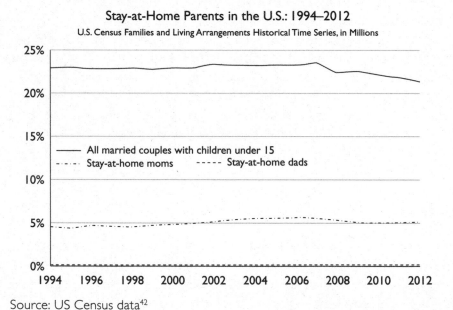

Stay-at-Home Parents in the U.S.: 1994–2012

U.S. Census Families and Living Arrangements Historical Time Series, in Millions

Source: US Census data[42]

The solution? If your son has the personality of a pioneer with a nurturing instinct, encourage him to weigh the trade-offs of being a full-time dad. But if working outside the home is part of his purpose, guide him toward investing in his children differently. In the past, dads often invested in their children by investing in stocks. Today, fathers are increasingly realizing that the best investment in their children is time. At APX Labs near Washington, DC, flexible schedules—or "dad time"— now rival stock options as the top perk.

Fathers' desire for involvement is more than a shift in attitude. Fathers have also shifted their behavior, nearly tripling their time with children since 1965.

And they're hungry for more. The Pew survey finds that twice as many dads as moms (46 percent vs 23 percent) feel they still spend too little time with their children. When given a chance, dads put their time where their mouth is: In the first ten years of California's paid family leave program, the proportion of claims filed by men nearly doubled, from 17 percent in 2004 to 30 percent in 2014.

In countries like Sweden and Canada, paid paternity leave policies make it financially more viable for the dad to attend to his child's emotional needs. In Sweden, 85 percent of fathers take paternity leave.[43] Why? In part, because if the dad doesn't take the leave, it is forfeited. And in part, because there is a culture of acceptance—even of expectation—of father involvement with infants. We are social beings: shifts in attitude shift behavior, and shifts in behavior shift attitudes.

Careers Are for Now; Children Are Forever

In the past, boys fulfilled their sense of purpose and mission via a career that was expected to last a lifetime. In the future, since careers will rarely last a lifetime, it is preparing your son to be a dad that is more likely to give him a sense of purpose for a lifetime.

Only a small fraction of men feel their souls are nurtured by their careers. For most men, the road to high pay is a toll road.[44] Tolls that involve time away from the family. Tolls that lead to the "father's catch-22": loving his family by being away from the love of his family.

There are few men who, on their deathbeds, say, "I wish I had spent more time at the office." But dads who nurture dad-enriched children receive the gift of a nurtured soul. And as his son feels he is contributing joy to his dad's life, he feels positive anticipation about the dad he can become.

This biological adaptability of our sons to fathering and the desire of our sons to be more involved as part of a lifetime's sense of purpose are pivotal to solving the boy crisis.

But because the disposability of boys is part of our heritage, solving the boy crisis will require our recognition that is not just boys' future that is at stake; it is the world's future. The world suffers from the emotional terror that results from dad-deprived boys and girls being seduced by ISIS and ISIS-type terrorists. Those psychological costs are then magnified by fiscal costs . . .

The Absence of Dad Creates the Presence of Government

In our attempt to restore emotional security after 9/11, we incur the fiscal costs of expanding the US government (e.g., NSA, TSA, Homeland Security, the Patriot Act, "extreme vetting," border walls, and immigration bans) and the psychological costs that accompany the loss of freedoms.

The War on Terror has added $2 *trillion* to America's debt as of fiscal year 2018.[45] What percentage of that cost might have been saved if ISIS did not have a supply of dad-deprived boys from which to draw?

Beyond these costs, scholars calculate that every *1 percent* reduction in family fragmentation would save taxpayers $1.1 billion *per year*.[46] For example, as we'll see, dad deprivation increases the likelihood of teenage motherhood, and *80 percent* of unmarried teen mothers become welfare recipients, costing more than $9 billion in tax dollars per year.[47]

As you read about dad deprivation's connections to the increase in crime, incarceration, school shootings, domestic violence, rape, drugs, problems in mental health, physical health, poverty, unemployment, and drop-out rates, keep in mind how each dollar we spend to bring in the government to clean up the tragedies of dad deprivation reflects multiple generations of psychic wounds that no amount of money can cure.

All Dad-Deprived Boys Are Not Equally Deprived

When a dad dies, or is killed in war, children do comparatively better than when their fathers are absent because of divorce or parents never marrying.[48] They do not fare as well as children raised in families in which both biological parents are present, but the likelihood of damage is less.

Why? When a dad is killed in war or dies at work or via a disease or accident, the father's absence does not leave the children feeling purposely abandoned. My own experience starting hundreds of men's and women's groups, spending weekends observing about fifty divorced dads with their children, doing my research for both this book and for *Father and Child Reunion*, plus conducting couples' communication workshops around the country, confirms this. Dads killed in war are portrayed as heroes. And in his father's absence, the oldest boy is sometimes told he is the new "man of the family," with special responsibilities. He often steps up to that new sense of purpose. In each case, the children retain a positive, even larger-than-life image of their dad, and the son feels a special responsibility to live up to his dad's memory.

When a dad dies, the children experience their mom's grief at his loss. Their mom often shows respect for their dad, and positive stories about him are enhanced by nostalgia. The children "inherit" that respect for him, and therefore for the half of themselves that is him.

In contrast, children of divorce report that they rarely hear their dad honored, and instead often hear their dad bad-mouthed. They "inherit" more negative feelings about that half of themselves, and often for men as a gender.

Children raised by moms who are single by choice tend to experience fewer problems than children of divorce. But these children are still more likely to struggle with delinquency, substance abuse, and depression (even when controlling for socioeconomic variables). For example, they are twice as likely as children living with both mom and dad to have problems with the law before age twenty-five,[49] more than two and a half times as likely to struggle with substance abuse,[50] and slightly more likely to experience problems with depression and mental health.[51]

Dad deprivation after divorce is such a big problem because it so often entails the child hearing negative things about the dad, and feeling that a dad who is available is purposely not making himself available, or so incompetent, unreliable, or narcissistic that he would do more harm than good.

Why It Cannot Be Said That Either Sex Makes the Better Parent

I want to be clear: the importance of dads does not imply that dads are *more important* than moms. Why? Men who challenge the stereotype—and in the case of divorce, often the courts—to be an equal or primary parent today are highly self-selected. We are comparing self-selected dads to the average mom.

Furthermore, dads are more likely to have the help of mom than moms are to have the help of dad. When a dad is the primary parent, he is more likely to invite mom in, and mom is very likely to accept the invitation. When a mom is the primary parent, while she usually wants dad involvement, it's more often conditional on him parenting the way she feels he should parent, and that "gatekeeping" becomes one factor in the dad withdrawing from involvement. (More on that in the next chapter.)

Reasons aside, a dad-rich family is more often a mom-rich family, too. Especially when both parents are involved, children are more likely to become emotionally rich, socially adept, physically healthy, and financially comfortable adults.

That said, millions of boys who are raised in homes without their biological fathers—whether homes with single moms, same-sex female parents, or stepdads—prosper, in large part because of the devotion, love, and wisdom of their nontraditional parents. Conversely, many who grew up with dads who abused them spend their lifetimes attempting to cleanse the toxicity of their early years. No single factor is a panacea, and the contribution of everyone who devotes themselves to raising or mentoring a child is a gift.

With that in mind, our focus here is on the degree to which father involvement is an underused resource in the family in the same way that female involvement has been an underused resource in the workplace.

Final caveat: what follows is true statistically, but not necessarily in any specific case. It can provide guidelines to prepare your son for the next evolutionary shift. Let it be a guide that deepens your wisdom, but never replaces it.

CHAPTER 14

Why Are Dads So Important?

The desire to be a father begins in the son, who sees in his own dad who he could become. We saw this when Ethan told his therapist he wasn't interested in becoming a dad because he and his dad couldn't see each other, and he didn't want to have children he couldn't see.

This chapter attempts to document the importance of dad. But there is another dimension that is not documentable; it is a blend of the spiritual, mystical, and unexplainable. We see it, for example, in the way many adopted children yearn to connect with something missing within themselves. I "got" this on a gut level when I watched this story of Justin Rozier on CBS News.[1] When Justin was nine months old, he lost his father in Iraq. He desperately yearned to touch and be part of something that had been a meaningful part of his dad's life. Justin's speechlessness when his mom made that happen, by tracking down the car that had been his dad's when his dad died and surprising Justin with it when he could drive, evokes what cannot be explained.

Here is how dad is crucial in more measurable ways.

Let Me Count the Ways

Appendix B lists some seventy ways that children benefit from significant father involvement—or put another way, seventy-plus ways in which dad-deprived children are more likely to suffer. We've already seen a few ways (greater vulnerability to sexual abuse, to ISIS, and to gangs) and still others will be described in the context of *when* dads matter (see the section "*When* Does Dad Begin to Matter?" in the next chapter) or what dads do differently (see "What Dads Do Differently," chapter 16). Let's start with fifteen that are more generally applicable to your son's life.

1. **School Achievement.** A study of boys from similar backgrounds revealed that by the third grade, the boys whose fathers were present scored higher on every achievement test and received higher grades.[2]
2. **The 3 Rs.** The more involved dad is, the greater a boy's increase in verbal intelligence,[3] and the better both boys' and girls' math and quantitative abilities.[4]
3. **School Dropouts.** The more years children spend with no or minimal father involvement, the fewer years of school they complete;[5] 71 percent of high school dropouts have minimal or no father involvement. Dad-deprived children are also more likely to skip school or be kicked out (expelled).[6]
4. **Employment.** While boys from two-parent homes are more likely than their sisters to be *employed* as young adults, boys who are dad deprived are more likely than their sisters to be *un*employed.[7] And when they are employed, dad-deprived boys are also less likely than their sisters to succeed as professionals.[8]
5. **Suicide.** Living in a home without a dad is more highly correlated with suicide among children and teenagers than any other factor.[9]
6. **Drugs.** Father involvement is at least *five* times more important in preventing drug use than closeness to parent, parental rules, parent trust or strictness, and is a stronger determining factor than the child's gender, ethnicity, or social class.[10]
7. **Homelessness.** Around 90 percent of runaway and homeless youths are from fatherless homes.[11]
8. **Bullying**. The American Psychological Association found in its review of 153 studies that father absence predicts the profile of *both* the bully and the bullied: poor self-esteem, poor grades, and poor social skills.[12]
9. **Victimization.** Children between ten and seventeen living without their biological dad were more likely to be victims of child abuse, major violence, sexual assault, and domestic violence.[13]

10. **Violent crime.** Every 1 percent increase in fatherlessness in a neighborhood predicts a 3 percent increase in adolescent violence.[14]
11. **Rape.** Among rapists who were specifically assessed as raping out of anger and rage, 80 percent came from father-absent homes.[15]
12. **Poverty and Mobility.** Children who were born poor and raised by both married parents had an 80 percent chance of moving to the middle class or above; conversely, children who were born into the middle class and raised without a married dad were almost four times as likely to end up considerably poorer.[16]
13. **Hypertension.** Among black boys, hypertension is reduced by 46 percent when dads are significantly involved.[17]
14. **Trust.** The more contact children have with their dads, the more easily they make open, receptive, and trusting contact with new people in their lives.[18]
15. **Empathy.** The amount of time a father spends with a child is one of the strongest predictors of the child's ability to empathize in adulthood.[19]

Any one of these items has enormous implications for your son's future. Take empathy.

Among the thousands of couples with whom I have worked, perhaps no quality fills the reservoir of love more than empathy.[20] I have never heard someone say, "I want a divorce; my partner understands me."

Think Republicans and Democrats. Israelis and Palestinians. Recall the lack of both fathers and empathy among the ISIS fighters.

Now think of litigiousness. Have you ever sued someone who empathized with you? Hospitals are learning the much greater power of empathy and apology over the doctor proving he or she did not make an error in avoiding malpractice suits.[21]

You get a sense, then, as to the negative impact of diminished empathy on marriage, war, and litigiousness, and on the quality of our sons' lives (even if he's planning to be a lawyer!).

The importance of empathy for your son's future employment is only growing. As the workforce increasingly evolves from muscle to mental, and rote tasks are increasingly handled by robots or computers, humans will be increasingly required for our emotional intelligence and empathy.[22] And boys, already behind in this area for reasons we will explore in part V, "Heroic Intelligence Versus Health Intelligence," will experience a greater gap in future employment opportunities if dad deprivation decreases their empathy, assertiveness, and emotional intelligence.

Women may still marry a man who has little empathy if he has lots of money. But if your son is less empathetic and also underemployed, especially if he meets a woman who wants children, his chances of rejection soar ("I don't need one more child").

Sadly, our "solution" to dad deprivation has been to reinforce it. Temporary Assistance for Needy Families (TANF) is available only if dad is *absent*, which then creates needier families and crowded prisons.

Prison Time

Many of the above effects of dad deprivation—violent crime, drug use, lack of empathy, rape—also increase a dad-deprived child's likelihood of going to prison as a young adult, especially if that young adult is a boy.

Prisons are the United States' men's centers (93 percent male). A staggering 85 percent of youths in prison grew up in a fatherless home.[23] More precisely, **prisons are centers for dad-deprived males**[24]**—boys who never became men.**

If your son commits a minor crime, he is also more likely to go to jail or prison than your daughter. First, if he has no criminal history and has committed a crime identical to that of your daughter, your son is more likely to be *charged*; second, he is more likely to be *convicted* of that crime; and third, **when he *is* convicted, on average your son will receive a 63 percent longer *sentence*.**[25]

We have discussed how, in an era of consciousness about racism in law enforcement, we are comparatively blind to the sexism that can magnify that racism. It is unlikely that your son will learn in school that **the gap in sentencing is *six* times greater for men versus women than it is for blacks versus whites.**[26] Black boys, of course, bear the dual burden of both racism and sexism.

In brief, if your son is dad deprived, he is much more vulnerable to committing a minor crime as a minor, and becoming a major criminal by systemic discrimination.

In an effort to spread awareness of the ripple effects of dad deprivation, in 2003 I ran for governor of California. While speaking at a prison, I was struck by how many of the men there were dads who, when they heard how important dads are, told me that gave them reason to live and get out of prison—"so I can teach my son how to not make the mistakes I made."

While my research on dads' importance gave many of the prisoners a sense of purpose, it also deepened their feelings of grief—grief that their children were suffering from their absence more than they had realized.

Daniel Beaty, whose dad suddenly disappeared to prison when he was a young boy, expresses his pain poignantly in a video describing the bond he and his dad created via a game called "Knock, Knock."[27] Like many father-son games, the bond was reinforced by a father-son "secret"—in this case, Daniel pretended to be asleep when his dad knocked, while knowing his dad knew he wasn't asleep. Daniel yearns for the routine of that game—a routine that once offered him feelings of security, love, and joy. After years of his dad's imprisonment, the adult Daniel pleads, "Papa, come home. I want to be just like you, but I forget who you are."

CHAPTER 15

Rediscovering Dad

The Generation of the Dad Rich Versus the Dad Poor[1]

One out of three children in the US live in fatherless homes.[2] I documented in *Father and Child Reunion* the damage of father absence to children of both sexes.[3] However, we have recently discovered that, over time, our sons are even more vulnerable.

For example, boys who grow up with either unmarried parents, absent fathers, or both were even less likely than girls to have had no education after high school. The education gap between the sexes was so much greater in this group than for boys and girls living with both parents that the researchers speculated that **the gender gap in education might really stem from sons' greater vulnerability to father absence.**[4]

Is Dad Deprivation the Problem, or Is It Poverty, Bad Schools . . . ?

When we hear that boys without dads do badly in so many ways, we wonder whether the cause is dad deprivation, or overlapping factors such as the greater poverty encountered by single moms in less-well-funded school districts.

Fortunately, two decades ago, two Harvard researchers sought to answer that question by reviewing four of the most methodologically well-designed national studies. They found that all four revealed the same thing: **even when race, education, income, and other socioeconomic factors are equal, living without dad *doubled* a child's chance of dropping out of high school.**[5]

More recently, leading researchers from Princeton, Cornell, and University of California, Berkeley, teamed up to dissect the most sophisticated research designs to determine whether the negative outcomes of children without dads was caused by father absence or by other causes such as poverty. They confirmed that **father absence is not just correlated with negative outcomes but actually *causes* negative outcomes.** Now, if you are not an academic, you may not know that it is exceedingly rare for leading academics to conclude that any single human factor such as dad deprivation would by itself cause problems. But as the researchers examined many different variables, such as children from poor homes with fathers, and discovered their mental health to be so much better than children from poor homes without dads, and also saw their much better social and emotional adjustment, they were able to conclude that dad involvement actually caused these more positive outcomes.[6]

Yet another study found that **students coming from father-present families score higher in math and science even when they come from academically *weaker* schools.**[7] Could America's decline in math and science have more to do with the decline in father involvement than the decline in schools? If so, a viable solution is working with schools to involve dads.

Similarly, we associate violent crime with poor inner cities—as if poverty is the primary cause. Yet a study of eleven thousand children in different urban areas found that the absence of dad contributed to violent crime as much as the absence of income.[8] That is, **when children in homes with less income and more father were compared to children in homes with more income but less father, there was no difference in the rates of violent crime.** Note the type of crime that is affected is violent crime—the type most likely to be committed by boys.

Of course, dad deprivation hurts our daughters as well. For example, in a study of inner-city Baltimore women who had been teenage mothers, one-third of their daughters also became teenage mothers. **But not one daughter who had a good relationship with her biological father had a baby before the age of nineteen.**[9] Note this is not just simple correlation: the study controlled for geography (Baltimore), economic variables (inner city), social behavior (parental history of teenage pregnancy), and mother's age. Even so, they found a drop in female teenage pregnancy from one-third to zero—making us fools if we fail to ask what we can do to be sure dads make loving connections with their children.

In brief, dad's presence enhances the lives of both girls and boys. That said, boys are more likely than their sisters to be damaged by any disadvantage—be it poverty or dad deprivation. And a longitudinal nationwide study from the University of Chicago finds that, of those disadvantages, "boys do especially poorly in broken families."[10]

Does Marriage Imply More Father Involvement?

Most boys don't want a lecture on the "immorality" of living together—as opposed to being married—when they have children. But it is crucial to let your son know that **when unmarried couples live together when their child is born, by the child's third birthday, 40 percent of those children will have no regular contact with their dad for the next *two years*—between ages three and five.**[11] Ask your son if he is willing to put his child at a 40 percent risk of having no regular contact with him prior to the age of nine, when the impact of that is not only a shorter life expectancy (as predicted by shrinking telomeres), but also those other 70+ risks to his well-being.[12]

For the first time in US history, more than **half of children born to mothers under thirty were born outside marriage.**[13]

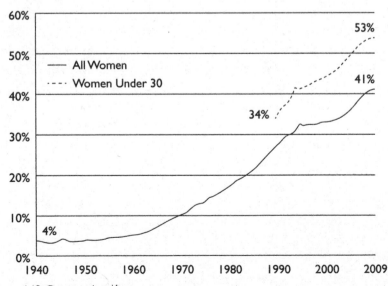

Percent of Non-Marial Birth to All Women, 1940–2009

Source: US Census data[14]

The implications? When we consider how children born to an unmarried couple are more likely to become dad-deprived children, it is no surprise that children born to an unmarried couple are less likely to succeed educationally, emotionally, and financially.[15] And the effects are a multigenerational vicious cycle: less-educated parents are less likely to marry. For example, women with only a high school diploma or less are less than half as likely to marry as women with a college degree (43 percent vs 92 percent).[16]

We got our first information a half century ago about the impact on children of their parents not being married from *The Moynihan Report*, directed by sociologist Daniel Moynihan, who also served under Presidents Kennedy, Johnson, and Nixon. **The Moynihan Report concluded that in a majority-black community the main predictor of growing up poor was not race but being born to parents who are not married. Why? A predictable outcome of no marriage was no father involvement.[17]**

Upward Trend

The percentage of births to mothers who are unmarried is twice as high for blacks as for whites, and across all groups, the rate has increased dramatically over the last 50 years.

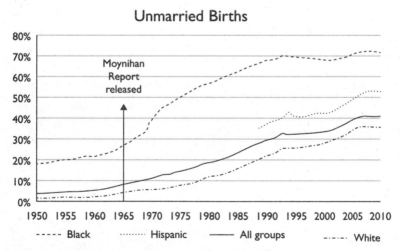

Unmarried Births

Notes: Prior to 1969, Black denotes all nonwhites, including Asians and Native americans; beginning in 1969, these data include blacks only. Respondents who indicated more than one race are not included in these data. Respondents of Hispanic origin are included in both racial categories and are identified separately beginning in 1989.

Source: National Center for Health Statistics; National Vital Statistics System

We have ignored Moynihan's warnings about our neglect of the challenges of dad-deprived children and its connection to unmarried births. Our blind eye has led to almost a tripling of unmarried births among blacks (from 25 to 72 percent),[18] and an expansion of the problem to white and Hispanic communities. We witness both in the figure on the previous page.[19]

While the Moynihan Report identified the quarter of black children born outside marriage as a crisis with a solution in 1965, today the percentage of *white* children born outside marriage is 36 percent[20]—more than a third higher than the 25 percent that had prompted Moynihan to label this a crisis. We ignored the crisis, and ignored the solution.

Why did we fail to identify dad deprivation as a crisis in the white community in 1965? Perhaps it was because in 1965 the percentage of *white* children born outside marriage was only 3.1 percent.[21] The 36 percent rate today represents a nearly twelvefold increase.[22]

Among non-college-educated white women under thirty who have children without marrying, the current 51 percent figure[23] is double what it was among blacks when the Moynihan Report alerted us to the crisis. Unfortunately, moms of Hispanic origin have followed the same pattern.

When Does Dad Begin to Matter?

Many people—including judges—feel moms matter more when children are younger, and that dads matter mostly as children get older. Legally, this has been institutionalized as the "tender years doctrine": the belief that moms are more important to children between the "tender years" of birth and first grade.

When Richard Warshak and 110 of the world's leading parenting experts examined the data, they found that, yes, early years are tender years—so tender that the infants and toddlers need both parents. The infants and toddlers who did best after divorce were the ones that had shared parent time with approximately equal father involvement. The data was so clear that the 110 world experts put their reputations on the line with a rare consensus report.[24]

So *when* does dad begin to matter? At birth? No. Prior to conception. Here's how dads matter from before conception through first grade:

1. **Preconception, for health.** The dad's preconception diet may be as important as the mom's. For example, inadequate vitamin B9 (folates, found in leafy green vegetables) damages sperm and results in a 30 percent increase in birth defects (e.g., skeletal abnormalities such as spinal deformities).[25]

2. **At birth, for adaptability.** The more frequently a father visits the hospital of an infant who is prematurely born, the more quickly the infant leaves the hospital and the better the infant's social-personal development and ability to adapt.[26]

3. **Birth to first grade, for IQ.** The more interaction a boy has with his dad before six months, the higher his mental competence.[27] By first grade, boys and girls raised in families with fathers present had significantly higher IQ scores than those with absent fathers.[28]

4. **First six months, for trust.** The more contact infants have with their dads before six months of age, the greater their ability to trust others.[29]

5. **First two years, for positive behavior.** When dad has positive contact with his children during the first two years, the children have fewer signs of uncontrolled and unwanted behavior.[30] (Dads and moms have equal amounts of positive engagements with daughters; dads have more than moms with their sons.)

6. **Between eighteen and twenty-four months, for regulating aggression.** Rough-housing, done much more frequently with dads, helps regulate both male and female toddlers' aggression, but "especially helps male toddlers control their testosterone-induced aggression by imprinting their left-brain circuits."[31]

7. **Preschool, for psychological health.** Eighty percent of preschool children admitted as psychiatric patients in two New Orleans hospitals came from homes without fathers.[32] Similar percentages of psychiatric patients emerge among dad-deprived children in Canada,[33] South Africa, and Finland, from preschoolers through teens.[34]

Ironically, of all the years that children need their dads, perhaps the tender years are the most important.

*Why the Quality of Care in the Tender Years Counts Even
More for Your Son*

The quality of care in the tender years is even more important for your son than your daughter. Why? Girls' right brain, frontal cortex, coping mechanisms, ability to make eye contact, and social skills are much better than boys' in the tender years.[35] Boys are far more dependent on the quality of childcare programs,[36] as well as on the length of parental leave.

Between quality childcare and longer parental leaves, the bigger contributor to a healthy and productive son is a longer parental leave. Without parental leave, parents often put children into childcare at about six weeks—"the exact time of the initiation of the postnatal testosterone surge found only in males."[37] From infant boys' first breath through six months, they have more problems adjusting emotionally—being angrier, and more likely to fuss and cry—and are in need of more calming.[38] Our cultural norms—that lead to less touching, cuddling, and speaking with male infants is, sadly, exactly the opposite of what is needed in a male child's very early years.

High-quality childcare for children from eight weeks to five years helps both girls and boys, but quality has a much greater impact on boys.[39] This is true not just in the short term. Boys with the high-quality care were making $19,800 more per year by age thirty, versus $2,500 more for the girls.[40] And whereas quality of childcare had only a minor impact on girls' drug use, arrests, or health, the boys who had high-quality childcare were 33 percent less likely to be drug users, as well as considerably less likely to be arrested or have health problems.

Stepdad or Bio Dad: Does It Make a Difference?

Your son's chances of becoming a stepparent are at least six times greater than your daughter's.[41] Why? Some 86 percent of families with a stepparent consist of a stepdad and a biological mom.[42]

And stepparent homes aren't rare: an estimated one-third of children will live in a stepparent home before the age of eighteen.[43] So whether your son is living with a stepdad, or someday becomes a stepdad, your teaching him how to navigate the stepdad minefield can be a gift to multiple generations.

Let's start with some potential good news for and about stepdads. First, remember, an involved dad triggers his "dad brain"—whether the child is biologically his or not. Second, a new stepdad almost always wants to support his new wife and looks forward to being of value in the lives of his stepchildren. Third, most moms want new stepdads involved—especially with their sons. Fourth, closeness with a stepdad decreases the likelihood that an adolescent boy's own marriage will someday end in divorce.[44] And fifth, if the stepfamily is long-standing and stable, the chances of the children adjusting are good.[45]

The bad news begins with the fact that most stepfamilies are not that long-standing and stable: the divorce rate for stepfamilies is 65 to 70 percent.[46] Stepfather involvement rarely reaches beyond the level of adviser. Stepdads usually become a "hierarchical dad" or a "conditional dad"—becoming equally involved only when he fathers the way the mom feels a good father should father. We'll explore that dynamic just below, but here's the result: after two years of marriage, most stepfathers are minimally involved and have little rapport with, control over, and discipline of their stepchildren.[47] When this happens, it undermines all five items of the good news.

Understanding that this process is predictable makes it less personal. But the real goal is to make the stepfamily work, so that your son is more likely to receive the contribution of his stepdad, or make a full contribution should he become a stepdad. Here's a GPS to the most precarious portion of the stepdad minefield: the slippery slope to the "hierarchical" (or "conditional") dad.

The Slippery Slope to the "Hierarchical" Dad

1. **Permissive love versus tough love.** The stepdad feels the bio mom is too permissive, and the bio mom fears the stepdad's greater strictness emanates from less caring. The kids resent the unwelcome restrictiveness of the stepdad, and make it clear, "You're not my dad; I don't have to listen to you"—their anger spiced with the sting of their parents' divorce.

2. **Kids exploit guilt.** The kids' pain stirs guilt in the mom; the guilt motivates more protectiveness. The kids exploit the fissure between the mom and the stepdad. The mom, feeling she needs to both protect the kids and reduce the conflict, increasingly marginalizes the

stepdad by discouraging tough love, roughhousing, teasing, the enforcing of chores and bedtimes . . .

3. **The "financial womb" dad.** The stepdad, usually a good earner (the more a man earns, the more likely he is to marry; conversely, the more money a divorced woman has, the less likely she is to remarry)[48] retreats to his only remaining contribution everyone values: providing a "financial womb."

4. **The hierarchical dad.** From this dynamic is born the hierarchical—or conditional—dad. That is, he feels he is permitted to be a father only as long as he fathers in the way the mother feels the father should father, and only as long as the children approve. The mom may not feel any of this, but it is his feeling that leads to his withdrawal.

Awareness of this four-part slope is the first step to preventing it. Family dinner nights are a second—to articulate the four-part dynamic and discuss it. Add road trips and camping—nature is conducive to father-child bonding. And find a family counselor with expertise in stepdad integration. See the counselor consistently, not just for emergencies. Make sure you're not trying to persuade the counselor to side with you, and that he or she facilitates each family member feeling heard.

Avoiding the slippery slope to the hierarchical dad is crucial to offsetting these more negative outcomes for children of stepdads:

- Children living with their married biological father do significantly better academically than those living with a stepdad.[49] They have fewer discipline problems, and are more likely to stay in school, attend college, and graduate from college.[50]
- Children between the ages of ten and seventeen who live with two biological or adoptive parents are significantly less likely to experience sexual assault or child abuse and are less likely to witness violence in their families compared to peers living in both single-parent families and stepfamilies.[51]
- Adolescents raised in stepfamilies face even higher incarceration rates than those raised in single-mom families.[52]

Of course, not every contributor to these stepdad challenges is preventable. Perhaps the biggest barrier to becoming an effective stepdad is that most stepchildren yearn for the reunification of their biological parents; many feel abandoned, angry, and depressed. Why? Every child wants to know who she or he is, and when children look in the mirror and see their nose, body language, hair, and eyes, they see their biological parents, not their stepparents.

While this obstacle can be the most challenging, the best way to address it is to ensure your stepchildren feel safe to express themselves. This is a five-step process. First, share what you've heard your stepson or stepdaughter say. Then empathize. Follow by asking if there's anything you are distorting or missing. Then invite him or her to say more. Last, after you've heard your stepchild in this way a few times, say something like, "Pretend you were a stepdad. What do you think would be the best thing you could do for your children if you really loved them a lot?" The most common result of this request is amazement at how stepchildren can release from arguing for their immediate gratification the moment you ask them to imagine themselves as a parent. A wisdom void is often filled with wisdom.

Becoming a great stepdad or dad involves communicating with mom as much as the children. Moms can't hear what dads don't say, so it is up to your son, whether bio dad or stepdad, to do three things (ideally before he gets engaged, but it's never too late):

1. Become a student of the value of what he, as a father, can contribute.
2. Make sure his future partner *desires*—not just agrees—to incorporate his contributions.
3. If a potential stepdad, spend a year or so caring for her children together, and make sure you can sort out any differences. If a potential dad, take care of other people's children together.

While the challenges of being a stepdad are clear, the challenges of being a same-sex parent are still emerging.

How Do Children of Same-Sex Parents Fare?

There are some studies concluding that children raised by same-sex parents fare as well as children raised by a male and female parent,[53] and other studies concluding that they do not.[54]

Both sets of studies are riddled with methodological shortcomings. As for the children of same-sex marriages, they are too young to aggregate longitudinal data in large enough numbers to have a reasonable claim on the most likely outcomes.

That said, some therapists working with same-sex parents report that many have some significant advantages.[55] When these are combined with my own observations and thoughts, five advantages emerge—most of which can be adopted by heterosexual parents as well.

1. **Self-selection.** Like dads who are the primary parents, same-sex parents—especially married same-sex parents—are highly self-selecting. Those who overcome societal prejudices have the advantage of high motivation.

2. **Planning.** Many same-sex parents plan for their children like many heterosexual women plan for their weddings. Those who plan for children and also plan for the stability of marriage magnify that planning advantage.

3. **Donor.** Many female same-sex parents carefully research and select the best possible sperm donor. And we do know that children of female same-sex parents seem to fare better than children raised by a heterosexual mom with a sperm-donor dad.[56]

4. **Experience with rejection.** The worldwide culture's dominant attitude toward gay people has left most gay parents with a lifetime of experience handling criticism and rejection. This is good preparation for raising children—especially adolescents!

5. **Honoring differences.** One of the keys to a stable and happy marriage is being able to honor the differences of our partner—and then make compromises. The same is true in successful child-rearing. Same-sex couples have had plenty of experience accepting the idea that others may have a different journey than their own—from childhood friends to their (likely) heterosexual parents. Their children, too, will benefit from seeing in early childhood that the predominant culture's way is not the only way.

Whether these advantages will in aggregate balance the disadvantages of not being raised with the checks and balances of different-sex partners is yet to be seen. Nevertheless, consciously implementing these advantages will very likely result in wonderful children.

Whether your son becomes a biological dad, stepdad, or dad in a same-sex marriage, he needs to be able to articulate the value of what dads are likely to do differently. And if that does not happen to be his style of parenting, he and his partner need to discuss how to incorporate that into their parenting.

CHAPTER 16

What Dads Do Differently

Dads and moms both love their children deeply, but differently. They have different ways of setting boundaries and enforcing boundaries; exploring in nature; roughhousing; creating teachable moments; challenging the kids' limits; using hangout time; and different attitudes toward teasing. Researchers have also documented dads' greater tendencies to

- walk a fine line between safety and risk-taking;
- juggle the roles of player and coach during play; and
- be creative, spontaneous, and silly.[1]

But when the value of each parent's contribution is not understood, tension results. If the parents learn to facilitate each other's complementary contributions, the child almost invariably benefits, and parental tension can morph into parental pride. The parents "get" that there is a reason nature created both moms and dads.

Of course, many moms are more like dads, and vice versa. Either way, though, there is a deeper problem. Moms tend to have talked about and read about parenting issues since they were young adults. Dads, not so much. So moms tend to articulate the value of their style more effectively.

Although researchers have observed some of the differences in dads' parenting style, a common way to observe parents and children interact is by bringing them into a therapist's office and watching them play together for about an hour with toys provided by the therapist. However, that misses most of mothering and fathering.

When I observed some fifty dads parent their children (before testifying on their behalf as an expert witness), my method involved observing them for between a full day and a weekend—and not in an office, but in parks, playgrounds, shopping malls, and restaurants, and at home. I observed children not just playing but helping at home, whether with cleaning up or preparing dinner. The length of time allowed me to see more than moments of fun; I also saw dads running errands, preparing the kids for bed, and getting them started for school the next morning. The dads were located not in one community, but in about fifty communities throughout the United States and Canada.

I discovered that what the therapist's office visits missed was dads' greater tendency to take their children to parks or playgrounds, or teach them by doing, such as being a "sous-chef" with dad in the kitchen. They also missed the games dads tend to create to make otherwise boring activities fun—such as turning a shopping cart into a basketball hoop and toilet paper into a ball. Few therapists have a Whole Foods in their office.

In dad's world outside the therapist's office, everything is a stage for an impromptu game: Something as boring as choosing a cereal becomes "Who can be the best nutrition adviser?" based on reading the nutrition label on the back of, say, Kellogg's Frosted Flakes versus Kellogg's Cocoa Krispies (you'll be surprised!).

In addition to turning life into a game, I observed seven other parenting styles dads tend to use with both their sons and daughters that create tension between mom and dad if their value to the children is not understood.

1. Boundary Enforcement (Versus Boundary Setting)

Moms often ask me, "Why is it that when I speak, nothing happens, but when their dad speaks, the kids drop everything and obey? Is it his deeper voice?" It makes moms feel disrespected and taken for granted. But it's not dad's deeper voice. Dads who don't enforce boundaries are also ignored.

Studies of single dads and single moms find that moms report themselves as considerably more stressed than dads—even though single moms are much more likely to receive financial assistance.[2]

Perhaps the most important reason is because moms are more likely to set boundaries, whereas dads are more likely to enforce boundaries. For example, although a mom is more likely to set an early bedtime, single moms are more than three times as likely as single dads to let younger kids get away with late or irregular bedtimes.[3] One boy half-joked, **"My mom warns and warns; it's like she 'cries wolf.' My dad gives us one warning, and then he becomes the wolf."**

Getting to bed late obviously contributes to health problems. That may be why frequent headaches and stomachaches are two to three times more common among younger children living with only their moms (versus with only their dads).[4]

Boys with poorly enforced boundaries also become boys with poor impulse control. When the University of Chicago Crime Lab examined why 610 Chicago public school students were shot by fellow students during a recent one-and-a-half-year period, they found that lack of impulse control and a lack of conflict resolution and social skills were characteristic of the boys involved.[5] However, what the study missed was that impulse control and social skills are some of the gifts of father involvement—and these boys' fathers were mostly absent.

We have seen that the amount of time a father spends with a child is "one of the strongest predictors of empathy in adulthood."[6] **Teaching a child to treat boundaries seriously teaches him or her to respect the needs of others.** Respecting another's needs contributes to empathy. Empathy doesn't trigger shooting.

Here are some of the outcomes of father involvement that are related to boundary enforcement and impulse control:

- Children living with dads are less likely to have discipline problems.[7] This is despite the fact that dads are less likely than moms to use physical discipline.[8]
- Five- to eleven-year-old children with moms are 259 percent more likely to go to the hospital.[9]

How does this mom-dad gap between *setting* boundaries and *enforcing* boundaries work in everyday life? Let's go back to bedtime in theory versus bedtime in practice . . .

When Harry was asked by a therapist why he thought he got to bed later with his mom than his dad, he explained, "With Mom, I can get away with it."

"How?"

"With Mom, I say, like 'I need water' or 'I have a tummy ache.'"

"So you manipulate her?"

Harry grinned.

"Don't those excuses get a bit old?"

Harry's grin expanded, as if delighting in his cleverness. "I have a whole bunch of excuses. Like, 'I have to get my homework done' or 'Just one more story.' Or I tell her 'I love it when you read me *Where the Wild Things Are.*'"

Harry paused, and then boasted, "I have a real sense of what will work. Sooner or later Mom gives in."

"Do you use those ploys with Dad?"

"No . . . They don't work with him."

"How's that?"

"He doesn't let me have any dessert or TV—or do anything fun—until I do my homework and chores."

"So he's more serious?"

"Well, sort of. He'll announce that bedtime is 9:30. But I know that whatever time is left after I do my homework and get all ready for bed is wrestle time or I get a story, or pretty much whatever I want—except no sweets. So I rush to get everything done."

"Doesn't that tempt you to just do a rush job on your homework?"

"Yeah, it used to. But when I got a C once from Miss Ahearn—she's real strict—then Dad started checking it while I get ready for bed. If it's OK, we get to wrestle or read. If it's not, I gotta go back to homework. But when it's 9:30, he gives me a big hug and kiss, and that's it."

Harry, like most kids, was like a prisoner vigilantly waiting for the guard to drop his guard, watching for a little crack in the prison door through which he could gain his freedom. Once Harry saw he could manipulate his mom for a better deal, it was just a matter of who had more energy. So Harry always won—and therefore lost: with a compromised immune system.

A weaker immune system also leads to a vicious cycle: Harry was absent from school, with a couple of trips to the emergency room, so his mom (and sometimes dad) became even more protective and guilty, allowing for more manipulation, and thus the cycle continued. But it all started with the more porous boundary.

What moms are more likely to bring to the family table is a deep-seated understanding that children need empathy (as does everyone).

Dad's contributions are more counterintuitive: first, that **empathy is a virtue which, when it only goes from parent to child, and is not required of the child, becomes a vice**. And second, that empathy for a child's desires does not imply being controlled by the child's desires.

That said, some dads give empathy too short shrift. When, then, do a child's desires count? At all times *before* the *setting* of a boundary. In fact, before setting a boundary, treating a child's input seriously and allowing him or her to have an impact when appropriate, plus giving an empathetic explanation when it is not appropriate, are crucial to her or his development of *empowering negotiating skills*. Empowering negotiating skills are best understood in contrast with *manipulative negotiating skills*.

A child who learns that a boundary that's been set is still negotiable develops manipulative negotiating skills. The child soon senses that if he or she doesn't "win" right away, with enough persistence they can ultimately exhaust the parent and "win." This second path is most frequently characterized by the exhausted mom finally yelling in frustration, "I said *no!*" The child then continues to press. The mom loses it and creates a punishment too big for the crime; then, feeling guilty, she fails to follow through on the anger-generated punishment, and in an effort to beg forgiveness, she bends over backward to please the child. The child soon detects exactly what worked to manipulate the mom into bending over backward and giving more than what was even asked for in the first place, and thus hones his or her art for the next iteration of the "cycle of the unenforced boundary."

The outcome? A disrespect for both boundaries and the parent who sets them. When the cycle of the unenforced boundary becomes a pattern, the result is a coercive relationship with the parent, and the child's disrespect becomes contempt. Just as important, the child "gets rid" of the parent who enforces boundaries—sticking with the parent he or she can manipulate. The child has won, and therefore lost. More on the cycle of the unenforced boundary in a chapter coming soon. But first . . .

How do dads enforce boundaries without their children wanting to "get rid" of them? It starts with his playing with the children. That play creates a bond. As we saw with Harry, the dad then often unconsciously uses that bond as leverage for boundary enforcement: "When you finish your homework and chores, and get ready for bed, we'll do whatever you'd like before bedtime."

Mom Can Enforce Boundaries, Too

Yes, dads tend to create games and enforce boundaries. But this is not proprietary dad behavior. For example . . .

A former assistant, Kacy, is a working mom. She has two teenage sons, which means that on school holidays they become "stay-at-home sons." Veterans Day had all the markings of a "when the cat's away the mice will play" day. But Kacy, a veteran mom, had a different idea.

The boys wanted to go out for lunch. Could Mom pay? Yes. But Mom hid the money in their apartment. Each completed chore earned the boys a clue in the form of a riddle as to the whereabouts of the money. The boys got lunch, and Mom got a clean house.

Well, actually, the boys got more than lunch. Instead of a feeling of entitlement toward their lunch money, they got the "holy trinity" of gifts: game playing, boundary enforcement, and postponed gratification. Throughout the day they got a sense of feeling cared for. And at the end of the day, Kacy got a paycheck. And I got to share this with you.

Boys Are to Dads and Boundaries as Bees Are to Flowers and Pollen

> *One of my most poignant memories is of my father stand-*
> *ing on the doorstep looking at his watch if I was late home.*
> *The fact that someone was looking out for me, and cared*
> *enough to do that, instilled a sense of security.*
>
> —Email from a reader of *Father and Child Reunion*[10]

When former TV talk show host Jenny Jones did a show entitled "Boot Camp My Pre-teen"[11] she brought on young boys who were giving their single moms far too many problems. She invited a marine sergeant to show them some discipline. As the sergeant railed at a ten-year-old boy, he concluded by asking the boy which he wanted: to shape up, or, he threatened, "Do you want me to be your daddy for the next eight years, son?"

The rebellious boy pleads, "Yes, sir."

The stunned-but-touched sergeant responds, "Why do you want me to be your daddy?"

The boy looked at him sadly. "I have no daddy."

Boys need dads who enforce boundaries like bees need flowers with pollen.

Do Kids Sense When a Boundary Will Be Enforced?

This segment from the *Today Show*'s Rossen Reports[12] offers a quick illustration of how kids pick up the difference between boundary setting and boundary enforcement.

The setup: A hidden camera records actors playing teenagers who are clearly under the drinking age. The underage teenagers ask unsuspecting adults to buy them alcohol (aka "shoulder tapping").

The finding: None of the men gave the underage teenagers alcohol; all but one of the women did. The women did express reservations, and a couple initially said no, but then they bought the alcohol for the kids anyway. When Rossen interviewed them after showing them the video of their responses, the women confessed that their desire to please trumped what they knew was right.

The takeaway: Kids pick up on how an adult's desire to nurture can be used against them; they can "feel it" if the adult has a need to please, and for many kids, their view of the adult as an "easy target" replaces respect for the adult. Men's vibe is more often "No lectures; No alcohol; Period."

Boys who live only with their moms become both more demanding and coercive[13, 14] toward their moms. Being worn down by this coerciveness leaves millions of devoted moms feeling "overwhelmed" and out of control.[15]

There are consequences outside the home, too: 4,700 adolescents below the drinking age are nevertheless killed each year in accidents while under the influence of alcohol. Many of them got the alcohol from shoulder tapping.

The gift of boundary enforcement is developing the ability to postpone gratification that is essential for the workplace. And especially for working from home.

Work-from-Home Starts with Boundary Enforcement at Home

One of the best options for your son to be both a fully-involved dad and a breadwinner is the option of working from home. But the work-from-home option is more complex than meets the eye—as IBM discovered.

IBM had long been the pioneer of work-from-home policies. But after twenty consecutive quarters of falling revenue, it reversed its policy in 2017, telling its employees to either work from the office or find a new job.[16] Bank of America, Yahoo, Aetna, and other corporate pioneers of work-from-home also reversed their policies.

In theory, the work-from-home option makes perfect sense for both your son and the future workplace. After all, the synergistic sharing of ideas that the proximity of the office facilitated is now viable via technologies such as Slack, Dropbox, Google Docs, and Skype. And working from home means avoiding stress-inducing and time-wasting rush hours; there's no cost of gas or wear and tear on a car, to say nothing of the billions of dollars saved by employers on office space.

Why, then, does working from home frequently fail to work at work? In part because **working from home requires self-starting. And children raised with poor boundary enforcement rarely master the postponed gratification that self-starting requires**. Especially boys.

Boundary enforcement that leads to a greater ability to postpone gratification and better social skills will help your son to work in either an office or from home. And if he wishes to work from home, he'll be more comfortable either starting his own business or proving to an employer that when he does work at home both he and the company are winning.

As for IBM and the companies that have reversed work-at-home policies? Don't worry. They will reimplement them, just more selectively— selecting employees with integrity who are disciplined self-starters.

2. Exploring Nature, Taking Risks

Dads often take their children to national parks and camping, where exploration comes naturally. But it is also often accompanied by a mom's understandable fear that the child could get hurt or lost. A dad needs to be able to contribute a countervailing consideration to mom's fear: the value of learning to explore with dad as a GPS as needed, so they don't get too lost.

And that value kicks in early. Toddlers whose dads encouraged exploring (while setting limits) had better social and emotional skills twelve to eighteen months later.[17]

3. Roughhousing: Dad as a Rough, Tough Cream Puff

During roughhousing, dads and kids are typically 100 percent energized, laughing, spontaneous, and, yes, silly. The dads were almost always able to distinguish between their son or daughter being excited-scared and scared-scared. When the dad picked up any sense of his son or daughter being scared-scared, he backed off. And when the excitement led to the kids getting out of control—which it usually did—or led to something unsafe, mean, cruel, or neglectful to a sibling or friend, the dad would pause and explain what needed to change: "Billy, how should you be treating your sister?" Yes, Billy would often defend himself by complaining about his sister, but the kids translated their dad's silence in response as, "Figure out a better way to treat your sister or the roughhousing ends." And Billy figured it out, or his dad ended the game.

After dads' tendency to tease, nothing creates more conflict between moms and dads than dads' much greater propensity to roughhouse. Roughhousing often scares a mom, because her fear for her children's safety is amplified by the appearance that dad is behaving like another kid, which mom translates as, "No one's responsible here."

The solution begins with dad. Dad should make it clear to mom that

- roughhousing can coexist with him keeping an eye on the kids' safety;
- *the kids themselves* know that dad may pretend to be a kid, but always returns to dad when needed; and
- what appears to be a bond of equals is never a bond of equals.

Almost all dads intuit their strength has two purposes: to excite and to protect. **Playing with dad is like being on a roller coaster—kids are excited because they feel safe.** They can take risks because they know the Clark Kent they're playing with can change into Superman, even without a telephone booth.

Dad's persona is a bit like a "rough, tough cream puff." They toss their children into water, or into leaves; they perch them on their shoulders, and then pretend to stumble as they launch them from shoulder to bed. Kids sense dad may be "rough and tough" on the surface, but at the center, he's a cream puff. Well, not quite—a cream puff who can revert to tough again if required.

4. "Teachable Moments": A Little Pain for a Lot of Gain

While I never heard a dad say this during my observations, most appeared to have an intuitive sense of the value of holding a safe space for "teachable moment" hazards. It's as if they had a different playbook for significant and insignificant hazards. I watched a dad in Ottawa, Canada, instigate a snowball fight by throwing a snowball at his son, and then, as his daughter picked up on the game, including his daughter, too. Both of his kids loved it. But soon his son began to form a snowball from some of the snow the sun had transformed into ice. The snowball was as hard as a rock.

The dad, Tom, teased, "Let me have that snowball . . . This is the one *I'll* throw at *you*, OK? Should I do that?" His son got the point. Significant hazard. Then his dad pointed to an area for softer snow, "Make your snowballs only from the softer snow. If you make a hardball, it gets tossed *at* you, not by you. Got it?"

His son got it. A few minutes later, some neighborhood kids joined them. Tom's kids took the lead in making it clear what was "fair game" and what wasn't. Soon a massively multiplayer off-line snow-throwing game broke out. After an intense half hour or so, Tom suggested, "Do you think you all have had enough for now?" While his daughter took that as permission to stop, no one else did. Tom said nothing more. Insignificant hazard. About twenty minutes later, his son, experiencing a massive in-eye snow event, was crying and blaming Jimmy for being too rough. Tom just announced, "OK, time for a hot bath."

Later Tom shared with me why he just offered a suggestion. "I wanted to give them a hint, but I feel they benefit more by monitoring themselves to discover the right boundary between doing and overdoing." Sort of a little pain for a lot of gain. Then Tom winked, and added, "And maybe next time I make a suggestion they might pay attention!"

In brief, dads tend to see themselves as a safety net so that kids can test their limits on the tightropes of life. Many dads almost instinctively allow the insignificant hazards to play out—creating what might be called "teachable moment" hazards.

When these aren't understood, the result is a boy like Alex being raised by mom and dad in two different worlds . . .

More on Roughhousing: Mom's World, Dad's World

Dad and Alex are play-wrestling. Dad typically lets Alex "win" at the last second. But this time, Dad feels Alex isn't giving it his all, so he doesn't. Alex starts crying. Dad teases Alex about being a bad loser, and after about a minute of letting Alex pout, playfully turns him upside down, after which Alex is back in the saddle.

During that minute, though, Alex's mom is thinking, "I could have predicted this would end up with Alex in tears!" Mom is angry at herself, feeling *guilty* for not fulfilling her responsibility of *proactively* protecting Alex.

Still feeling that guilt, Mom watches as Dad continues the same roughhousing after Alex has cried—after Dad "should have learned his lesson." Moreover, she is dismayed the roughhousing is continuing *as if nothing had happened*—barely acknowledging Alex's tears, being more dismissive than nurturing.

This triggers Mom's second maternal emotion: a fierce resolve to not repeat the earlier mistake of allowing her child to get hurt. However, since she knows Alex loves and needs his father, she represses the impulse to stop the roughhousing outright, and bends over backward to give Dad a second chance. She shares with Dad how and where she believes it's safe for him to roughhouse, and how not to go too far.

While Mom is feeling pride for having supported—even improved!—Dad's parenting, Dad experiences a different feeling.

A dad rarely says this—and moms can't hear what dads don't say—but in this context Dad feels that Alex's occasional crying is a *healthy* part of a three-part cycle:

1. "losing"
2. crying
3. moving on

Alex's dad feels some crying can be healthy if he is able to use it to teach Alex how winning in life involves losing and moving on—even crying and moving on (or falling and moving on; or not getting one's own way and moving on). For most dads, this three-part cycle is unconscious, so moms never hear this perspective.

Something else reinforces this mom-dad gap between "I'm bending over backward" and "I'm being snuffed out as a dad." When speaking to Mom, often Dad tries to underplay Alex's crying. He doesn't want to call it to Mom's attention. However, this underplaying just reinforces Mom's perception of him as dismissive and insensitive.

Ironically, when Mom is not there, Dad is more likely to nurture Alex. Why the difference? When Mom is gone, Dad feels that each minute of soothing Alex is a minute of soothing Alex—not another minute of Mom judging Dad for hurting Alex.

Last, if Alex feels a little extra crying will get Mom and Dad to compete to give him a few extra goodies—dessert and extra attention—he often exploits their tension like water seeping into a fissure on a roof. The gap between Mom and Dad widens further, and Alex unconsciously learns "victim power."

If mom and dad are in a custody battle, dad often "snuffs himself out" for fear his children will report that they cried at dad's, and this will be told to a psychologist and reported to the court, thus jeopardizing his time with them. Kids often do reveal their crying because they may have experienced it bringing them extra empathy and goodies from mom.

If dad tells his children to not say anything, it can make things even worse. When they say nothing for a while, but do eventually reveal their crying, mom feels dad is hiding things from her, reinforcing her feeling that dad cannot be trusted.

In different ways, mom, kid, and dad can each unwittingly contribute to the "killing" of dad. One reason is that while the risks of roughhousing are obvious, the benefits are not.

The Benefits of Roughhousing Rough-Tough-Cream-Puff-Style

Researchers consistently find that fathers who spend time with their children give their children the gifts of self-control and social skills.[18] Might the roughhousing component contribute to this? Studies of baby rats that engaged in rough-and-tumble activity find they become less aggressive and have more social skills as adults.[19]

Among humans, we've seen dads' tendency during roughhousing to be responsive to their children's cues, thus teaching the child that the two components of setting boundaries to protect oneself—tuning in to one's own needs, and speaking up—pays off even when otherwise getting "carried away" with the excitement of roughhousing or a game. This is sometimes called "emotional intelligence under fire."[20]

5. Challenging the Kids' Limits

"Enough is enough," Betty complained to Arnold, Marcy's dad. "This is only Marcy's fourth time skiing, and you're bringing her to the intermediate slope with kids who've been skiing for years. And when she fell, you didn't get the point, you just kept her out there. Suppose one of those faster skiers had run right into her? Didn't you see how exhausted and scared she was?"

Arnold retorted, "And did she wake up early this morning, all excited to go back out there again?"

"Sure, yeah, but she's a teenager," Betty said. "You're supposed to be the adult!"

Arlene told me about a similar problem with her husband, Martin, who would use a verbal equivalent to challenge the limits of their kids, Marty Jr. and Maggie. "Martin uses vocabulary that he knows Marty Jr. and Maggie don't understand. He knows it, but when I point it out, he's dismissive."

"I'm not dismissive. I've explained to Arlene that this is the way they learn new vocabulary."

"That'll just frustrate and discourage them."

"Well, I do it whenever you're not around, and they come back for more." Arlene and Martin both looked my way.

I shared with Arlene the research about the positive impact that using vocabulary beyond the child's current grasp has on children's ability to express themselves.[21] When I explained that no vocabulary is understood when first heard, and that part of building language is to keep introducing new words and ideas until the context builds the child's vocabulary, Arlene was more at ease. Since she was the household Scrabble champion, she gave herself permission to try it on the kids herself.

Whether in sports or school, dads will often encourage their children to challenge their limits.[22] When a dad sees his kids trying hard, he typically lets them win, but if they are not trying to their capacity, he may let them lose. The same dad whose ego might get involved when it comes to competing against peers is characteristically selfless when he engages in competition with his child. He feels no reward from winning with his child; his victory is teaching his child to both lose and win.

A dad's tendency to turn everything into a game is the way dad makes it palatable to challenge his children's limits. Often the competition is "last time you ran the hundred-yard dash in fifteen seconds—let's see if you can beat that." The laughter and the energy created by friendly competition may well lessen for dads the stress and sense of feeling over-whelmed that moms so often report.

While it is challenging for many moms to "get" roughhousing and the degree to which dads challenge kids' limits, what even fewer moms get is how a dad's propensity to challenge takes time to process and therefore requires more hangout time with dad.

6. Hangout Time

Boys have to hang out before they let their feelings out. This is not neces-sarily true with mom, but it is with dad.

When Rick's dad picked him up from soccer and asked him how the game went, Rick answered, "Fine." Rick's dad couldn't pry another word out of him.

That evening, Rick was doing his homework on the dining table while his dad was cleaning up in the kitchen. Rick wandered into the kitchen. Eyeing up the options in the fridge, he wondered aloud, "Hey, if you do a good job playing goalie one week, but then the coach asks someone else to play goalie the next week, what's that about?"

That was the start of a half-hour conversation. The relief Rick felt with honest feedback about his disappointment over being replaced as goalie gave him enough security to ultimately broach a half dozen other disappointments that had been quietly poisoning his psyche and unwit-tingly leading him down a slippery slope toward depression. Had Rick's dad just picked Rick up from soccer and delivered him to his mom, that conversation would never have taken place.

Wouldn't the conversation have just taken place with his mom instead? Probably yes, and perhaps with even *less* hangout time. Why? Rick is likely to have anticipated reassurance from his mom, but a challenge from his dad. It takes less time to prepare oneself for reassurance than for a challenge. That is why hangout time with dad is so important—to balance mom-style input with dad-style input.

When two researchers examined the many possible reasons *why* children do so well psychologically when they either have about equal parent time or live primarily with dad, high on the list for boys was hangout time with dad.[23] Hangout time with dad, though, was *number one* on the list for girls. Although girls express their feelings more easily, what they receive most often from girlfriends and mom is reassurance. Unlike boys, who are frequently challenged by their friends (as we'll see below), girls are less likely to have anyone besides dad to go to with the anticipation of being challenged by someone who has her best interest at heart. [24]

That challenging takes many forms. Perhaps the one that creates the deepest mom-dad divide is teasing.

7. Teasing: Emotional Intelligence Training, Dad-Style?

The verbal equivalent of dad-style roughhousing is dad-style teasing. While dad-style boundary enforcement teaches children the meaning of a red light, dad-style roughhousing and teasing provide practice with interpreting the nuances of a yellow light.

Arlene also complained to me, "The kids love playing with their dad, but Martin often teases them, and sometimes both Maggie and Marty Jr. break down crying. Especially Maggie. I can't believe Martin doesn't learn from their crying and stop. It makes me afraid to leave them alone with Martin. Especially Maggie."

Martin responded, "You make it sound like they're crying all the time. The crying is rare—and they're over it in a few seconds and back to playing again. Besides, people in the world make fun of you; you have to know how to take it."

Arlene didn't buy it. "People in the world are also bullies; our job is protect our kids, not bully them."

Who is right? Arlene *and* Martin. But because Arlene's perspective is easier to understand—no good parent wants to bully their kids—let's start by looking at the positive functions of teasing.

A dad teasing a child is like a doctor inoculating a child: the vaccine "teases" the child with a version of a real virus to help the child's immune system grow strong enough to fight off the virus in the real world. However, while teasing can be a virtue, any virtue taken to its extreme becomes a vice.

Wait. Why did I say, "A *dad* teasing a child is like a doctor inoculating a child"? Because children are used to their dads teasing them as a part of play. Once, when Arlene tried to tease, Maggie broke into tears almost immediately. Maggie was used to her mom being empathetic and more serious—so in mom language, Maggie translated teasing as a serious criticism.

Maggie's tears convinced Arlene she was right—"teasing is borderline bullying." She couldn't get what Martin thought he was teaching when he teased.

When Martin teased, he taught Maggie and Marty Jr. to interpret the meaning of a twinkle in his eye, slight alterations of his voice, shifts in his facial expression. Teasing is a core component of teaching emotional intelligence, dad-style.

Arlene was fighting for the children to be protected at the moment of impact. Martin felt he was preparing the children to be protected for a future moment. The children need some of both.

Arlene still argued that teasing did not make kids feel loved. And certainly, when teasing comes from the mouth of a nonteaser, it does get misinterpreted as criticism. But when the kids were around Martin, they learned dad language. They sensed that when Martin teased them, it was *because* he loved them.

Bonding Through Teasing and Wit-Covered Put-Downs

Teasing in moderation doesn't just inoculate us against criticism. It is also male-style bonding. The commerce of masculinity is the trading of wit-covered put-downs. Your son will experience it in junior high school. And he'll experience it even more powerfully if he joins a fraternity.

Despite the negative stereotypes, fraternity brothers often bond for a lifetime, sometimes becoming among the few long-lasting friends men have. Fraternity brothers look more forward to their fraternity reunions than their college reunions. But no one plans bully reunions. So there's clearly a bigger distinction between teasing and bullying than met Arlene's eye. Since it's better to understand a language than to be on the "outs," let's take a deeper dive.

Why is it that fraternities trade in teasing and other wit-covered put-downs? **The exchange of wit-covered put-downs is boys' and men's unconscious way of training each other to handle the criticism it takes to become successful.** Try running for president if you can't handle put-downs.

For guys, the more hazardous the profession, the more its members trade wit-covered put-downs. They're ubiquitous in "the death professions"—in the military and among coal miners, construction workers, police officers, and Alaskan crab fishermen. For these men, a put-down isn't harassment; it's their diet. Women who rise in their ranks understand the meaning of their language.

What is the meaning of their language? When, for example, a firefighter enters a burning building, he needs to know his partner will risk life and limb to save him. A partner who cannot be teased—who takes himself too seriously, who is too thin-skinned, fragile, or narcissistic to take a joke—also can't be trusted to risk his life to pull a partner out of the rubble after the ceiling collapses.

Among the armed services, by far the most hazardous is the Marine Corps. A marine knows that if he's wounded, a thin-skinned narcissist won't risk enemy fire. Testing each other to see who is not just willing to die but also strong enough to drag a fellow marine to safety, creates a lifelong bond: "Once a marine, always a marine."

Second, what is common to male-on-male teasing is identifying something that is unique to that man that might hint either at his weakness, or, alternatively, a strength that other men fear will make him think he's better than the others—a prima donna. He cannot be trusted to risk his life for a "lesser" being.

When, for example, Peter became the newest firefighter in the firehouse, Peter enjoyed the unique strength his dad's position as fire chief conferred. The other men feared that they might have a prima donna on their hands. They feared that if a burning roof collapsed, Peter would call for help instead of immediately risking his life to help them. So they started teasing him—stepping to the side of the washroom sink so they wouldn't block Prima Donna Pete from the mirror.

Once, when Peter was having dinner at the firehouse, one of the firefighters handed him a pike pole (a pole with a hook on the end), and teased him that Peter Piper would need that to pick a peck of his pickled peppers. When Peter casually pretended to use it to pick his nose, his colleagues could see that he could laugh at himself. When he calmly asked the ringleader, Frank, "Prefer yours pickled or plain?" the guys were clear that he could tease back—that he could good-naturedly play the game.

This example demonstrates multiple subtleties of emotional intelligence Peter learned from his dad's own teasing:

- By using a playful tone, Peter proved he "got" the meaning of the game. Had Peter said in an *aggressive* tone, "Prefer yours pickled, plain, or deep up your flat-ass asshole?" he would have failed the test. Aggression is evidence of being out of control, defensive, and unable to handle criticism.
- By giving the pike pole to Frank, Peter signaled that he was happy to play *with* Frank as opposed to dividing the workforce by gathering up a group to defend him against Frank. That would also have demonstrated defensiveness.
- By responding playfully with Frank in front of the others, he was letting the others see he knew how to be assertive without being aggressive—that he didn't need to run to daddy for protection, and that his "strength" would not be used against them.

Peter's dad, Joe, had prepared his son to know that a certain amount of hazing is the price of admission for acceptance, not rejection. **The trading of wit-covered put-downs is boys and men training each other to handle criticism, unconsciously knowing that the ability to handle criticism is a prerequisite to success.**

When the hazing was happening, Joe was careful to not interfere, knowing it would only reinforce the firefighters' fear that Peter was to be protected, and therefore couldn't be trusted to protect.

Joe had also taught Peter to know his limits—to have the guts to speak up against *too much* hazing. But teasing and hazing are the rusty edges of accountability: if you're a little bit off, we'll flash you the yellow light—and we'll see if you can be accountable rather than defensive.

Translating Men's Language of Hazing as Acceptance into Women's Language of Hazing as Rejection

After some early testing, Peter was accepted as part of the firehouse team. But hazing became an issue again when the first woman applied to enter their all-male force. The guys were hesitant to haze her for fear of being sued for discrimination. But they knew that if they did not, that *would* be discriminating against her—she wouldn't get the same opportunity to bond and become part of the team. Joe concluded, "We're damned if we do, and damned if we don't."

What the firefighters missed was asking themselves, "Could we solicit from her or other female firefighters ideas for alternatives to hazing that could nevertheless vet for a rookie's willingness to risk her or his life to save theirs?"

(One of the ways to prepare your son for leadership is to prepare him to hear the perspectives of everyone, while encouraging him to search for out-of-the-box perspectives that he has not yet heard.)

In groups of men unified by either physical danger (e.g., hazardous professions), significant responsibility (e.g., C-suites), or competition (e.g., team sports), put-downs are not a sign of disrespect but a prerequisite to bonding. The subject of the teasing *does* indicate a potential problem, but men in these groups tend to tease only if you are a candidate for being one of the team. If the person being teased responds with the emotional intelligence that Peter demonstrated thanks to his dad's preparation, he earns the teasers' trust, which is the key to the inner circle's inner circle.

In brief, **among guys, if you can't tease 'em, you can't trust 'em.**

Teasing in Marriage

When Martin teased his kids, he was not just preparing them for interactions with peers from junior high to the workplace but also for a happy marriage. **Married couples who tease each other during conflict feel more connected and happier after the conflict than those who criticize in a straightforward way.**[25]

If humans' Achilles' heel is our inability to handle personal criticism, especially from a loved one, then teasing, when part of the package of playfulness, often feels less toxic. In the past, jesters were paid to tease—and were highly respected when they did it well. A king who could handle it put the court at ease: the court gained trust that they could speak their mind and keep their head.

It would be impossible to appreciate *Saturday Night Live*, Steven Colbert's *Late Show*, or *The Joe Rogan Experience* if we did not know how to read satirical smiles, switches in voice tone, the roll or wink of eyes, a raised eyebrow, a stare held an extra second—signals that there's a grain of truth, a pinch of exaggeration, and, above all, time reserved to get off our high horse of judging and dividing and share a minute of laughing and uniting.

Hearing all this was helpful to Arlene. Teasing was still a hard thing for her to do herself, but she did register that, for guys, "if you can't tease 'em, you can't trust 'em." And she wanted both Marty Jr. and Maggie to have the emotional intelligence to be able to be trusted by boys and men. Realizing the value of teasing allowed her to at least see Martin as making a contribution rather than as just being insensitive.

That said, Arlene was still wary that teasing and hazing might too easily morph into harassment and bullying. On a gut level, she felt it devalued the person being hazed. And she has a point . . .

Teasing: Preparation for Hazing and Harassment, Dad-Style?

Hazing is most ubiquitous in the death professions because a willingness to die involves preparing oneself to go from being valued at home to being devalued at work and in war. **Especially in the military, hazing helps recruits amputate each other's individuality because the war machine works best with standardized parts, not with people who say, "I'm special."**

Preparing your son for the male–female workplace dilemma is most challenging in times of relative peace—when men are told both that the women are equals *and* if they harass and haze the women as equals the men will ruin their careers and destroy their families. This reinforces the men's beliefs that women want to "have their cake and eat it, too." And when women are subject to hazing, it simultaneously reinforces their feeling devalued and their beliefs that men are only paying lip-service to equality.

For Joe and Martin to most effectively impart emotional intelligence about teasing and hazing to Peter and Marty Jr., they need more than just an understanding of the male culture of teasing and hazing; they also need to appreciate its differences from female teasing culture. While women of certain backgrounds and cultures tease each other, when it comes to the powerful teasing the vulnerable—as in a dad teasing kids, or women being teased by men in a mostly male workplace when they fear not being respected at work—there is considerably more hesitation. And even among women, teasing may have different unwritten rules.

Many women will relate to Sadie's experience:

> When I'm having lunch with a couple of my girlfriends, we'll be talking with each other—even talking while the others are talking—all hearing each other's stories, and all supporting each other. It's a great time.
>
> But if one of us goes to the restroom, there's a good chance the others will say something about her—it could be a concern, or a criticism. When our friend returns, we're all smiles and act like nothing's happened. Hmm . . . Maybe that's why when I'm with my girlfriends and I have to use the ladies' room, I wait until one of them gets up to go, and then I join her.

"So that's why women all go to the restroom together!" I laughed. Then I asked, "Do you ever share your criticism or concern directly?"

"If it's a concern, for sure. Usually right there, in the group. But if it's a criticism, maybe not. And if it gets too bad, we just don't invite her next time."

The process among many women, then, might be thought of more as antihazing, and antiteasing. **If female-to-female teasing and hazing does occur, as in *Mean Girls*, it signals that the woman being teased and hazed is on the outs, not that she's being vetted for inclusion.** It often occurs *after* the women have vetted for friendship via other means (e.g., sharing their vulnerabilities or being supportive of each other), not as a way of vetting for friendship.

The male-female gap in the understanding of hazing is exacerbated by one of male-style hazing's primary rules: target whatever is different. Marine recruit Raheel Siddiqui was a Muslim, thus labeled a spy, and forced to strike other recruits on the neck to simulate what Muslim spies allegedly do.[26] What makes every woman different is that, as a woman, she is suspected of wanting to be protected rather than subjected to harassment and hazing.

The more a workplace's mission is to physically save lives at the risk of their own, the more likely it is to be predominantly male. And the more a woman in such a workplace faces the type of testing that Joe faced when other firefighters feared he'd be protected by his dad. Women often experience it as sexism against women; the men often experience it as fighting the sexism of protecting women from hazing—sexism they fear would undermine female coworkers' readiness to protect their country.

Arlene's biggest fear when Martin teased the kids was that the teasing would go too far and have a lifetime effect of trauma, as it did with Raheel Siddiqui. Raheel committed suicide. And for Maggie and Marty Jr., she didn't see its relevance: neither was likely to enter a "death profession," so she initially only saw the potential for trauma, not training to read life's yellow lights and increase the kids' emotional intelligence.

While Martin and Arlene remained at odds about teasing versus protecting, Maggie and Marty Jr. benefited from the checks and balances. And as Martin and Arlene embraced the value of those checks and balances, the emotional tension between them lessened, and Maggie and Marty Jr. loved the greater security they felt at home.

The Conditional or Hierarchical Dad

Just as the power hierarchy in the executive suites of many workplaces may leave a woman feeling left out, so the power hierarchy at home— paired with a lack of awareness of the benefits of dad-style parenting— may leave a dad feeling left out. The Pew Research Center reinforced what most people know from experience: women still run the home that men still financially support. Even "in dual-income couples," they report, "it is the woman who has more say, regardless of whether she earns more or less than her partner."[27]

And while your son will hear a lot about women being left out in the workplace, he will hear little about the ways that his potential as a dad can be snuffed out. Some of his unique contributions, instead of being valued, may be used as a reason to "kill" him as a dad. Though rare in serious discussion, this topic is occasionally broached via humor, as in the old *Dennis the Menace* cartoon in which Dennis explains to a female friend, "You can't win 'em all—unless you're my mom arguing with my dad."[28]

The difference is in expectation: at work, everyone expects to be in a hierarchy—even the CEO reports to the shareholders. And that CEO knows his or her employment is conditional. But your son isn't expecting to be in a hierarchical relationship to his wife. His vows said "for better or worse," not "conditional upon her approval only." This hierarchical-dad

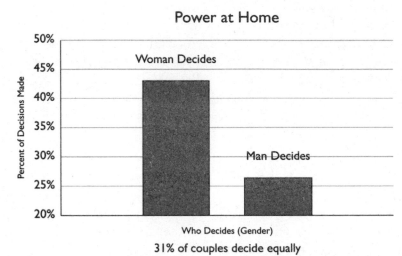

Power at Home

4 decision areas: weekend activities; big home purchases;
household finance; what to watch on TV

Source: Pew Research Center[29]

feeling often becomes much more pronounced when your son becomes a
dad himself. How, then, can you alert him to speak up before it is too late?

Litmus Tests of the Conditional or Hierarchical Dad

There are two quick litmus tests your son may well observe as to whether
his dad is valued and therefore whether he is likely to be valued as a dad.

A first litmus test is a mom saying "*my* son" or "*my* daughter"—not
"our son" or "our daughter"—or, worst case scenario, saying "my son"
when she is proud and "our son" when she is disgusted.

A second litmus test? If your son notices that his dad is playing differently when mom is around, he may unconsciously fear that he may
also become a "conditional dad"—a dad who feels he has to modify his
parenting to satisfy mom's conditions. Or, put another way, a dad who
feels like a "hierarchical dad"—able to father as long as he fathers the way
a mom feels a father should father.

If your son is bright and sensitive, he may intuit there is a "glass ceiling" in his home—a dad who can never be more than a vice president of
the family in which mom is the CEO. But while the women's movement

has made one glass ceiling visible, the glass ceiling your son senses, he cannot see.

One of the best ways of catalyzing your son's ability to see that glass ceiling is to encourage his involvement in a men's group in which everything shared is confidential. In the three hundred or so groups I have formed with men between seventeen and ninety, I find this to be one of the most helpful ways to free him to express vulnerability without feeling he will lose respect. This doesn't have to cost anything. Boys as young as junior high schoolers get involved in all-male groups, usually with a mentor or teacher's supervision. By the time your son is in his twenties, he can join peers.

So if you've ever wanted to know your son more deeply by being a fly on the wall of a men's group, here's your chance. Don't expect it to always be politically correct. But do expect it to offer you an honest view of the cues a boy often absorbs from the dynamics between his mom and dad—and the ability to use a men's group's feedback to discover what he wants to emulate and what he wishes to change.

Don's Dad, Don's Son

As each of us did our brief check-in at the start of one of my men's groups, Don revealed that his dad had just had a heart attack. When the check-in was complete, we asked Don to talk about his dad more deeply than he had in the past . . . starting with his best memories:

"My best memories are going with my dad to his country music gigs. He was no big celebrity, but he had a following, especially around Nashville, where we lived. He did it full-time before he met my mom, and by the time I was three or four he was doing small tours here and there.

"My fondest memory? It for sure was going with him to some of the gigs just before my sister was born. He'd escort my mom and me backstage with him, and we'd meet all the producers and some fans. Man, the fans treated him like he was God. It made me feel like I had the best dad.

"But my favorite part was when he would introduce me and Mom to the audience. He did it at different times each set. So every song I'd think, 'Will he introduce me and Mom after this song?' When he finally introduced us, he'd always lift me up onto the stage and into his arms. He'd hold me real close. And then he'd say, with this loving look in his eye, 'Here is the joy of my life.'

"I could feel his pride as he looked back and forth between me and Mom, and as Mom smiled back at both of us. It made me feel like we were all so connected. I felt so secure. Once I remember him holding back tears, and my asking him, 'Are you crying, Dad?' He told me those were tears of love."

Don paused, it seemed with tears in his eyes. "I guess those are more than my favorite childhood memories. They're probably the best moments of my life."

Don's face was glowing with the memory, but a few seconds later one of the guys in the group noticed a slight change in his demeanor. "Share more about your sadness, Don."

"I think the real jolt I feel from my dad's heart attack is that he might die a broken man; or maybe even because he's been broken. He hasn't had a spring in his step—or, it seems, much joy in his heart—for years. That's such a contrast to the dad I knew when he took me up on that stage."

"What happened?"

"I remember—maybe I was about five or six—my parents told me that Mom was pregnant and that I would be having a brother or sister. I was pretty happy, but then I overheard Mom and Dad agreeing she would have to put off her return to teaching, and how they would also need a bigger home. They discussed my dad having to give up playing music full-time, maybe just do it on weekends. I could hear them talking about how they were both sad about that, but they felt there was no other way.

"After that, there was a long period where my dad was applying for jobs with one company after another. That was the first time I ever saw him irritated. I never thought about it before, but I think I get it now."

"Yeah, I get it for sure," one of the guys muttered, and then, remembering our rule to focus on the speaker, asked Don, "What do you get about it?"

"I'm imagining him being rejected every day, and being rejected applying to do something he didn't even want to do. He lost if he got the job, and lost if he didn't get the job. God, how depressing."

"Did he finally get a job?"

"Yeah. He eventually took a job selling insurance . . . with CNA."

"Was your dad any happier when your sister was born?"

"Sort of. He was crazy for her, and for sure being with her was when he was happiest. But my sister became the center of everything. Of course, I had the typical ambivalence about that." Then Don drifted a bit.

"What's happening, Don?"

"I was just piecing two and two together—it was about that time that I also recall sensing a distance between my mom and dad. Oh, God. And that's the same thing that happened with me and Barbara [Don's wife at the time] when David was born."

"You became more distant from Barbara after your son was born?"

"Definitely."

One of the men interrupted, "That happened for me and my wife too—when our first daughter was born." All the guys in the group who were parents nodded in recognition.

"What was the feeling, Don?"

Don's long pause seemed to walk a tightrope between letting the question slide and digging deeper, as if into an uncomfortable space. "This is awful to say, but I felt like I was working harder so my wife could have a new lover that I was paying for."

"Wow, that's graphic . . . powerful. Did you tell Barbara that?" one of the men asked.

"Not the world's best idea!" another guy half-joked, and half-advised in pain.

"No, I could never say that. I could only say that here. I probably wouldn't even allow myself to think it if I wasn't here."

The men nodded. Then one returned to Don, "Why did you feel it was awful to think that?"

Don paused again. "I'm ashamed—I am supposed to be thinking of my son, not myself."

The group broke into a ten-minute conversation identifying with that feeling and how we would never have the guts to say that to our wives, or in any other setting—or even have allowed ourselves to think it.

"You said your dad's heart attack might be because he's feeling like a broken man?" one of the guys prompted, returning to Don.

"Yeah, that's what I'm thinking; I don't know. It seems like the better my dad did at CNA, the more he was traveling, and the more depressed he got. He was gone a lot at night, and took to drinking. When he lost his temper, he seemed sorry right afterward, but then a week or two later he'd lose it again.

"By the time Dad retired, he and Mom had long since lost that love feeling I remembered from when Dad used to hold me onstage. Nowadays they seem happier to be playing with David [Don's son] than to be with each other."

"Don, that's a bummer. With his heart attack, that's gotta be tough. But at least he's alive, and you can still deepen your connection with him."

"And what about you, Don? You seem to love your music more than your chiropractic practice, yes?"

"For sure my favorite moments now are practicing music with David, and seeing him do a gig or two—even though, at fifteen, I worry that if he becomes too successful that he'll get all caught up with the adoring girls! He's not so worried about that!"

"What are you doing to make things different for you and David—so you don't 'become your dad'?"

"Well, aside from getting divorced—" The group laughed. Don continued, "On the good news side, first I'm having an open discussion with David about the trade-offs between doing what he loves, which could make him a 'starving artist,' and doing something he likes—but doesn't love—that pays the bills."

"What are you actually modeling for him?"

"Trying to do it all." Don laughed self-deprecatingly. "But I'm within a few years of the end of alimony and child support payments, and in six more years college tuition should be paid. In the meantime, I am marketing the CD I showed you guys last month, and trying to teach David how to create and market CDs so there's some source of 'income while he's sleeping.' David *loves* that idea! I'm also helping him develop a backup career that won't make him depressed like my dad became—and like I can occasionally be.

"I'm also trying to get David to think about what it means to have children. It's a tough discussion, 'cause when we drifted into it he asked, 'Are you glad you had me?'"

"Yikes. What did you say?"

"I said it was the best thing his mom and I ever did. I think he could tell that I meant that. Then I told him that he'd be a great dad, but that ultimately everyone has to answer that question for themselves."

"Unless your wife wants a child; then it's answered for you!" one of the men half-joked to the tune of knowing laughter.

"Well, you're getting quite sage, Don. Since you've gotten divorced, did you talk with David about how to avoid that?"

"Not directly. But I told him to focus on finding a woman who thinks of others . . . to watch how she treats waiters, her parents, that type of thing."

"But apparently that didn't work for you . . ." one of the guys teased.

"I got addicted to Barbara's beauty and charm, and high maintenance came along for the ride. But I can't tell David that, and I don't want to parrot a bunch of sound-good euphemisms like 'focus on inner beauty,' so I'm trying to get David to value women who, for example, pay for themselves, have career ambitions . . . that type of thing."

"Get women to pay for themselves? Aren't you setting him up to be rejected?"

"I do worry about that, yeah. You think so? But I guess I just want to plant the seed that the best way to find a girl who doesn't expect him to be her wallet is to not be her wallet."

Brad said, "I wish my dad had told me that," and a couple of the guys rolled their eyes as if to say, "Good luck with that."

"Basically, I guess you're right, Brad, I'm trying to have the discussions I wish my dad had with me."

I smiled. "When you and David played as a duo together at your Super Bowl party, you definitely both seemed to exude so much joy and love, Don. I could see it from David, too. I think you've broken the cycle."

The Worrier and the Warrior: The Checks and Balances of Parenting

Shortly after our men's group had asked Don about his favorite memories of his dad, we all did a brainstorming of the other men's favorite memories.

Glenn started, "*My* favorite memory is trying to outwit my dad when we were playing hide-'n'-seek. I started by hiding under the bedspread. When I got bigger and Dad caught on, I hid behind clothes in the bedroom closet. When he caught on to that, I put pillows under the bedspread so he'd think it was me, then hide somewhere else. When he caught on to that, I'd set an alarm that would go off next to the pillows. No excitement thrilled me more than when I 'fooled' Dad. And the longer I fooled him, the longer he'd toss me in the air, as a reward, and then he'd either catch me or not catch me and I'd land on the bed. My mom would freak about how high he threw me. I think maybe that made it all the more fun—like it created a bond."

Jim offered, "My favorite memory was playing horsey."

"I'd kick my dad on the side so he'd buck harder—like a horse. I'd always want to see how long I could stay on before I got dumped."

"What did your mom think of that?"

"Ha. I'd be saying, 'Buck harder,' and Mom would be saying, 'Don't buck so hard.' Poooor Dad." Jim laughed. "Once I fell and cried, 'cause I loved how Dad cuddled me when I cried. But then my mom yelled at Dad for making me cry, and we didn't get to play horsey for a long time. So after that if I fell I made sure to not cry."

As a boy in a dad-rich home roughhouses, is coached, or is read to at bedtime, his dad's love and support becomes part of him the way syrup becomes part of a pancake. It reshapes him like the syrup reshapes the pancake, and neither is the same again.

As your son gets older, he needs to know that the blend of laughter, roughhousing, and matching of wits dads offer is a recipe for a paradoxical bond: the bond of being on the same team by being on different teams. And he needs to be cognizant of how he, too, can use this paradoxical bond when he is a dad, as leverage for his children to do homework or get to bed on time, or to successfully encourage his child to get up and try again when something goes wrong.

Part of being a father warrior is to listen when mom worries, thus clearing the path for her to tap into her inner warrior—something that can be done whether married or divorced if, in the event of divorce, you adhere to the four "must-dos."

CHAPTER 17

In the Event of Divorce . . .
The Four "Must-Dos"

If divorce is in your best interest, what are the four "must-dos" to also foster your children's best interests?

If children of divorce are to have a reasonable chance of doing as well as children in an intact family (one where the biological mom and dad are married and living in same home as the children), these four must-dos must all occur consistently and simultaneously:

1. **Equal time.** Children have approximately equal time, including over-nights, with each parent.
2. **No bad-mouthing.** Neither parent bad-mouths the other in a way that the child can detect, either verbally or nonverbally (e.g., eye-rolling and emotional withdrawal).
3. **Proximity.** The parents live close enough to each other that the child does not need to forfeit friends or activities to see either parent.
4. **Counseling.** Consistent couples' counseling occurs even when there is no emergency.

Here is why each is important—one at a time:

I. Time

Time trumps dime. An analysis of 63 studies published in the *Journal of Marriage and the Family* concluded that children benefit more from quality of time with dad than quantity of money from dad.[1]

The more equal the time, the better. A meta-analysis of the best studies found that if children cannot live with both parents together, a minimum of one-third of a child's time should be spent with each parent. However, "additional benefits continue to accrue up to and including equal (50-50) time."[2] And a separate meta-analysis concludes that the only children of divorce who are "about as well off as those in which the parents remained married"[3] are the children who have about equal time with both parents.[4]

Overnights are important. One hundred and ten of the nation's leading researchers and practitioners issued a recent consensus report stressing the importance of not only more time with fathers, but more overnights in particular.[5] Overnights allow children the full benefit of both parents' styles of parenting.

Parenting plans should be consistent. Parenting plans that include both parents having "bedtime and waking rituals, transitions to and from school, extracurricular and recreational activities"[6] increase children's facility at creating friendships.[7]

In short, children benefit from approximately equal time and overnights with each parent.

The studies referenced above mostly concern the benefits of shared parent time for children in the United States. In the United States, as in most developed countries, the law is way behind the science.

The few countries practicing equally shared parenting are witnessing the benefits for both the children and parents, and are responding by making equal time the default. For example, in 1984, only 1 percent of the children of divorce in Sweden experienced equal parent time; however, as the benefits became apparent, by 2011 that figure had increased to 37 percent.

A recent Swedish study also found that parents whose children were in their "tender years"—under four years of age—felt their children were benefiting from equal time. *And this held true even among the higher-conflict parents.*[8]

Did the parents' perceptions accurately reflect their children's reality? Yes. A Swedish study measuring the well-being of 172,000 children found that the children in equally shared parenting did much better than those in sole-parent or primary-parent arrangements, and almost as well as those in an intact family.[9] The study measured the children's psychological and social well-being, and their physical health.

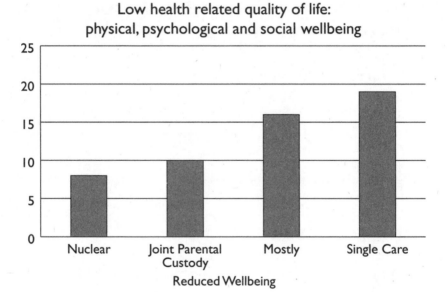

Low health related quality of life: physical, psychological and social wellbeing

Reduced Wellbeing

Source: BMC Public Health[10]

The same study found that parents in equally shared parenting arrangements were also happier than parents in a sole-parent arrangement on all seven measures the researchers reviewed: their children's social network, the family's housing, work arrangements, overall economic health, physical health, family type, and ability to have a positive impact on their children.[11]

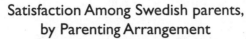

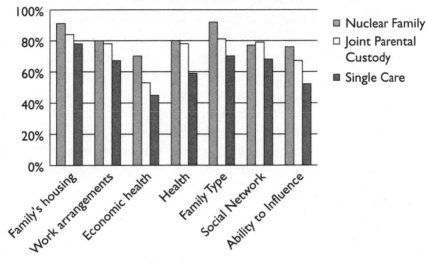

Source: BMC Public Health[12]

Divorce's biggest disaster from the child's perspective is loss of contact with a parent.[13] **Children express intense dissatisfaction with the traditional arrangement of every other weekend.**[14] While both boys and girls found it a loser, the greatest feelings of deprivation and depressive behavior were observed in the boys.[15]

Children with equally shared parent time liked the length of time they were with each parent because they didn't feel that one parent was really more like an aunt or uncle.[16] The children who expressed the greatest interest were under ten.[17]

Boys' overall well-being in shared parent time arrangements was similar to that in happy, intact families.[18] As was both sexes' relationship to their parents—especially to their dads.[19] And they created better relationships with stepparents.[20] Even within the first few months after separation, shared parent time results in less sibling rivalry and fewer negative attitudes toward the parents.[21]

From the parents' perspective, shared parent time leaves each parent feeling less stressed out.[22] One of mothers' biggest complaints after divorce, when they have the primary or sole care of the children, is that they feel overwhelmed; shared parenting time leaves mothers with more time for themselves, and more time for the emotional benefits of social support.[23]

When a single mom has to be the "tough guy" with her son, she has to play both the female role and the male role. She often experiences the single-mom paradox: feeling like she is losing her femininity even as she plays the most feminine role. Shared parent time liberates a mom from having to be the "man of the house." And for some moms, it gives them an opportunity to rediscover their femininity.[24]

However, there are two nagging questions to be answered before judges and moms can feel at peace with equally shared parenting time after divorce: In high-conflict relationships, shouldn't one parent be in charge? And won't switching homes so regularly destabilize children?

In High-Conflict Relationships, Shouldn't One Parent Be In Charge?

I often hear judges in family court worry that if the parents' conflicts are great enough to bring them to court that they should probably assign one parent as the primary parent. But an analysis of forty-three studies concluded that "children in shared parenting families had better outcomes on measures of emotional, behavioral, and psychological well-being, as well as better physical health and better relationships with their fathers and their mothers, benefits that remained even when there were high levels of conflict between their parents."[25]

Won't Switching Homes Destabilize Children?

Judges and parents often worry that the instability of divorce will be magnified by the constant switching of homes required by equally shared parenting. Since this worry is perhaps greatest for preadolescents and adolescents, a large study of such children sought to uncover the reality. Its conclusion was that children in equally shared parenting arrangements had better psychosomatic health (physical health affected by emotional and mental stresses) than children living mostly or only with one parent. (They did not, however, have as good psychosomatic health as those living in an intact nuclear family.[26]) In brief, **two-parent stability trumps geographical stability**. Put another way, two parents in two homes is better than one parent in one home.

2. Bad-Mouthing

Shortly after I spoke on the boy crisis at the University of Toronto, some-one posted a YouTube video of the presentation[27] that seemed to be a stimulus for the letter I've excerpted here:

> Hello Dr. Farrell,
>
> My name is Ned and I'm a currently unemployed 29-year-old . . . I'm writing you because I feel like no one around has an ear to what is going on with me.
>
> My parents divorced when I was about two, and since then **all I have heard is how my dad is a horrible person . . .** After the divorce and the loss of my father, video games became my world.
>
> I seem like sort of a poster child for the type of problems you talk about, namely finding it hard to communicate, lack of focus and motivation, and a disconnect to the outside world. My personal relationships always fall apart, and I can feel the resentment from my family for not "manning up." I also notice that when I am criticized I will retreat and attack my criticizer from a distance.
>
> In the past five years I have been able to create some commu-nication with my dad . . . He always tells me about how different I was when I was a child: confident, loving, inquisitive, invested. Those traits seem like another person to me.
>
> **Truthfully, I hate who I am . . .** I must change because otherwise I can only ruin for myself and those invested in me if I continue this way. Any advice would be greatly appreciated.
>
> Ned[28]

Two sentences in Ned's letter reflect the seeds of the problems expe-rienced by many children of divorce, and especially by boys: "All I have heard is how my dad is a horrible person," and "I hate who I am."

Children who hear that their dad is a jerk, irresponsible, or a liar eventually look in a mirror and see their dad's nose, hair, or eyes in their own. As they learn their genes are 50 percent their dad's and recall a lie or two of their own, they begin to fear that they are the jerk, liar, and irresponsible loser that they have been told their dad is.

Of course, for a boy, this is even more haunting since, as we've seen, desire to be a father begins in the son, who sees in his own dad who he could become.

"Your father was a jackass."

While both moms and dads can be guilty of bad-mouthing the other parent (including using negative body language), Glynnis Walker's research interviewing children of divorce found that moms are almost five times as likely to bad-mouth dads as dads are to bad-mouth moms.[29] This doubtless contributes to three other crucial findings about children of divorce:

- Children living with their dad felt positively about their mom; children living with their mom were more likely to think negatively of their dad.[30]
- When children live with only their moms, the parents are nine times as likely to have conflict as when children live with their dads.[31]
- Children living with their mom are less than half as likely to have contact with their dad.[32]

The less involved a biological parent is, the more dangerous bad-mouthing becomes, because the child begins to experience the less-involved parent only as a straw parent, and to view that half of her or himself that is that parent as a straw child. Especially damaging to the child is calling the other parent a liar, irresponsible, or manipulative. Even worse is "diagnosing" the other parent with a personality disorder (e.g., "your dad is a narcissist" or "your mom has borderline personality disorder").

This does not mean that a parent cannot defend her or himself from a false accusation made by the other parent, but restrict your defense to creating a clearer picture of your intent, not a disparaging picture of the other parent's personality.[33] For example, if a child recalls, "Mom said, 'Once again, Dad didn't care enough to come to my soccer game,'" it's fine to clarify, "I was on a business trip last week so I could make enough money to hopefully send you to the finals." But refrain from adding, "And mom knew that." The discipline to stop with the defense and to refrain from a counterattack will allow your children to experience what maturity is, and to earn you your children's long-lasting respect.

Of course, some parents have good reason to minimize their children's contact with the other parent. But as a rule, a true parenting instinct includes fighting for the other parent to be involved with the children as if the children's lives depended on it.

Since dad is most at risk of being both bad-mouthed and less involved, let's look at three reasons the bad-mouthing sin is in conflict with your child's best interests:

1. Your children grow up feeling, "I hate who I am."
2. Your children fear that "loving dad is betraying mom."
3. Bad-mouthing undermines dad's motivation to invest money and time in the bank of love and to become responsible in response to the hope for love.

3. Proximity

If children live in separate homes, proximity to the other parent has been found to be the single most important factor determining a child's likelihood of success.[34]

What is the optimal distance? In my observations of children in fifty families for between a day and a weekend, the optimal distance between parents' homes appeared to be between five minutes and twenty minutes' drive time.

Children tend to resent going to another parent's home if it is far enough away that they cannot keep up with their soccer or gymnastics practice, thus depriving them of the benefits of team or individual sports. Similarly, after a divorce, stability is important; missing the birthday party or slumber party of a friend can destabilize friendships, sometimes triggering withdrawal or depression. Farther than twenty minutes created stabilization problems. Closer than five minutes—within easy walking distance—tends to tempt children to use proximity as leverage in undermining parental discipline—"You're mean, I'm going to daddy's/mommy's."

4. Counseling

A major study following children of divorce for ten years[35] found that the children whose parents were randomly assigned to do consistent couples or relationship counseling did much better than the children whose parents were randomly assigned to the control group with no counseling. This study was not conducted in privileged communities with a choice of high-priced psychologists but in low-income communities with community center counselors.

Limiting counseling to moments of crisis after divorce means parents are often in contact only when their conflict is the greatest and deadlines are imminent, and therefore when emotions are the most frazzled. That contact then becomes a breeding ground for reinforcing the misunderstandings that contributed to the divorce.

Here's why counseling time should always be on the calendar, and at short intervals (e.g., once every week or two): When it is, couples tend to save what bothers them for that calmer and more centered time rather than get into arguments whenever they are most triggered. And when they do convene, they tend to dig deeper and more compassionately into the underlying issues; they are more amenable to creating win-win solutions, and are more motivated to follow through.

If Shared Parenting Isn't Possible, Are Children Better Off Primarily with Mom or Dad?

Although equally shared parent time works best to maximize your sons' and daughters' chances of success after divorce, if we must stop at one of the inns of last resort—primary-parent time or sole-parent time—which is better, mother time or father time (ahem)?

While most studies suggest that, if a choice is forced, children of *both* sexes do better when they are primarily with their dad (though remember, primary-parent dads are more self-selected than primary-parent moms), our sons are even more vulnerable to not having dads than our daughters: "Boys do especially poorly in broken families," [36] particularly in single-mother families after divorce.

Compared to his sister, a boy experiences greater vulnerability when he is raised by an unmarried mother with little education, as well as when he attends a poor-quality public school. The boy is likely to have many more behavioral and cognitive problems, be less likely to graduate from high school, and be more likely to commit serious crimes.[37] However, there are a few studies, such as one in Sweden, where children who lived primarily with their moms did better.[38] We'll put this in perspective in a minute, but first there's something counterintuitive that you need to know about dad involvement.

More than one-third (36 percent) of fathers who are living at or below the poverty line are single dads.[39] The more money and the more education a dad has, the more likely he is to be used to raise money, not children. Only 7 percent of dads with bachelor's degrees are single dads (compared to 26 percent who do not have a high school diploma).[40] So when we read how children do with single moms versus single dads, remember that *both* single moms *and* single dads tend to be poorer and less educated than average. This helps us see that we have somewhat comparable populations for comparing how children do when they live with a single mom or dad.

Dad, Self-Esteem, and Warmth

Boys who live with their dad after divorce tend to be warmer, have higher degrees of self-esteem, be more mature, and be more independent than boys who do not.[41]

Dad Versus ADHD

Thirty percent of children living only or primarily with their mom had problems with concentration, versus 15 percent who live with their dads.[42]

Dad Versus Being a Victim

Children living only with their dads were less likely to experience problems related to feeling like victims.[43] For example, they were

- one-third as likely to feel victimized by other children;
- half as likely to have frequent nightmares;
- one-quarter as likely to experience frequent seizures of fear; and
- half as likely to have feelings of low self-worth and lonesomeness.

They were also less sensitive to criticism and had fewer temper tantrums.

And perhaps as a result of all the above, children living with dads also had more playmates,[44] which, of course, makes them less likely to be depressed or feel victimized by other children and thus better able to avert the cycle of victimhood.

Dad-Only in the Early Years

Kyle Pruett of Yale studied infants living with just their dads—compared to just their moms—and found that in the areas of personal and social skills, they were two to six months ahead of schedule. The results with older babies followed suit.[45] The infants also performed problem-solving tasks at the level of babies four to eight months older.[46]

Dad-Only in the Dangerous Years

Millions of divorced parents worry as their son substitutes video games, drinking, drugs, or porn for friends and the risk of rejection when reaching out for love.

These dangers reach their peak (e.g., school shootings and suicide) in the late teenage years. Fortunately, there are solutions.

In a study of more than twelve thousand teenagers after divorce, children living with single dads fared better than children living with single moms. (Note, though, that the same study found that when teenagers lived equally with both parents after divorce, they were more easily able to make friends than even the children in intact families.[47])

Do Boys Do Better with Dads and Girls with Moms?

The prevailing wisdom has been that, if boys and girls must be with one parent or the other, boys should be with dads and girls with moms. As we've seen, this isn't true—both boys and girls do better with their dads. At all ages. Even when the dad has no advantage in income.[48] Yet we've also seen that only living with dad is also not the ideal.

Divorced Dads' Depression—and Suicide

While depriving children of their dads is a tragedy for the children, the purpose void it creates for a dad can lead him to depression.[1]

Divorced men are almost ten times more likely to commit suicide than divorced women from similar backgrounds.[2]

Obviously, a dad's suicide has a devastating impact on all the children. But even one of a dad's red flags of suicide—depression—leads to children being 72 percent more likely to experience emotional or behavioral problems.[3]

Whether a dad disappears by suicide or by depression, when a dad disappears, a son disappears.

But it *is* true that the advantage of father time is greater for boys than for girls. However, this has not been found to be the case in all studies. Researchers who focused more on how well children did in school found that while both sexes do better with dad, it was not any greater for the son than the daughter.[49] But, for example, boys do *much* better psychologically with their dads than with their moms; girls also do better when primarily with their dad, but not much better.[50]

Do Children Do So Well with Dads Because Dads Only Take the Easier Children?

The evidence actually suggests the opposite.

US census data revealed that when children with developmental delays are under the age of one, dads are more than *fifteen* times as likely as moms to take those children into their care.[51] As well, nearly half the children who ultimately live with their dads full-time initially lived with their moms. Why did they move? The mom often felt overwhelmed and out of control[52]—often because the children resorted to drugs, drinking, delinquency, depression, and disobedience (including vicious swearing at the mom), or what I refer to as the 5Ds.

In brief, whether infants or teenagers, developmentally delayed or delinquent, dads are more likely to get the children who are challenged, and the children who are challenging. Yet the children do very well under their care. Which opens the door for more young men to define their future purpose as a "father warrior."

The word "warrior" is not added lightly. A warrior makes himself aware of the barriers to achieving his purpose. Then, rather than focus on what is standing in his way, a warrior focuses on how to get past those barriers. Which is exactly what he'll be teaching his children.

CHAPTER 18

The Father Warrior: Why Fathering Will Be a New Male Sense of Purpose

Remember when I shared my conversation with John Lennon and the impact that the men's group I formed had on his decision to take a five-year leave from his work to raise Sean—how he told me that raising Sean was the best decision of his life? His account of his transition from "earning love" to "being love" was touching to me. And that was before I knew who he was!

Wait. Consider that last sentence: "And that was before I knew who he was!" Here I was getting to know John as a human being. Yet both you and I knew exactly what I meant when I wrote, "And that was before I knew who he was!" My statement was all the more ironic because John was basically saying to me that John Lennon as dad to Sean *was* who he was: John as human being, not John as human doing. John as dad, not John as success object.

The social bribes that seduce us—especially boys and men—into becoming success objects are ubiquitous. Once my autographing fiasco made me aware of John's celebrity status, I became conscious of the whispers around us at the party—the whispers of "Look, look over there, there's John Lennon."

The courage it takes for a man who has the wherewithal to make himself a success in the world outside the home to nevertheless resist the chorus of social bribes and instead to become a full-time dad, is the courage that earns him my appellation "father warrior."

Practically speaking, though, if a dad has talents that could make him a star, is it realistic for him to choose "being love" over "earning love"? Well, you probably have not heard of the Irish musician Michael Laffan. That's because, when Michael and his wife, Rhiannon Giddens, had children, he gave up his career to raise them. He now focuses his musical talents on lullabies.

Are there millions of Michael Laffans out there, men who would happily nurture their wives' careers and their children—maybe earning some money from home, maybe not? Men who would choose to do so not only if being the primary parent becomes the new in-vogue warrior but because it is his inner warrior?

Your son is unlikely to choose to be a "father warrior" if he doesn't feel two things: first, a sense of purpose; second, that his contribution will be pivotal. So his role in the checks and balances of parenting requires a deeper dive.

Moms and Dads, Checks and Balances: A Deeper Dive

The nurturing instincts of mom and dad are often complementary. Metaphorically, a mom tends to give a fish to someone who is hungry—even if she has to eat less fish herself. A dad's nurturing instinct is more prone to be guided by the old adage, "Give a man a fish, and you feed him for a day. Teach a man to fish, and you feed him for a lifetime."

Instead of giving a hungry person the fish, many dads see the hunger as an incentive for the hungry person to learn how to fish—an opportunity to be taken advantage of before the person satisfies his hunger and loses the incentive.

Which nurturing instinct is better? Or is there a way to do both? And if so, what's the way? We can get a clue from Jack's experience . . .

Jack was three weeks into first grade. As his mom, Jessica, and his dad, Joshua, finished reading him his last bedtime story, Jack started crying, "My teacher doesn't like me."

"What makes you say that, Jack?" his dad asked.

"She picks on me, and she's mean."

Jack's mom and dad both listened and held him. Then his mom assured him, "Sweetie, I'm so sorry you're not liking your teacher. I don't want you to worry, though. I know there are two first grade teachers. I'll call Ms. Robbins [the principal] and see if we can get you a transfer to Ms. Beatty. Would you like that?"

Jack seemed mollified. Joshua had different feelings, but decided not to say anything until the morning. At breakfast, Jack's dad queried, "Jack, remember how you didn't get along with Robbie when he first moved in across the street . . . and now you're best friends?"

Jack resisted. "Ms. Moyers is different. The other kids think she's mean, too."

Jessica didn't like the "learn to get along" direction she saw the conversation going. "Josh, this is Jack's first year. A bad experience can affect his attitude toward education for years." Joshua and Jessica argued for a minute, and then told Jack they'd talk about it more and give him their thoughts tomorrow.

The next morning, Jack's dad took the lead. "Jack, here's what Mom and I will do. We will meet with Ms. Moyers first. Then we'll talk with you about what she says, and we can all decide together what to do from there."

Jack hesitantly agreed. And then his dad asked him the crucial question: "Jack, what do you think Ms. Moyers will say to us about you?"

Jack was taken aback, but his hesitation was trumped by his desire for his dad to know that Ms. Moyers hated him. "She hated it when I talked to Robbie—even though we didn't talk or pass notes until she was writing on the board. And she moved me away from Robbie even though I was just answering Robbie's note. Why didn't she make *him* move?"

"So did you stop passing notes to Robbie?"

"Yeah. Well, sort of. Ms. Moyers moved Jerry to where I was. So I pass my notes to Jerry...and he passes them to Robbie. And now Jerry, he's friends with us, so he and Robbie and I all pass notes." Jack grinned, then sobered. "That's when Ms. Moyers started getting mean, and she read one of my notes to Jerry in front of the class. You see, first it was just me she moved, and then just my note that she read . . ."

Jack concluded, "I guess that's probably what Ms. Moyers will tell you—about the notes."

"If Ms. Moyers agreed to become less mean and not pick on you, is there anything *you*'d be willing to do differently?" Jack's dad asked.

Jack thought, then reluctantly volunteered, "I guess maybe I could stop doing the talking and note passing, but I'm still quite sure Ms. Moyers doesn't like me."

After Jessica and Joshua's meeting with the teacher, they all agreed to meet directly with Jack. Ms. Moyers was able to let Jack know why she thought he was an exceptional boy, yet also to explain how it was hard for her to keep everyone's attention when the other students were distracted by whispering and notes. Jack softened at Ms. Moyers' praise, and seemed to get that the note passing was distracting others, but added, "I just get fidgety."

Ms. Moyers offered, "Would it help if there were some more short recess breaks during the day, Jack? And if we made up more little skits based on the stories we read—and things like that?" Jack brightened up.

Ms. Moyers complimented Jack for letting his parents know what was bothering him, and then offered, "I'd like to invite you to continue being in my class, but let's make a special agreement, if it's OK with you, Jack. Will you agree that if you or I are having a problem with each other, that one of us will ask for a little 'special time' and we'll each know what that means—and then we'll talk about it real honestly, like you did?"

Jack agreed. His attitude shifted, and he felt Ms. Moyers now liked him.

Jessica and Joshua are an example of the value of checks and balances. Jessica's initial approach was to fix the problem for Jack; Joshua's initial approach was for Jack to fix the problem for himself.

Because both parents treated each other with equal authority, Jack gained experience with what it takes to achieve a win-win outcome: speaking and listening to everyone who is involved, compromise, and creating a safe way to continue communication.

Jack, like most kids, has desires that are paradoxical: he naturally wants the security of parental harmony, but will also naturally seek to widen any fissure he sees if it strengthens his hand with the parent who is "on my side." If, however, he successfully exploits the chaos of the storm to widen the fissure, he experiences mixed emotions: he is superficially delighted, but underneath, the degree to which he can exploit that fissure is the degree to which he feels unprotected in the next storm.

Match.com: The Father Warrior Meets the Have-It-All Woman

Women often feel it is unfair that men can "have it all"—a powerful career, a great marriage, and well-raised children—but they can't.

If "well-raised children" means children raised full-time by her while she is also engaged in a powerful full-time career, she is right. In that way, she can't have it all. Neither can a man. But if "well-raised children" means that she is as willing to have her husband raise their children to the degree that many dads have their wives raise the children, then the opportunity may be right in front of her: an unemployed man who has great social skills, nurturing abilities, and the desire to be a father warrior.

A traditional role of raising money may be part of your son's path to purpose. But if that makes your son feel like a "dad-the-wallet," and raising children would make him feel more like a father warrior, use family dinner nights to help him develop an ability to articulate to an aspiring have-it-all woman that he may be her answer: a minimally employed dad who has plenty of time for the children.

Part of the family dinner night discussions needs to prepare your son for meeting an aspiring have-it-all woman who may feel guilty about potentially "neglecting the kids." Role-play your son asking her if she would always make time to be with the children. Since her answer will almost invariably be yes, she need not feel guilty. Second, encourage him to inform himself, and then her, about exactly why children who are raised primarily by dads tend to do extremely well on every psychological, social, academic, and health measure.

In brief, coach your son to help her to get rid of her guilt—not your son!

That may take care of the guilt. But what about the money?

If Men Get Paid More, Is It Realistic for a Dad to Be the Primary Parent?

Even if your son helps temper the guilt of an aspiring "have-it-all" woman, he may encounter yet another barrier: the fear that the combination of him earning less and her facing discrimination in both pay and promotions, could result in their family suffering financially. They may rationalize that it makes more economic sense for him to be the primary breadwinner, since the cards are stacked in his favor.

Fortunately, when I spent seven years researching the gender pay gap (resulting in the book *Why Men Earn More: The Startling Truth Behind the Pay Gap—and What Women Can Do About It*), I discovered some startling facts that may allow your son's potential wife to let go of that fear—*if* she's the right partner for him.

The full reality has many layers, which is why it took a book to unravel. But here's the first clue: **the male-female pay gap is not a gap between men and women; it is a gap between *moms* and *dads*.** Or more precisely, between men and women's work-life decisions when they become moms and dads. More on that in a minute.

This is the second clue: women who have never been married and never had children earn 117 percent what their male counterparts do. (This is true even when years and hours worked, and education, are considered).[1] That creates some sense that the issue is not an undervaluing of women per se.

Some elaboration. For *Why Men Earn More*, I calculated the impact of twenty-five differences in the typical work-life decisions of men and women, each of which leads to men receiving higher pay, but to women experiencing more balanced, flexible, and fulfilling lives. For example, women in general are much less likely to take hazardous jobs (e.g., firefighter), dirty jobs at bad hours (e.g., garbage collector), jobs with less fulfillment (e.g., engineer over librarian), specialties involving extensive technical training (e.g., surgeon over general practitioner), or fields with high financial risks (e.g., venture capitalist over teacher).

Once children arrive, these differences are accentuated, and three other general differences become enormous: moms *cut back* hours at work, while dads *increase* their hours, especially at nights and over weekends; moms travel less, dads travel more; moms commute fewer miles, accepting jobs that pay less, while dads commute more miles for jobs that pay more . . . This can create some fascinating discussions for family dinner night (see appendix B).

FAMILY DINNER NIGHT
High Pay as a Toll Road

Which careers attract you, and what trade-offs would those careers likely incur if you had children (e.g., becoming an Amazon executive, but with less time for children versus becoming a teacher, and getting home when your children do)? What are the trade-offs of jobs versus pay when it comes to hazards (e.g., roofer), dirty environments (e.g., cleaning sewers), less fulfillment? Or would your trade-off be to not have children, or not get married, or get married to someone who would support you but who you are less attracted to than, well, you know who . . .

Ask: Is the road to high pay a toll road? Then take it deeper: Is high pay necessarily about "power" or "privilege"? Or is there a "pay paradox"—that is, is pay about the power we forfeit to get the power of pay?

As your son becomes comfortable enough with these discussions to take the lead with a potential partner, two of the core conclusions of my decade of research for *Why Men Earn More: The Startling Truth Behind the Pay Gap—and What Women Can Do About It* may be most helpful:

1. Among the twenty-five pivotal decisions that determine high pay, when women and men make the same decisions, women earn slightly more than their male counterparts.[2]
2. Career-focused women are promoted more quickly to executive levels in large companies than their career-focused male counterparts.[3]

Nevertheless, if your son's potential wife is nontraditional, he does need to acknowledge that she does face a special burden: a company's assumptions about the work choices she may make after giving birth. So how can your son let her know he wishes to be a partner in overcoming that special burden? Here are a couple of ways:

1. Discuss with her having people from work over for dinner as *he does most of the cooking and serving.* Creating for a selection of executives above her at work a real-life experience of how a man can give a

woman's career the support traditionally given by a woman to a man's career has a deeper impact than making the argument in theory. And besides, people are far more empathetic and open-minded after they've eaten dinner.[4]

2. Encourage her to express to the dinner guests the dilemma faced by the company: that if she is young, married, and planning to have children, the company has to weigh the possibility of investing in training her only to lose their investment as she potentially leaves for months, years, or forever. When she can empathize like that, she lets the executives know that she is thinking of the company's best interests. They sense she is someone who is on their team.

If your son wishes to consider being a primary parent in a good marriage, he'll want to do a deeper dive, but initiating these discussions with a woman in whom he has an interest can catalyze a five-part sequence for her: At first, she may not be sure whether he's an original thinker or a kook. Second, if he shares the facts while also listening to her perspective, she discovers the answer is "original thinker"—plus a guy with social skills. Third, this frees her to see his courage, which earns her respect. Fourth, if she's attracted to him, the power of attraction plus respect may—or may not—begin to melt three biases:

1. That a man earning less would be too insecure to handle a woman earning more.
2. That a husband who earns less is "another child"—a burden.
3. That a man who doesn't pay for her dinner doesn't really desire her.

Fifth, she becomes free to imagine their children being raised primarily by your son.

Your son needs to know this won't work with just any woman—but he's not looking for just any woman. Like Babe Ruth, he may strike out a lot before hitting a home run. But unlike Babe Ruth, he only needs one home run. While helping his prospective partner envision a life with your son as the primary caretaker is only part of a long checklist. She may still have to deal with her friends' and parents' biases. **If your son is nontraditional, he needs to know that the most important work of his life is selecting a woman who is free enough from social constraints to free him from social constraints.**

But Will Companies Hire Your Son as Father Warrior?

Brandon lived in Encinitas, California, just north of San Diego. His joys were surfing and golfing, and Encinitas had both. One day he noticed that his company needed a new branch manager in its Minneapolis location:

> The jump in pay interested me for a minute, but then I thought of the cold Minneapolis winters and I shivered that minute away!
>
> A week later, though, my wife, Lauren, announced she was pregnant. I was delighted, but Lauren wanted to care full-time for the baby prior to kindergarten and have at least two kids. The following day, I found myself checking to see if that Minneapolis job had been taken—the pay was higher, and the cost of living lower, so we'd be able to afford a four-bedroom home in a good community.
>
> The job was still open, and after a couple of weeks of seeing if I could find anything that paid comparably in the San Diego area, I applied for and received the job in Minneapolis. We moved.

That was eighteen years ago. Brandon took the traditional route, with one exception: before he moved, he searched for flexibility that would allow him his lifestyle.

Traditionally, companies knew that the more children a dad had, the more he would feel the need to work extra hours with extra responsibilities to earn extra income. So companies did not develop family leave policies, they developed "leave the family" policies. **Dads were user-friendly for companies, because they could most easily be used.**

Since Brandon and his family made that move, companies are increasingly facing a different reality. Adding to the women's movement's push for flexible work schedules, and the fear of losing female employees when they become mothers, companies are also now facing 49 percent of full-time working dads saying they would prefer to be full-time with their children. And since it is the best and the brightest young men who tend to feel this way, companies are adjusting. For the first time, in addition to lists of companies friendly to women and mothers, we are beginning to see lists such as *Fatherly's* 2017 ranking of "The 50 Best Places to Work for New Dads."[5]

If your son might be open to being the primary parent, and he is into gaming and tech, he's off to a good start. The tech industry dominates the list (e.g., Netflix, Etsy, Spotify, Facebook, Twitter). Companies in the financial industry—such as American Express and Bank of America— also offer generous flexibility for new fathers.

We can get a sense from Netflix and Etsy as to how the companies wishing to attract the best and brightest dads are doing it. Netflix not only offers the option of a year of paid paternity leave but individualizes other options to fathers' needs and desires. Etsy offers "dedicated parents' rooms decorated with the artwork created by Etsy sellers, and a rooftop garden overlooking downtown Manhattan."

It's a new world, one that will be increasingly open to your son as father warrior if he can change consciousness as he changes diapers.

That's the good news. But I wouldn't be calling it father *warrior* if there were not some insidious "enemies" your son will have to fight. Many companies have a less flexible consciousness. And if you think of discrimination as applying only to women, get ready to be introduced to a whole new world: discrimination against dads. (Who said parenting wasn't humbling!)

CHAPTER 19

DAD: Discrimination Against Dads

"It Doesn't Feel Right When I See Them Together"

Imagine taking your son on a summer vacation to Jefferson's Monticello in Virginia. Now envision him staring at the billboard shown below, with a picture of a man's hand holding a child's hand, and reading, "It doesn't feel right when I see them together."

Source: Virginia Department of Health

The ad suggests that a man holding a child's hand is, in itself, something inappropriate—something "not right." How might this make your son feel about someday being a babysitter, mentor, tutor, childcare provider, elementary school teacher, or even just a dad taking his child to the park around noon on a weekday?

As you search for a way to lighten the impact of the bias, you look for evidence that this billboard is from some fringe group. Instead, you notice the letters VDH and, with a squint, read "Virginia Department of Health."

That exposes a new layer of implications: For this billboard to be put up, it would have been reviewed by about a dozen layers of government bureaucracy, none of which protested spending taxpayer dollars to imply that a dad touching a child's hand might not "feel right."

In an era of "See something, say something," today's bias becomes tomorrow's police report. Mike Stillwell, cofounder of National At-Home Dad Network in Virginia, shared in the *Washington Post* an experience of an at-home dad at a park with his child who was approached by some mothers and queried as to why he wasn't at work. Although the dad explained, the mothers nevertheless called the police.[1] Today's bias, tomorrow's police report. A police report that may not just jeopardize his ability to raise his children but also to raise money for his children.

When it comes to men as daytime dads, we have yet to confront some of the guilty-until-proved-innocent sexism that in many ways parallels the guilty-until-proved-innocent racism that millions of black people experience when Driving While Black (DWB). If your son becomes a father warrior he will be part of a movement that will face the sexism of PWM (Parenting While Male). And should he consider becoming a preschool or elementary school teacher, he will likely fear the sexism of TWM (Teaching While Male).

It takes just one suspicion to become a police report. And just one police report to make a school feel it needs to let your son go lest other parents be afraid to send their children to that school. That may end his teaching career. Or worse. When a school feels no option but to ignore the sexism against your son to preserve itself, that's a perfect example of systemic sexism.

That risk of disposability, the price of the fight to rescue children from male-deprivation, is why your son will earn the title "father warrior" (or, if a teacher or mentor, "father figure warrior").

Moms Have the Right to Children, Dads Have to Fight for Children

This bias against men as caregivers may also affect your son should he get divorced. The frequency with which he sees his children—and you see your grandchildren—often hinges on the recommendation of one professional. Judges generally follow the professional's recommendation to determine your son's future involvement with his children.

The problem? A 2016 study of social workers documented a key obstacle to custody that dads encounter worldwide: **"Social workers tend to consider the children's wishes as long as their preference is for maternal custody. When children express a paternal preference, their wishes carry no weight."**[2]

This professional bias against dads did not come out of nowhere.

The feminist movement, initially supportive of father involvement, began opposing equal rights for dads of divorce in the early 1970s. In the first year or two that I was on the board of NOW in New York City (1970–73), Gloria Steinem used to tell me, "What the world needs is more women at work and more dads at home."

Betty Friedan was even more father-positive. While the first stage of Friedan's message, *The Feminine Mystique*, was about the need for women's liberation, Friedan's *The Second Stage* was about the need for the liberation of men to complete the liberation of women. **In *The Second Stage*, Friedan predicted women's career goals would never be achieved if men were not more incorporated into the fathering role.** Fortunately, Friedan's first book catalyzed more flexible roles for our daughters; unfortunately, her second did little to catalyze more flexible roles for our sons.

However, around 1972–73, something changed. NOW was getting pressure from divorcing and divorced moms to the effect, "I know what's best for my children. I want the right to raise my children as I see fit." Or, "The new man in my life will be a better dad; we need the freedom to move for his job, to an area with better schools, and to start my life anew." Or, "I thought NOW was about expanding women's rights. I cannot continue my membership if NOW is lobbying to limit women's rights."

We debated. I argued that children were the priority, not women or men, and that even the nascent evidence we had at that time suggested that children did better with both parents. Many board members were sympathetic, but they felt that NOW's primary mission was to support women and that if NOW undermined its political base it would undermine its ability to support women. Since the midseventies, then, the National Organization for Women's chapters nationwide have almost universally supported a mother's right to choose who parents a child of divorce. Mothers' rights trumped equal rights.[3] Politics trumped equality.

This feminist political position fed the professional bias against dads and, along with court battles feeding a lucrative family court system, led to a universal feeling among divorced dads worldwide: that **a mom has the right to children, but a dad has to fight for children.** NOW's decision added to the impetus for the emergence of "fathers' rights" groups and turned what was a potential alliance of the sexes into the current battle between the sexes.

We are seeing how this affects our sons. But it also damages our daughters. As I was writing this chapter, I received a letter from Brianna Neese, who gave me permission to share these excerpts here. Brianna is twenty-four, and recently graduated from Smith College in biology and neuroscience. She shared this . . .

> I have gained much perspective from being raised by a father who struggled to raise me alone, without any community support. I have a perspective of having survived and stood up to an abusive mother, and an extremely biased family court system whose aim is to separate fathers and children. I faced unyielding custody evaluators, psychologists, emergency screeners, and judges. I have watched how this whole process has affected, and continues to affect, my father. And now, after finishing Smith College, I understand a little more about Gloria Steinem's feminism, and can compare that to the feminist ideas I encountered at Smith College . . .
>
> Many young women are raised to feel contempt for men, and ultimately restrict themselves by classifying themselves as perpetual victims. I find it difficult to find friendships among women my age. Most young men I have met in college have serious emotional problems I feel ill equipped to navigate. I wonder how I can partner with men . . .
>
> You provided my father with the words and language to discuss these complex issues with me in age-appropriate ways.

This allowed him to develop his own convictions and ethics in order to stand firm in the face of incredible scrutiny, criticism, and ostracism, which ultimately allowed him to push through a seven-year, egregiously litigated court case so that I might have a better future, and help me decide how to become the best woman I can be.[4]

How Did *Father Knows Best* Become *Father Knows Less?*

Parenting while Male didn't always evoke fears of incompetence or sex abuse. Before the Industrial Revolution, boys assisted their dads in their work and became apprentices (as farmers, blacksmiths, shoe makers, coal miners, etc.). In wealthier families, when there was the rare divorce, the father usually had primary custody. He may have delegated the day-to-day responsibilities to a nanny, but the buck stopped with dad. Even today, in some cultures, such as the Aka tribe of Africa, fathers spend 47 percent of their days holding their infant children or keeping them within arm's reach.[5]

So how did *Father Knows Best* become *Father Knows Less*—or *Father Molests?* As divorces broke families apart, the 1950s forces of the era of *Father Knows Best* morphed into the forces of the era of *Father Knows Less.* The bumbling Homer Simpson inspired the longest-running prime-time sitcom in American TV history, with over six hundred episodes to date, bridging the presidencies of Reagan through Trump. Perhaps second place in the *Father Knows Less* contest goes to the clueless dads in *Everybody Loves Raymond.*

This confluence of image, politics, and professional and legal biases influenced our making more progress for women at work than for men at home. We hear this in our everyday use of language. For example, in the past, when a doctor was a woman, we used qualifiers—we called her a "female doctor." Now we commonly call a woman who is a doctor a doctor. Yet for a man who is a dad full-time, we still use qualifiers—calling him a "full-time dad"—or even "Mr. Mom." We'll know we've made progress if, in the future, when your son is asked his profession, should he choose to be a full-time dad, he automatically responds, "I'm a dad," as easily as our daughter might respond, "I'm a doctor."

The Image of the Deadbeat Dad

If your son becomes a dad without being married, he joins a group that has a reputation for being deadbeat dads: "Sex? Yes, please. Responsibility? No, thank you." Deadbeats generate little empathy. The law treats them accordingly. Obviously, your son could in fact be a deadbeat. But this is his more likely reality . . .

When a dad agrees with the choice to have a child, he almost always wants to be involved in the life of his child. And as we have seen, 49 percent of dads who are working full-time to support their children would prefer to be full-time with their children.[6] Worldwide, fathers' groups are fighting for the right to be *with* their children; I am aware of no fathers' groups fighting for the right to be with*out* their children.

When divorced dads are denied equal time, many offer to pay legal child support—in addition to sharing the everyday expenses, and even when they earn about the same as the mom—on the condition that they see the children about equally.

The deadbeat dad image persists in part from ignorance that **70 percent of child support debt is owed by parents with incomes of less than $10,000 per year** (*parents* almost always means "dads").[7] Many of these dads are then imprisoned because of owed child support, deepening their arrears and undermining their ability, when they do get out, to hold a job and pay child support!

If your son becomes unemployed and receives a check for unemployment insurance, it will arrive with his child support deducted. The same is true of tax refunds. All that may leave him unable to secure a decent apartment to which he can bring his children. Thus, while the government is using taxpayer money to help moms who fall on hard times (e.g., the Women, Infants, and Children program), it is taxing the dads who fall on hard times.

It doesn't have to be this way. We've seen the evidence in chapter 17 that "time trumps dime." Child support needs to be redefined: supporting the children with the two resources children most need: time and love. More on that later.

FAMILY DINNER NIGHT
Sex as Destiny

Family dinner night discussions with your son about how the image of dads being deadbeats leads to laws that create greater consequences should he become an unwanted dad, will help him put two and two together: **when your son has sex with a woman, he puts his life in her hands.**

The good news? This can encourage him to really get to know a woman before having sex, ultimately developing a much more positive appreciation of women. Since there are few more powerful forces than your teenage son's sexual desire, you'll need the most persuasive approaches for your son to use birth control rather than have a birth control him.

Deadbeat Dad Yesterday; Dorito-Distracted-Disconnected Dad Today

Should your son contemplate becoming a more involved dad—not necessarily even an equally involved or full-time dad—his motivation will be tested by a perpetual bombardment of *Father Knows Less*. He will notice that **virtually 100 percent of TV ads that portray only one sex as a jerk portray the man as the jerk**. Yes, even the show watched by more than 80 percent of US men while almost 70 percent of US women laugh at them, in front of them: the Super Bowl.

For example, this 2016 Super Bowl ad for Doritos[8] portrays mom and a female doctor entranced at the ultrasound of the infant-to-be while dad is similarly entranced—with his Doritos.

Mom laments to the doctor, *"Really*? He's eating Doritos at *my* ultrasound? See what I have to deal with?" The doctor empathizes, "I know"—as if to say, "Yes, sister, I've been through this a thousand times; dads are hopeless."

Sure enough, the ultrasound reveals the womb-bound baby is *imitating* the dad's preoccupation with Doritos. And surprise, the infant bursts from the womb with the addictions of the father, grabbing for the Doritos.

The message your son gets: a dad is less than useless; his uselessness is contagious.

Of course, the ad is hilarious. Why? Because it magnifies our biases. Not convinced? Try the reverse. Imagine the dad and a male doctor entranced at the ultrasound, while the *mom* is entranced only with her Doritos. It wouldn't resonate with our biases.

Is there a way for a similar Dorito ad to be positive toward fathers and spark equal hilarity? Yes. It just takes a little out-of-the-box—or maybe out-of-the-bag—thinking. Try this . . .

Mom, the doctor, and dad are all entranced with the ultrasound. But as the doctor gives mom, dad, and herself "her best medicine"—a bag of Doritos for everyone—each bite escalates their ecstasy. Ravel's "Boléro" gives a rhythm to the ecstatic escalation. As the cadence of their chorus-of-rapture peaks, suddenly mom's rhythm is alternating between labor pains, and, after grabbing a Dorito, a *When Harry Met Sally*-type orgasm—at which point the infant bursts from the womb to grab all three bags of Doritos. The dad exclaims, "You go, girl!"

The out-of-the-bag ad accomplishes five things: viewer laughter; Dorito profits; jump-starting the dad brain; support for an empowered daughter; and no message either that father knows less or father cares less.

Is there hope in the real world? Yes. A real ad maker (as opposed to my unreal ad) created this series of dad-inspiring Pantene ads.[9] Although aired only in a regional market during the 2016 Super Bowl, it featured three NFL dads (DeAngelo Williams, Benjamin Watson, and Jason Witten) doing Pantene "dad-dos" on their daughters. The father-daughter bond in each is palpable, and you can see the love deepen even within the course of the brief commercial. Each ad concludes with a message that connects the heart with the mind: "Girls who spend quality time with their dads grow up to be stronger women."

Soon the Instagram hashtag, #dumbstuffdadsdo, can be replaced with #stuffdadsdo. Touchdown.

Guiding Your Son to "Make a Difference"

Whenever your son spots an injustice, it's a potential "teachable moment" toward scoring a different type of touchdown. If he is disgusted with the image of the deadbeat dad, you can help him to have a direct impact on the images of boys and men we see in the media.

Take, for example, a 2013 Clorox ad that proclaimed, "Like dogs or other house pets, new dads are filled with good intentions but lacking in judgment and fine motor skills." When your son hears ads like this one, it doesn't inspire him to develop his dad brain.

Haven't seen this ad? That's because some viewers organized a protest. And it was withdrawn.

Below is one of the protest visuals:

Source: www.daddydoctrines.com

You have leverage. Companies don't want a bad image. And when you exercise your leverage, you teach your children how to be effective in the world—even as you increase their respect for you, for not just paying lip service to discrimination against dads but actually helping to close the door to discrimination, and open the door to dad.

CHAPTER 20

The Best Parent Is Both Parents, *But...*

Fortunately, lack of father involvement is a crisis with a solution: father involvement.

Eating sugar is also a problem with a solution: eating no sugar. Sometimes doing the right thing is so within reach, and so out of reach.

Let's look at what we can do to support father involvement when it is within reach, and what to do when it is out of reach.

The Best "Parent" Is an Attitude Shift

To integrate women into the workplace, we required a still-in-process attitude shift toward women and work. To integrate men into parenting requires a yet-to-evolve attitude shift toward both dads and marriage.

Escaping the "Psychological Divorce" Trap

While marriage is the best way to ensure that a boy has an involved dad, your marriage will not inspire him to marry if he feels you are legally married but psychologically divorced.

Nor will it inspire him if he discovers later in life that his parents suffered through "staying together until the children get older."

Psychologically divorced parents who are just biding time until their children's graduation often feel like they are in a "minimum-security-prison

marriage." It's depressing for the parents, and provokes anxiety in the children.

Many couples blame the failure of their marriages on money, children, or lack of sex. **But a happy marriage is less about money, children, or lack of sex than about how we communicate about money, children, or lack of sex.**

So why don't we communicate better? It begins with that Achilles' heel of humans—our inability to hear personal criticism from a loved one without becoming defensive, especially if the criticism is given badly. (And for most of us, all criticism from loved ones is "given badly"!)

Why doesn't our love overcome our defensiveness? Because the more deeply we love, the more our partners' criticism hurts, the more fragile we feel. So when our loved one's criticism increases our fragility, we may respond with defensiveness and anger. But our partners, not aware that our anger is our vulnerability's mask, are both blinded to the vulnerability that would soften their hearts and intimidated by our anger. So our partner responds by "walking on eggshells." Slowly, our passion's flower wilts. Raising children and the money to support them leave us too fatigued to communicate, and they intensify our interlocking dependencies even as the lack of communication weakens our interlocking hearts. Hence psychological divorce and the minimum-security-prison marriage.

Active listening—verbalizing to your partner what you heard her or him say—is a good starter solution. But it is rarely used outside a therapist's office. Why? Active listeners are expected to not only drop defenses but to repeat the criticism without the defenses. The problem? Defenses feel most crucial *when* you are feeling criticized by someone you love.

To sever this Gordian knot, I developed a method by which we can learn to feel safe on the inside when being criticized because we emotionally associate our ability to provide a safe environment for our partner's feelings with a golden opportunity to be more deeply loved.[1] The anticipation of feeling more loved by someone we love requires no defenses. I offer some starter steps as to the methods I've developed to communicate nondefensively in chapter 27 on healing hurt people.

Even when couples do master the art of communicating nondefensively most of the time, I am often asked, "When we do argue, is it healthy to fight in front of the kids?"

Fighting in Front of the Kids

Elijah recalled,

> I remember being seventeen and asking my parents if I could use the car on Friday evening, but neither of them liked the crowd I was hanging out with. My mom was arguing that I should get to use the car, but with an 11 PM curfew. My dad said "no car until"—until I get my grades up and find a better crowd. At first I was adding arguments to support my mom, but as their disagreements got nasty, I began rooting for them to just stop fighting.
>
> When I later got involved with a woman who became my fiancée, and she and I had our first significant fight, she fell apart and broke off the engagement. Turns out her parents never fought—at least not in front of her. And then they got divorced. So she thought that if she and I were "worse" than her parents—having this fight—we must be doomed. Well, we sorted it out, and in the process I realized I have a deep wound from my parents' fighting turning nasty, and she has a deep wound from not knowing how to handle any disagreement.
>
> I'm bringing all this up because now we're about to have a kid and I'm wondering, Dr. Farrell, do you think it's good to fight in front of our kids?

Here's the litmus test, Elijah. The answer is yes, *if* . . . if the way you disagree is the way you would want your kids to disagree with their future partners.

The ability to transform disagreements into love rather than resentment is the most important inheritance you can give your children. If you can't pass the litmus test, then

- keep the process behind closed doors;
- get couples' communication training—not to solve a problem, but to learn how to problem-solve; and
- learn the art of appreciating each other.

The art of appreciation is a valuable currency—with a special twist when it comes to the impact on your son of appreciating his dad.

Appreciation of Dad, Inspiration for the Son

> *Nobody appreciates daddy . . . Nobody ever says, "Hey, Daddy, thanks for knocking out this rent!" "Hey, Daddy, I sure love this hot water!" "Hey, Daddy, it's easy to read with all this light!"*

> —Chris Rock, comedian

Your son is more likely to say "Thank you for making dinner" than "Thank you for making the money without which this dinner could not have been made."

In a world of working moms, is the traditional division of roles—mom raising children and dad raising money—still likely? Yes. The *Harvard Business Review* reports dads are more than three times as likely as moms (29 percent vs 9 percent) to work more than fifty hours a week outside the home.[2] This means the person whose contributions to the family are left unappreciated is usually dad.

Just as moms often feel unappreciated for the dusting, laundry, and dishes, dads often feel unappreciated for working the hours necessary to pay for car payments; insurance for the car, home, and health; rent or mortgage and property tax; utilities . . . When, instead, he is criticized for coming home late or "bringing the office home" with him, he often feels damned if he does, and damned if he doesn't.

The problem: **When the house is clean and the bills are paid, the effort our partner makes to keep things the same are invisible exactly because things are the same.** Nothing empties the reservoir of love faster than when only the getting-home-late-type trade-offs are criticized. A reservoir filled with stress has no room for love.

The solution: Nothing fills a reservoir with love faster than when the invisible is seen. Fortunately, to make the invisible visible, we just need to acquire the discipline to look for it—looking for the effort it took to combine shopping yesterday for tonight's dinner with picking up your son from his friend's playdate.

The stressors that are hardest to see are the ones either camouflaged by the illusion of power or the ones that result in "kicking the dog," therefore directing our empathy only to the dog. We see both in the men of *Mad Men*.

No One Asked Why the Men Were Drinking

Mad Men illustrated well the way women's intelligence, people skills, and potential contributions to the workplace were undervalued in the 1960s and '70s. In contrast, its portrayal of men as perpetually drinking, self-inflating, blatantly sexist, unfaithful, womanizing, territorial, power hungry, money obsessed, and deadbeat dads reinforced our retrospective perspective that we had lived in an era of man-the-oppressor versus woman-the-oppressed. We were less likely to feel for men being driven mad and more likely to feel mad at the men.

Mad Men deepened our anger at the straightjackets of stereotypes on women's lives. And deepened our anger at how men perpetuated those stereotypes at the expense of women.

Consider your son's takeaway for his role in the world: his dad or grandpa is being portrayed as a role model for a role your son doesn't want to play, the oppressor. **If your son sees being an oppressor as his future, being a failure to launch might look like progress.**

Two unasked questions can catalyze your son's ability to break the stalemate between seeing himself as a potential successful oppressor versus a failure to launch:

Question one: Why were the men drinking?

Question two: What drove the mad men mad?

Drinking numbs stress. Consider how stress was built into the way the ad executives in *Mad Men* were raised by their parents. Did their parents teach their sons to ask themselves, "What creates the glint in your eye?" or, "What do you think will fulfill you the most?"

And how many of the women to whom these men were most attracted—women who almost invariably expected children that these men would be expected to support—said to these men, "I am attracted to your soul; if becoming a lawyer or advertising a product you may not believe in in order to support me and the children in any way compromises your soul, then let's not have children, and I will earn at least half of the money we will need. And a small home in a cheap area, with an old car—that will be great if it allows you to keep your soul intact"?

Of course, in the 1960s, a woman's ability to earn half the income was severely limited by the biases that affected her income. What *Mad Men* got was the biases that limited a woman, but not how those very biases that limited her also limited him. Feeling obligated to earn money that someone else spends while not appreciated for the earning can make a good man a mad man.

If your son assimilates the pressure to earn money and does so without asking what most fulfills him, he may, like the men in *Mad Men*, find himself drinking. And if he follows his bliss and finds it's the money he's missed—and then finds the woman he loves is looking elsewhere for the money *she* misses—he may feel he's a failure and, yes, start drinking.

Family dinner nights can broach with your son the question of whether power is feeling obligated as a male to earn money someone else spends while he dies sooner, or whether it is the freedom to embark on a discovery of what is fulfilling, then find a way to make a living doing that, and selecting a partner who supports a work-life balance that works for both of them.

Your son may have the personality to blend high pay with high purpose, but if, for him, the road to high pay is a toll road, 'tis better that he takes the road that doesn't drive him to drink as he's paying the tolls. Driving under the influence of alcohol is often a symptom of being driven under the influence of social bribes.

If you are the type of person whose friends tend to talk with you about their families' challenges, including thoughts of divorce, then how do you use what you've learned in *The Boy Crisis* to best support your friends?

How to Support a Friend When Divorce Is Underway

What would be your response to this situation?

A good friend of yours, let's call her Amanda, is sparkling with happiness. She has found the best attorney in town to represent her desire to have primary custody of her and her husband's children after her divorce. She feels this will allow her to move a few hundred miles away with her new soon-to-be fiancé who is "a much better dad"; she's especially excited to share with you that "Bill just loves Alan and Cindy—he wants to adopt them."

Take a moment to contemplate your response.

Really, take a sixty second pause. I'll wait. ☺

Does your internal response include letting Amanda know that children of divorce do much better with equally shared parenting with the biological dad? That they do better when their biological dad lives within about twenty minutes? And that for a boy, especially, moving even to a better neighborhood can be deeply disturbing?

Did you recommend that instead of spending between $100,000 and $200,000 on attorneys, evaluators, and expert witnesses, that she and the dad use a fraction of that money toward couples' counseling either to give the marriage another chance or to help Amanda and her husband negotiate an out-of-court separation?

Most of us agree that the best parent is both parents.[3] In theory. But if there is a divorce, we experience some cognitive dissonance: on the one hand, we believe that "the best parent is both parents"; on the other hand, we feel that the best "parent" is whatever arrangement the mom feels is best. That is, we are empathetically drawn to give unconditional support to a friend of ours who is a mom to have primary custody and even move away if that is what she convinces herself is best for the children because she feels it is best for her.

The underlying solution to the dad deprivation that often accompanies divorce begins with an attitude shift. **"The best parent is both parents" means mommy is no substitute for daddy, money is no substitute for daddy, and another man is no substitute for daddy.** Just as daddy is no substitute for mommy, money is no substitute for mommy, and another woman is no substitute for mommy. Divorce doesn't change that. The best parent is still both parents.

Stability Versus Flexibility: Fathering for a Future Father

In the past, parenting your son for his future meant preparing him for stability—for a career that would last a lifetime. Today, parenting your son for his future means preparing him less for stability and more for flexibility. He and his partner both need to be comfortable rowing on both sides of the family boat: raising money and raising children.

Since boys are especially prone to learn by doing,[4] preparing your son to have a sense of purpose as a future dad might start, for example, with teaching him how to feed his infant or toddler sister or brother and help him or her get dressed, bringing your son shopping with you for what his sibling needs, and teaching him how to cook. As he gets that experience, recommend him as a babysitter. If he worries, "A kid at school called me a sissy. Am I a sissy?" answer, "You're a future dad. You're a future leader."

The biggest gift of preparing your son to both raise children and raise money is that you will have prepared him for finding a soul mate rather than a role mate. That is, he'll be free to discover the type of partner he is most attracted to rather than be confined to partners who are good at only one role: raising children *or* raising money.

That said, few moms will be happy being married to a full-time dad who earns no money. Fortunately, as we've seen, **the future will increasingly see the home place becoming the work place.** So part of the preparation to be a more engaged dad will be experimenting with flexible ways of making money from home even before the children start school.

If your son is good with computers, one of those ways might be freelance design or coding. If he's good with numbers, but also loves nature, he might do tax work during tax season and landscaping in the late spring and fall. If he loves research and risk (and his wife makes enough money, or they've inherited some), he might manage investments.

When your son's children reach school age, your son might start working away from home—perhaps teaching in elementary school or a preschool, where the schedule would allow him to remain the primary parent, and where the need for males, and especially males with experience with children, is considerable.

If your son wants a fulfilling career, let's say as a musician, you can share with him two truths-in-tension:

1. When you follow your bliss, it's the money you'll miss. In the past, authors like me would have to tour our books nationwide or worldwide in order to translate our bliss into a mortgage payment. And therefore, the most successful writers and other artists (remember John Lennon) were MIP: missing in parenting.
2. Technology will allow your son to follow his bliss with a lot less money being missed. Or more precisely, technology (e.g., digital production, distribution, and promotion), creative persistence, and a capacity for flexibility, plus a flexible, supportive partner, can allow your son to follow his bliss while raising both money and children.

If balancing work and family interests your son, introduce him to the Families and Work Institute—it will help him navigate the challenges of work-life flexibility.[5] And if he wishes a deeper understanding of why the road to high pay is a toll road and ways to balance earning more with loving more, introduce him to my *Why Men Earn More*.[6]

While technology opens flexibility's door, hangout time with dad can, as we've seen, create psychological stability for both our sons and daughters. Here are some great ways to start . . .

Cheap Fun for Dad and Son

Since boys love to learn by doing, and dads learn to teach by doing, check out the PBS site ZOOMsci (http://pbskids.org/zoom/activities/sci/). It offers more than a hundred games and activities that teach your child how to do things like design something (e.g., a door alarm or water filter), experiment with his or her senses (e.g., blind spots or reaction time), work with energy (e.g., making a hot air balloon or a lemon juice rocket), use fingerprints or snowflakes to detect patterns, create a string telephone or guitar, and build a bird feeder from a milk carton or a bridge out of toothpicks.

Your son may or may not discover a penchant for engineering, but *you'll* certainly discover that, when it includes "doing," bonding with your son can be both cheap and fun.

Dad-Inspiring Movies

One of the best ways of both spending quality time with your son and inspiring your son to eventually activate his dad brain is to gather the family together for a dad-inspiring movie. But to turn passive time into active time, introduce a postmovie family discussion, with a treat like ice cream to help foster the beginning of a ritual. (Contribute your favorite movies and the discussions they inspire on *The Boy Crisis* website at www.boycrisis.org.)

Finding Nemo (2003) – G	*Evelyn* (2002) – PG
The Lion King (1994) – G	*Fandango* (1985) – PG
Back to the Future (1985) – PG	*Father of the Bride* (1991) – PG
Cheaper by the Dozen (2003) – PG	*Field of Dreams* (1989) – PG
East of Eden (1955) – PG	*Goodbye Christopher Robin* (2017) – PG

The Incredibles (2004) – PG

It's a Wonderful Life (1946) – PG

October Sky (1999) - PG

Big Fish (2003) – PG-13

Catch Me If You Can (2002) – PG-13

Click (2006) – PG-13

Courageous (2011) – PG-13

Dear Frankie (2004) – PG-13

Family Man (2000) – PG-13

I am Sam (2001) – PG-13

Juno (2007) – PG-13

Life is Beautiful (1997) – PG-13

Mrs. Doubtfire (1993) – PG-13

My Life (1993) – PG-13

The Pursuit of Happyness (2006) – PG-13

American Sniper (2014) – R

About Time (2013) – R

Billy Elliot (2000) – R

Boyz n the Hood (1991) – R

Chef (2014) – R

Foxcatcher (2014) – R

Good Will Hunting (1997) – R

He Got Game (1998) – R

Life as a House (2001) – R

Road to Perdition (2002) – R

Southpaw (2015) – R

Absent (2011) – NR

Bicycle Thieves (1948) – NR

Dear Zachary: A Letter to a Son About His Father (2008) – NR

Father of the Bride (1950) – NR

To Kill a Mockingbird (1962) – NR

Men's Group (2008) – NR

When the Best "Parent" Cannot Be Both Parents

While the *best* parent is both parents, it doesn't take both parents—or even one parent—for a boy to experience a role model of a caring man. My father-in-law volunteers as a reader at a local school; good friends are mentors with rite-of-passage programs such as the ManKind Project and Young Men's Ultimate Weekend; and I served as a counselor with the Y and Boys Clubs when my primary credential was recently having been a boy. In addition to being wonderful opportunities to contribute to a boy's life, they are a great way to discover whether the adoption option or being a stepdad is for you.

Programs like these are especially useful for single moms or female same-sex parents, because keeping your son *consistently* connected with male role models is essential. For example, we have seen that the most predictable area in which boys fall behind is reading. Children who have fallen behind in reading by third grade are only one-quarter as likely to graduate from high school.[7] Bringing a male volunteer into such a boy's life to help him with his reading can provide him with a trove of benefits: a father figure, higher reading proficiency, increased odds of high school graduation, and higher self-esteem. It also touches the heart of the volunteer with the blessing of purpose.

A father figure does not need to be part of an organization. *CBS News* featured the touching story of a neighbor of a five-year old boy, Brian Kelly.[8] Brian's favorite moments were gardening and riding the lawn mower with his dad. Then Brian's dad, a captain in the air force, left for six months of overseas deployment. When Brian knocked on his neighbor's door to see if his neighbor would garden with him, his neighbor not only said yes but gardened with him every day for the six months his dad was away. All of us can look out for these *carpe diem* moments to give a boy an opportunity to experience male-style fathering.

OK, you're sold, but think you're too old? The AARP begs to differ. Their Experience Corps thoroughly trains volunteers who are fifty and up to tutor children between kindergarten and third grade who have reading challenges. Studies show a 60 percent improvement in kids' critical literacy skills in *one school year.*[9]

My Most Life-Changing Camping Experience

Some of the most enriching experiences of my first thirty years of life involved being a leader for the Boy Scouts and Boys Clubs, a counselor for the Y, and the founder of Liberation Camp in Rowe, Massachusetts— where we did role-reversal exercises that helped both older and younger campers, and men and women, "walk a mile in each other's moccasins."

My most life-changing camping experience, one that may have planted the first seeds for this book, was as a counselor with the Y in Ridgewood, New Jersey. One of my summer campers was a boy I'll call Nathan. Nathan had no social skills and a lower-than-average IQ. Within a day, Nathan had alienated all seven of his cabin mates, who pleaded for me to "do something about him." So I did, sort of—I did something about the other seven campers.

On our second night, I found a special assignment as an excuse to get Nathan out of the cabin for about an hour each evening. During that first absence, I convened with the other campers and, after empathizing with their complaints, asked them to guess whether Nathan was happy. The very question—asking about Nathan's happiness—took them by surprise. Yet everyone concurred that he must be miserable.

I asked, "If you could all do something this week as a team to make him happier than he had ever been, would you do it?" Every boy said, "Sure." Then I asked if they were willing to become a team in a mission to give Nathan positive feedback.

The first problem was that no one could think of anything positive about which to give him feedback. I couldn't either. But I was the camp's riflery instructor, so I promised I would teach Nathan to be a good marksman if they would agree to display Nathan's best targets on the cabin wall and compliment him even if they had better targets that would not be posted. They loved the conspiracy . . . er, mission!

The next day, Nathan's first target was posted, and the compliments began. By the following day, one of the boys reported Nathan's first smile. Another reported that he was being nicer, and yet another observed that he was walking with a bit more confidence. The boys were amazed, and were competing to show what they had said that they felt might have contributed to the change. The boys were glowing with that "mission accomplished" feeling.

I then asked, "Do you think Nathan has ever in his life been sought out by anyone for his advice?"

One of the boys mocked, "You mean, like, 'Nathan, how can I be a doofus?'"

After allowing a little outlet for their shadow-side laughs, I asked them how they felt when someone asked them for advice. Then I requested that they visualize together how Nathan would respond to, say, their asking Nathan *to help them* be better marksmen.

One of the boys objected, "But we're all better than he is." Another volunteered, "That's not the point." Slowly, they saw the possibilities. The next evening, the two boys who had asked Nathan for advice were noticing that Nathan was walking even more "straight up," rather than slouched, more confident than depressed and angry. One boy volunteered, "He actually taught me how to breathe as I was pulling the trigger, and it worked—I improved my score."

Before we said good night, we plotted that the following morning one of the boys would show Nathan how to make a hospital corner with his bedsheet, and shortly after another boy would ask Nathan to show him.

By the end of the week, the esprit de corps in the cabin was palpable. The boys were saying how sharing a cabin with Nathan was the best thing that could have happened for them. For *them*, not just for Nathan.

At the end of camp, one of the boys' parents circled back to me as they were about to leave with their son. They said, "I don't know what's happened with John, but he's being so kind and thoughtful—what a joy. What's happened?"

My response was a bit distracted by another couple, who seemed to be crying as they approached me. They stuttered through their tears that they were Nathan's parents, and clarified that their tears were tears of happiness. "Nathan has never been happier. He's walking like he's confident and joyful, and he's talking with the kids like he really has friends. He's never had any friends."

While that summer was a good experience for Nathan and the campers, it also could not have been a more life-enhancing experience for me. And it is that type of experience that is waiting for other men who take leadership roles in the scouts, Y, Boys Club, ManKind Project, and Experience Corps.

As with Nathan and my campers, the benefit to boys' skill development is less important than the benefit in character development. These findings about Cub Scouts tell us why . . .

The Cub Scouts and Character

Most of us, if we had to choose between our children being trustworthy, kind, and cheerful on the one hand, and financially successful on the other, would choose the positive character traits. Of course, the wisdom of life experience tells us that boys with those positive character traits enhance their chances of career success, relationship success, physical health, and spiritual happiness.

A study of the impact on a boy's character of his involvement in the Cub Scouts started by dividing boys into two groups, each with equal scores on six character traits—trustworthiness, kindness, cheerfulness, obedience, helpfulness, and hopefulness. After three years, the boys who were actively involved in Cub Scouts scored considerably higher on all six character traits than the ones who did not join the Scouts.[10]

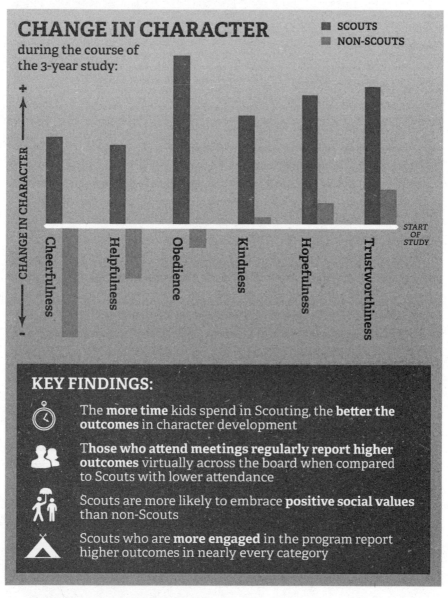

CHANGE IN CHARACTER
during the course of
the 3-year study:

■ SCOUTS
■ NON-SCOUTS

+

CHANGE IN CHARACTER

–

Cheerfulness   Helpfulness   Obedience   Kindness   Hopefulness   Trustworthiness

START
OF
STUDY

KEY FINDINGS:

The **more time** kids spend in Scouting, the **better the outcomes** in character development

Those who attend meetings regularly report higher outcomes virtually across the board when compared to Scouts with lower attendance

Scouts are more likely to embrace **positive social values** than non-Scouts

Scouts who are **more engaged** in the program report higher outcomes in nearly every category

Source: Boy Scouts of America[11]

Since dad-deprived boys are more likely to be depressed and angry (as opposed to cheerful and hopeful), destructive and bullying (as opposed to kind and helpful), and disobedient, the Cub Scouts offers a powerful source of hope for boys deprived of dads.

Although the study did not extend to the older Boy Scouts, I can identify from my experience with the Boy Scouts seven ways the Boy Scouts channels young male energy that boys without dads are often missing:

"The Seven Ways" the Boy Scouts Channels Boys' Energy

1. **Clear oaths, mottos, and "laws"** for duty to self, and to others build boys' foundation for manhood. These are
   a. *internalized by repetition;*
   b. *externalized by saying them aloud in unison among peers; and*
   c. *channeled by male leadership for constructive use in real life.*
2. **Merit badges** provide the opportunity to learn in a way to which boys respond: through doing, competing, and tangible measures of respect.
3. **Weekly meetings** reinforce each of these processes, inspiring further productive masculinity.
4. **Matching your son to the merit badge.** With about 120 merit badge options—including new ones on game design, robotics, programming, digital technology, animation, and sustainability—it is easy for any boy to find something positive that interests him.
5. **Matching your son to a mentor.** The actual work toward the merit badge often puts a boy in consistent contact for guidance with a male adult with similar interests.
6. **Mastery of content that is measurable, tangible, and translates into respect.** Because each merit badge puts him closer to his next increase in rank (e.g., six toward Star; eleven toward Life), he is inspired simultaneously by his sense of mastery at learning new content and the anticipation of a future, tangible acknowledgment that will increase his respect among peers, leaders, and parents.
7. **Leadership and social skills** are also rewarded with titles—ranging from Assistant Patrol Leader to Junior Assistant Scoutmaster.

In brief, over the course of more than a century, the Boy Scouts have honed what Margaret Mead had articulated—that boys are shaped by social reinforcement. Titles that offer measures by which boys can gain the respect of both male peers and adults are crucial motivators for boys to channel their enormous energy constructively before a purpose void seduces them to channel it destructively.

Titles and ranks are often derided as "hierarchical," and as reflections of men's obsession with power. Yes, titles and ranks are "social bribes." But those social bribes are the way we inspire boys to serve others and often sacrifice themselves—which is not exactly "power." The Scouts use social bribes to channel male testosterone toward competence, character, leadership, and service, preparing them for the best of traditional masculinity. Which, by the way—not irrelevant to many of the boys—also increases their appeal to girls! (And as of 2018, of course, girls have the option of learning all these as the Boy Scouts also opens its doors to girls.)

Ys and Boys Clubs

This constructive channeling of "boy energy" is also facilitated by Boys & Girls Clubs and Ys, with a few additional twists. Starting in the first grade, some Boys & Girls Clubs offer flag football, with both boys and girls permitted to play. For boys eleven to fourteen, there's a Passport to Manhood program. And by age thirteen, a Date Smart program offers both sexes joint activities and ways to communicate with each other.

Many of the Ys offer programs for children as early as preschool age, and also offer childcare. Their after-school academic programs can be helpful for dad-deprived boys' significantly greater challenges at school. During the most challenging years—grades six to twelve—the Ys help boys (and girls) channel potentially destructive energy into creative leadership by encouraging good social skills and service to others. The Ys also provide mentorship programs for youth and teens.

Mentoring and Rite-of-Passage Programs

Sending your son to a mentoring or rite-of-passage-type program is generally a life-enhancing experience for an already motivated boy, and often a turnaround experience for a boy who is rudderless, angry, or electronically addicted.

The most widespread and well-tested of the rite-of-passage programs is the ManKind Project (MKP).[12] Their signature program is its New Warrior Training Adventure. It is designed to immerse young men in a series of outdoor adventure experiences. The bonding and sense of camaraderie emanates from participants experiencing the best of traditional masculine values of service and courage without the facades of strength that have typically been men's weakness. The program encourages authenticity and emotional intelligence.

The MKP has also formed small groups of Men Mentoring Men (currently serving about ten thousand men around the world), called Integration Groups, in which young men learn communication, relationship, and conflict-resolution skills. The groups foster no-bs, empathetic-but-honest bonding, rather than bonding by hazing or bonding by creating in- and out-groups.

Other rite-of-passage programs include the Young Men's Ultimate Weekend,[13] Young Men's Adventure Weekend,[14] and Mountain Quest,[15] which all focus on outdoor adventure, team building, social skills, spiritual values, connection to nature, and the transmission of values such as responsibility and service to others. The Young Men's Ultimate Weekend offers a simultaneous course for parents to help them capitalize on the growth their son experiences during the program.

Mountain Quest, in Seattle, works with sixth-grade girls and boys to create a safe environment to share and process their feelings in real time. Their all-male program uses ceremony and initiation rites to lend the program a timeless, archetypal spirit, while encouraging comfort with "letting loose" and being goofy and exuberant.

No demographic groups are in greater jeopardy than African American and Native American boys and young men. My Brother's Keeper, formed by President Obama in 2015, focuses on their needs. Since President Obama arranged for its funding to be from private sources, he will be able to fulfill his pledge to continue My Brother's Keeper as one of his lifelong missions. If your son qualifies, it is an opportunity made for him. The program's goals include mentorship or support "from cradle to career."

The Adoption Option

The logic of adoption is that two caring parents who are highly motivated, well-educated, and financially sound will give a child better opportunities in life than a birth mother (and sometimes father) who cannot keep or does not want that child, whether because of her age, health, education, or finances. And that is likely accurate.

However, for many adopted children, that isn't the whole story.

My stepdaughter, Erin, was adopted at birth by my wife, Liz, and Liz's former husband. I think Erin best summarized her challenge being adopted—and therefore her adoptive parents' challenge adopting—when a rancher friend from New Zealand joined us for dinner.

We asked our friend to describe some of his life on his ranch. His eyes flooded with nostalgia as he recalled how two of his ducks had recently been killed shortly after their ducklings had hatched:

"But almost immediately one of my female chickens took the ducklings under its wing, and began nurturing and raising them. It was so touching. Then one day the ducklings were big enough to venture out of the barn. I'll never forget them struggling to waddle down the hill, and so proud to get to the lake at the bottom.

"Then one duck immediately jumped into the lake. The 'mama' chicken went into a frenzy—chickens can't swim. Then another duck jumped in; well, the mama chicken went berserk. Then—"

Erin, eight at the time, interrupted: "That's the way I feel. Like a duck raised by a chicken."

We sat in stunned silence.

This is the challenge for adopted children, and therefore for the parents raising them: no matter how loving the adoptive parents, the child can still feel "like a duck raised by a chicken." Many adopted children seem to experience some of the same "search for self" that befalls the child who loses his or her biological dad.

Adopting a child can mean that child will someday feel as if she or he has been kidnapped from their own world, and expected to adapt to an alien family. All of the adoptive family's love is sometimes unable to completely heal that wound, although compassion aids the healing.

And there is doubtless more to it than that. Kathryn and Dan Kay, good friends of mine in Connecticut, who are nuanced in their parenting skills, adopted a daughter. They felt tested—and often overwhelmed—by the challenges they faced.

One day, when their daughter was in her twenties, she joined an adoption-focused group that read *The Primal Wound* by Nancy Verrier. Their daughter immediately felt understood, and recommended the book to her parents. They too experienced the solace of seeing their family dynamic on the written page, allowing them to deepen still further their compassion for, as Verrier puts it, the "fears an adopted child suppresses and the terrible hole in their hearts and souls due to the fact that they are separated from their birth mothers even if they were adopted at one day old."

Verrier explains both the science and her opinion of the psychology of primal attachment: how in the womb embryos become attached to the mother in primal ways. Adoption, even at birth, tears the child away from everything to which it is connected on a primal level, creating a primal wound. Therefore, the trauma of being abandoned by the mother to which the embryo was biologically and psychologically attached trumps the theoretical joy of being adopted by loving and devoted parents.

No one can say for certain what creates the challenges that many adopted children and adoptive parents face. We do know that many—and probably the great majority—of adopted children are doing better than they would have had they not been adopted. Erin is very clear about that, that she sometimes feels guilty that her life has so much more opportunity than her half brothers and sister who were not adopted.

But what we also know is that, no matter what the reasons, adoptive children's struggles are measurable. By eighth grade, children of adoptive parents were more than three times as likely to be suspended from school than children of the same gender and racial-ethnic background from intact families with equal family incomes and education.[16]

Why, then, would a family adopt? Because our sense of purpose, and our need to care and be cared for, are activated, as can probably best be witnessed with the transformation of a tough Pittsburgh detective named Jack Mook who discovered two boys being abused in a foster home. Jack ultimately adopted the boys legally and became a full-time parent. He called it, like John Lennon, "the best thing I ever did in my life."[17]

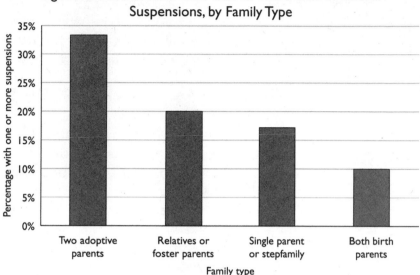

Eighth-Grade Students with One or More Out-of-School Suspensions, by Family Type

Source: Institute for Family Studies[18]

Jack seemed to possess characteristics that are common to those of successful foster homes: high standards, considerable responsibilities, maximum affection, minimum medication, and boundary enforcement.[19]

Wanted: a few good men.

Grandfather Time

I was feeding quarters into a parking meter. As I was about to select a tarnished old quarter as my first contribution, I recalled my numismatist friend, and thought it would be fun to have him check its value. Turns out, its tarnished looks were but a reflection of its age, which contributed to this particular quarter being worth eight times its face value. In many Native American cultures, the community is the integration of all beings—grandparents, grandchildren, parents, relatives, men, women, nature, and the cosmos. Listening to each other, and to the world around them, is what allows for a transfer of love.[20]

In nonindigenous culture, our grandparents' "tarnished" look often leads us to overlook their value. And half of our grandparents are especially likely to be as dismissed as a couple of old quarters: grandfathers.

But grandpas can be of special value when a boy is in need of a role model, particularly if:

- the boy's dad is, because of his work, experiencing the father's catch-22—earning the love of his family by being away from the love of his family;
- the boy's dad is divorced and cannot get equally shared parenting, or is in the military, prison, or otherwise unavailable;
- grandpa always felt sad that he was experiencing the father's catch-22 when his son was growing up, but now has more time;
- devoting time to raising his grandson would reignite grandpa's sense of purpose and his inner child;
- grandpa is feeling the awakening of his "dad brain" and cherishing what he is discovering about himself; or
- grandpa loves nature, kidding, teasing, and tossing a ball, and finds that the discussions he has with his grandson after he's won or lost a game makes watching his grandson more meaningful than rooting for professionals who will never hear his advice and whose love he will never feel.

When the Biological Father Is Missing, Can God the Father Help?

After giving a sermon/workshop at St. Paul Community Baptist Church in one of the country's poorest communities, Bedford–Stuyvesant in Brooklyn, I met with a few men's groups the church had sponsored. Of the approximately twenty-five young African American boys, about twenty had four more things in common:

1. They had little or no time with their dad.
2. They spent time in jail.
3. They found Christ and a strong church community with a committed reverend.
4. They felt inspired to discipline themselves toward constructive rather than destructive lives.

Did faith in God help these young men? Yes. Almost all the young men said that they would still be involved in the life that landed them in jail if they had not been redirected by their faith in God the Father.

I saw in that experience how dad deprivation seems to engender a spiritual deprivation. The guidance, approval, and boundary voids the boys felt from their fathers' absence led to their receptivity to guidance, approval, and boundaries from gang leaders and other pseudoauthorities, as we saw earlier in the case of ISIS. The Bedford–Stuyvesant community was one of the most dangerous in the country. When Reverend Jerry Youngblood came in and organized a strong church community with a strong message, he offered the boys the guidance, approval, and boundaries that helped fill that void.

Between dad involvement and each of these alternatives to dad involvement, almost everyone who cares can participate. Yet that participation can either be facilitated or made more challenging by the culture we create toward the challenges boys face: do we continue our "cultural shrug," or create a cultural shift?

CHAPTER 21

From "Cultural Shrug" to Cultural Shift

In this era of fires and floods, during which about 98 percent of the first responders who sacrifice their lives to save ours are men, a cultural *shift*—one that teaches boys to value their lives rather than protect ours—literally threatens our lives. Since a reconsideration of the social bribes that contribute to the boy crisis may put our lives at risk, it is understandable that a boy crisis would be met with a "cultural shrug."

And as we've seen, caring equally for our sons also means confronting the psychological detachment we have needed to cope with our sons' potential disposability in war in the past, and in floods and fires in our future.

FAMILY DINNER NIGHT
Behind the Cultural Shrug

Try this question for an intriguing family dinner night discussion: "If our daughters were 98 percent of the first responders sacrificing their lives in floods and fires, would global warming be treated more seriously?" (Be especially sure to follow the guidelines in appendix A on this one!)

If we do wish to move from a cultural shrug to a cultural shift, can policy changes help? Yes. Legal and policy changes shift a cultural shrug like tossing a stone into a lake can shift still water. For example, in two of the states with the largest African American populations—Maryland and Virginia—policy differences have contributed to a radical divergence in the unemployment rate of twenty-five-year-old black males: only 35 percent in Maryland, versus 65 percent in Virginia.[1] Employment's ripple effect reaches from a lower crime rate to the creation of taxpayers out of tax drainers.

So how can you help shift the cultural shrug? Parents who organize can have a significant impact on three things: first, laws and policies; second, as your son watches what you do that works and fails to work, you'll be teaching him how to be effective in the world; and third, you'll be helping him make a transition from a potential purpose void to a sense of purpose—creating something bigger than himself. That transition is the core of the journey from boyhood to manhood.

The best way to shift out of a cultural shrug is to start with what we have most detached from that most deserves our love and attention: veterans. And especially the veteran who is a dad.

Kill Today, Love Tomorrow: The Military Dad Dilemma

Andrew, a marine completing his first tour of duty, lived for his "Skype days"—the days he would see on Skype how Megan, his wife, was teaching their four-year-old daughter to "count the days 'till daddy comes home." He could barely wait—it was the reward for which he was risking his life: his family's love.

Andrew did not wish to be the Lone Ranger Dad that seemed to make some of his marine friends not care if they lived or died. He wanted to be both integral to and integrated with his family.

Finally, Andrew's plane landed. Although Andrew had only once met his one-and-a-half-year-old son, Andrew's version of hide-and-seek charmed his way into his son's graces. Within a week of his return, Andrew's heart was opened. "The only thing I care about is being a loving dad and husband."

But Andrew soon realized that, while he admired Megan's devotion as a mom, he also felt Megan was too permissive. And Megan felt

Andrew's "overemphasis" on rules, goals, and discipline was overdoing the "tough" part of "tough love." Even the way Andrew played with the kids scared Megan.

While Megan's "permissiveness" bothered Andrew, it also delighted him to discover something his experience away from the family would allow him to contribute to the family. And his experience was most informed by boot camp and marine culture.

Boot camp and the marines had allowed Andrew to experience how he could do things he never thought he could do. He knew that was because he was required to do more than he wanted to do every day. Andrew felt he was a better, more confident person as a result. Now, as a dad, Andrew could "pay it forward" for his children.

Andrew talked with Megan about preparing the kids to reach beyond their comfort zones and discover capabilities that he felt Megan was failing to nurture when she would give in to the children's first "I don't want to." Sometimes Megan agreed, but when her children said, "I don't want to," or cried, Megan's first instinct was to listen and solve their problem with the least pain.

Within a month, Andrew was feeling that exactly what he thought he had to contribute to his family was creating conflict that was tearing his family apart. Megan felt the insecurity of not having dad around was being replaced with the insecurities of *having* dad around. Both felt hurt and sad.

No one had prepared Andrew and Megan for the "military dad dilemma": speak up or shut up. Speaking up risked creating conflict that poisons love, and shutting up was a surefire way to raise spoiled children who will always feel dependent. No one had taught Andrew and Megan how to extract from the training to be a warrior those elements that could make their children stronger, and balance that with a mom's experience and instincts.

If we wish to alter the cultural shrug facing young men's transition from being trained to kill effectively to being trained to love effectively, we need to explore policy changes that prevent postdeployment from becoming predivorce. We use boot camp to train our soldiers to kill in war. When our soldiers return home, we need a postdeployment boot camp to train our soldiers and spouses to integrate the best of each other's skills to succeed on their next mission: building a strong family.

Postdeployment Boot Camp

In the military, when the going gets tough, the tough get going. It's not an option. In a postdeployment boot camp (PDBC), a veteran would learn how and when to uncork emotions rather than liquor bottles. And a boy would see his dad integrated into the family rather than become the victim of a dad-alienated family.

How? By starting with the positive: helping our sons and their wives translate the many strengths our sons learn serving our country in war into serving their family at home. For example, in the process of learning how to serve, veterans also learn to adapt, deal with crises and emergencies, and both lead and follow. They develop or strengthen qualities such as loyalty, alertness, stamina, and waking up as needed at any time of the night. Each of these are either necessary or helpful in the raising of children.

A PDBC would also help veterans revisit what they learned that was more functional in war than in love. In war, mistrust and paranoia are functional; at home, they are dysfunctional. A PDBC would call upon veterans' capacity to adapt—to adapt from functional paranoia to trust.

Similarly, in the heat of battle, if someone in his unit is wounded, if it takes a facade of strength to rescue him, that strengthens the military unit. But at home, if his wife or children are sick, the facade of strength that's perfect for the moment of emergency must be followed by knowing how to ask for help and empathize in order to strengthen his family unit.

In wartime, things like family therapy, couples' communication training, and marital counseling distract from a necessary focus on winning the war; after wartime, they're necessary tools to help the soldier and family reunite.

The length of this training? If a soldier has been engaged in combat, a PDBC needs to provide retraining to love at least as extensive as the veteran's training to kill. The gift to children who wait for a dad to return and love them is a dad who knows how to give them that love when he returns. And the gift to his son is a role model whose sense of purpose in war isn't followed by an alienation from purpose when he returns for the love for which he was willing to die.

Being at war—or at work—unconsciously prepares the entire family to think of dad's contribution to be his dime, not his time. Both our family consciousness and our laws need to incorporate the value of a father's time.

From Father's Dime to Father's Time

We have seen the conclusion from sixty-three studies that children benefit more from quality of time with dad than the quantity of money from dad.[2] Yet . . .

The world recently saw Walter Scott, reportedly a loving dad who had four children, though no job, shot in the back eight times by a South Carolina police officer as he ran from his car. Walter Scott was unarmed.[3]

The media jumped on Scott being shot because he was black. Good. They missed how people shot by police are twenty-four times more likely to be male. Bad.

Some people argued that Scott got shot because he was running away from the cop. But we missed how policies that focused more on Scott's dime than Scott's time are what led to him running to begin with. Because these dad-as-wallet policies can easily affect your son should he become a divorced dad, and therefore discourage your son from becoming a dad, we need to take a look . . .

Walter had previously served *six months* in jail after falling behind in child support by $6,800.[4] When Walter ran from his car that day, there was another warrant for his arrest because of unpaid child support. Walter's older brother, Rodney, told MSNBC that Walter had told him he would run rather than go to jail again. So when he was stopped (for a broken taillight), he ran.

What's wrong with this picture?

Three-quarters of dads who were in South Carolina jails for being behind in child support suffer from extreme poverty.[5] **And *one-eighth* of all South Carolina inmates are in jail for being behind in child support payments.**[6] No dad is imprisoned for not spending enough time with his children. And it is rare for a mom to go to jail for preventing dad from spending enough time with his children.

Although the director of that inmate study, Libba Patterson, was also the former director of the South Carolina Department of Social Services, she called the system "a modern-day debtors' prison."[7] More accurately, a prison for indigent dads.

We've discussed how this pattern holds nationwide, and is perpetrated by this self-defeating logic: nationwide, with 70 percent of parents who owe child support having incomes of less than $10,000 per year,[8] and many of these dads too poor to pay child support nevertheless imprisoned because of failure to pay child support, the state deepens their arrears and further damages these dads' ability to hold a job and pay child support!

Yet the self-defeating logic continues, driven by a federal budget of $2.9 billion to get dads to pay more money ("Child Support Enforcement") while in contrast, the federal budget to ensure dads have more time ("Access and Visitation") is only $10 million.[9]

Practically speaking, then, for every dollar spent to assure a child gets father time, $290 is spent to assure a child gets father's dime. In brief, **we spend billions to get from dads the money few of them have, and virtually nothing to allow dads to give the time they do have—the time their children need.**

Imagine your son becoming unemployed as a divorced dad and his former wife claiming that the very qualities that make your son unemployed at work make him unsuitable as a dad. Is there a policy solution that would work for your son while still treating the mom's fears with respect? Yes. Make any government financial support, for your son or his child's mother, dependent on him *and the mom* taking classes in communication and parenting skills, plus state-of-the-art job training that emphasizes jobs that can be used by businesses in their community. Then connect both dad and mom with job placement counselors.

If an approach like this were taken, what's the evidence it would work without just becoming one more government entitlement program? Let's go to where it has been tried: Chattanooga.

Implementing Child Support as Dad Time Over Dad Dime

Chattanooga, Tennessee, is in Hamilton County. In 1996 Hamilton County had a divorce rate 50 percent higher than the national average. Chattanooga decided to lower the rate of divorce by improving communication skills, increasing awareness of family responsibilities *before* pregnancy, and increasing father involvement. The program was appropriately called First Things First. Instead of using government money, for the first decade the program raised all its money (about $1 million) privately.

Rather than focus on girls who had become pregnant, First Things First started in junior high schools to create an understanding of what responsibility for a child meant among both girls and boys before pregnancy.

Then First Things First went to where many of the kids' dads were—jail, mostly for not paying child support. In cooperation with Chattanooga judges, the program enrolled 168 of these dads through its courses on relationship and communication skills, and father involvement. It offered the dads job training, and then helped them find jobs.

The payoff? In the end, only 5 of the 168 returned to prison for non-payment of child support.[10] First Things First supported the dads, and the dads supported the children.

First Things First catalyzed a cultural shift in Chattanooga. Between 1997 and 2015 divorce filings decreased by 33 percent. First Things First created solutions that prevented the divorces: developing prepregnancy programs that resulted in a 63 percent decrease in teen births (from 242 in 1997 to 88 in 2015) and increasing father involvement when teens did have children.[11]

The Government: As Problem, as Solution

Does the absence of dad create the presence of government, or does the presence of government create the absence of dad?

As in South Carolina, the presence of government can certainly create the absence of dad. But can Chattanooga-type solutions be adapted by governments to increase the presence of dad and reduce the presence of government?

President Obama, proof that a boy can have an absent father and still be a success, has nevertheless said that no government can fill the hole in the psyche of a boy with an absent dad. So the solution means involving dad, not replacing dad.

But will the long-term effect of involving dad cost or save the taxpayers money? And will it increase or decrease the size of government? Here's why Chattanooga-type programs will both save the taxpayers money and decrease the size of government:

We've already gotten some sense of the trillions of dollars spent on homeland security and defense emanating from dad-deprived boys joining ISIS. Dad deprivation creates a threat to our freedom, and then we discover government needs to erode our freedoms to protect our freedoms.

Beyond homeland security, though, father-absent households also receive most of the $100 billion dollars per year spent on welfare programs.[12] Temporary Assistance for Needy Families (TANF) distributes

87.5 percent of funds—or $15 billion—to father-absent families. Medicaid spending on father-absent families is another $23 billion.[13] Head Start and school lunch programs follow the same pattern.

The title of the Women, Infants, and Children (WIC) program makes apparent which sex's inclusion could lead to additional government exclusion. There is no fathers, infants, and children program. Although theoretically fathers with custody can also receive assistance through WIC, the WIC website lists data only for the 9 million mothers served, never mentioning a single dad or man.[14] And of course, the program's name would not invite a single dad to enter a WIC office to inquire.

That $100 billion spent on welfare doesn't include the $39 billion spent annually on prisons.[15] Nor the much greater use of mental and physical health services by children in father-absent families. Nor the cost of a reduction of income tax payments resulting from the lower earnings of children of father-absent families.[16]

You get the point.

So the big question is this: Can the government effectively facilitate dads' presence, so it needs to pour less into cleaning up problems catalyzed by dads' absence?

Well, **our "cultural shrug" toward both the boy crisis and father involvement has led to no significant government effort to reduce the presence of government by increasing the involvement of dads.** The government has begun programs in cooperation with a few cities, but no wide-ranging study of effectiveness has been completed as of 2017.[17]

The one study of efficacy that has been completed was of the InsideOut Dad program, a parenting program for incarcerated fathers.[18] It concluded that InsideOut Dad had increased the imprisoned dads' effectiveness and contact with children. But that's only one program. We still have a long way to go in our journey from cultural shrug to cultural shift.

Creating a White House Council on Boys and Men

Clearly, government involvement, through social programs and new policy, has the potential for great impact. It's worth your time to advocate for. But creating change through government isn't easy.

Two of the biggest challenges of working with the government are, first, that the left hand often doesn't know what the right hand is doing;

and second, there's little incentive for government employees to avoid duplicating efforts if it eliminates their job.

The problems generated by fatherlessness and the boy crisis are handled by different departments of the government: the Departments of Health and Human Services; Education; Labor; Housing; Veterans' Affairs; Defense; Homeland Security; and so on.

To begin to solve these problems, a central coordinator—one with no incentive for duplicating jobs—is needed. And since the White House is the only part of government that does not inherently favor one of these departments over the other, creating a White House Council on Boys and Men would be the best assurance that the necessary changes would take place, while also addressing the first two challenges of working with government: ensuring that the left hand knows what the right is doing and that employees are not fighting to continue programs that overlap with those of another department.

A White House Council on Boys and Men could search for the programs around the world that have most successfully turned father absence into father presence by training both parents to integrate dad wherever possible, and, when father absence is necessary, how and when to integrate male teachers, mentors, and programs such as scouting. It could look for the best approaches to paternity leave, veteran reintegration, and so on.

But most important, a White House Council on Boys and Men could catalyze a cultural shift from our current dismissive shrug of the boy crisis. It would publicize the problem and also lend it credibility—not just in the United States, but worldwide.

An executive order creating a White House Council on Boys and Men would, by itself, motivate professional conferences and private funding for the solutions we need to the problems created by the connection between fatherlessness and the "purpose void" (as well as the disconnect between heroic and health intelligence, which we'll discuss in the next part of the book). It will lead to conferences on diverse topics such as the futures of retraining boys for the option of traditionally female careers, making schools more boy-friendly, male birth control, crime, guns, the impact of our image of boys, and male work-life harmony.

As I noted in the introduction, I have chaired a coalition (including John Gray, Michael Gurian, Leonard Sax, and many others) to create such a White House Council on Boys and Men (see WhiteHouseBoysMen.org).

It seeks to shut off the faucet that's flooding the floor with single-parent families, rather than only cleaning up the flood of problems generated by father absence in our communities.

If we get more of what we pay for, then let's pay to get more dads, rather than pay more when dads are absent.

Our Dads, Our Sons, Our Guns

No matter our perspective on guns, if we care about our sons, we need to connect the dots among our dads, our sons, and our guns. And then develop some win-win solutions.

Start with the *father* of Stephen Paddock, the 2017 Las Vegas massacre gunman. Stephen's father is Benjamin Paddock, a notorious bank robber. In Benjamin's psychological evaluation, he reported that he was an only child, pampered by his mother and not disciplined by his father.[19]

The missing ingredient in Benjamin's life: someone making the typically dad contribution of discipline and postponed gratification.

The predictable outcome: in Benjamin Paddock's words, "I went where I felt like it, disrupting everybody's schedule." [20] He was driving a car by age twelve. Although a self-described genius, he dropped out of high school by age fifteen, and soon served a five-year stint in prison.

Upon release from prison, Benjamin married. Stephen was his first child. But by the time Stephen was seven, he lost his dad to federal prison. He visited his dad in prison, but as Stephen's brother Eric shared after Stephen was killed, Stephen was angry at his dad for being "more interested in crime than his family." [21]

Stephen's mom initially told Stephen that his dad had been killed in prison. But Stephen later learned that his dad had, in fact, used his alleged genius to escape and was on the lam.[22]

Here is where the dad deprivation takes on a deeper dimension of abandonment, as it does in divorce when the father is available but not available. The fact that his dad could have completed his sentence and been able to reconnect with his family, but chose instead to leave them behind by using his brilliance to escape from a federal prison, must have infused Stephen with excruciating pain, driving him to search for how he could be recognized by his dad—as if to say, "Dad, look at me, I'm like you; I'm worthy of your attention."

Whether or not that is an accurate assessment of one of Stephen's underlying motives, what is clear is that he used twenty-three guns, including an AR-15 assault rifle (designed to mimic the rapid-fire sound of a machine gun), to kill fifty-eight people and injure more than five hundred in a matter of minutes.

Now let's connect those dots. The worst mass killing in modern American history, Stephen's massacre, was not caused by guns, but would have been impossible without guns. The cause? I would suggest that one catalyst was the role of Stephen's grandparents, with no one playing the traditional father's role of boundary enforcement, discipline, and postponed gratification.

A dad like Benjamin, without this discipline, is less likely to be able to fulfill his responsibilities as a dad. So his son, Stephen, becomes a boy who suffers the slings and arrows of dad deprivation. And boys who are hurt hurt us. Since emotional wounds do not disappear as boyhood disappears, Stephen became a hurt boy who hurt us as a hurt man. The most effective way boys and men who are hurt can hurt us is with guns.

Guns don't cause the initial damage, but they expand the ability to inflict damage. Guns magnify the degree to which a boy who feels devoid of power and purpose, because he has not had his testosterone and intelligence constructively channeled by the love and discipline of his dad as role model, can fantasize a moment of power to compensate for his black hole of powerlessness. Whether via ISIS, a school shooting, or a Las Vegas massacre, nothing promises a magical compensation for the powerlessness of fatherlessness more than the power of guns.

Creating Win-Win Solutions

Once a lack of parental discipline leads to a Benjamin Paddock–like entitlement and purpose void, is there any hope? Yes. Filling that purpose void with purpose . . .

For all of Benjamin Paddock's problems, he nevertheless wanted to use his troubled background as a resource to help other troubled youth do a turnaround. Evidence? Benjamin "walked into the sheriff's office and offered to counsel troubled youths."[23]

In Benjamin's words, "I only took the incorrigibles . . . I told them I had a degree in social psychology and nobody bothered to check." The result? Benjamin's evaluator said that Benjamin assessed that not a single young man assigned to him ever ended up back in court.[24]

The opportunity to rechannel boys without purpose into a life of purpose often comes from rechanneling their particular expertise of destructively channeled energy into constructively channeled energy in the same field. However, the institution that is facilitating the redirection of the boy's energy must be vigilant that the young man internalizes how his new purpose as a role model will be lost if he returns to his destructive ways. In Benjamin's case, there was no such program. Perhaps, if there had been, Stephen would have been able to prove himself to his dad as a counselor rather than a killer.

Would solutions like this take care of the problem—allowing us to not have to address the issue of guns? Well, we are faced with a Gordian knot. Mass shootings do more than kill people—they kill psychological security. Psychological *in*security magnifies our willingness to trade in freedoms in exchange for an expanded government as protector. And ironically, the guns that lead to more government and less freedom also lead to the demand for more guns to protect us from big government and the loss of freedom!

Is there a way to cut this Gordian knot? A way that has worked? In 1996 Australia had experienced thirteen mass shootings in eighteen years. Given the size of the Australian population, that is the equivalent of 180 US shootings in eighteen years. John Howard had just become prime minister. He led the charge for a major mandatory gun buy-back program that led to more than seven hundred thousand privately owned weapons being surrendered (the US equivalent of about ten million), and additional weapons seized.[25]

The legislation also banned the sale and importation of automatic and semiautomatic weapons. This led to a 75 percent reduction in gun ownership.

The first massive study examining the impact was published in 2016. The results? **In the almost 20 years following Australia's change in gun policy, mass shootings fell to *zero*.**[26] And boys who hurt, hurt themselves less as well: there was a 74 percent reduction in gun-related suicides.[27] There was also a decline in total non-firearm suicide and homicide.[28]

Guns are not the cause of the boy crisis, but as we are working on the causes, the control of guns can limit the damage of dad-deprived sons.

CHAPTER 22

Creating Dad-Enriched Families

Responsible fatherhood starts with our being responsive to fatherhood. When boys and men are told they are needed, they respond, and become responsible.

A mother can tell a boy he is needed, but a boy sees himself in his dad. If his dad is involved, he feels inspired; if he is absent, he feels abandoned. He becomes vulnerable to being recruited by gangs or by ISIS. Boys who are in desperate need of a father figure are also vulnerable to sexual exploitation, whether by male Catholic priests or female juvenile detention staff.

Perhaps the most significant human accomplishment in the United States during the twentieth century was our awareness that defining our daughters in one way led to our daughters feeling confined to one way. It can be our most significant human accomplishment in the twenty-first century to create an awareness that defining our sons in one way leads to our sons being confined to one way.

For both sexes, it can no longer be said that biology is destiny. Biology is not destiny; biology is the potential for adaptability. The "dad brain" lies dormant—until a dad makes a social decision to be involved with a baby. Then neurons are triggered, hormones are stimulated, and his dad brain awakens.

Our grandmother needed to know she could matter at work. And our son needs to know he can matter at home. From the diet he eats before contributing his sperm and the intelligence he can stimulate in a baby born prematurely, and at every other age and stage of life, his contributions are important.

While dad matters amid the stability of an intact family, he appears to matter even more amid the instability of a family of divorce. Fortunately, the "four must-dos" of divorce—equal time, no badmouthing, proximity, and couples' communication—can ensure the interests of the parents do not negate the best interests of the child.

The father warrior of the future is one who will fight to not slide down the slippery slope to "conditional dad." This means your son becoming a student of the nature of his contributions—whether via boundary enforcement, or bonding through roughhousing and sport; by sharing with mom how he uses that bond to create leverage for their child to get to bed on time, or do homework, or chores, or be kind to his sister.

A dad must do his homework, but not just his homework. He must also deliver findings to mom. Moms can't hear what dads don't say.

Being a father warrior also means confronting not just the slippery slope to conditional dad in the home but also the image of dad as deadbeat outside the home. Each affects the other.

And being a father warrior means introducing your son to scouting, mentor-adventure weekends, and, if you have a male partner or your son's mom has remarried, being sure they are also integrated into your children's lives as part of the parenting checks and balances that are as necessary to parents as to governments.

Next to war, nothing calls for the presence of government more than the absence of dad. And nothing limits the need for the presence of government more than the presence of dad.

But ensuring dad's presence means replacing the era of the no-option man, in which we value him only if he works full-time, with an era of the multi-option man, in which we demonstrate our respect for him whether he works full-time, fathers full-time, or does some combination of both.

Few of our sons will complain to a psychologist, "I didn't get enough money from my dad." The gift of a father's involvement—the gift of a glimpse of life's blueprint—is the gift of fewer male midlife crises and more lifelong marriages, of fewer alcoholic dads and more devoted dads.

Your son having real power begins with supporting him to create the harmony between work and life that is appropriate to his personality, cognizant of the trade-offs of each decision, and true to the commitments he makes as he takes the journey from boy to man. And it is supporting him to create his own heroism—one that, for the first time in history, makes his heroic intelligence compatible with his health intelligence . . .

PART V

Heroic Intelligence Versus Health Intelligence

Boys' Weakness as Their Facade of Strength

Heroic Intelligence Versus Health Intelligence

Bill watched his friend Pete jump off a bridge into a shallow stream. His other friends cheered, as did a girl Bill had a crush on. Pete, in his moment of glory, turned to Bill, and pointed: "You next, Bill!" Everyone watched in anticipation. Pete teased, "You chicken?" A few of his friends joined Pete, chanting "Sissy!" "Chicken," "Sissy," "Chicken."

The chant got to Bill. He was shaking as he looked down from the bridge. But he said nothing. He dove. His head splattered against a hidden rock. Pete was the first to get to Bill, but he could only cry helplessly as blood streamed from Bill's head through Pete's fingers. Pete never recovered from the guilt of "causing" Bill's death, or the grief of never being able to tell Bill how sorry he was.

Since training to become a hero is socialization for a short life, and "health intelligence" is socialization for a long life, heroic intelligence is in tension with health intelligence.

Even when Petes aren't yelling "chicken" so Bills can hear, Bills are still internalizing the "chickens" they've already heard, trying to prove themselves so they never hear it again. The chorus of social bribes to "prove himself" is just one way a boy's "heroic intelligence"—what he absorbs about how to be heroic—undermines his "health intelligence"—what he absorbs about how to take care of himself. A boy who tries to prove himself is at risk of losing himself.

Of course, risk-taking can be a virtue. Our inventors, entrepreneurs, Navy SEALs, Nobel laureates, and Olympic athletes are risk-takers. But risk-taking for boys is that sometimes-virtue taken to its extreme that becomes a vice. And since few boys reach heroic status, the need to "prove oneself" to become that one in a million becomes a social bribe to take risk-taking to its extreme. This contributes to your son being about twice as likely as your daughter to be killed in an accident.[1] And overlapping stressors—such as the stress a boy experiences as he fears physical failure if he jumps, yet fears social failure if he doesn't jump—can be instrumental in your son being more likely than your daughter to:

- be addicted to drugs or alcohol.
- be addicted to drugs prescribed to counter his addiction.
- be addicted to video games or video porn.
- be addicted to gambling.
- be injured or killed while driving drunk or recklessly.
- be injured in a dangerous sport (e.g., football, boxing, wrestling, rock climbing, rodeo, lacrosse, skateboarding, snowboarding, free-style motocross, ice hockey, car racing).
- "lose it" and act out physically.
- join a gang.
- commit a crime.
- murder.
- be murdered.
- be on-the-street homeless (vs in a shelter).
- be incarcerated.
- be obese.
- be diagnosed with ADHD.
- commit suicide.
- die at a younger age of one of fourteen out of the fifteen leading causes of death.[2]

But isn't some of this just biological?

Biologically, Girls Just Live Longer, Right?

When your son hears in school that women live longer than men, if he asks why, he will probably be told: "It's (mostly) a biological thing." He'll feel the way his mom may have felt when she saw only male presidents in her history book and perhaps silently assumed that "biology is destiny" or "I don't have a chance."

If more than seventy countries have challenged the limits of female biology with female heads of state, how can we also challenge your son's unconscious assumption that "biology is destiny"—or, more precisely, the assumption that a boy's biology is a shorter destiny?

Begin here. In 1920 American boys and men lived just one year less than women;[3] today, American boys and men live almost five fewer years (females, 81.6; males 76.9).[4] Yet **the male-female life expectancy gap has grown almost 400 percent.**

Take your son's thinking overseas. If a shorter life expectancy is just a matter of the genes, and not environment, boys and men in Switzerland would not live to eighty-one even as males in the Philippines live to sixty-five, and in Sierra Leone, to forty-nine.[5] If boys and men in Switzerland live almost 25 percent longer than in the Philippines, and 65 percent longer than in Sierra Leone, your son can see that his biology is not his destiny.

When can you start giving the gift of a longer life to your son? Before you conceive. Before the beginning, as it were.

Before the Beginning...

We've seen (in part IV) that a dad's diet and health can have a significant impact on the health of his sperm. Therefore, **both parents' cumulative health creates your son's health; your son's health begins before his beginning.**

There is probably no better way of helping your son see his health as part of his sense of purpose than to know that, should he someday wish to have children, his health today will contribute to his son's health tomorrow. And that he will be his son's best hero not by risking death, but by developing an intelligence that supports both his physical and emotional health. Intelligence he can pass down to his son.

But this means adjusting parenting that has evolved to raise sons prepared for the disposability of heroic intelligence—parenting that begins the moment your son cries. For example, parents take longer to pick up their sons than their daughters.[6] The lesson your son may experience? Expressing his feelings—as in crying—is futile. He is learning step one of his unconscious hero's journey: his feelings don't count. **To be a hero is to be emotionally constipated.**

And as developmental psychologist Erik Erikson posits, infants whose basic needs for cuddling, diaper changing, and feeding go unmet are at risk of developing a lifelong mistrust toward other human beings—which may manifest in later life as excessive jealousy, a need to constantly check up on his or her mate, and other behaviors that undermine intimacy.

We are also less likely to sing to our son. Or tell our son stories. Or read to our son.[7] **A desire to be nurtured is in our son's nature. But it's a nature we don't often nurture.**

Consciously, we tell our sons, "Don't get hurt." We make sure they get to bed on time and eat healthfully. Unconsciously, we send a different message.

We've seen how virtually every society that survived did so by preparing its sons to be disposable—disposable in war, and disposable at work.

This prepares us to unconsciously undermine our son's health in three ways:

1. Teaching our son to be sensitive to *his* health is in competition with *our* survival instinct. Encouraging Pop Warner football becomes a form of dad/son intimacy without consciousness of how its past purpose of preparing a boy for disposable heroism may be in tension with our son's future health.
2. If you fear you may lose your son, it helps to unconsciously protect yourself from forming too deep a psychological attachment. This can deprive your son of the health benefits of being picked up and held when he cries, thus depriving him of the emotional security that expressing his feelings will attract empathy and intimacy.
3. You want to raise a son who can respect himself and be respected, as well as a son you can be proud of for raising. So you cheer for him at sports your community cheers for that put him at risk—be it football, lacrosse, wrestling, or ice hockey.

Becoming a man is associated with power. But once we teach our son to not cry, he learns to be ashamed of his feelings, and therefore of his nature. That shame undermines his health. When a boy learns to both undermine his health and psychologically distance himself from himself, he doesn't have real power. He is a hero without himself. Preparation for becoming a statue, not a person.

There is now less need for our sons to die for us to survive. We have finally reached a point in history when parenting for manhood can integrate parenting for heroism with parenting for health. We can integrate the healthiest aspects of traditional heroic intelligence to make it part of the package of emotional and physical health intelligence. But before your son can pursue the healthy parts of masculinity, we need to take a deeper dive into the power of social bribes to prevent your son from even considering what is healthy.

Social Bribes: Hollywood—Heroic Health Versus Mental and Physical Health

Hollywood is a potent voice among the sirens of your son's social bribes. For Halloween, among his top choices for costumes may be Spider-Man and Teenage Mutant Ninja Turtles. His masks, capes, and "weapons" shout "Respect me!" and "Fear me!"[8]

What is the subliminal message Hollywood sends? First, that a hero must so fully sacrifice himself that others only recognize his facade as a quasi-human doing, not himself as a fully human being. That is, others recognize Superman, but no one knows the real Clark Kent. And even Lois Lane is only interested in him as Clark Kent after she discovers he is Superman. Similarly, others recognize the quasi-human doing Batman, but not the human being Bruce Wayne; they recognize the quasi-human doing Spider-Man, but not the human being Peter Parker. As a Ninja Turtle, your son learns subliminally that he is to complete heroic missions aboveground, but live belowground: that is, the human being need not be known, either to others or even to himself.

Hollywood's message for your son is that a hero is never fully integrated within himself.[9] He lives a double life. James Bond is anonymous to himself.

Your son absorbs, then, a gap between his heroic health and his mental and physical health. And to the degree we don't know him as a human being, that human part of himself is less missed if his heroic acts in real life do result in him losing his life. His anonymity allows us to be less guilty about his disposability.

But wait. With Hollywood increasingly producing female heroines, does this mean that the new female heroine will prove herself a heroine by risking her life to save the men she loves? Or, at the very least, that your son will no longer be expected to risk his life for her love?

Let's look at what your son may unconsciously discover, and how you can help him bring it to the conscious level so he can make conscious choices.

Does the New Heroine Mean Your Son Won't Have to Risk His Life for Her Love?

Before we begin, one caveat: Each family member will see the same movie differently—which is what makes movies like these perfect catalysts for great family dinner night discussions (see appendix).

Let's start with *Star Wars: The Force Awakens*. (Spoilers below—but if you haven't seen it by now, you probably don't care!)

In *The Force Awakens* your son sees that the former Princess Leia is now a general. Yet Han Solo, not the heroine as general, is the one who dies in the process of attempting to fill General Leia's request to bring their son home.

As for your son's lessons in finding love, when the male lead and easily presumed romantic interest Finn takes Rey's hand to help save her, she chastises him for taking her hand without asking. Punishment for taking a woman's hand without first asking for and receiving consent is now the law on college campuses in many states. It is called "affirmative consent"—that a young man needs to ask for verbal or written permission before he touches a young woman. (The law is gender-neutral, but really . . . !)

How could the scene have been handled that would have encouraged your son to respect a woman more than seeing a male hero being chastised by a female heroine for taking her hand to potentially save her life? First, Finn being thanked by Rey. And second, if Finn later reaches for Rey's hand and she is ambivalent or not interested, seeing Rey say something to the effect of "I appreciate your interest, but I'd prefer to not hold hands. *I promise that if I change my mind, I'll initiate.*" Since Rey already knows Finn is interested, her risk of rejection would be close to none. Then your son would see Rey taking responsibility for what she desires rather than just chastising Finn when he tries to save her.

If Hollywood were really progressive, how might it have developed the scene to allow your son to feel that a strong woman is one who shares equal responsibility for protecting him and equal responsibility for risking rejection? First, by instead having Rey reach out for Finn's hand as she tries to save his life. And second, by showing Rey as more romantically interested in Finn than he was in her, but nevertheless initiating and risking his rejection of her.

At the end of *The Force Awakens*, Finn lies in a coma facing possible death after being thrashed in a lightsaber battle—to ward off a threat to Rey, in whom he clearly remains romantically interested. Rey is unscarred; Finn is rewarded with a kiss on the forehead.

In the old Hollywood fiction movies, the man who risks his life for a woman's love is almost always rewarded with her love. As opposed to a kiss on the forehead. The message your son may absorb is that a young man today cannot possibly do enough to please a woman who is already super powerful.

The problem? **If your son is unclear as to what a highly powerful woman wants from him, he is more likely to go for a woman who is less powerful who has some need for him**. In the meantime, your son sees little variety among his heroes and heroines about what different women and men want and need from each other.

The male hero's kryptonite

Female superheroes, like their male counterparts, have physical strength, mental acuity, and sexual allure. But unlike their male counterparts, they are without the Achilles' heel of virtually every male hero: sexual neediness. Every James Bond, past and present, has a sexual neediness that often leads to him being sidetracked and putting both his mission and himself in jeopardy. But Rey, for example, expressed no sexual neediness. Finn did. The Hunger Games trilogy reveals the same pattern: its heroine, Katniss, was not interested in a romantic relationship. Peeta and Gale were. **The female superhero's lack of sexual neediness makes her a "super" superpower.**

Hollywood plants the seeds for male-only draft registration

We saw the heavy price your son pays if he does not register for the draft. Hollywood plants the seeds for your son's acceptance of only males signing up to potentially risk their lives not being an option but an obligation. From *Star Wars'* seven episodes in aggregate your son may subliminally surmise that **if the life of a beloved woman—whether romantic partner or mother—is at risk, his life is at risk.** His first job is to save her life. He is born male. That's what he signs—or rather, is signed—up for.

Suppose he does risk his life to protect a woman, but fails? Your son witnesses Anakin Skywalker's transformation into Darth Vader when Skywalker was unable to rescue his mother from death. The message: **Even if your son tries to use his power to save a woman, if he fails, that power will implode**, becoming an anger that festers and sucks him into the dark side.

How male and female heroes die: Let me count the ways

The biggest male stars are allowed to die for your children's entertainment, as with Han Solo. Or be left in a coma, as with Finn—with the movie ending without your son knowing whether he will live. Uncertainty about his future life is OK *if* the star is a male. None of the female stars die—or are left in comas.

In contrast, when a recent female fictional character *is* killed in a Hollywood movie, it almost always occurs for one of two reasons:

- **She killed other (good) women** and therefore was a force for evil—not a "real" woman.
- She is being used so that the movie can focus on men being killed to avenge her death. In this case, in fictional Hollywood movies she will almost always **be killed within her *first three significant appearances*,** so you develop a little attachment to her, but not too much.

Now, though, a third, more insidious, reason is rising like a phoenix out of Hollywood fiction: **if a good woman is killed, a man is to blame.** For example, in *The Hunger Games: Mockingjay—Part II*, the plan of the male character, Gale, to help win the war did not follow the advice of the woman he loved, Katniss. The result? Prim, a good woman and Katniss's sister, was killed. Although Gale risked his life to save Katniss's sister (and the rest of Panem), he did not follow Katniss's plan. He could not be forgiven; he lost Katniss' love.

FAMILY DINNER NIGHT
Hollywood—Image Versus Reality

Here are some starter questions for family dinner night. Before you begin, revisit the images of the one man viewed four ways in appendix A:

1. What dilemmas does your son's sexual neediness create for your son?
2. In which Hollywood fiction movies have heroines who appear in more than three significant scenes been killed? In which ones have their male equivalents been killed?
3. Is *The Hunger Games: Mockingjay—Part II*'s message to your son that he must not only risk death to protect a beloved woman, but if he doesn't follow the woman's way of doing it, he will lose her love? Or is the new message that the woman's plan is more likely to be right than his? If so, does this send your son the message that he's still valuable for risking his life, but a woman has the superior mind?
4. What messages do other movies send about what it takes to earn the love of the other sex?

In real life, you will want your son to both listen and be listened to. How, then, can your son keep the best of heroic intelligence while avoiding the restraints of heroic intelligence in order to create health intelligence?

Transforming Heroic Intelligence into Health Intelligence

When Cody asked his dad, Ryan, if he could walk to the school to pick up a game of basketball or something, his mom cautioned, "I've heard stories there's a rough crowd that hangs out there." But his dad persuaded his mom to let him go.

When Cody arrived, a pickup game was underway. It was apparent to Cody that some of the guys had been drinking. When Cody asked if he could join the game, one of the better players, on the JV team, teased that they'd prefer a bottle, but OK. When Cody was offered some swigs, he accepted so he'd be accepted.

As Cody saw that the game was as much "fouling practice" as a game, he felt nervous. He missed his first few shots—the last one was an airball. The guy who had said he'd prefer a bottle to Cody mocked, "Hey, the team that has Cody gets a handicap." Another chimed in, "You mean a 'Codycap'!" Right after that, the same guy purposely fouled him. Cody released his pent-up anger with a fierce punch, fracturing a bone in his own hand.

Cody panicked and ran home. His mom started to get ready to take him to the emergency room, but his dad said he'd take responsibility, since he had been the one to persuade her to let Cody go. While they were waiting for Cody to be attended to, Cody gave his version of what went down. When Cody volunteered he had accepted the drink as a way to be accepted, Ryan, to make sure Cody did not feel shamed, empathized by sharing his story of when he had done the same thing in high school.

Then, Ryan asked Cody to recount the "top five" red flags he had detected prior to the fight. Ryan asked Cody in a tone of voice that made the "top five" seem like a game. Cody eventually concluded: the drinking; being told the guys would prefer a bottle to him; the game looking more like "fouling practice"; the escalation of the mocking; and being purposely fouled. Ryan eventually asked Cody what he would do differently if a similar situation were to occur in the future. Although Cody had missed heeding his mom's caution to avoid the school, his dad was able to turn the experience into a teachable moment.

Health Intelligence Inventory

Teachable moments on the pathway to your son's health intelligence are nurtured by mom and dad as a crockpot, not mom and dad as a microwave. Since what's *in* the crockpot also counts, take this health intelligence inventory by giving yourself one point if you've tried to teach the following to your son—two points if he's absorbed it!

(continued on next page)

My son has been taught/learned to:

___ respond to an insult with respect rather than with another insult, a fist, or a gun.

___ leave electronics behind at family dinner.

___ consider playing flag football rather than tackle, even if his parents are less likely to come to the game and there are no cheerleaders.

___ have the courage to refuse to get drunk or to excessively haze or be hazed in order to "belong," as with a fraternity.

___ check in with himself as to what would uniquely make him happier—for example, being a third-grade teacher, or an engineer.

___ have the courage to refuse to jump off a cliff into a stream even as boys are calling him "chicken" and a girl he has a crush on is watching.

___ refrain from racing a car, or racing down a dangerous, unknown slope on skis.

___ spend about as much time with his dad as his mom—especially if he is a child of divorce.

___ associate being a man with salad as much as with barbeque.

___ never hesitate to ask for help.

___ never ignore a concussion in order to "win" peer respect, parental pride, or a girl's "love."

___ respect, but never glamorize, a hazardous job with "elite" status (e.g., Navy SEAL; Special Forces; astronaut; CIA Special Operations).*

___ understand that many people offering a social bribe respect someone who has the courage to quietly articulate why giving in to the pressure doesn't work for him.

___ expect himself and a woman friend to protect each other rather than expect himself to be an "unpaid body guard."

It's a tough test—if you scored a ten, you're doing well.

---

*If your son wants, for example, to be an astronaut, it does not imply low health intelligence if he's making sure that the reason he's doing it is not a result of social bribes.

Boys' Weakness as Their Facade of Strength

In my freshman year in high school, I aspired to earn my way onto the varsity track team. At an early practice session of the half mile, I spotted the coach watching. At the sound of the starter gun, I immediately jumped out in front of the other runners—including our best. But the coach seemed less than impressed. I soon petered out. Coach Foster, wiser than I, quietly took me aside: "Pace yourself. Save your strength, then explode with your speed at the end."

As I integrated his save-my-strength strategy and dropped my facade-of-strength strategy, I experienced less weakness and more strength. In the process, I had learned as much about my weakness being my facade of strength as about running.

I had no trouble learning this strategy not because I was special but because I was like every other boy: I wanted the best formula for crossing the finish line first. I needed an authority figure to care enough to take me aside and reinforce what my dad had told me but that didn't sink in until I had lost in real life by ignoring it.

That a facade of strength weakens boys and men is affirmed by science. Each time a frequent rescuer, like a firefighter, responds to an emergency, his testosterone increases, which weakens his immune system. [10] His adrenaline (or epinephrine) also spikes, which makes him vulnerable to blood clotting, and therefore to heart failure.

When your son feels pain, he's more likely than your daughter to "tough it out" and less likely than your daughter to go to the doctor. But if he finally does go, although his situation is by that time more likely to be severe, he is nevertheless less likely to follow up on the doctor's instructions,[11] including advice to avoid strength-depleting activities such as drinking and consuming a lot of sweets. As a result, our sons are 62 percent more likely to have to be readmitted to a hospital than our daughters.[12] His weakness is his facade of strength.

Why do boys do this? **We have taught boys that, while building strength is considered masculine, preventing its loss is feminine.** Thus, moderating drinking and sweets, getting to bed early, pacing ourselves, crying, going to a therapist to reduce stress—all of which can prevent your son from losing the strength he has worked so hard to acquire—have less "cred."

The solution? Make it your contribution on family dinner nights and in other teachable moments to help him contemplate a paradigm shift in what it means to be a man.

Manning Up: A New Paradigm

A boy increases strength by building it up.
A man increases strength both by building it up and preventing its loss.

A boy thinks his facade of strength is his strength.
A man doesn't need a facade.

A boy "toughs it out" by blocking out his weakness.
A man knows that finding his weakness takes strength and is the first step both to adding to his strength and preventing its loss.

Is it really possible to get this new paradigm into the head of a boy obsessed with proving himself? Yes. But it is not easy. It is parents versus a myriad of social bribes. Versus political leadership that doesn't "man up." Which is why parents are paramount.

While the journey from boy to man was not designed to make a man live for long, it *was* designed to make a man strong. So let's look at the social bribes of traditional masculinity that can *enhance* your son's health.

Health-Enhancing Social Bribes

Using "The Tough Get Going" to Enhance Health

Almost everything the chorus of social bribes teaches your son to do are virtues that get taken to the extreme and become vices. For example, when the mantra "When the going gets tough, the tough get going" is linked to male heroism, we bribe our sons to take "the tough get going" to its extreme. Should your son not become the one-in-a-million male who achieves heroic status, he can be disappointed in himself.

In balance, though, "the tough get going" mantra can teach your son to persist after missing a game-defining layup in basketball; after breaking a leg skiing; or after being rejected, whether in a job interview or on Match.com. In these cases "the tough get going" mantra does more than help him reengage. It also:

- expands the synapses of his brain as he searches for new ways to succeed.
- embeds in his brain a memory of when he has successfully reengaged, and how he did it—creating, in a sense, his own emotional rehab center.
- increases his dopamine and his stamina as he searches for the motivation and energy to reengage.
- assures him that he can hold his own among his peers, which encourages him to be more social.
- facilitates his transition from a boy whose parents will fix it to a man who can fix it himself.
- enhances his self-respect.

So how will your son know when to stop and when to continue? By tuning in, not out. Once a boy sees becoming a man not as tuning out his pain but tuning in to it, he becomes open to making more nuanced decisions. For example, he can substitute "no pain, no gain" with, as yoga master Iyengar taught, distinguishing between pain that deepens his strength and pain that weakens his strength. Pain he experiences when his body is not active is pain that needs attention. When a boy experiences some pain when he's mindfully working with his body to reach his "edge," that's "good" pain—pain that deepens strength, until he reaches his "edge." Tuning in to his "edge" is the baby that needs to be kept as the bathwater is drained.

Not Holding a Grudge

Jim slid into second base. Ralph, the shortstop, called him "out." Jim said, "No way . . . You're blind." The shortstop insisted that Jim was, in fact, out, and that Jim was a cheater. The dugout on Jim's team unloaded, with everyone insisting Jim was safe. The other team's dugout also unloaded, insisting Jim was, in fact, out. Soon shouting turned into shoving.

The following afternoon, Marty slid into second base. Jim and Ralph were now on the same side—playing second baseman and shortstop—and both called Marty "out." Marty insisted he was safe. This time both Jim and Ralph were calling *Marty* "blind."

After years of playing on opposite sides one day, and the same side the next, it never occurred to either Jim or Ralph to hold a grudge. They would never have put it this way, but they both intuitively understood that "where you stand depends on where you sit."

The aspect of heroic intelligence that encourages competing in pickup games, during which the sides are constantly changing, helps boys learn that disagreements—even swearing and shoving—are often a function of role. They are not to be taken personally. Holding a grudge today will undermine your ability to be a teammate tomorrow.

How do we know this benefit accrues to boys? Studies of videos of men and women from forty-four countries playing sports—from table tennis to boxing—find that after the game male opponents spent more time talking with each other, patting each other on the back, and embracing each other than did female opponents. Even the male-to-male handshakes were warmer and tighter than the female ones, which were described as "frosty."[13]

This study, by Joyce Berenson of Harvard, was inspired by similar studies of male chimpanzees, who would fight one day and work together the next. Berenson also cited studies showing that "when two females compete in the workplace, they feel much more damaged afterward."[14]

When boys get into conflicts, parents tend to break them up and teachers tend to exact a punishment. But a positive aspect of heroic intelligence is the tendency of boys and men to "fight with their all" but not hold grudges afterward—to sense that the source of the conflict is different roles and goals, not a bad person.

Boys are more likely to treat life as a game—whether in virtual worlds or the real world—and know that today's opponent may be tomorrow's partner.

Preserving the best of traditional masculinity should be a priority of parents because your son is preoccupied with the paradox of learning how to simultaneously fit in and stand out. Guiding your son through masculinity's virtues before they become vices can help your son resolve that paradox in a way that suits his personality.

This is no easy task: the social bribes that prepare your son for heroic intelligence are so deeply embedded that very little about your son's body is his choice—and often, not *your* conscious choice, either. Since a choice that is not conscious is not a choice, let's dig deeper into those social bribes so you have choices for your son that your parents did not have for you.

Your Son's Body, Not His Choice

There was never a time when your daughter did not hear "a woman's body, a woman's choice."

There was never a time when your son heard "a man's body, a man's choice."

There's a reason for that. Had your son heard "a man's body, a man's choice," your daughter might not have had a body about which she could make a choice. That is, our daughters' lives—all of our lives—were dependent on our sons' requirement to risk theirs.

It all begins when he begins . . .

Circumcision: To Cut In, or Cut Out?

> *Before my son was circumcised, he was a calm, peaceful baby. After he was circumcised, he was very different.*
>
> —A frequent parental comment reported by Dr. Vanessa Dahn, Founder of Safe Landing[15]

Were these boys' transformations from calm to "different" a result of the circumcision? Until recently, we didn't know. Few cultures cared enough to ask. We just did it. Thus, in the United States, about three-quarters of newborn boys are circumcised—usually *without* anesthetics. (Anesthetics are considered dangerous for a newborn.) Worldwide, billions of infant boys' blood-curdling screams mark their protests, but, nevertheless, they're circumcised. A boy's body, not his choice.

Yet some countries—and medical associations—are rethinking circumcision. The Denmark Medical Association says circumcision should not be performed under eighteen: it should be a young man's choice.[16]

What is male circumcision about? The more a society prepares its boys for disposability, especially in war, the greater the role circumcision plays in that preparation. Circumcision is the primal preparation for disposability.

In many warrior societies, such as the Maasai (of Kenya and Tanzania), a boy is still not considered a man until he is circumcised *shortly after puberty*.[17] The boy must first exhaust himself by herding cattle for seven consecutive days, and then on the eighth, he takes a cold shower, and marches in the cold weather to the place of circumcision. On the way, he is exposed to both social bribes of encouragement, and social pressure such as being threatened with death if he runs away from the knife. Then, with *no anesthesia*, he becomes a man only if he *does not flinch* as his penis is sliced open.

If the boy fails this test, which proves his preparedness for physical disposability, he is socially disposable. Social disposability means failing to gain the respect of those he respects. Which implies either not being eligible to marry, or at least not being able to marry one of the community's desirable women. Ironically, the boys who are the most disposable physically can compete for the girls who are the least disposable socially. In this way, the disposable males and the desirable females create the next generation's disposable males and desirable females.

In the twenty-first century, the Maasai have stopped circumcising girls, but not boys. For girls, the practice had a different goal: to desensitize them to sexual pleasure so their sexual desires did not influence their choice of mate. (Which also means they would have less desire to give the males sexual pleasure.)

Now here's the rub. I asserted that preparing boys for pain in preparation for heroic disposability is so integral to many cultures that until recently very few studies ever asked the crucial question: Does circumcision have any negative impact on a boy's life? Now we know it does.

If your son is circumcised, preliminary research on three hundred men suggests he may have about a 20 percent greater chance than intact boys of experiencing alexithymia,[18] a condition that makes it difficult not just to express feelings, but to identify them to begin with. Boys with alexithymia tend to have less imagination and intuition. In practice, this also tends to mean they have less empathy. With less empathy, there is less intimacy—they are likely to have fewer real friends.

At moderate to high levels, alexithymia can also inhibit your son's ability to respond to therapy, the same process that would help allow him to express feelings and increase empathy. And as a circumcised boy with alexithymia gets older, he may be more than four times as likely to use a drug to counter erectile dysfunction.

The percentage of adults suffering from alexithymia is estimated at between 10 and 28 percent, depending on the study.[19]

Circumcision shortly after birth is also considered by many research-ers to cause neonatal trauma, which is linked to aggressive behavior both toward others and toward oneself—as in suicide.[20]

Knowing that our failure to study the impact of circumcision ema-nates from our not questioning male disposability will hopefully free you to study the pros and cons without assuming that because most Ameri-cans do it, there must be a good reason. It may be "your son's body, not his choice," but it can be your choice.

"First and Ten, Concussion Again!"

"First and ten, do it again!" cheerleaders yell. They might as well yell, "First and ten, concussion again!"

Until recently, the NFL denied any connection between playing foot-ball and brain injury. But in 2017 the *Journal of the American Medical Association* (*JAMA*) published the findings that more than 99 percent of the former NFL players whose brains were examined at autopsy suf-fered from chronic traumatic encephalopathy (CTE), a neurodegenerative disease that can lead to dementia.[21]

That's the NFL. If your son gets involved in football, his chances of becoming a professional player are low. But what about college football? The *JAMA* study found that **among former college players, 56 percent suffered from severe CTE pathology, which was associated with signs of dementia 85 percent of the time.**[22]

About three million boys between the ages of five and sixteen par-ticipate in youth league football such as Pop Warner Little Scholars.[23] And it is when your son is of Pop Warner age that he is most likely to ignore the danger of a concussion, sometimes returning to the field within twenty-four hours.[24]

The danger with your son returning to the field too early—or perhaps at all—is the multiplier effect: each concussion weakens his resistance to the next. By high school, one-third of players report two or more concussions *per season*.[25] And if your son experiences three or more concussions *total*, the risk of suffering a reduced ability to form new memories increases more than fivefold.[26]

Concussions are linked to the thinning of brain tissue. In addition to undermining memory, brain tissue thinning is associated with an inability to sustain attention and, perhaps most important, a loss of executive function. New research on college players shows that this brain damage remains for years after their final college game.[27]

With this much danger, why would anyone "in his right mind" play football? Mind you, I say this as someone who took my coach's side when he tried to persuade my dad to let me be the kicker for our high school team. Although I had other sources of acknowledgment, I wasn't about to refuse more! Fortunately (only in retrospect), my dad won, and it was a boundary he enforced. But many dads play a different role . . .

Remember how invisible Jack felt when his dad kept "son-dropping" at his brother's football games, boasting that the boy who just caught the pass was his son, Jack's brother Kyle? To this day, Jack recalls how when his dad *did* introduce him to those near him in the stands, there was no excitement in his dad's voice—not like there was when he talked about Kyle. Jack recalls, "I felt like the 'extra baggage' son."

Because boys experience the cheers of parents, friends, and cheerleaders prior to the age of consent, these sirens of social bribes become a straightjacket of social bribes that reinforce consciously the message sent by circumcision unconsciously: "My body, not my choice."

Even if one school medically disqualifies your son because of repeat concussions, investigations find that this won't stop another school from recruiting him.[28] At Syracuse University, when A. J. Long suffered his third concussion, the doctor ordered him sidelined, saying that his situation predicted an increased risk of dementia by age forty-five. Six other universities immediately pursued Long. If your son has developed heroic intelligence but hasn't learned from you to balance it with health intelligence, he won't learn to do so in college. Few colleges will put your son's health over their glory.

If you are having trouble getting your son to absorb his potential risk, take an evening to gather the family around the movie *Concussion*.

Based on a true story of the NFL's denial of concussion research, when the gifted high school tight end John Castello watched it, he was alarmed to the tune of turning down twelve full football scholarships to colleges like Holy Cross.

Decisions like John Castello's are so rare because collectively **we teach boys to associate being abused with being loved**—whether adolescent circumcision among the Maasai, or football among the Americans. Other boys support this; parents and teachers support this; taxpayer money supports this (meaning we all support this). And, oh yes, girls support this . . .

When your pubescent son is transfixed as the high kicks of his school's most beautiful girls call the gaze of his eyes beneath their skirts, he yearns to fulfill their siren call—"First and ten, do it again!" He may need your help for what's lost in translation: "First and ten, risk a concussion again."

Flag Football: "Use Your Head. No, Not That One."

Football is perhaps the game most brilliantly designed to prepare your son for life. It requires mastering a multitude of complex plays, yet, as one player after the other is either tackled, blocked, or veers off course, he needs to create or adjust to a new play in a nanosecond—a play that is somehow coordinated with everyone else. The infinite possibilities for improvement require constant postgame review and, yes, introspection. Virtually every player needs a combination of physical strength, mental flexibility, and an ego secure enough to focus on the team before himself. If a boy's initial gifts are less than extraordinary, physical and mental discipline, plus a team spirit, can allow him to add value. And that's just for starters.

The question is, Is there a way to retain the game *and* your son's body and brain?

Yes. Football's body-and-brain depleter is tackling. Tackling is the cause of more than two-thirds of football's catastrophic injuries.[29] But football without tackle—flag football—is growing quickly, and with the support of the NFL.

Like tackle football, flag football uses both the mind and the body. But there's a difference: **tackle football is a *body*-mind sport; flag football is a *mind*-body sport.**

By eliminating tackling, flag football may preserve your son's body and brain. But I wondered whether it provided the same outlet for boys' energy. To get some insight, I arranged to get up close and personal with a team that was practicing in San Francisco for the 2016 national championship for NFL-sponsored flag football. The team was Mo Steel.

As Mo Steel was practicing, I learned that their exceptional quarterback, Will Poses, was a high school freshman who switched on and off between playing flag and tackle football. I asked Will's mom, Sarah, to share the biggest difference she observed about Will's tackle versus touch experiences. She knew immediately: **"Flag football is so much more about strategy. You can't 'take someone out' with your body, so it's more about your mind."**

"Does the loss of physicality deprive the boys of some of their bonding?" I asked.

Sarah pointed to the boy playing center. "He's played touch ball with Will since they were both eight years old. They can tell what the other needs just by the way they breathe."

Will loved both versions of the game. But Sarah and Will's dad were experiencing a dilemma about whether to support Will in playing tackle football in his sophomore year.

I empathized with that dilemma. I mentioned above how, as a high school student, I sided with my coach's desire to have me be the team's punter and kicker for points after touchdowns—as opposed to my father's objection that, as a 6'1" and 149-pound beanstalk, I'd either be bad enough to be ignored, or good enough to be worth being crushed by a 250-pound guy.

Each year something happens that triggers my appreciation of my dad fighting both the coach and me—what I now see as fighting for me. For example, after my wife, Liz, and I bought a three-story home, the owner, who was in his sixties, was graciously giving us a more intimate tour when I noticed he was limping up the stairs. With sadness, he volunteered, "I was hoping to live in this home until my wife or I died, but I got too many knee injuries from high school football, and the three stories are more than I can handle."

The difference between then and now was that when I went to high school neither the NFL nor my high school sponsored flag football. And most probably, neither does your son's high school. But today, with the NFL's support, that can change.

Will Your Son's School Adopt Flag Football?

If you approach your son's school to adopt flag football, you'll find your arguments will resonate with many educators. The passion of educators is to develop students' minds; tackle football risks students' minds. Most educators will also agree that it's a bit of a mixed message to punish boys who wrestle on the playground and then cheer for them to bang heads on the football field.

The most practical approach with your son's school does not involve asking them to forfeit tackle football. It can *supplement* tackle football with flag football teams that are all male, all female, and coed. And you and your school can do it at virtually no cost, with the help of the NFL Flag division.[30] (The fact that it's an NFL-sponsored option suggests that the NFL is preparing for a new definition of masculinity—while simultaneously offering flag football the credibility of the NFL's "manliness.")

However, if your son's high school is so slow to respond that you fear your son will have graduated before there's a change, discuss with an attorney this legal approach: **tackle football is using taxpayer money to risk the minds and bodies of only our *sons* before the age of consent.** That arguably makes it a violation of the Fourteenth Amendment's "equal protection" clause—the clause from which emanates the civil rights legislation that guarantees the equal protection of minorities, and Title IX legislation to protect the equal rights of women. Now it may be time to use it to protect our sons' bodies and minds.

The goal is not to sue your son's school, but sometimes the threat of a lawsuit creates an incentive for an institution to cut through the red tape—in this case, before your son graduates. Should you take this approach, don't just do it for your son, do it *with* your son—so that he'll learn from it whether the effort succeeds or fails. This implies that before you do this, your son is on board. If he is scared off by social bribes—such as, "What, *fag* football?"—you've got to first deal with his vulnerability to social bribes. Only then can you create teachable moments for both your son's school and your son.

The availability of a flag football *option* encourages your son's body to be your son's choice. When the use of his body becomes a conscious choice in high school, you've laid the groundwork for making his next decision conscious as well: to join the military, or not.

My Son Wants to Join the Military. Is This Good News or Bad News?

The most potent message to your son that it's his body, but not his choice, is male-only draft registration and the life-altering array of penalties should he fail to register (see chapter 9). Yet, should your son announce that he *wants* to join the military, chances are you'll have mixed emotions . . .

The military offers the discipline that dad-deprived boys suffering from lack of boundary enforcement tend to need. So if your son could benefit from discipline, but you don't wish him to come home either in a body bag or alive on the outside but traumatized on the inside, how can you help him have the "best of both worlds?"

First, make sure he understands that **even if a soldier lives, the risks of war come home with the warrior—that for every soldier killed, about twenty-five veterans kill themselves.**[31] Share with him the stories of young men like Michael Yurchison of Ohio, who was motivated by 9/11 to protect his country. Although he came home alive on the outside, when his mom joyfully greeted him at the plane after his discharge, she soon realized she was greeting, well . . . "it was like he was an empty shell."[32] He began drinking, doing drugs, and sleeping with the same type of gun that had been his sleeping partner in Iraq. Tragically, for Michael, like so many veterans, serving his country was followed by his country failing to serve him. His efforts to receive help were met largely by delay and dismissiveness of his psychological torture.

If your son remains interested, there are specific ways he can lower his risk. First, he is likely to be a *lot* safer in the air force, navy, or army than in the marines.

Second, avoiding the *elites* of the air force, navy, and army (e.g., Green Berets/Army Special Forces, Army Rangers, Navy SEALs, Air Force Pararescue) will vastly decrease your son's likelihood of both death and coming home "alive but dead."[33]

Here's where your sowing seeds about how "social bribes" prime boys and men for disposability can reap benefits. Being seen as an "elite" is a social bribe for your son to risk death, PTSD, or brain damage. **The more your son wishes to be part of the elite, the more he will abhor being pitied. Yet boys who join the elite today are often the ones who are pitied tomorrow.**

Your Son's Body, Your Son's Choice: Resisting the Sirens of Social Bribes

Here's the big question: Since we still need to fight ISIS, build skyscrapers and underwater tunnels, clean out sewer systems, and protect our homes from fire, if we teach our sons to resist the sirens of social bribes and make his own choice, do we forfeit these benefits?

Mostly no. But the more your son values himself, the more he will want to be paid in order to take these risks and jobs. And the more he will want his safety protected (e.g., safer oil rigs, as in *Deepwater Horizon*). Introducing your son to each of the sirens that are meant to seduce him into disposability as heroism doesn't mean he won't become a soldier, or construction worker, or firefighter. He's still free to be a soldier by choice. He just won't be a soldier by bribe. He will have the same type of choice your daughter has. (Your daughter is not told, "You'll be more *feminine* if you are a marine.")

How do we do this? Topher is a good example . . .

Seventeen-year-old Topher was in awe as a squadron of air force fighter jets flew in perfect formation over the Super Bowl arena as the high notes of "The Star-Spangled Banner" reached their peak and the cameras focused on marines in resplendent uniforms framing their serenely confident faces.

Topher's dad, a high school teacher, noticed his son's transfixed body language. Topher was nearing graduation and was considering college versus other options. His dad could see Topher's awe leading him in the direction of the military, perhaps Annapolis. His dad did not say anything, knowing he couldn't hold a candle to Topher's anticipation of the Super Bowl game.

On the next family dinner night, though, Topher's dad brought up the Super Bowl and asked Topher if he could identify any social pressures to be in the military that Topher had noticed during the Super Bowl.

Topher had not thought about it, but when asked, he lit up. "Those jets soaring over in unison were awesome . . ."

"Yeah," his dad agreed. "Anything else?"

"Well, maybe how confident all those marines looked—I don't have that confidence, and maybe they're just pretending, I don't know, but it made me think that being a marine or in the air force or something could also give me that confidence."

With a little help from his dad, Topher was also able to identify the power of "The Star-Spangled Banner" and the majesty of the marines' uniforms.

His dad then asked if he saw any connection between the military, the Super Bowl, and the cheerleaders.

"Huh," Topher muttered, "I guess that the best-looking girls cheer for the toughest guys?"

Topher's dad listened, then added, "And perhaps, 'If you cannot make it as one the world's best football players, you can still be a real man that women will desire by being in the marines or air force?'"

"I never thought of it like that!" Topher laughed.

Topher and his dad bonded over their ability to see how the jets, uniforms, patriotic music, confident faces, cheerleaders, and the ceremony were, in essence, a confluence of social pressures—a choir made up of the sirens of social bribes.

Caveat: Even if your son can identify each siren intellectually, he is unlikely to be able to resist them unless he is blessed with two support systems:

- The love and support of both his parents. Without it, social bribes flourish in the fertile ground of your son's emotional void.
- Boundary enforcement that fosters the discipline required to perform well in school and sports, and to master social skills, so social bribes aren't needed to make him feel he's worth something.

With these foundations, your son is freer to explore his potential for making social contributions in non-life-risking ways: whether as a healthcare worker, IT guy, sous chef, teacher, or a full-time dad. He may still choose a profession that risks his life, but then it will be your son's body, your son's choice.

CHAPTER 24

Emotional Intelligence and Mental Health

Heroic intelligence teaches a man to kill, not to listen: to repress feelings, not express feelings; to take risks more than assess risks; to fake confidence rather than acknowledge fear; to pretend he knows what he doesn't know; to not ask for help—from parents, from peers, from God, from therapists, from his partner, from . . .

Each of these had a purpose. If a man faked confidence and pretended to know what he didn't know, although he might be killed, he could die as a leader, not as a follower—perhaps as a hero, not as a loser. And until he died he would have hope of respect, love, and sex—better than benign neglect and being both the hundredth choice of his wife's fantasy life, and her being the hundredth choice of his.

The price of heroic intelligence on a boy's emotional intelligence is even greater than the price of heroic intelligence on his physical health intelligence. The great majority of physical health problems—whether a broken leg, virus, or poor diet—are easier to resolve than the problems resulting from a lack of emotional intelligence. For example, taking unassessed risks and faking confidence can lead to the greater propensity of boys to be diagnosed with disorderly conduct,[1] which is linked with antisocial personality disorder, aggression and violence, repetitive lying, theft, destruction of property, and conflicts with authority.[2] The cumulative results of a lack of emotional intelligence, such as the boy-to-girl ratio of fourteen to one in correctional institutions among eighteen- to twenty-one-year-olds,[3] haunt a boy for the rest of his life.

In addition to these mandates of manhood that damage boys' emotional intelligence, four other major contributors multiply that damage: father absence, physical abuse by parents, verbal abuse by parents, and parental neglect. The challenge is minimizing those problems before they minimize our sons.

As a parent, you do more than see your son's vulnerability. You feel it. But few others do, because his method of dealing with vulnerability—acting out, anger, delinquency—distract us from his vulnerability. And distract him from his vulnerability. And as a parent, **you can easily feel judged and alone if you are the only one to understand that your son's anger is the mask of his vulnerability.**

The Barriers to a Boy's Emotional Intelligence

A Boy's "Compassion Void"

Most boys experience a "compassion void." Why? For starters, boys' peers rarely listen; boys resist church, its fellowship, and the faith that someone will always hear him and love him; they resist therapy and its confidential disclosure that reduces isolation and alienation; and a boy senses that revealing insecurities to a potential girlfriend is only appealing if his Lois Lane first sees him as Superman, not as Clark Kent. And yes, that's just for starters.

As a boy's journey enters the road toward manhood, he discovers (if he is heterosexual) that the girls he is attracted to and the boys he befriends have different ways of communicating the same message to him.

He notices, usually unconsciously, that should he express fears or complain about a problem, a potential girlfriend hears whining. And girls fall in love with alpha men, not whining men.

Guys, on the other hand, give him a maximum thirty-second window of opportunity to air a fear or complaint, after which he opens himself to ridicule, and a loss of peer respect.

In short, he notices that complaining doesn't generate empathy; it generates pity. Or loss of respect. He absorbs that both sexes' experience of him complaining is the same: like hearing nails scrape on a chalkboard.

So he stops listening to his own complaints as well—hearing himself would make him feel less of himself.

In contrast, should a boy hear the girl that he's interested in complain, he sees an *opportunity*: an opportunity for him to solve her problem, to "rescue" her. His hope? To be rewarded with her respect, and with the slice of her love that emanates from her respect. And, oh yes, with the invitation for his body to be part of hers.

To whom can a boy express his feelings without either losing status among his peers or getting advice that he feels is often accompanied by a loss in respect? Often, no one.

His best chance for empathy is from his mom. How is it that a mom can hear her son express fears, but his potential girlfriend cannot? Because **when a potential girlfriend hears a guy complain, it violates her instinct to *be* protected; but when a mom hears her *son* complain, it triggers her instinct *to* protect.**

With his dad it's a little different. His dad is likely to empathetically protect him until he reaches an age where dad expects him to start acting like a man. And then, even though dad's heart may empathize, he fears that too much empathy will decrease his son's ability to be tough enough to be respected and loved. So he helps his son create a mask he feels his son will need to be respected as a man who can provide for his family, even as he desperately wants to experience the vulnerable and sweet boy hidden beneath his mask.

So how do we get behind the mask boys live in—the mask of masculinity?

Behind your son's mask: Filling the "compassion void"

New research reveals that a parent's **compassionate listening positively affects the development of an adolescent's brain in a way that** *affects the rest of his or her life.*[4] When twelve-year-olds with argumentative and angry moms were compared at age sixteen to those with moms who were warm, affectionate, and approving in the face of disagreements, the sixteen-year-olds with the affectionate moms showed *changes in the amygdala and prefrontal cortex that predicted less sadness and anxiety, plus more self-control.*[5]

While the research with the twelve- to sixteen-year-olds only looked at their mothers, studies cited in the chapters on dad-deprived boys show

how, for example, hangout time with dads was pivotal to both boys' and girls' psychological health.[6] While both parents' compassionate listening, then, is paramount for both sexes, it may fill an even deeper "compassion void" for your son.

However, compassionate listening to your son is more easily said than done. As Peter and his parents, Felicia and Frank, explain . . .

"I'm fine . . . Just leave me alone."

Whenever Peter told his mom, "Just leave me alone," she felt helpless and withdrew. Peter lacked the social skills to say what he really felt.

As Peter reflects back on his early adolescence, he recalls, "Whenever I opened up to my mom or dad about some problem, they just gave me a lecture. I was already stressed out, and their lectures just stressed me out more."

As Peter got older, he developed the social skills to say that directly to his parents. But he felt it didn't solve the problem:

> Both my mom and dad would tell me, "OK. I got it. I'll just listen." My mom even apologized. And at first, they would listen. Both of them. But it didn't last for long.
>
> Soon they just went back to giving me lectures. They think that by making the lecture a little briefer, they can call it advice. But when I'm stressed it just feels like criticism. I hate it because it makes me feel like they don't believe I can think for myself.
>
> And that isn't even the worst part. When they lecture me, **they use everything I've just been saying to criticize me more than they would have if I had said nothing.** It's like they're using what I say against me. They feel it's to help me, but I feel betrayed . . . like the promise to listen was really just a bait and switch.
>
> So that's why I don't trust their claims that they'll just listen!

Peter's parents had a different perspective: "If we say anything—even a few words—he calls it a lecture. The only school he'll attend is the school of hard knocks—you can't tell him anything."

Peter's mom and dad did eventually make headway with Peter. Frank reported, "We made the most progress after I began immersing myself in his video game *League of Legends*, asking Peter what each character meant to him. His reasons impressed me, and I sensed that he could feel my respect. It opened him up."

Felicia added, "I think what also helped, Frank, was your setting up the basketball hoop and our getting the outdoor Ping-Pong table, and you and I challenging Peter to games at Ping-Pong. It seemed like as Peter developed confidence in his playing basketball and Ping-Pong that he began to be receptive to inviting over some friends. He became more social. The video game characters weren't his only 'friends.'"

Felicia hesitated, then recalled, "Another big step forward came when our family counselor worked with Frank and me to appeal to Peter's strengths, not his weaknesses. For example, we shared with Peter how impressed we were at how quickly he solved problems in *League of Legends*. And so, when Peter did eventually allude to a problem, we affirmed his problem-solving skills and then asked him how he would solve that problem if it was occurring with one of his favorite characters. It worked— every time we appealed to his strength it seemed to make him stronger."

"The toughest transition," Frank cautioned, "was making sure we didn't let playing with Peter lead to our trying to keep close by being friends rather than parents. We had to move back to expectations of Peter and boundary enforcement. I can't say it's been a road without bumps, but it's sure a lot better than it was a year or two ago."

A Boy's Gap Between the Need for Peer Approval and the Skills to Get It

One of the biggest challenges for children around ages thirteen and fourteen is the gap between their need for peer approval and the social skills necessary to get it. Children who develop social skills effective in bridging this peer approval–social skill gap also develop positive changes in their brain's circuitry that last a lifetime.[7]

Empathy is the most important single social skill. **Between ages thirteen and sixteen, boys show a temporary decline in empathy on a biological level—a decline not suffered by girls.**[8] This decline is then reinforced by the tension between heroic intelligence and emotional intelligence.

For Tom, this empathy deficit was reinforced during his freshman year of college as he was entering the hazing ritual stage of his dad's fraternity, and his potential fraternity brothers were hazing a new recruit by having him drink a large glass of whiskey in which a few other frat members had peed. Tom knew he'd be the next in line. He wanted to stop the process, but was afraid he'd be ridiculed, be rejected by the fraternity, and be a disappointment to his dad. So he just laughed and cheered.

Tom felt ashamed of himself for not having the courage to at least speak up, but also worried that maybe his desire to stop the process meant he couldn't hack it as a man. "I felt caught between a rock and a hard place: was 'courage' the courage to confront the fraternity, or was 'courage' the courage to drink the pee? It didn't help that this was my dad's fraternity, and he had had the guts to get through their hazing. I guess I saw this as a defining moment—if the fraternity saw through me, so would my dad. So would some girlfriend. If not today, then someday."

Fortunately, some national fraternities, such as Delta Tau Delta, are already making this shift from heroic to emotional health intelligence with newsletter cover stories like the recent "Power of Connection: Enhancing Well-Being Through Brotherhood."[9]

Helping Your Son Take Risks in Life Without Risking His Life

Around age fifteen or sixteen, a boy's brain will typically encourage risk-taking by releasing increased amounts of dopamine—the "feel good" hormone—when he takes risks. Comfort with risk-taking is healthy for any boy (or girl). Leaving home is risky, as are getting married, having children, starting a business . . . However, since the increased chemical reward from risk-taking in boys leads to your son being much more likely than your daughter to be killed or permanently injured during adolescence, we need to know what encourages a boy to take risks in life without risking his life.

A study of teens uncovered that fifteen-year-olds who became closer to their parents by talking through problems without arguing or yelling activated a region in their brains that allowed them to feel good without taking excessive risks.[10] (This is why family dinner nights are so pivotal, using the guidelines in appendix A.)

How Heroic Intelligence and Emotional Intelligence Play Out in Everyday Life

Moving to Better Neighborhoods Helps Girls and Hurts Boys

The children of 4,500 families were randomly chosen by the Department of Housing and Urban Development to move to *better* neighborhoods as part of its Moving for Opportunity program. When the children were studied ten to fifteen years later, **the rate of PTSD among boys who moved to better neighborhoods was like the rate found among soldiers returning from combat.**[11]

Chloe and Gabriel were typical of the children participating in the program. Chloe's social skills allowed her to "cry out" her grief at moving, and then use her social skills to integrate among her new classmates.

In contrast, Gabriel had trouble getting past the knowledge that the new neighborhood was "better." In his old "worse" neighborhood, he felt he had less to prove. That made it easier for him to feel comfortable and confident enough to be tested and teased, and to test and tease back. Here, when he was mocked for where he came from and how he dressed, he forgot that being tested was part of the male way of vetting *any* new candidate for friendship, not just "inferior Gabriel." Gabriel became depressed, pretended not to care, and rejected help from the school's counselors.

As with Gabriel, ten to fifteen years after their participation in the Moving for Opportunity program, the boys were more likely to experience post-traumatic stress disorder (again, *comparable to that among soldiers returning from combat*), plus higher rates of depression, conduct disorder, and juvenile delinquency.

The deeper observation here is the boys' vulnerability. **Counterintuitively, when it comes to a loss of friendships and love, your son is the more vulnerable sex.** Why? Gabriel needed security and attachment before he could feel good about being tested, but heroic intelligence has no room for coddling. Coping with a loss of friendships and love requires emotional intelligence, and creating new friendships and new romantic relationships requires good social skills.[12] When it comes to love, heroic intelligence does not protect boys; it weakens boys. And makes a boy even more in need of love.

Emotional Intelligence: The Smile Is Mightier Than the Sword

In poorer neighborhoods, gangs compete to replace dads. Not just for boys, but also for girls. We can get a glimpse of the effectiveness of heroic intelligence versus emotional intelligence by looking at how boys' heroic intelligence and girls' emotional intelligence plays out in gangs. No surprise with boys—they achieve respect and status by acting tough. "The rougher, tougher and nastier they are, the higher their status."[13]

In contrast, girls gain high status in gangs via their people skills and their facade of innocence.[14] After a street fight they will pick up mobile phones, glean information about who is doing what and when, and help their gang use the information to their advantage. This can minimize the risks of the boys—and sometimes girls—smuggling weapons and drugs.

Because gathering information rarely requires the girls to shoot or kill others, the girls can remain a "clean skin"—without a criminal record. That facade of innocence allows the girls to be less likely to be detected by police when, for example, they hide something in a baby carriage next to a baby.[15] It also means they get let go more quickly when they are part of a group the police is cross-examining.

In gangs, as in the rest of life, boys' tendency to limit themselves to a facade of strength often fails to protect them. Girls' emotional intelligence allows many girls to both derive protection from boys' physical strength as well as from a facade of innocence and weakness.

There is, though, for boys, yet another way of being strong some would see as weakness—a way I inadvertently discovered when I was in seventh grade.

The Bully and the Bullied

To this day, I vividly recall Jimmy standing across from me with a brick in his hand, threatening to smash my skull. Like Gabriel, I had just moved to a new neighborhood, in Waldwick, New Jersey, and had spent too much time talking positively about my old neighborhood in Paramus. Jimmy didn't like me "threatening" his territory, and, as his brick hovered over me and my mind raced with visions of a brick smashing my skull, I was blessed to access my limited reserve of seventh-grader emotional intelligence: searching for something I respected about Jimmy.

Eureka! I recalled that Jimmy had formed a small club of neighborhood friends. I offered, "Jimmy, you're a leader. You got Bobby and a lot of the kids in our neighborhood to join your club, and then they made you captain. *Why do you think they made you captain?*" I don't recall what Jimmy answered; I do recall that as he started telling me why they wanted him to be captain, that his arm kept lowering the brick, until he dropped it into the gutter.

Because so many of us have experienced the damage of being bullied, and are disenchanted with the lose-lose choices we thought we had as boys—get beaten up, run away, or fight back—it is easy to believe it is our job as parents to keep expanding the punishment of bullies until the bullying stops.

In my encounter with Jimmy, though, I unwittingly discovered an alternative to getting beaten up, running away, or fighting back: seeing the bully as someone in search of respect, knowing that if we can help the bully find what he can respect about himself, the brick of anger will fall.

In brief, I inadvertently found that one way to fight disrespect is with respect. I couldn't have put it that way in seventh grade, and it wasn't my leading instinct—but somehow, in my search to survive, I accessed that option, and doubtless it has stayed with me so long because it worked so well.

Later I learned that bullies are often being abused at home by a bully parent,[16] or are neglected and rudderless with little or no father involvement. I discovered that, counterintuitively, bullies and the bullied often have a lot in common: **they are often both underachievers with low self-esteem.**

If we are to bridge the gap between health intelligence and heroic intelligence, it starts with compassion not only for the bullied but also for the bully.

Helping both the bully and the bullied

When it comes to bullying, your son is growing up in the Expand the Punishment era. For example, school districts in Missouri as of 2017 are required by mandatory reporting laws to report to the police as a potential felony any behavior that causes another student "emotional distress." Note the student is not charged with a misdemeanor but a felony.[17] To "lock up the problem" is to just repress the problem, then increase the problem, then release the problem. Especially if the boy is a preteen or early teen.

A better solution? Emotional intelligence training for everyone in school. Boys who hurt hurt us. **The bully who is healed is the best protection for the bullied.** But until those programs are put in place, studies of boys around ten to twelve find that one of the best ways to decrease your son's likelihood of getting into a fight, or being anxious and sad, and to help him develop friends, is to *discuss with him issues like bullying over dinner.*[18] (Sound familiar?)

Often a discussion will emanate from an experience like this . . .

Aikido for the bullied

When Sarah inquired about the scratch on her son David's face, she sensed David was covering something up when he said he got it playing soccer during lunch hour. When Sarah pressed him, David eventually admitted he was shoved by a few kids who, he said, pretended that he kicked them to give them the excuse to shove him. Sarah hugged him and asked if it had happened before. With some prodding, David eventually acknowledged he'd been being teased about being fat, but begged his mom, "Don't tell anyone! Don't make me regret I told you."

Later that night, Sarah told Daniel, David's dad. Daniel asked *why* they were bullying him. A bit annoyed, Sarah responded, "It's not important why. These days they suspend kids who bully. We need to make an appointment with the principal."

Daniel pressed, "But what's provoking the bullies?"

"They're calling him 'Dumpy David' and saying he should play goalie 'because he's bigger than the goal' or something cruel like that. Besides, he's not that overweight. Austin [David's friend] is fatter than he is. And this isn't about David. It's about the bullies."

"Instead of calling the principal, why don't we use this as an opportunity to get David to change his diet and exercise?" Daniel asked.

"Dan, they're physically shoving him around by his tummy, pretending to be sorry in case he's 'pregnant.' Being ridiculed like that could leave David with psychological scars for a lifetime. And look at how his face is bruised."

Daniel and Sarah argued it out. They eventually struck a deal: they'd call the principal about the bullying but also sign up as a family for six months at Weight Watchers, and the whole family—including David's sister, who was also overweight—would attend.

Finally, Dan and Sarah agreed that while David was in Weight Watchers, he and his dad would play soccer and basketball together until David lost the weight—at which point he could get more involved in sports at school without being mocked.

Daniel helped David to not use the excuse of criticism-given-badly to ignore what he could learn from the criticism. By teaching David to use even something as reprehensible as bullying as a growth opportunity he was helping David to expand his emotional intelligence.

And by calling the principal, Sarah used the system to stop the bullies' behavior, sensing that few parents would know how to turn bullying into personal growth.

Daniel and Sarah ultimately used the checks and balances of male-female parenting to both stop the bullies and make sure David did not just stop at being a victim.

In the process, Daniel and Sarah were teaching David mental aikido: how to use the negative energy as a force to both empower himself and to strengthen the system. Aikido for the bullied.

Eighteen Steps Toward Integrating Emotional and Physical Health Intelligence into Heroic Intelligence

The bad news is that the gap between your son's heroic and health intelligence is a million or so years in the making. The good news is that, for the first time in history, with less social pressure to be increasingly proud of your son only to the degree that he is a heroic warrior or successful sole breadwinner, we are freer to help him differentiate between knowing himself and being seduced by the sirens of social bribes.

If, after this process, your son chooses to be a Navy SEAL, firefighter, or a CEO who works seventy hours a week, he is more likely to have made that decision by conscious choice—as a choice aligned with who he is rather than the need to prove himself. Then he will be a hero who has integrated health intelligence with heroic intelligence.

That said, the power of our brain's rostral cingulate zone to make us responsive to the sirens of social bribes will always make the discovery of our unique selves a challenge—even if we are a full-time Buddhist monk. So here is a little arsenal of eighteen practical steps you can take to begin to integrate emotional and physical health intelligence into your son's heroic intelligence:

1. If possible, keep both parents about equally involved in your son's upbringing—whether married, divorced, or never married. If impossible, get your son involved in the Boy Scouts, Mankind Project, or the programs described in chapter 20, "The Best Parent Is Both Parents, *But . . .*"
2. If dad and mom have different parenting styles, treat them as healthy checks and balances.
3. Model great listening skills—if you tend to become defensive when criticized, get help.[19]
4. Roughhouse, coach, and play. Make everyday activities like shopping into a game, with fun competitions.
5. Routinely get your son's input, and then use the bond of roughhousing and playing as leverage to set and enforce boundaries. Don't set any boundaries you do not enforce. Enforce boundaries sooner rather than later—repeated threats without follow-through lead to escalation, arguments, and blurting out consequences you won't enforce, breeding your son's disrespect and even contempt.
6. Impart a sense of sacredness for family dinner nights and "The Five Essentials" in appendix A—especially these next two.
7. Discuss at dinner meaningful life issues and dilemmas, and issues in the kids' lives; make sure no one dominates, and interruption is taboo. Your advice comes last, and is discretionary.
8. Make no topic taboo at dinner. Boys love to be challenged; they'd rather only half-understand a conversation than be bored.
9. Use the invitation of friends (yours and his) to occasional family dinner nights to help your family develop a supportive social network and a leadership group for self-discovery.
10. Frame empathy as manly—as the emotional equivalent of rescuing, healing, and protecting someone.
11. Frame respectfully speaking up to peers as courage—after he has the courage to listen first.
12. Develop questions you ask your son about every new friend (so that no one friend is seen as being picked on). Is that friend someone you respect? Why? What does that person encourage in you that you feel will make you a better person? Is there anything that magnetically

attracts you to her or him that you feel may lead you to a place (physically or psychologically) that you will ultimately regret? Do you think this person will be a trusted friend five years from now?

13. Make exercise part of your son's daily life—not as an option, but as a top priority. Be sure three types of sports are integrated into your son's life: team sports, individual sports, and pickup team sports. Each makes a distinct contribution to his development.

14. Introduce him to meditation, yoga, and prayer, and do them with him. In addition to providing your family with some quiet moments to extract deeper thoughts from the noise of life, they can also become a part of your family's connective glue. If your son doesn't believe there's a God that listens, no matter—let him know that prayer has value even if he only listens.

15. Set up opportunities for him to develop friendships with girls in which neither he nor the girl have a romantic interest (e.g., via school paper, student government, debating, or coed sports like tennis, Ping-Pong, running, soccer . . .).

16. Teach him to listen to music that soothes, and seek to understand why he loves the music he loves. Ask him to listen to why you love the music you love.

17. Create enough pressure to teach him how to handle pressure. Frame "failure" as a prerequisite to success—part of the gift of risk-taking and being a man. But make sure he "gets" that you love him as a human being, not a human doing, and that "failure" as a human doing is but an opportunity to grow as a human being. Knowing that allows pressure to be part of life's game, but not his life. (Only when he "gets" that will sports and video games in moderation reinforce that.)

18. Treat the family as a team, with your son's chores and consciousness of your needs being what gets him to "make the team." Children don't develop empathy from parents who are only empathetic. When we consider only our children's needs, they also consider only their needs. Let him know the benefit to him: parents who are less stressed contribute to happier, more successful children.

Given *The Boy Crisis'* focus on your son, step eighteen—family team consciousness—is pivotal. So let's conclude with a deeper dive into the science behind why "If anybody ain't happy, ain't nobody happy."

"If Anybody Ain't Happy, Ain't Nobody Happy"

Moms have a big influence on boys' mental health. But the old maxim "If mama ain't happy, ain't nobody happy" needs a companion: "If papa ain't happy, ain't nobody happy."

Stressed and depressed parents—moms or dads—create major problems in young children, including poorer social skills, hyperactivity, and behavior problems such as lack of self-control and less cooperativeness. These problems show up even in toddlers, but become especially prevalent by fifth grade and beyond.[20]

Stressed and depressed parents also have a disproportionate impact on inhibiting language skills of boys.[21] As we've seen, boys are especially vulnerable to stress and family turmoil in many other areas.

Of course, an unhappy, stressed child can also trigger unhappiness and stress in parents. So family team consciousness is the awareness that "If anybody ain't happy, ain't nobody happy."

Easily said, but how is it done—this "family team consciousness"? Jordan, fourteen, put it this way, "When I hear 'time out for Mom' or 'special time for Dad' that jolts me out of my 'me' focus." Then Jordan recalled with excitement, "Once Dad was afraid he'd be home too late for the start of one of the NBA finals. I figured out which play-off he meant and DVRed it. I was so happy when he got home late, and I could bring him a beer and let him see the whole game. He was elated and seemed to feel so loved by me for just doing something so simple, it made me want to do more; it made me feel happier than pretty much anything—except maybe a later curfew!"

Jordan did not articulate the connection, but introducing Jordan to "time out for mom" and "special time for dad" was an example of what laid the groundwork for the family team consciousness that led to Jordan thinking of surprising his dad with DVRing his game. When the consciousness of "If anybody ain't happy, ain't nobody happy" becomes "If everybody's happy, everybody's happy," you've achieved family team consciousness.

CHAPTER 25

Reversing Depression, Preventing Suicide

You may feel that your son would never commit suicide. If so, why not just skip this section? For the same reason that we learn how to drive safely even though we are unlikely to be killed in a car accident.

Every parent and educator needs to know suicide's red flags so we won't need to lower the school flag.

Throughout the developed world, where boys and men are experiencing a purpose void, plus dad deprivation and the other causes of the boy crisis, suicide has soared. Especially among white boys. In the United Kingdom, suicide accounts for three times as many deaths as road accidents—more than leukemia, and more than all infectious and parasitic diseases combined.[1] The price of the stiff upper lip.

We think of the male-female suicide gap as greatest during an economic depression. **Yet the male-female suicide gap in the United States has *tripled* since the Great Depression.**[2]

Since a leading red flag of suicide is depression, and our understanding of depression has been via the way it manifests in girls, not boys, many parents are blind to our sons' warning signs.

Suicide Young, Suicide Old

The two times in a boy or man's life that he feels most alone and most vulnerable are:

- in his early twenties.
- after sixty-five, increasing with each year.

When a boy is in his early twenties, the gap between the expectations on him as a man and his fears that he won't meet those expectations is the greatest. In this age group, boys' suicide rate is 5.4 times that of girls.[3]

But it's even worse after retirement. As men retire, the human doing is left behind; only the human being remains. Men disproportionately feel they aren't worth much as a human being. They sometimes feel they are worth more to their family as an inheritance than as a person. **By age eighty-five, men's suicide rate is 1,650 percent higher than that of women the same age.**[4]

Why is a statistic on the suicide of older men relevant to your young son? Let's look.

First, grandpa may be a direct influence on your son. If grandpa commits suicide, it can haunt the whole family. When my mother committed suicide at age forty-eight, although my sister and I were just starting our twenties, the closer my sister and I got to forty-eight, the more we feared that could also be our destiny.

Second, knowing as a boy that suicide is in his gender can be as preventive as knowing that cancer is in his genes. It encourages him, for example, to use tools like the Warren Farrell Male Depression / Suicide Inventory, later in this chapter, like a marine might use a map of a minefield.

Causes of Suicide

Women Cry, Men Die

> **Item.** Women constitute 75 percent of those who seek professional help to prevent suicide; men constitute 75 percent of those who commit suicide.[5]

There is no better example of men's facade of strength being a weakness, and women's permission to express weakness being a strength, than the fact that women seek help to prevent suicide more frequently, even as men commit suicide more frequently.

Don't girls and women attempt suicide more frequently? Yes. *Attempting* suicide is a way of preventing suicide—by asking for help.

Do women register more suicide attempts but fewer completions because they use pills more and guns less? No. Girls and women are as capable of pulling a trigger as boys and men.

Here's the difference: the person who *attempts* suicide usually believes that someone cares enough to help—and knows how to help. It is a way of pleading for those who love her to pay attention—to move her pain from the back burner of their lives to the front burner.

In contrast, a boy or man who *commits* suicide generally believes, usually mistakenly, that no one cares enough to help—especially no one who would know how to help. Or, more specifically, he believes:

- No one loves him who knows who he really is—both his best and worst selves.
- No one really needs him.
- There's no hope of that changing.
- If he shares what he is feeling or things he is ashamed of, whoever he talks to will lose respect for him, which will only increase his shame.

These are only the tip of his iceberg—or the gateway to his hell.

If No Human Doing, No Human Being

Item. Each one-percent *de*crease in GDP leads to an almost one-percent *in*crease in suicide.[6]

Item. In Glasgow, those from the poorest areas are ten times more at risk of suicide than those from the richest.[7]

When your son is single, the more he expects himself to pay for a woman's five Ds—drinks, dinner, driving, dates, and diamonds—the more an economic slump that leaves him unemployed can make him feel hopeless, potentially translating into his greater vulnerability to depression and suicide. If your son pays for the five Ds when he is single, it is also psychological preparation for becoming a sole breadwinner, and becoming depressed or suicidal if he faces long-term unemployment and disappoints his family and himself.

We have seen that when men retire at age sixty-five and above, their suicide rate soars, reaching 1,650 percent that of women his age by age eighty-five. If your son identifies himself by the way he makes a living ("I'm a doctor"), he can experience the loss of his job as the loss of himself. And by age eighty-five, he's also often lost his wife—giving us another clue as to male vulnerability to the loss of love. His vulnerability, to loss of love or purpose, never dies. Until he dies. **Whether via forced unemployment, retirement, or loss of spouse, men's response of suicide can just be the killing of what has already been killed.**

Suicide Is Contagious

Guy was depressed. Since his parents got divorced, Guy's anger was rising and his grades were falling. Good colleges were accepting his buddies and rejecting him. He felt he was a massive disappointment to everyone, especially himself. He hated that when he even hinted at his problems to his parents, he either got a lecture or a dismissive pep talk ("I know this is hard, but why don't you just join . . . call . . . try . . ."). His friends' responses felt more like pity than empathy, especially since, after sharing with them, he noticed he was invited to even fewer get-togethers.

Then an acquaintance of his in his high school committed suicide. At school assemblies and the memorial service, the boy's peers and family sang his praises, wishing they had spent more time trying to understand him. Guy fantasized being mourned and praised, too—being the focus of remorse for those who wished they had persisted even as he resisted. Suicide felt like a way of bringing life to his death.

Suicide is contagious—as in the copycat Palo Alto suicides in 2015.[8] So what can a community do to minimize copycat suicides? First, yes, express fully the sorrow at the loss and honor fully the existence of the boy or girl who commits suicide. And then, add a second step: honor those who have used the community resources that do exist, and invite them to share how those resources have given them strength. Familiarize the community with the people behind those resources.

Why do we often see more suicides among boys in privileged communities like Palo Alto, than in poorer communities like Bedford–Stuyvesant or Watts?

In a poor community, in the battle to survive, boys are killed by others. Surviving without imprisonment can be a source of pride. In a privileged community, the expectations are higher; failing those expectations generates shame. And asking for help begets pity. Especially to a boy, privilege on the outside can mask his fears of failure to measure up on his inside.

Once we see the connection between heroic masculinity and suicide, the next step is to distinguish between a happy hero and a boy who is walking on the stepping stones toward suicide. Here's how to diagnose the danger . . .

Diagnosing Danger: The Warren Farrell Male Depression/Suicide Inventory (WFMDI)

Molly was feeling suicidal and depressed. She reported herself to her college's psychologist, and got help. Last year she graduated from college.

Tom was feeling suicidal and depressed. He didn't even think about reporting himself to the college's psychologist. Last year he killed himself.

By reporting her depression, Molly became part of the statistic that depression is a girls' and women's problem. By not reporting his depression, Tom also became part of the statistic that depression is a girls' and women's problem.

In *The Myth of Male Power*, I challenged the assumption that depression was predominantly a woman's problem—saying that if suicide is so predominantly male, that it is improbable that depression is predominantly female. As we saw above with Molly, the fact that women report depression more may reflect women's greater health intelligence: Molly recognized the problem; she knew of friends and institutions that would listen to her; and she proactively used those resources to ask for help.

Molly's emotional intelligence flourishes due to the responses she experiences from others: when a woman breaks down, cries, and asks for help, she triggers a rescuer instinct in men and emotional bonding with women that reinforces the value of her seeking help in the future. When a man breaks down, cries, and asks for help, he triggers pity.

Since the publication of *The Myth of Male Power* in 1993, researchers at the University of Michigan and elsewhere have agreed that, while many of girls' and women's ways of expressing depression apply to boys and men, boys and men were also prone to manifesting depression differently. So they tested men for womanizing, and both men and women for anger, substance abuse, risk-taking, self-destructive behavior, gambling, and workaholism. When they added these criteria to those more typically used to diagnose depression (e.g., low energy or spirit, sleeplessness), their findings, as reported in *JAMA*, were that **there is almost no difference in the percentage of men versus women experiencing depression:** 31 percent men and 33 percent women.[9]

That's progress. But the criteria the researchers added here are only the tip of the iceberg.

Their new criteria focused on destructive and self-destructive *externalized* male behavior (e.g., gambling, womanizing). Missing are a large range of *feelings* that boys and men often *internalize*—feelings like not living up to expectations, not having a sense of purpose, or not feeling needed, loved, or understood. Of course, adding these criteria will also help identify depression in some girls and women.

Future inventories also need to probe for *situation-catalyzed* depression, since boys' and men's feelings are more likely to be acknowledged in the context of a specific situation that catalyzes the feeling. Examples include a boy finally asking out the girl he desires, being rejected, and then overhearing gossip that makes him feel mocked for trying; losing significant contact with his dad after a divorce or death; and feeling so socially awkward that transitions like moving to a new neighborhood become emotionally isolating. As we've seen, each of these creates more problems for boys than girls. As he gets older, we need to probe for different situations, like being fired, or, after divorce, being restricted to "visitation" even as he feels the children have been turned against him.

Common to most of these internalized feelings is believing that *no one loves him, no one needs him,* and there's no hope of that changing.

Future inventories must also inquire whether the male is a member of a group that tends to use suicide as an end to depression: Caucasians, Native Americans, affluent young men in their twenties, men over sixty-five, those with access to guns . . .

The inventory below includes more than sixty red flags, or stepping stones toward suicide (fortunately, many are only a concern when combined with others). This inventory is my first step toward incorporating these ways of understanding depression in a way that is more male inclusive, but not female exclusive. Use the inventory for the whole family as a discussion starter for a family dinner night.

Should your son (or daughter) see a question that "hits the nail on the head," he intuits *it wouldn't be on the questionnaire if it wasn't also a problem for others.* He is released from the fear that "I'm the only one" and "something is wrong with me."

The result? He feels seen, and freer to share his version of that experience. Which is a prerequisite toward reporting depression—which is a step toward a solution.

The Warren Farrell Male Depression / Suicide Inventory (WFMDI)

___ Do you feel no one loves you who knows the real you?

___ Do you feel no one needs you?

___ Do you feel there is no hope of people loving you or needing you in the foreseeable future?

___ Do you feel that if you discuss your real fears with someone you may lose that person's respect?

___ Do you feel ashamed of something you've done that has recently been or may soon be exposed (e.g., cheating on a test, or on a significant other, or in business)?

___ Have you recently (last year or two) dropped out of school?

___ Are you unemployed?

___ Have you been unemployed for more than a year?

___ Have you been unemployed for more than a year with family to support?

___ Are you unemployed with family to support and less than three months' worth of savings?

___ Do you feel you were let go from work because the employer wasn't happy either with your work, with you, or with both?

___ Are you Caucasian or Native American?

___ Do you often feel you are disappointing your parents' high expectations of you?

___ Is your family middle class or above?

___ Do you feel isolated from local friends whom you could potentially see in person?

___ Are long-distance, online friends (e.g., from video game playing, Tumblr, Reddit) pretty much your only friends?

___ Did your family recently move to a new neighborhood while you were in school?

___ Are you uncomfortable communicating with others?

___ Do you think about your problems more than you think about the problems of all your friends and family combined?

___ Does the thought of talking about depression or suicide—even to a professional—make you feel ashamed?

___ Do you feel aimless or without purpose?

___ Do you wish you had a better relationship with your dad?

___ Do you wish you could see your dad more frequently?

___ Are you angry at your dad and glad he is not in your life?

___ Do you wish you had a different dad?

___ Do you wish you knew who your dad is?

___ Have you often been told that you are a "mama's boy" and are overprotected?

___ Are you between eighteen and twenty-six, or older than sixty-five?

___ Have you recently been divorced?

___ Do you have less contact with your children than you would like?

___ Have you lost a custody battle in court?

___ Do you feel your children have been turned against you?

___ Do you feel hopeless about having a good relationship with your children while they are still young enough to benefit from you?

___ Have you recently experienced a significant romantic breakup?

___ Was the breakup initiated by your former partner?

___ Do you wish you could get back together, but feel there's no real hope of that?

___ Do you feel you have ADHD?

___ Do you "live" to compete in a highly competitive way in a sport (e.g., skiing, swimming, basketball, mountain bike racing)?

____ Do you "live" to compete in a sport likely to cause damage to your body (e.g., football; motorcycling; cliff, rock, or ice-climbing; ice hockey; X Games; skateboarding or snowboarding)?

____ Have you gotten a ticket for speeding or driving recklessly in a car or motorcycle more than once in the last ten years?

____ Are you an avid marathon runner?

____ Are you an avid triathlete?

____ Are you so involved in video games that you neglect work, responsibilities, frequent exercise, friends, or family?

____ Are you so involved in porn that you have problems getting an erection with real women or have been rejected by real women who felt you wanted more extreme sex than they were comfortable with?

____ Do you feel that if you ask out a potential romantic partner that you are more than likely to be rejected?

____ Do you identify as a member of the LGBTQIA community and have been afraid to share that with your parents, or at school or work?

____ Are you very overweight or obese?

____ Do you exercise or play sports less than three times a week?

____ Do you gamble frequently enough that it either creates tension with someone you love or, at the end of the year, you wish you had the money you lost?

____ Do you drink or use drugs more than you feel is healthy for you?

____ Do you root for a team with such devotion that when they lose the big one, you feel depressed and sometimes angry?

____ Do you experience frequent bursts of anger (more than once every couple of months) that seem to come out of nowhere?

____ Do you frequently experience sleepless nights?

____ Do you experience chronic fatigue?

____ Do you experience chronic digestive problems?

____ Do you experience chronic headaches?

___ Do you "work morning, noon, and night" because it gives you an excuse to avoid family, friends, or other responsibilities?

___ Do you have easy access to a gun?

___ Have you written or thought through what notes you'd leave your family if you ever committed suicide?

___ Have you thought of covering up suicide with an accident—such as a car accident or "falling" by "mistake" off a cliff?

___ Have you ever felt that your insurance policy is more valuable than you are?

___ Have you ever attempted suicide?

___ If you have attempted suicide, was a part of you hoping that you would fail and, as a result, people would reach out to you?

___ Have you noticed a lot of suicides in the news recently, or attended memorials for local suicides?

___ Have you ever been in prison or a juvenile detention facility?

___ Have you ever been a victim of physical or sexual abuse?

___ Was your mom or dad seriously depressed or suicidal?

If any family member or friend answers yes to seven or more questions—or even once on a crucial question like contemplating the specifics in a suicide note, or feeling no one needs them—then be certain they receive the help of a therapist, ideally one who has read *The Boy Crisis* in full for context.

Preventing Suicide

If you intuit that suicide is imminent for someone you love (including yourself), reach out to a trained counselor at 800-273-8255 (the National Suicide Prevention Lifeline). Or text "help" to Crisis Text Line at 741-741.

Talk It Out

Boys and young men between fifteen and twenty-four who ask for help are only half as likely to commit suicide.[10]

If you are worrying about your son committing suicide, you may be afraid to say something for fear of "putting ideas into his head." But research finds that talking directly about suicide works better than ignoring the elephant in the room.[11] For example, depression ran in Gordon's family. In addition to making sure his son, Howie, was good at sports and had plenty of friends, he consciously let Howie know about his own struggles, who had been helpful to him, and that "asking for help" was a mark of courage (as in "the *courage* to ask for help"). As a result, Howie did not feel like a disappointment to his dad when he was fighting bouts of depression and came to his dad for comfort. In fact, Howie sensed how his openness deepened his bond with his dad.

If talking about suicide seems daunting, start by talking about depression, not suicide. Your son in particular is more likely to open up in response to a *specific* question ("Are you having suicidal thoughts today?" "Were you thinking about using a gun?") than to proactively volunteer that he's depressed. You can jump-start the specific question approach even as you make it less personal by having the whole family—not just your son—fill out the inventory above as a family dinner night project.

Trickle-Down Neglect

Three characteristics of suicide—being male, being between eighteen and twenty-four, and having parents with high expectations that one is failing to meet—are all found among boys who make it to top-rated colleges but are much more likely to be failing.

The most important sources of news for families sending sons to these top-rated colleges are outlets such as *PBS NewsHour*, NPR, the *Today Show*, and CNN. These sources most frequently adapt stories from the *New York Times*. The *New York Times* has, in essence, trickle-down power.

The *New York Times* often covers suicide but ignores boys and men. For example, in its approximately three-thousand-word article on campus suicide, not one word mentioned any of the challenges that might lead to the four-to-one ratio of male-to-female suicide on campuses.[12]

To the contrary, **every example used in that 2015 story in the *New York Times* on campus suicide was of girls**.[13] And every example of suffering from the pressure to meet standards of perfection was an example of a girl's suffering. There was no hint in the *New York Times* article that suicide even affects boys.

How might the *New York Times* have used its trickle-down power to be more helpful to your family? For example, by interviewing boys about the shame they feel when they appear to be likely to fail out of college. How does a young man face his girlfriend—who is statistically likely to be doing better, and unlikely to be interested in a guy who is less disciplined, especially if he becomes a "failure to launch?" Does he fear failing out of college will prevent him from succeeding in the job market, and therefore damage his opportunity to be loved and married?

How does he communicate his disappointment in himself to his parents? If a boy feels his parents stress his being a human doing, does his failure mean he is disappointing them as a human being?

The *New York Times* does not neglect your son more than any other popular source of news. It just has more trickle-down power, and therefore more moral responsibility to not be the purveyor of trickle-down neglect.

The impact of this caring void is a funding void. Few foundations and governments fund what people don't care about. And even professionals whose job it is to care—such as social workers and suicidologists—need funding to dig deeper. But . . .

Suicide: Mostly About Boys, So Let's Study Girls

When the National Association of Social Workers studies suicide, *they study only female suicide*. When social worker Tom Golden asked why, he was told by the executive director that it was because the *funding only allowed the study of girls*.[14]

But wait. What about the American Association of Suicidology? Its executive director lamented, "As much as I would love to lead the charge (in finding out why boys kill themselves), try to go out and get funding for it."[15]

Funding comes from caring because caring produces the political pressure that creates funding. The media's coverage of boys' suffering can go a long way toward our caring.

The Suicide Gene: SKA2

If your son's answers on the Warren Farrell Male Depression / Suicide Inventory send up red flags, in addition to being sure he has a good therapist, you may also want to get him a blood test for the presence of what might be called the "suicide gene": SKA2. The latest research, from Johns Hopkins University, found that the presence of SKA2 predicts suicidal thoughts or behavior with about 80 percent accuracy.[16] If your son or daughter has this gene, he or she is likely to be less able to suppress cortisol following stress; this inhibits his or her ability to keep emotions from running amok.

If your son (or daughter) does prove to be vulnerable, what next?

Henry Ford: Putting the Brakes on Suicide

We associate Henry Ford with cars, but he has also put the brakes on suicide. The Henry Ford Health System in Detroit has reduced the rate of suicides from the average inpatient suicide rate of 230 per 100,000 patients, to as low as 0 per 100,000 patients in 2010.[17]

Many of their methods, while not designed to help their male patients specifically, nevertheless address some of the issues that particularly impact boys and men.[18] For example, their patients-helping-patients program, in which patients use their history of challenges to help other patients with similar challenges, has the by-product of giving boys and men a sense of purpose and feeling needed, which reduces anxiety about being rejected and paves the way for building friendships. With a suicide rate of as little as zero, it is evident that these antidotes to depression and suicide also apply to girls and women.

As we discussed above, a boy is more likely to open up in response to a *specific* question ("Are you having suicidal thoughts today?" or "Were you thinking about using a gun?") rather than proactively volunteering that he's depressed. The Henry Ford program has also found that the discussions that emanate from direct and specific questions are preventive.[19] This is one of the functions of the Warren Farrell Male Depression/ Suicide Inventory as well.

And for boys especially, engaging with someone who is credible, who cares, and who follows through daily, are three key elements of suicide prevention. Ford's inpatient program does all three.

Of course, the best "treatment" for depression is prevention. Among the eighteen steps outlined in chapter 24, "Emotional Intelligence and Mental Health," I recommend both boys' and men's organizations, and groups. Both will foster your son's emotional intelligence, but in different ways.

Should Your Son Join a Men's Organization, or Group?

We have seen the effectiveness of organizations such as the Cub Scouts and Boy Scouts. And many boys have benefited from the sense of purpose and fellowship their dads discovered via service organizations such as Kiwanis, Rotary, and the Lions Club. The fact that they are now open to women expands their ability to model for your son how men and women can be effective partners on common projects. I've even seen boys in junior high look forward to the time when they could be part of these organizations.

These organizations use service as the vehicle toward a sense of purpose. As the group works through the interpersonal dynamics from creating goals to fulfilling them, each member's emotional intelligence is honed. While the sense of purpose these groups engender is still based on being a human doing rather than a human being, a man is freer to be his real self than he is at work because the organization is voluntary, and what he does there is not as necessary to supporting his family as his workplace.

In contrast, more informal groups for boys and men of all ages build male emotional intelligence more directly. I mentioned in the introduction how, in the early '70s, the National Organization for Women in New York asked me to form a men's group. It was to be the first of hundreds of men's (and women's) groups I would form. In most of these groups, about eight guys gather in a circle at each other's homes, usually about once every other week, and share what is happening in their everyday life.

With confidentiality as the key, men's groups open the door to men opening their hearts. This type of group can give your son a safe space where he feels supported as he shares self-doubts. The support comes as he discovers that beneath their "I'm cool" mask, many of the other guys feel the same as he does. The security to remove his mask is to his emotional intelligence what water is to a flower.

These informal men's groups serve a very different purpose, then, from the Boy Scouts, or from the Kiwanis or Rotarians. Those long-established organizations are not designed to help their members share their fears or feelings of vulnerability. Why? Part of the reason for joining those organizations was to be respected; each member knew that sharing marital troubles, lack of confidence, or an affair could undermine his reputation.

In contrast, the purpose of the informal men's groups is for boys and men to express what men in the formal groups repress. The informal groups' key—confidentiality—diminishes the fear of reputation loss, allowing for genuineness, the discovery of self, and therefore the building of emotional and spiritual intelligence.

Both types of groups build male strength, albeit differently. We saw in my informal men's group that John Lennon had joined that it was one of the most important contributions to John's life—and perhaps *the* most important contribution to the life of his son Sean.

Here's the bottom line: **in my forty-five years of forming men's groups, I have never heard of a man who was actively involved in a men's group being hospitalized for depression, or commit suicide**.

If your son is a teenager, he can learn how to join or form a group for teens from organizations like The ManKind Project and Boys to Men, or, perhaps with your help, start one with a faith-based organization. The instructions in Bill Kauth's book *A Circle of Men* are still relevant.[20]

If your son is older, have him check into the men's group movement called men's "sheds," which are particularly popular in Australia and Europe,[21] and ripe for being adopted in the United States.

Veterans: Caring for the Ultimate Caring Profession

The military might be thought of as the ultimate caring profession. But their graduates—veterans—are among the least cared for. We now have more tools to care better—if we care enough.

Rebooting Boot Camp

No group suffers more than veterans from the gap between heroic intelligence and health intelligence.

For every veteran who suffers from PTSD or commits suicide, there are many others who suffer injuries or death that are avoidable but for the acceptability of disposability—like the shocking experience Vanessa Dahn shared with me about her husband:

> My hubby was completing his last night of repel school in the army. He was expected to do night repels followed by a night run of sixteen kilometers. But when he was coming down on the ropes, the helicopter pilot mistakenly went straight up, forcing my husband to free-fall at least thirty feet. The damage would end up requiring three foot surgeries and a stem cell transfer, and lead to a hearing loss, a calcified tendon, and hip problems. Yet rather than being sent directly to the hospital, *he was told he would fail the course if he did not immediately run the sixteen kilometers.* And just as bad, he agreed to continue—only to be paying the price for the rest of his life.[22]

The social bribes of the military—from boot camp training to the lure of becoming a five-star general—teach him to identify his purpose with his disposability. The social bribes become so ingrained that they are as difficult to remove as syrup from a pancake. To do so would require at the very least walking him through every step of the training that originally prepared him for heroic intelligence, to retrain him for health intelligence.

So even once the need for a soldier's disposability ends, when he returns home, that training remains. This is a large part of why, as we have seen, one US veteran commits suicide every sixty-five minutes.[23]

Although inpatient treatment programs often have six-month waiting lists and infamous bureaucratic nonresponsiveness, the Department of Veterans' Affairs (VA) has at least established a suicide hotline with trained staff. And since 2001, while the rate of suicide among veterans who do not use VA services increased by almost 39 percent, the rate of suicide among veterans who **do** use VA services increased by only 9 percent.[24]

Since a 9 percent *increase* is not exactly encouraging, it will help to look into some of the more effective programs for vets—such as the Time Cure and the Veterans' Transition Program, both of which call upon a veteran's mental discipline to win a new war: the war in their mind. A 2012 video, "A War in the Mind,"[25] demonstrates the process.

For a military man, this reframing of war to include the psychological is pivotal because military culture has trained him to "just get over it" and, if he is being destructive in any way, to take personal responsibility for stopping his destructive behavior. Everything his friends died for—and he almost died for—was about taking personal responsibility. **When a veteran internalizes that he's failed to take personal responsibility, he is a step closer to suicide.**

While this reversal of attitude toward the psychological is pivotal, new evidence points to the connection between the physical and psychological. If your son is within about 150 feet of a blast, even if he appears completely unharmed physically, he is nevertheless at a high risk of brain damage.[26] Specifically, he is likely to experience a scarring in his brain that does not diminish with time but grows like an embryo, leading to the likelihood of your son suffering from memory loss, cognitive problems, inability to sleep, and profound, often suicidal, depression. As time passes, and as the embryonic scar spreads, these dangers increase rather than decrease.[27]

Restoring Purpose: Restoring Service

Eric Greitens had recently returned from Iraq, where he had witnessed several friends being killed after their barracks were bombed by al-Qaeda. After some recovery time, he spent a day visiting severely wounded veterans at Bethesda Naval Hospital. He asked each wounded veteran, "What do you want to do now?" Each wounded veteran's answer had one common denominator: serve. Serve with their unit, or serve in their community[28]—for example, as a teacher or coach, or by building something like a home for disabled children. In essence, they wanted their mission to continue.

So their mission became Eric's mission. He founded Mission Continues.[29] For example, Team Rubicon has sent some seven thousand veterans to help with disaster relief, including the 2016 floods in West Virginia and the 2016 earthquake in Ecuador.

If your son returns from military service depressed, a natural response is to "cut him some slack." But a boy whose purpose was to serve most often has his purpose restored by serving. By being needed, either within the home or outside the home. Preferably both.

A key to understanding veterans is to know that **many veterans are "rough, tough cream puffs."** Their idea of caring is not words but deeds. And making themselves tough enough to do those deeds is their definition of love.

Veterans harden themselves so others don't have to. In this way, they "civilize" all of us. **Veterans create privilege for all those who have not had to serve.** Veterans put out the fires in my life, so I can feel protected enough to write about them putting out the fires in my life. Whereas the spiritual leader and philosopher civilize us from the top down, the soldier civilizes us from the bottom up.[30]

This understanding is necessary to move beyond seeing the returned veteran as serving only in the outdoors—building homes and rescuing. If we cut through to his caring heart, we also open up the possibility of his entering the "caring professions"—being a coach, a teacher, a full-time dad, a social worker, or working in emergency medicine or health care.

If we build on the warrior spirit within him, we can transfer that spirit into his becoming a "tech warrior," à la Gates, Jobs, Zuckerberg, or the veterans who founded GoDaddy and Google-acquired Skybox Imaging.

Bringing service home

We're used to calling veterans heroes for their service away from home. But almost all **traditional men make their sacrifices in significant measure in the hopes of being appreciated when they come home, and having their learning experiences integrated into their homes.** The degree to which men's—or women's—mission defines their purpose is the degree to which the end of that mission can create a "mission void," or depression. Hence the suicide rate among male veterans and retirees.

War may create PTSD, but the process of becoming a soldier teaches a man to become a standardized part who does not take everything personally, so that he may work more efficiently—so that he may be the ultimate team player.[31] He needs to know he is valued for his ability to be a team player in his own home. Hopefully, part IV made it clear how the first priority of returning from service is knowing how to help dad serve not where his friends' hearts have stopped, but where his heart is.

CHAPTER 26

Hidden Hazards to Your Son's Health

Because the survival of our sons has long been in tension with the survival of ourselves, our fear of coddling and protecting our sons has allowed for more pleas to save whales than to save males. Thus, many of the hazards to our sons' health have remained hidden. Let's begin at the existential beginning . . .

The "Sperm Crisis": To Be, or Not to Be

In the beginning, there was sperm. Sperm in search of an egg. Yet even prior to 1990 men's sperm count was down by 50 percent.[1] Now **one in five *young* men are not fertile.**[2]

The consequence? **Men with lower sperm count, even if they can reproduce, are likely to have a shorter life.**[3]

Because the quality of sperm is an indicator of the quality of the environment, it is also an indicator of environmental problems that have an impact on girls and women. Sperm is the canary in the coal mine. Whether or not we ignore the sperm crisis may pose the ultimate existential question: to be, or not to be?

A New SOS: Save Our Sperm

If you wish to enhance your son—or future son's—sperm, what can you do? Here's what we know:

- **Before pregnancy.** Dad, don't do marijuana. Mom, don't smoke. Also, the quality of dad's diet affects the quality of his sperm. And both parents' lifestyle choices, like exercise and stress, affect their future son's health and sperm.
- **Pregnancy.** Dad, support mom to do all of the above by doing all of the above with her. Dad, do the three Ls: listen to her, love her, and, oh yes, listen to her. Mom, do the three As: appreciate, appreciate, appreciate (*him*, that is).
- **Soon after birth.** Don't make your son's baths too hot. Keep up that great diet—especially by limiting high-fat foods and sugar that isn't in fruits and veggies. Check the quality of your drinking water; if it's not great, check for the best filtering system. Or move.
- **Dad In, Fat Out.** Obesity, diabetes, and erectile dysfunction are your son's *un*holy trinity. The quality of the father-son relationship matters far more than the mother-son relationship in preventing a boy from being overweight or obese.[4] But exercise also weighs in heavily.
- **Know what to check for.** If your son is taking drugs for hypertension—or any other drug—check for their impact on infertility. Teach him—or ask his pediatrician to teach him—about checking for enlarged veins on his scrotum (varicocele); about 40 percent of infertile males have varicocele. Keep the lid on recreational drugs, including marijuana—heavy use affects fertility. If he takes steroids to make himself appear like more of a man on the outside, he's likely to have less potent sperm on the inside.[5] See the section on page 295 on testicular cancer prevention.[6]
- **And about that cell phone.** Cell phones can impair sperm's viability and motility (its ability to move toward an egg).[7] They may also create gliomas in the brain (tumors that are likely to be malignant) and heart tumors. More studies are in progress, but one thing is already clear: his pocket should be cell phone free, unless he wants his life to be child free.

Our progress has created more hazards to our sons' health than cell phones.

Plastics: Growing Girls, Shrinking Boys

About half a century ago, in the film *The Graduate,* Mr. Braddock revealed to his son, Benjamin, played by Dustin Hoffman, that the key to future success was "plastics." Today, the future is here, and while plastics did become a key to our future success, that success came at a price.

Plastics leach phthalates. Like the great majority of modern chemicals that leach into our waters from plastic bottles and pesticides, phthalates mimic the action of *female* sex hormones. These phthalate esters catalyze the onset of premature puberty in human girls, and are also associated with the *shriveled testicles* of alligators in Lake Apopka (the watershed that serves Orlando's Disney World), according to the US Fish and Wildlife Service.[8]

Is Lake Apopka an isolated example? No. The emasculation of both fish and a large variety of mammals has also been found in other parts of the United States, such as the Great Lakes, Idaho, and the states of Washington and Alaska, as well as in other countries such as England and Greenland.[9]

The *male* smallmouth bass swimming in the rivers of Virginia, Maryland, and DC have begun making eggs, not sperm. And it's not just the occasional male smallmouth bass. It's at least 80 percent of them.[10] Scientists have tested seven sites in the tributaries of the Potomac. In both DC and the rivers surrounding DC (more than one hundred miles up both the Conococheague Creek and the Monocacy River in Maryland), the outcome was the same. Apparently, there is also no difference in these smallmouth basses' sperm whether Democrats or Republicans are in office!

Is there an impact on our sons? Estimates are similar from experts from Duke and MIT to the University of Minnesota: between 1990 and 2006 there has been an increase in erectile dysfunction from about zero to 25 percent among the male students they counsel.[11] Maybe a connection, maybe not.

Preventing Testicular Cancer

Testicular cancer can manifest in young boys, but half of the cases occur in young men between twenty and thirty-four. And it is four to five times more likely to occur among white males than black or Asian American males. The risk is highest among US and European males.[12]

The bad news: the testicular cancer rate has doubled in recent years.[13] There are now 8,850 new cases of testicular cancer each year. For reasons you now know, neither the school system nor general public awareness is likely to clue your son in to how to check for early indicators. So a parent needs to take the lead.

The good news: if it is caught early, testicular cancer's cure rate is 99 percent.[14] And it can be caught early by, first, checking for an undescended testicle. By middle school, have your son check his scrotum once a month for lumps, in the same way you would have your daughter test for breast cancer. And have him check for enlarged veins. Let him know that if caught early that the 99 percent cure rate makes it a hazard he can avoid. The very process of having your son do this is perfect training to help him see growing up male as being inclusive of taking responsibility for his health.

Drinking and Drugs

Boys and men are nearly three times more likely than girls and women to abuse alcohol, and twice as likely to abuse recreational drugs like marijuana and cocaine.[15]

The key word is "abuse." Whether the issue is video games or cannabis, boys whose testosterone is not channeled constructively channel it destructively. Testosterone tends to surge toward the end of high school—the same time that drug use (as well as the suicide rate) in boys soars. Between eighth and tenth grade, boys and girls use drugs about equally. But by senior year, 8.5 percent of boys use marijuana *daily*, versus only 3.3 percent of girls.[16]

Testosterone is best channeled by creating an infrastructure for your son to do so before adolescence, when he's still receptive to your suggestions. We have seen how each of the many infrastructure building blocks—whether team sports, family dinner nights, boundary enforcement, two-parent involvement, or the nineteen steps toward integrating health and heroic intelligence—contribute differently to the network of pipelines for channeling your son's testosterone effectively when adolescence opens the floodgates.

The Unholy Trinity: Obesity, Diabetes, and Erectile Dysfunction

Fat spreads. Obesity is king of an unholy trinity, inviting the addition of both diabetes and erectile dysfunction. This unholy trinity in turn predicts a future of problems with heart disease, poverty, and self-esteem. Because erectile dysfunction is the most challenging of these for a boy to discuss—especially in the form of premature ejaculation or failure to become erect—let's dig in there.

While premature ejaculation is embarrassing to a boy, and can make his partner feel he cares only about getting himself off, it has the saving grace of at least some partners being able to interpret it as the result of their own irresistible attractiveness!

In contrast, if your son's obesity begets failure to become erect as a teenage boy, few of your son's partners will interpret his flaccid penis as the result of their own attractiveness! Instead, your son is likely to experience quintuple jeopardy: fear that his partner believes his inability to get an erection is a reflection of his lack of attraction to her or him; shame at not being able to get hard; shame at not being able to control his weight; fear he'll not only be rejected by his potential lover but also be laughed at behind his back ("He's fat *and* flaccid!"); and isolation from feeling he cannot discuss this with anyone.

For your son to experience this quintuple jeopardy when his sexual identity is in its fragile formative months can be life altering. It can lead to him turning to pornography rather than risking rejection from real women or men. Pornography predicts even more erection problems,[17] and feelings of loneliness, isolation, depression, and obesity. Fat spreads.

The rate of obesity among adolescent boys is increasing. (Fortunately, girls' has stabilized.) Obesity among boys is the dominant cause of 75 percent of young Americans being unable to meet even the basic standards for military service.[18]

Why? For starters, lack of boundary enforcement around diet, exercise, and video game use has contributed to American boys and men being among the fattest in the world. When 70 percent of adult men are overweight[19] and a third are obese,[20] it means a boy is exposed to unhealthy food and lifestyle at home. Most important, obesity *as a boy* predicts problems for your son as a man—from metabolic challenges to cardiovascular complications.[21] Fat spreads.

The Message the Affordable Care Act Sends to Your Son

Heroic intelligence encourages risking life; health insurance protects against the risks in life. Logically, men, in greater need of that protection, would be more likely to seek insurance. Yet boys and men are only 43 percent of the eligible insured. That is, they are 16 percent less likely to be insured than females. For millions of boys and men, the impact of social bribes trumps logic. And trumps life.

I consulted with the Obama administration about how to increase male participation in the Affordable Care Act. It was then that I discovered that something even more surprising was going on.[22] And still is. It may play out in your son's life as it did with Ted . . .

When Ted had his first serious girlfriend in college, he let her know that he wanted to share responsibility for sexually transmitted diseases and birth control. Kathy had her antenna tuned for just such a guy. They agreed they would both check out what was available on campus.

A couple of days later, Kathy volunteered, "I had my first 'Well-Woman Visit.' The counselor—Susan—was great. She gave me a lot of info about the best doses of estrogen for birth control and the best methods for avoiding STDs or STIs."

"That sounds great." Ted nodded.

Excited, Kathy continued, "Then she took my entire health history. I had to check in with my parents, and I found out that my grandmother had suffered from both depression and breast cancer. So Susan gave me info about breast cancer genetic tests—they're called BRCA tests—and the latest research on the value of mammography screenings. I'll get a comprehensive screening every year. For free. And all my pap smears are free, too.

"So what did you find out, Ted?"

"I found out that there's no such thing as a 'Well-*Man* Visit'—none of that comprehensive family history stuff, no screenings, and," making light of it, "no free pap smears . . . but maybe that's the case because your reproductive health stuff can be more complicated than a guy's, eh?"

"Yeah," Kathy added, "but don't guys commit suicide more and deny a lot of stuff? Seems like there should be a special effort to reach guys. And besides, if we're going to be real partners, we both have to know about both of our problems."

In fact, Kathy and Ted were correct: the Affordable Care Act provides all those provisions for women, and none of those provisions for men. And all those provisions for women are free.[23]

Moreover, with Kathy's Well-Woman Visits being annual, once the comprehensive initial history allows her university doctor to have her baseline, every year they can quickly detect any sudden changes. That comprehensive initial visit also allows for that baseline to be acquired while Kathy is young enough that her parents are available to give her the details.

Kathy's Well-Woman Visit also included a *mental* health history. For free. When Kathy recounted her own bouts of depression, the fact that her grandma had also suffered depression informed the next phase of her Well-Woman Visit—setting goals for prevention. Kathy and her doctor agreed to goals of exercising daily, including doing yoga, and a diet that would counter depression. Kathy learned her BMI. Kathy recalled, "Knowing I'll be evaluated next year has definitely increased my motivation to follow the plan."

And yes, you guessed it: there's no free mental health history for Ted.

When flu season was approaching, Kathy had already had a briefing on the risks and benefits of a flu shot—and the fact that she could get them for free. *For Ted, the ACA provides none of that for free.*[24]

On an unconscious level, the free annual Well-Woman Visits give Kathy a sense that someone cares. And most important, that *she* needs to care.

For Ted, none of this was true. His heroic intelligence was left undisturbed by health intelligence. As Ted put it, "When it comes to guys, it seems like there should be a sort of affirmative action to get us to pay attention to our health, given how bad we are at it. My dad only goes to the doctor to get my mom off his back!"

More important for Ted, though, was his gnawing feeling that he wanted to be a partner with Kathy in their sexual decisions, but he knew he wasn't. Both their parents were quite religious. Talking to his parents about the need for money to go to the doctor to discuss his and Kathy's sexual health was awkward at best. These services were free to Kathy, so she didn't have to ask her parents for the money and launch an equally challenging discussion.[25]

What Ted also doesn't realize is that, like the ACA, virtually every state also offers considerable resources for women and maternal care, while almost no state dedicates specific resources for men, or paternal care.[26]

And Ted is lucky, because Ted is white. Boys and men of color fare worse on all twenty-two indicators of health and well-being—from AIDS to cancer, heart disease, and diabetes.[27] They are also less likely to have insurance coverage or receive health screenings. Less financial and emotional support are being provided to the gender that needs it more—and even less to those of that gender who need it the most.

Should the law be changed to prevent gender discrimination by the ACA? No. The ACA itself already makes gender discrimination illegal. It is in violation of its own law![28]

Hospitals' "Glass Ceilings": Men's Health

The traditional male role of hero creates men's "glass ceilings" in hospitals in the same way that the traditional female role of mother has reinforced women's glass ceilings in the workplace. That is, the traditional role of mother did not lead to workplaces envisioning women as working seventy-hour weeks as is expected of many CEOs. And women's traditional role also led to few women thinking of themselves that way. In a complementary way, the social bribes of heroic intelligence led to hospitals seeing many fewer male patients. Many men in pain felt that "when the going gets tough, the tough get going"—to anyone but a doctor. Until it was too late.

In hospitals, those glass ceilings include the presence of women's centers but the absence of men's centers.

Your son is growing up in a world where his health is caught between two perspectives:

Perspective one: Because boys and men die sooner from fourteen out of fifteen of the leading causes of death, hospitals should have men's health centers in the same way they already have women's health centers.

Perspective two: Health research is already about men—the whole world is about men—so why would we need men's health centers?

The dominance of perspective two created long delays in the formation of Miriam Hospital's men's center in Rhode Island, even when it limited itself to men's sexual health.[29] A professor of women's health protested, "Men's health? That's got about as much relevance as white liberation."[30] Her perspective was solicited by the American Medical Association.[31]

So how can this problem be a solution? **It is exactly this men's health void that creates your son's men's health opportunity.**

Men's health centers such as those at the Cleveland Clinic and NYU Langone's Preston Robert Tisch Center for Men's Health are finally being formed as your son is now seen as part of a neglected market. That is, capitalism (your son as market share) is beginning to chip away at ideology (it's only your daughter who is neglected and needs to be protected) just in time for your son to benefit.

The good news for your son is not just the potential to be a future recipient but also the potential to be a future participant. And to do so, he does *not* need to become a doctor. He can become a physician's assistant, or a nurse practitioner, and increasingly develop a specialty in one of the below-mentioned areas of men's physical or emotional health. He can do this in two ways:

First, by getting in on the ground floor in men's centers. Find the gaps, and fill them. Most men's centers are focusing on men's physical health (e.g., issues of the prostate, erectile dysfunction, diabetes, colorectal cancer, heart disease, urinary tract infections). They are weak on emotional health. Your son's awareness of the sixty-plus red flags on the Warren Farrell Male Depression / Suicide Inventory, for example, may motivate him to develop programs for hospitals that identify the stepping stones to male depression and suicide in time to redirect young men toward more life-enhancing paths.

Second, even in the areas of physical health, there are many diseases to which men are far more prone than women and that are nevertheless neglected by hospitals. Liver cancer, one of the most lethal forms of cancer, is three times more common in men than women. Young men are about four times as likely to contract tongue and throat cancers as women are—especially sexually active young men who consistently engage in oral sex.[32] And the same four-to-one gap exists with male deaths from cancers of the esophagus, larynx, and bladder.[33]

Third, your son can also develop his expertise by becoming an intern at places such as the Men's Health Network,[34] or if he has a talent for writing, at *Men's Health* magazine, or if he's a doer, with worldwide organizations such as the Mankind Project.[35]

Nor does your son need to wait for a job to be advertised. He can proactively create his own job with a hospital's men's center by, for example, interning as a coordinator of community outreach to schools, Ys, and scouts, using the sixty-plus questions to kick-start a men's group.

If your son is handy, he can form a "building a man" program to work with vocational schools to teach boys to build homes, or do repairs for those in need. As we've seen, boys build purpose by doing, and build health when they've built purpose.

To fill hospitals' void in developing the preventive medicine of emotional intelligence, your son may wish to develop programs that coach boys on how to empathize, and ultimately become an EM (empathy mentor). Never heard of an empathy mentor? Well, there isn't a lot of competition for the job your son creates!

One of the pioneering contributions of the late Richard Bolles's classic, *What Color is Your Parachute?* is the much greater success achieved by those who create a job than by those who apply for an advertised job. The first step is what we just did: identify what is needed; then develop some proficiency; and then present to a hospital how he can fulfill the needs he's identified.[36]

I know this works. When I was doing my PhD at NYU, I contemplated becoming a university president. But I didn't want to spend my career climbing to the top of a ladder only to conclude it was bringing me to the wrong ceiling. It was the late '60s and student protests were haunting universities. So I sought out the president of NYU, James Hester, and proposed to write a small book on how students could participate in university governance rather than just protest. He loved it, and appointed me as an assistant to the president. It introduced me to every school in the university, and in four months I knew that being an author was more for me than being a university president.

The Government as Glass Ceiling

Should your son be inclined to explore the field of men's health, he will discover that the neglect of male health intelligence is so institutionalized in the government that it might be called government approved. The bias against boys and men in the Affordable Care Act is just the outcome of a deeper institutionalization. For example, although your son and the men you love predictably die sooner than girls and women, the US government has seven federal offices for women's health, but none for men's health. Each contributes to legislation that is tuned into the needs of girls and women, but not that of boys and men. Once the legislation is passed, it spreads the word via webpages for womenshealth.gov and girlshealth .gov, but none for menshealth.gov or boyshealth.gov.

As we take a brief look at these seven offices of women's health, I'll be asking you to help your son view these inherited biases as part of the present that he has an opportunity to change in the future.

How is that realistic? The absence of equal services for boys and men is arguably unconstitutional—a potential violation of the Fourteenth Amendment's guarantee of "equal protection" to both sexes. This discrimination can only survive with apathy. If your son and his peers care, your son will be in on the ground floor of a massive change.

Too big a project for your son? No problem. Young men who are not inspired to lead a mission are often inspired to be soldiers in a mission. Here are some entry points . . .

Your son might intern in one of the seven offices of women's health, where the money already is. If he has a bent toward technology and is inventive, he can help develop the future of healthcare: robotic aids that can do the laundry, clean the house, and pick up dishes.

Because the money is in women's health, the women's health agencies will be developing these with older women in mind, but your son can help develop adaptations that will make older men laugh (e.g., Alexa or Siri engaging in playful, wit-covered put-downs that are both quasi-outrageous and a tad off-color).

As your son works to help elderly women use virtual reality to reconnect with their past (e.g., their sorority or first home), he can be mindful of creating adaptations that will be user-friendly to men, such as returning to their high school's football game, or college fraternity. Virtual reality is especially conducive to play, entertainment, games, excitement, and fun—all of which can enliven the lives of any aging person, and has special appeal to men (who never quite lose their inner boy!).

Developing these adaptations where the money is will introduce your son to thinking of the neglected aspects of men's health that are the equivalents of what is being funded for women. As you'll see among the following women's offices, whether your son is interested in biomedical research, the testing of food and drugs, agriculture, social work, or domestic violence, there is a male equivalent that is being neglected (e.g., domestic violence against men). As he writes articles and memos, he can build an expertise that will allow him to both further the health of women *and* be on the ground floor of men's health centers and the eventual male equivalents of the already-developed women-centric agencies below.

Your son doesn't have to move to Washington, DC, for these kinds of jobs. There is also likely a regional federal office near him. For example, the Department of Health and Human Services (see number 3) has ten regional offices for women's health, none of which currently has an equivalent for boys and men.

1. **Women, Infants, and Children (WIC) Program, US Department of Agriculture**
   This is the program that almost exclusively funds poorer moms if they don't have a dad in the home. If a dad doesn't give the mom more money than the government would, it's the government in, the dad out. Or the government as substitute dad. As we've seen, this dad deprivation increases the likelihood that the woman, infants, and children will remain poor and be more prone to suffer in some of about fifty other ways, thus continuing into the next generation the cycle of the need for government as daddy for women.

   Your son's mission as part of this agency? To get dads more involved so children receive more love, the family earns more money, and ultimately both our sons and daughters contribute more to the world.

2. **Office on Violence Against Women, US Department of Justice**
   Research for the past half century has been consistent in its findings that domestic violence between the sexes is about equal—although in dating years it is much more female on male.[37] However, since all the $5 billion that fund some twenty-one grant programs are focused only on helping girls and women, this leaves an opening for your

son to create two types of programs: first, programs that also help boys and men speak up about physical or sexual abuse; and second, since a person is rarely violent toward someone from whom she or he feels empathy, programs that teach both sexes to handle personal criticism by becoming supportive rather than defensive—like the program on couples' communication described in the next chapter. This will allow his professional contribution to also contribute to his emotional intelligence in his personal life.

3. **US Department of Health and Human Services' Office of Women's Health**

   The Department of Health and Human Services has ten regional offices for women's health, with about 60,000 employees, and four agencies with separate offices of women's health listed below.[38]

4. **National Institutes of Health's Office of Research on Women's Health**

5. **Center for Disease Control and Prevention's Office of Women's Health**

6. **Food and Drug Administration's Office of Women's Health**

7. **Health Resources and Services Administration's Office of Women's Health**

None of these has an equivalent for boys and men.

Again, it is the men's health void that creates your son's men's health opportunity. Necessity is not just the mother of invention; it can also be the father of invention. Your son shouldn't feel like an antihero if he seeks to be a pioneer in men's health. When we protect boys and men, we also protect girls and women.

CHAPTER 27

From Hurt People Hurting People to Healed People Healing People

The solution to hurt people hurting people? Healed people healing people.

Refilling the Empathy Void

One of the best ways to heal is to hear. To empathize.

Empathy doesn't come easily. We're all born thinking only of ourselves. No infant stops crying when hungry because she or he senses that their twin brother or sister needs food or attention more than they do. However, while we are wired to be self-centered, we are also wired to serve ourselves by being receptive to the needs and wishes of others. This is reinforced by our brain's rostral cingulate zone, which gets a spike of the feel-good drug dopamine when others respond appreciatively after feeling our empathy. It's all part of being wired to adapt.

Empathy is like eating our veggies. We have to learn it is good for us. And then adapt.

But if you are a parent who consistently empathizes with not only your children's needs but also their desires, without also emphasizing with others' needs and desires, it will tend to leave your children focused just on their needs and desires and, therefore, less empathetic. That is, they have no need to adapt.

The era of overempathetic parents has had consequences: the empathy level of college students has dropped about 40 percent between 1979 and 2010.[1] Less empathy has a cyclical effect: fewer friends leads to more depression and alienation, which leads to more video games and more video porn, which leads to more desensitization, more objectification, and less empathy, which leads to fewer friends . . . Parental empathy is another one of those virtues that, when taken to an extreme, can become a vice.

So how can you transmit the virtue of empathy without creating the vice of self-centeredness? We've seen that, worldwide, the more a father is involved, the more empathetic the child. And we've seen why—for example, the tendency of dads to use roughhousing and game-playing to develop a bond, and then use that bond as leverage to enforce boundaries that require the child to develop postponed gratification and think of his dad's needs, too (like not being scratched or poked in the eye while wrestling).

But what if significant father involvement is just not possible for your son? You can jump-start empathy by first being empathetic, and then requiring your son to hear you, too—as well as his siblings and friends. Whether you're a mom or a dad, the best way to begin is by "catching him" being empathetic—even if it's to a frog. Find a seed, and water it. Then, after watering the seed, channel his energy: help him write a thank-you note, take care of his sister when she's sick, or invite a kid at school who seems lonely to join him for lunch.

That is, empathy can be taught. The Danish school system offers one hour of empathy building each week for all their schoolchildren, ages six to sixteen. During that hour, the students talk with each other about who is being left out, bullied, or rejected. By talking through bullying and being mocked, it allows both the bully and the bullied to replace their low self-esteem with compassion. The emphasis is on acknowledging each other, hearing others' viewpoints, and considering things from many perspectives. The goal is to create what the Danes call *hygge*[2]—a supportive atmosphere. From this program's consistency emerges a sense of community and feelings of security and confidence. Which also free children from spending the rest of their lives trying to prove themselves.

If you have a son (or daughter) who is both caring and competitive, introduce him to the Caring Contests sponsored by Unified Caring. A mom I interviewed described how after her autistic son, Seth, read the essays of previous contestants, and then wrote his own, he experienced a significant and permanent increase in his empathy.[3] She felt it has allowed him to navigate the world effectively enough to now be entering college. Invite your son to catalyze an increase in his caring intelligence by reading the essays, submit one of his own, and win some prize money.

Yes, empathy can be taught.

Couples' Communication: Your Children's Best Inheritance

Shortly after Liz and I married, her daughter Alex, then a ninth grader, had her first boyfriend. Soon, though, they ran into problems. Since I had been conducting couples' communication workshops, they sought my help.

As I began introducing them to how to listen nondefensively, Alex interrupted me midstream, exclaiming, "Wait, this is what you and mom do!" Because Liz and I tended to work through our areas of tension in private, I was surprised at the nuance Alex had absorbed from our nonprivate communication.

Alex's reaction also deepened my awareness of how, even though Liz and my style was distinct from Liz and her ex-husband's—the style to which Alex was exposed in her first five years—it was nevertheless being absorbed. Although things did not work out with that boyfriend, Alex and her second boyfriend, Hutch, did come to my workshops, eventually got married, and have just had a son who will hopefully avoid the boy crisis!

So what is the connection between the boy crisis and couples' communication? The most important cause of the boy crisis is the divorces that lead to dad-deprived boys. But the solution is not to make divorce harder. It's to make marriages better. And, as mentioned earlier, a happy marriage is less about money, sex, or children than about how we communicate about money, sex, and children.

But if everyone wants to communicate well, why isn't everyone doing it? Why can't we all just get along?

Because historically, when we heard criticism we feared an enemy. To survive, we "got up our defenses." Or we killed the enemy before the enemy killed us.

The good news? Your great-great-grandparents survived.

The bad news? Your partner most likely "walks on eggshells" for fear of saying what she or he thinks will make the relationship better only to have you respond defensively. After their desire to be heard leads to an escalating argument a few times, they start becoming more focused on just keeping the peace, but with little pieces of themselves—and their love for you—being lost in the shadow of their fear.

As you read that paragraph, did you feel yourself getting a little defensive? See if that defensiveness dissipates as you read that paragraph in reverse:

When you say to your partner what you feel will make the relationship better, your partner too often responds defensively. Soon you find yourself "walking on eggshells" for fear of an escalating argument. You slowly find yourself more focused on just keeping the peace, but with little pieces of yourself—and your love—being lost in the shadow of your fear.

If the second paragraph is easier for you to hear, that means that you are, well, human. The downside of our surviving by "getting up our defenses" is that, as we've seen, the Achilles' heel of human beings is our inability to handle personal criticism from a loved one without becoming defensive. **Love doesn't eliminate defensiveness, because love creates vulnerability, and defensiveness is vulnerability's mask.** When our defensiveness doesn't shut our partner down or "win" the argument, we may become angry. Anger is the mask of vulnerability we use when defensiveness fails to work.

Much of my recent life's work has included inventing a work-around to the hard wiring of defensiveness. Since defensiveness is biologically natural, couples create a special "caring and sharing" time of two hours per week when, prior to hearing their partner's concerns, they *alter* their biologically natural mindset with a six-step meditation that allows them to temporarily do something unnatural: associate feeling criticized with an opportunity to be more deeply loved. It is only during that two-hour period that they are asked to alter their natural state and temporarily associate the criticism with being loved. The couples are then taught how to both create and sustain a "conflict-free zone" during the remaining 166 hours of the week. These are just two components of what creates "the art and discipline of love."

Whether you achieve it via my method[4] or another, the internal security and emotional intelligence of a loving marriage becomes your children's best inheritance.

Sharing the Caring

An extensive study comparing men who are not the primary breadwinner to those who are the primary breadwinner finds that **the primary breadwinners have:**

- poorer psychological health.
- poorer mental health.
- their poorest psychological and physical health during the years they earn the most.[5]

Moreover, a woman who *shares* the financial burden feels psychologically *healthier.*[6]

So we've found something that increases the health of both sexes: sharing the financial burden.

However, what is healthy is still at odds with the pressure many dads feel to accommodate the mom's choice, whether that's to work full-time, work part-time, or be full-time with the children. If mom has three options, whatever she chooses can feel less like a pressure and more like a choice. And dad usually accommodates with one of his "three options": to work full-time, work full-time, or work full-time (which often means working two jobs if he is a working-class man, and overtime if he is an executive). If your son does not know how to identify social bribes, and therefore cannot separate social pressure from his deeper desires, he will be unable to talk about what he's feeling, and his health will suffer.

We've missed this because the message of the past half century has been how a mom often makes a sacrifice *of* her career. We remained virtually unconscious of the way a dad often makes sacrifices *in* his career.

Nor did we consider how a dad's entire career might be a sacrifice: the loss of the glint in his eye. By equating high pay only with power and privilege, we missed how it was also pressure and expectation. This made us oblivious to how the road to high pay was often a toll road.[7] The tolls of losing family time, personal time, time to develop friendships . . . the tolls that drove the sad men of *Mad Men* to drink.

The solution to this, then, is a serious contemplation of having both sexes share both the raising of money and the raising of children. While each parent's individual personalities are the more important factor in determining the best arrangement for them, it is at least good to know that in general this approach will make both the mom and dad healthier, and the children do better—as the chapters on dad-enriched boys make clear.

If anybody ain't happy, ain't nobody happy.

Prescription Drugs, or Another Prescription?

In the past, the prescription for raising healthy boys was some blend of an intact family, boundary enforcement, discipline, and purpose fulfilled by roles. Today, as those prescriptions have gone unfilled, drugs are prescribed to fill the void. Not all the symptoms were positive: inability to pay attention, bullying, harassment. But instead of harnessing them with boundary enforcement and channeling them with purpose, **the negative symptoms of the male culture are harnessed by the prescription drug culture.**

Prescription drugs can help a boy who is suicidal or has ADHD past a tough spot and assist him in discovering a competence that gives him a sense of control and self-worth. However, too often they also atrophy his brain, damage his liver, throw his mental health out of balance, and create deeper addictions, which are then addressed by creating new prescriptions and renewing old ones. In the process, those family values–based prescriptions from the past that helped prevent the problem in the first place are forgotten.

The era of prescription drugs by default is now de rigueur. Fortunately, there are places like Safe Landing Group Center in Colorado that fight the propensity of psychiatrists, nurses, and judges to take the drug route. They create a supportive family-like community that uses positive reinforcement to encourage boys twelve to eighteen into sports, music, physically demanding chores, and other life-enhancing alternatives.

If your son is addicted, whether to alcohol, street drugs, or prescription drugs, Saint Jude Retreats has a more than 60 percent long-term success rate with addiction recovery.[8] And if he has ADHD, John Gray presents a plethora of little-known nonprescription solutions in part VI.

While many of the prescriptions from the past need updating, there is one that has been tossed out that is easy to rescue. Recess.

The Solution to Recess-Deprived Boys? Recess

Just as the solution to dad-deprived boys is dads, the solution to recess-deprived boys is recess. Here's the problem—and the solution . . .

Recess, usually less structured than physical education, allows more flexibility to decide what to play and how to play. Therefore, when it comes to boys and recess, schools face a dilemma:

- Boys are more likely to use recess to bully, but
- boys are in dire need of recess.

To schools, recess bullying is about even more than bullying—it is also about litigation. And beyond bullying and litigation, recess takes away from classroom time to prepare students for state and federally mandated testing. Is there a solution?

Paradoxically, the solution to recess as a problem is recess. And not just for our sons. Evidence?

A 2017 report by the CDC finds that recess:

- enhances students' memory, attention, and concentration.
- helps students stay on task in the classroom.
- increases academic achievement.
- reduces disruptive behavior in the classroom.
- helps control weight and strengthens bones and muscles.
- reduces anxiety, stress, and depression.
- improves students' social and emotional development (e.g., learning how to share, problem-solve, communicate, cooperate, and negotiate).[9]

Take the last point alone: recess improves social and emotional development. The greater a boy's social and emotional development, the less likely he is to bully. So **while recess provides the playground in which bullying may be found, it is also the laboratory for reducing bullying.** And the more bullying is reduced, the more litigation is reduced. To eliminate recess in order to reduce bullying is like eliminating talking in the classroom to reduce arguing.

The impact of recess on academic achievement, memory, and attention makes it clear that the best way to prepare your son for federally mandated tests is to strike a balance between the discipline of sitting and studying and the rejuvenation of recess and running.

By providing the atmosphere for self-starting activities, recess has a special appeal to boys' tendencies to be self-starters and entrepreneurs.

We want to proactively encourage this for our daughters, and nurture this spirit in our sons.

Let's not throw out the *boy* with the bathwater.

Traditional heroic intelligence is about taking care of others; health intelligence is about taking care of self. The new hero knows that he takes better care of others in the future when he takes better care of himself in the present. Healed people heal people.

PART VI

ADHD: Treatment With or Without Medication

CHAPTER 28

The New Neural Crisis

The many reasons we have explored in previous chapters for the escalating boy crisis—the purpose void, dad deprivation, an outmoded
focus on heroic intelligence over health intelligence—not only influence
our children's thinking and patterns of behavior but directly contribute to
a biological change in the brain. This shift has given rise to a new neural
crisis. This neural crisis not only derails normal brain development in
our children but also limits their ability to receive parental support in
overcoming these new challenges.

When we fail to equip children with the emotional support they need
to cope with the stress of our modern lifestyle, we directly change their
brains and prevent their normal development. But even when a child does
get that emotional support there are many other lifestyle factors common
to our modern world that inhibit normal brain function and development.

These modern lifestyle factors include air and water pollution, farming practices that include powerful pesticides and fungicides, processed
foods, nutritional deficiency, antibiotics, over-the-counter and prescription drugs, and overstimulation from TV, YouTube, and video games.
These new changes are directly linked to the new boy crisis. And as we
will see, boys compared to girls have an increased vulnerability to these
common lifestyle changes.

Did you know that one out of ten American children have been diagnosed with ADHD? Yet, twice as many boys as girls are diagnosed.[1]

Did you know that one out of nine American students seriously
contemplate suicide every year?[2] In just three decades, mental illness

has increased thirty-five-fold in America. Yet, as pointed out previously, teenage boys are four times more likely than teenage girls to actually commit suicide.[3]

Did you know that one out of six American children have a developmental disability?[4] And on average, boys have twice as many learning disabilities.[5]

In addition, boys are dramatically falling behind girls when it comes to completing their education; more girls will graduate from high school,[6] and twice as many women will graduate from college as compared to men.[7]

The rate of autism in children, as well as other development disorders, has been dramatically rising. In 1980 only one in ten thousand children was diagnosed with autism.[8] But in 2016, one out sixty-eight children—but one out of forty-two American boys—was diagnosed with an autism spectrum disorder.[9] Boys were nearly five times more likely to have autism than girls.[10] This new neural crisis is affecting everyone's brain health, but boys today are most at risk.

The most common symptom of the new neural crisis in boys is the rising rate of ADHD.[11] Because ADHD is not only the most common but also the most researched symptom, we will focus primarily on its many symptoms, causes, and—most important—practical solutions that do not necessarily require medication.

A New Spin on ADHD

There is still much confusion about what the term ADHD really means. The name of the disorder itself—attention deficit hyperactivity disorder—is actually misleading and prevents many parents and adults from recognizing or relating to this condition. The common symptoms identified by the medical industry are often varied and even contradictory, and as we will explore later, many symptoms have yet to be defined. While some children with ADHD are distracted and disorganized, others are restless and impulsive, and some are both.

In most cases of ADHD there is not an actual deficit of attention at all. Instead, there is an inability to allocate attention appropriately. Children with ADHD that are inattentive, distracted, or "spaced out" find it hard to allocate their attention to what their teachers are saying; instead, they are stuck in a daydream. Other children with ADHD, those who are hyperactive, impulsive, or restless, are also unable to focus on the teacher but for different reasons. They are simply not that interested in what the teacher is saying. They would rather be somewhere else. They can't sit still in class, but they can certainly sit still in front of a TV or video game.

Dr. Martha Bridge Denckla, a clinician and scientist at the Kennedy Krieger Institute and Johns Hopkins University, says she faces this confusion regularly from parents who bring their children to the ADHD clinic where she practices. "I am constantly having to explain to parents that ADHD is not a deficit in the sense of, say, a budget deficit or a thyroid deficiency, where you don't have enough of something. Rather, it's the control over attention." A briefing paper of the Dana Foundation summarizes, "The question, Denckla says, is: 'Where is the child's attention being allocated? Is it where it needs to be to meet the demands of home, school, and society?' . . ."[12]

"Allocating one's attention appropriately for success in school requires a degree of willful control—what might be thought of as will power—to turn away from a preferred activity and focus on an activity that may not be as compelling or immediately rewarding."

People with ADHD have plenty of attention. That's why they can play video games for hours, or get lost in their Legos, or devote endless attention to biologically stimulating activities like eating junk food, taking drugs, risk taking, watching TV, using digital tablets, and consuming internet pornography. They may have plenty of focus, but they are unable to easily shift their focus to less stimulating activities.

Over time, this inability to focus on less stimulating normal activities causes them to focus even more on activities providing extra stimulation. For example, children are easily distracted from cleaning their room or doing their homework by the increased pleasure that comes from the higher biological stimulation of playing video games. As their brains adapt to this increased stimulation, they disconnect further and further from their natural internal motivation to cooperate with and please their parents and teachers. In practical terms, children with ADHD may become more motivated to play video games and less motivated to earn their parents' approval.

The One Cause

There are a host of modern lifestyle changes over the last three decades that contribute to this new neural crisis, but ultimately it all comes down to one cause. By understanding and addressing this one cause, ADHD and the many other symptoms of the new neural crisis, like anxiety, depression, learning difficulties, oppositional behaviors, and addictions, can be corrected.[13]

The cause is most simply understood as inhibited dopamine function in the brain.[14] **Dopamine is the reward brain chemical that gives us pleasure while increasing our motivation, focus, and interest.**[15, 16, 17] The reason children are often more motivated to play video games than clean their room is because video games, like an addictive drug, stimulate the production of more dopamine.

For many researchers, the cause of the dramatic setback we've seen in mental wellness is still a mystery. But at the same time, a wide range of peer-reviewed studies demonstrate a clear link between inhibited dopamine function and lack of mental wellness.[18]

In my experience working with hundreds of parents and children, improving dopamine function in the brain can correct the many symptoms of this new neural crisis. In some cases, parents and children can reap positive benefits within days.

However, these positive changes occur primarily when children are also receiving the emotional and behavioral support they need. Children require loving attention and specific educational support for normal brain development, but this support is not enough if they are burdened with toxic overload, nutritional deficiencies, and overstimulation.[19] Understanding how to restore normal dopamine function in a boy's brain is the key for recovery.[20]

Inhibited Dopamine Function

Dopamine function is intricately related to brain health because it is the brain chemical that regulates our focus, interest, motivation, and pleasure. When dopamine function in the brain is inhibited, we experience a lack of focus, interest, motivation, or pleasure in response to normal and healthy life experiences. With reduced dopamine function, in order to feel good we become dependent on more intense experiences to stimulate higher levels of dopamine production.[21] In the absence of more intense experiences, a boy begins to feel bored, restless, impulsive, distracted, or distressed.

For clarity and simplicity, instead of referring to these symptoms as ADHD, I call this condition inhibited dopamine function. As we have seen, the standard description of ADHD as a deficit of attention can be very confusing: a boy with ADHD who is mentally distracted in the classroom owing to a short attention span may also become hyperfocused on his video games. Inhibited dopamine function is a broader definition and is inclusive of nearly every symptom of this new neural crisis.

For someone with inhibited dopamine function, routine experiences that would typically be peaceful, relaxing, or fulfilling such as reading, learning, playing, talking, loving relationships, healthy eating, exercising, socializing, and working can quickly become boring, empty, dissatisfying, or tiring. The brain then requires higher-than-normal stimulation to experience normal levels of pleasure, focus, interest, and motivation.

High dopamine stimulators are simply experiences that are more intense. Here are some common high dopamine stimulators that affect children and adults: [22]

- speed and rushing[23]
- immediate gratification[24]
- loud music[25]
- risk and danger[26]
- fast food and overeating[27, 28]
- stress and trauma[29]
- challenge, achievement, and accomplishment[30]
- a new romantic partner[31]
- new and different activities or experiences[32]
- more money[33]
- new and different digital stimulation[34]
- sensational news and thrilling experiences[35]
- video games, movies, and TV[36]
- success or winning[37]
- bright colors[38]
- sex and orgasm[39]
- online porn and one-night stands[40]
- emergencies[41]

- procrastination[42]
- fighting and shooting guns[43]
- sugar and desserts[44]
- coffee and caffeine[45]
- intense exercise[46]
- intense pain or pleasure[47]
- drama and strong emotions, positive or negative[48]
- loss and grieving[49]
- worrying and stress[50]
- alcohol, amphetamines, heroin, and other addictive drugs[51]

High dopamine stimulation (positive or negative) stresses the brain and over time kills brain cells.[52] Occasional high dopamine stimulation doesn't injure the brain as long as we give the brain the opportunity and support it needs to recover.

To recover from high dopamine stimulation, the brain needs to find balance, not only by relaxing with low dopamine stimulation, but through extra nutrition from a healthy diet, plenty of restful sleep, and the support that comes from stress-reducing loving relationships and social bonding. Without this extra support for the brain after high stimulation, the brain cannot find balance and tends to crave more dopamine stimulation, resulting in further imbalance.[53]

One of the many contributing factors to the increase of ADHD symptoms in our children is the new emphasis on test scores in reading, writing, and math. This focus in modern education increases dopamine stimulation. At the same time, schools are excluding the more traditional emphasis on low dopamine stimulators like art, music, drama, dancing, singing, physical play, and exercise. **This dramatic shift from valuing the arts and exercise prevents the brain from finding dopamine balance.**[54] Eventually, even high dopamine stimulators like math, writing, and reading may become boring, tiring, or tedious.

As schools have decreased the different expressions of the arts along with opportunities for physical activity, the different symptoms of inhibited dopamine function (and, of course, ADHD) have increased.[55] This imbalance in the modern school curriculum, along with increased access to junk food and sugary soft drinks at schools, is a major contributor to inhibited dopamine function. (**Junk food and soft drinks are high dopamine stimulators, just like taking stimulant drugs.**[56])

With increased exposure to high dopamine stimulation the brain becomes more dependent on it, just as heroin addicts begin to depend on their fix just to feel normal.[57] With this dependence on higher dopamine stimulation to feel alive and motivated, dopamine function in the brain gradually goes more out of balance.

There are many other modern lifestyle conditions that inhibit normal brain function—such as environmental toxicity, concussions, antibiotics, and nutritional deficiency—but it bears repeating that overexposure to high dopamine stimulation over time will cause inhibited dopamine function in the brain. (In chapter 31, we will explore in greater detail the many other contributing factors that lead to inhibited dopamine function.) **Simply put, too much high stimulation inhibits normal brain function.**

To understand this more fully, let's explore a more dramatic example that we are witnessing today when our sons who join the military return home after spending many months in combat situations.

The brain of a soldier radically changes after living and working in a challenging, stressful, and dangerous combat situation for many months. As mentioned in the list above, risk and danger are major stimulators of dopamine production. **Working in a combat zone produces levels of dopamine comparable to taking cocaine or heroin.[58]** Even if soldiers leave home with normal brains, they may return home with inhibited dopamine function. Then, without high dopamine stimulation at home, they feel bored, lifeless, and unmotivated.

To feel alive and motivated again, they commonly crave some form of intense dopamine stimulation, like riding motorcycles at high speed or other risky behaviors; drinking too much coffee, energy drinks, or alcohol; taking illegal recreational drugs; overexercising; promiscuous sex; and the intense drama of barfights and domestic violence. In many cases, the outcome is depression, addiction, divorce, and suicide.

This extreme and tragic example of what is happening to many of our returning soldiers reveals how vulnerable our brains are to consistent high dopamine stimulation without the balance of low dopamine stimulation. Normal brain health, performance, and function depend on a balance of the two.

ADHD, Children, and Brain Performance

Children are especially vulnerable to our new neural crisis because their brains are still in the process of developing. Our brains continue to undergo significant brain development until the age of twenty-five.[59]

When talking about ADHD, children, and brain performance, the first question I always get is, Do you think ADHD is overdiagnosed?

My answer is not a simple yes or no. Why? Because what some people are really asking is, Should we be giving our children all these drugs? My answer to that question (in most cases) is a clear and definite no. Most experts today, including doctors and researchers from the Centers for Disease Control and Prevention of the United States, recognize that **ADHD drugs are dangerously overprescribed.**[60]

Brain-enhancing drugs like Ritalin have short-term benefits but cause long-term brain injury.[61] They actually worsen the brain condition that originally gives rise to ADHD symptoms.[62] Harvard researcher William Carlezon and others have identified dramatic and long-lasting behavior and molecular alterations in the brain's dopamine system as a result of taking stimulant drugs. This impaired dopamine function gives rise to boredom and a host of mental and emotional challenges, along with a general dissatisfaction in life.[63, 64, 65]

ADHD drugs and other stimulants not only further inhibit dopamine function but, with continued use, they provide less and less benefit.[66] Researchers at the Brookhaven National Laboratory have published a study showing that, **after only one year of using a stimulant drug to treat ADHD, dopamine function in the brain is inhibited by 24 percent.**[67] This change explains why medical doctors frequently need to increase their patients' dosage.

These drugs worsen the condition that leads to ADHD and, even for temporary symptomatic relief, are not necessary in most cases.[68] In chapter 32, we will explore the many nondrug solutions validated by peer-reviewed scientific studies that can heal the brain and restore normal brain function without side effects—or at the very least reduce a child's need for prescribed medication.

Other times, when I am asked this same question, "Is ADHD overdiagnosed?" people really mean, "Do you think that this condition is real?"

The answer to that latter question is a resounding yes! Certainly, **ADHD drugs are overprescribed, but the underlying condition of**

inhibited dopamine function is very real. Researchers have found that the brains of children with ADHD are actually different from children without ADHD. It is a real condition. And it is widespread.

In our fast-paced digital age of immediate gratification and information overload, we are *all* experiencing, to some degree, a neural crisis related to inhibited dopamine function. In some children it gives rise to ADHD and in other children it causes learning challenges, while in adults it gives rise to a lack of passion in relationships, low energy levels, and depression.

Inhibited dopamine function affects brain performance to different degrees in nearly everyone, but doesn't always interfere with our ability to be successful or creative, or even to feel love. It does, however, still interfere with our ability to be happy, healthy, and fulfilled.

While inhibited dopamine function in some children will give rise to learning challenges, for others it may motivate them to become hyperfocused on achievement. Many high achievers today also have inhibited dopamine function, and to the degree they experience a dependence on high dopamine stimulation they will experience higher stress, relationship problems, depression, anxiety, or become vulnerable to addictions. Pick up any magazine and read the countless stories of broken families, violence, and drug addiction among some of the most successful, smart, and influential people in the world.

Increased boredom and dissatisfaction from inhibited dopamine function can lead to a variety of symptoms, from addictions to caffeine, alcohol, video games, junk foods, and online porn to sedentary lifestyles, procrastination, or an inability to sustain long-term intimate relationships.[69] **While one person with inhibited dopamine function becomes a drunk when they grow up, another becomes a financial success but addicted to porn and unable to sustain passion in a loving relationship.** There are thousands of outcomes that may result when a person has an impaired ability to be motivated or satisfied.

Low dopamine function is affecting our children, but it is also creating new challenges in adult relationships, work, and marriage. From this perspective, ADHD, which is only one of the many symptoms of low dopamine function, is actually *underdiagnosed.*

So, is ADHD overdiagnosed? The answer is no: **ADHD is overmedicated, but underdiagnosed.**

Most parents and their doctors are not aware of the substantial evidence that giving children drugs for ADHD and other mental problems has long-term side effects. Even more disappointing, most doctors are not aware of the many natural solutions for ADHD, which do not have side effects. For most children, there is no reason to give drugs with known side effects when studies have shown repeatedly that natural solutions can be just as effective.

Even when the brain has been injured by ADHD drugs, I have witnessed its ability to heal itself, given the right nutritional and behavioral support. And by addressing this one condition, inhibited dopamine function, you will have the key to a much more fulfilling future for your children.

One Cause with Different Symptoms

Research is increasingly showing that **every mental or emotional challenge we see in children and adults is inextricably linked to low dopamine function**.[70] The same inhibited dopamine function in the brain that gives rise to ADHD in other children gives rise to anxiety disorders, learning disorders, sensory disorders, mood disorders, and self-esteem disorders.[71, 72, 73]

As mentioned before, dopamine is the brain chemical of focus, interest, motivation, and pleasure. Low dopamine function inhibits focus, interest, motivation, or pleasure in a wide range of symptoms. In general, it shows up as a dependence on hyperstimulation to increase dopamine levels—for example, rather than feel bored from a lack of interest, a child seeks out the hyperstimulation of a video game, TV show, or high-carb snack to feel pleasure, interest, and motivation.

But when children are dependent on higher stimulation to feel good, they are also more likely to ignore their parent's wishes and misbehave, since the normal dopamine stimulation of pleasing their parents is not enough to motivate them to cooperate. **To motivate children to "listen," parents often bribe them with ice cream or the threat of punishment.** Both the anticipation of sweets or the fear of punishment temporarily generate high levels of dopamine to then motivate a child to cooperate.[74, 75]

Inhibited dopamine function not only derails normal brain development but also diminishes a parents' influence to lead, guide, and nurture their child. **With easy access to high dopamine stimulators, children are less dependent on their parents for dopamine stimulation.** As a result, a child's brain is biologically rewired to seek out more intense dopamine experiences like sweets, video stimulation, and even negative attention caused by emotional drama, fighting, and resistance.

When you restore normal dopamine function, children automatically become more cooperative with their parents. Bribes of sweet rewards or threats of punishment are no longer needed to motivate a child. The satisfaction that comes with pleasing their parents is a big enough dopamine stimulator. Children feel more connected to their parents and automatically become more confident and responsible in all areas of their lives.

CHAPTER 29

The Four Faces of ADHD

As we've seen, ADHD is better understood as a symptom of inhibited dopamine function—a tendency to hyperfocus on those activities that provide increased dopamine stimulation like immediate and easy gratification. In fact, **add the prefix *hyper-* to almost any common personality trait and you get something that is often diagnosed as ADHD:** hyperactive, hyperfocused, hyperimpulsive, hypercontrolling, hypersensitive, hyperdistracted, hyperintroverted, hyperextroverted, hypersocial, hyperreclusive, hyperindependent, hyperpassive, or just hyper-spaced-out and unable to focus at all.

With ADHD, a naturally introverted child becomes *hyper*introverted and thus excessively fearful of social interactions. A naturally extroverted child becomes *hyper*dominant and can be insensitive to others.

Another common difference among children is that some are playful and others serious. A naturally playful child with ADHD becomes *hyper*playful and spontaneous to the extent that they don't finish things and become disorganized. A naturally serious child becomes *hyper*responsible and serious but often resistant to change and overjudgmental of others.

The way each child manifests ADHD or inhibited dopamine function is unique, but **all "hyper" temperaments can be roughly grouped into the four faces of ADHD—creative, responsible, bold, and sensitive:**

1. A **creative child** who likes to start new things becomes **hyperfocused** on what is new and exciting and is easily distracted from attending to what is routine.
2. A **responsible child** who loves order and following rules becomes **hypercontrolling** and as a result may become oppositional, defiant, or resistant to change.
3. A **bold child** who is naturally more assertive or action oriented becomes **hyperactive or impulsive**. While such children mean well, they may easily become inconsiderate of others. They often act or talk without including or considering others.
4. A **sensitive child** who is more in touch with their emotional needs by nature becomes **hypervulnerable or moody**. Unlike a bold child, such children may be overconsiderate of others. As a result, they become easily hurt when others are inconsiderate of their needs, feelings, and wishes.

The Basic Symptoms of Low Dopamine Function

Understanding the functions of dopamine can provide greater insight into how one condition, low dopamine function, can affect different people in so many different ways. The four characteristics of dopamine function, as we saw in the last chapter, are

1. focus
2. motivation
3. interest
4. pleasure

All the different symptoms of low dopamine function come from having too little of any of these four characteristics.

Here are a few examples of what it looks like when a child is experiencing too little of any of these four characteristics and what happens when dopamine function is corrected:

- Tommy lacked the **focus** and **motivation** to do his English homework. "My whole life, I thought I didn't like reading. It would put me to sleep. Now, I enjoy it and read often. **I don't suddenly get tired or bored when I begin reading."**

- Brice lacked **interest** in school. "I could not comprehend what I was reading. The information just didn't stick. I thought I was just stupid. **Now, I love school, I can understand so much more. I am really smart."**
- Willy lacked **focus**. He was often distressed by his inability to organize his life. "I used to be stressed all the time because I didn't know where I had put things. I was always losing things and then telling myself I should be better. Now, I have an easy system. **I put things away in their proper place so I can remember where they are."**
- Casey lacked **pleasure**. He was often depressed. "Nothing was as good as it was in the past. I would always compare my present life with my past. Now, I feel like **my life is exciting and interesting and my best years are yet to come."**
- Jason lacked **motivation**. He had lost his reason for living. "My life was boring and I was too fat. Kids made fun of me. I was eating too many desserts and watching too much TV. I never left the house. Now, **I am taking risks and doing new things. I joined a choir and even started to ski, which is great fun.** I am getting to know a new part of me."
- Stevie lacked **focus**. He was always forgetting things. "I was not getting anything done. I would even go into a room and forget what I was going to do. I would get distracted and do something else. I was always starting things but not finishing them. **Now, I finish what I start and remember what I am planning to do. I feel proud of my accomplishments.** I focus on one thing at a time. I feel clear and more organized."
- Jack lacked **pleasure**. He was having trouble relaxing and enjoying his life. "I was worried all the time and having trouble falling asleep. I was afraid of change. You name it; I would worry about it. Now, I can let it go and trust that I will handle it when it shows up. **I enjoy going to sleep. I feel grateful for the support I have in my life rather than worrying all the time."**
- George lacked **focus and motivation**. He had difficulty finishing his projects. "I would start one thing and then, before I could finish, something else would capture my attention. I would lose my

motivation to finish something. **Now, every day I review my goals and check them off at the end of the day."**

In short, each of the four characteristics of low dopamine function is filtered through a child's unique temperament, resulting in different symptoms.

As we explore the four different faces of ADHD or low dopamine function, keep in mind that your son may have a little of one or more of another. No child will fit any one face precisely; we are all different. But using the four faces below as a framework can help us recognize our tendencies when we are out of balance, as well as help us have more compassion for others when they are out of balance.

The Four Faces

There are endless ways to describe and categorize our natural and healthy differences, but to best discuss the impact of low dopamine function we will focus on four broad categories of temperament: creative, responsible, bold, and sensitive.

Every parent or teacher knows that one child may be more "bold" while another may be more "sensitive." Another child may be a combination of many temperaments. Most children have one dominant temperament and one or two secondary temperaments. In addition, children often move from one face to another at different times in their development, or shift faces according to different circumstances. For example, a child might be hypershy in personal situations but hyperbold when selling lemonade to strangers.

In each of the four temperament categories—creative, responsible, bold, sensitive—children may also be more analytical, emotional, physical, or intuitive. In addition, these categories will commonly manifest differently according to natural gender differences, which are then conditioned in different ways by social norms and circumstances.

Although every child has a dominant temperament, different situations and circumstances will bring out or activate their secondary temperaments. For example, when **creative** children feel supported they shift to their secondary temperament and become more **responsible**. When the circumstance changes and they feel needed, they become **bolder,** or when they are challenged to solve a problem, become more **sensitive**. In this way, over time, a more creative child is able to gradually develop and integrate each of these four temperaments.

ADHD or low dopamine function does not determine a child's unique balance of temperaments but it does radically alter its expression. With a deeper understanding of how ADHD affects the expression of our natural temperaments, we can be more patient, accepting, and supportive of our children, as well as other family members and ourselves.

1. The Creative Temperament

Children with a **creative** temperament have a greater need to feel supported with encouragement, patience, and acceptance. With this support, they eventually become more **responsible** and finish things. When they feel needed, they may become more **bold** and expressive. When they feel challenged to solve a problem, they become more **sensitive** or vulnerable and reach out to others for support through cooperation and collaboration.

To get the support they need, these children require extra stimulation, variety, and the opportunity to explore different interests. They thrive in the role of student, researcher, or problem solver. They seek happiness.

But with low dopamine function, children with a creative temperament become hyperfocused, seeking too much new stimulation. These happy, playful children have a higher risk than those of other temperaments of becoming distracted and disorganized. They have difficulty finishing projects and get bored easily.

When faced with the responsibility to finish a task, they become the opposite of more responsible: they become forgetful, scattered, and disorganized. When they feel needed, instead of becoming more bold and motivated to serve others, they become unproductive, overcautious, and resistant to taking risks. They will tend to wait until the last minute to do things. Think of the creative writer who spends years never finishing their book or the artist who doesn't want to sell their work.

When challenged to solve a problem, instead of reaching out for help to collaborate with others, they become completely and unintentionally indifferent to others. You can talk to them and they don't hear a word you are saying because they are so focused on solving a particular problem. Think of the absent-minded, forgetful professor.

2. The Responsible Temperament

Children with a responsible temperament have a greater need for the support of routine, rules, and regularity. They feel secure when they know what to expect and when they receive messages that they are good, loving, and caring. With this support, they eventually become bolder, willing to take more risks. When they feel needed, they become more compassionate and sensitive. And when they feel challenged to solve a problem, they become more flexible and creative.

To get the support they need, these children require more security, stability, and a regular eating and sleeping routine. They thrive in the role of judge, organizer, or manager. They love order, as in "order in the court." They want to do what is right.

But with low dopamine function, children with a responsible temperament become hypercontrolling and compulsive. These organized, orderly children have a higher risk than those of other temperaments of becoming too controlling and critical of others. They can be resistant to change and have difficulty taking risks.

When faced with making a decision or taking a risk, instead of becoming more assertive or bold they become the opposite: overcautious and resistant to change.

When they feel needed, instead of becoming more sensitive to the needs of others, they become cold as ice, sternly adhering to their idea of the rules or what they consider to be right or fair. Think Judge Judy when her buttons get pushed.

When challenged to solve a problem, instead of becoming more creative, they become uninspired and unimaginative, sticking to the status quo.

3. The Bold Temperament

Children with a bold temperament have a greater need to feel successful in making a difference. With extra praise, appreciation, and acknowledgement of their contributions, they eventually become more compassionate and considerate of others. When they feel needed, they become more flexible and creative. When they feel challenged to solve a problem, they become more accountable and responsible.

To get the support they need, these children require greater acknowledgment for what they do and increased opportunities to

feel successful in making a difference. They thrive in the role of leader, boss, or protector. They seek the power to make a difference.

But with inhibited dopamine function, a child with a bold temperament becomes hyperassertive. These busy, highly motivated children have a higher risk than those of other temperaments of becoming inconsiderate or mean to other children. They can go too fast, acting or speaking without thinking of consequences. To avoid feeling bored, they can be impulsive thrill seekers.

When confronted with the different wishes, wants, needs, and feelings of others, instead of becoming more sensitive, selfless, or compassionate, they become indifferent or arrogant.

When they feel needed, instead of becoming more creative and motivated to solve problems, they become easily bored and unmotivated to do anything unless they "have to" or it is a big emergency. They are easily addicted to playing video games.

When challenged to solve a problem, instead of becoming more responsible and considering the right thing to do, they become impatient, impulsive, and irresponsible, taking too many risks.

4. The Sensitive Temperament

Children with a sensitive temperament have a greater need to feel understood and heard with reassurance and validation of their feelings. With this extra support, they eventually lighten up and become more playful and creative. Sometimes all they need is to have a good cry, and then suddenly they feel happy and carefree. When they feel needed, they become more responsible and accountable. When they feel challenged to solve a problem, they become more confident and bold.

To get the support they need, these children require greater empathy and attention to their feelings. They also need to feel helpful and supportive to others in need, but should be careful to not overgive. These children thrive in the role of nurturer, supporter, and team player. They seek to be good.

With inhibited dopamine function, a child with a sensitive temperament becomes hypervulnerable. These caring, considerate children have a higher risk than other temperaments of feeling needy, depressed, anxious, unhappy, and overemotional. They may unconsciously seek out negative attention.

In the process of giving and receiving in their relationships, instead of becoming playful, light, and creative, they start to keep score. They may become moody, resentful, heavy, or fixed. They resist all encouragement, support, and good advice. "Yes, but . . ." is their automatic response.

When they feel needed, at first they give more, but then they focus more on what they are not getting in return and give less as a result.

When challenged to solve a problem, if they are stressed, instead of becoming more bold and assertive, they become more fearful and defensive. They focus on what they don't want instead of what they do want.

Finding Balance

Every child has a unique balance of creativity, responsibility, boldness, and sensitivity. The many different challenges and circumstances of growing up help children to access, develop, and integrate their different temperaments.

The inhibited dopamine function that gives rise to ADHD derails this natural process. To varying degrees, it creates a chronic imbalance in brain function that inhibits normal self-expression and development. By restoring normal dopamine function, our children are able to freely express, develop, and shift between their natural temperaments according to what is appropriate to the different circumstances in their lives.

There are many ways to restore healthy dopamine function. But we can't dive headlong into a solution without first exploring the many contributing factors that give rise to inhibited dopamine function.

CHAPTER 30

The Many Causes of ADHD

If you have a headache, no solution for the pain will work for you if you continue to hit yourself in the head with a hammer. In a similar way, the natural solutions for low dopamine function won't work as well unless you first address what may be causing the condition.

This is also why research trials of natural solutions or prescribed medications rarely show a 100 percent success rate. **No matter how effective a solution is, it is not enough to just provide it. You must also change the actions that are causing the problem.**

Listed below are sixteen contributing factors that can interfere to varying degrees with healthy dopamine function. Unless these contributing factors are addressed, restoring normal dopamine function is not possible no matter what therapies are used to heal the brain.

1. Acetaminophen

Fever suppressants and cold, flu, allergy, and painkillers like Tylenol, NyQuil, Percocet, and Vicodin, all of which contain acetaminophen, inhibit dopamine function. In the long run, acetaminophen's use has been linked to the brain's inability to restore normal dopamine production.

Over six hundred medicines contain the active ingredient acetaminophen. Tylenol, the biggest selling over-the-counter medicine in the world, has only been widely used since 1980, which is also when the incidence of ADHD, bipolar disorder, and autism began to increase. Several studies have demonstrated that a boy's risk of ADHD or inhibited dopamine function increases when a mother takes fever suppressants or painkillers with acetaminophen during pregnancy.[1, 2]

Acetaminophen inhibits the natural production of glutathione, which is produced by your liver to protect the brain from free radical damage.[3] When used to suppress fevers or pain, this common medicine suppresses your brain's natural ability to heal itself.[4, 5] (We will explore later the important role that fevers have in restoring normal brain function. Most parents are not aware of the fact that even a fever of 105 degrees Fahrenheit won't cause any injury to the brain, but instead helps to heal the brain and improve brain function.)

Children and adults with ADHD, bipolar disorder, and autism, as well as those who suffer from dementia, Parkinson's disease, and Alzheimer's disease, have low glutathione production.[6, 7, 8] Low glutathione levels inhibit the growth of the myelin sheath, which is what insulates your nerves and protects the brain from overstimulation. *Demyelination* caused by high dopamine stimulation in the brain is the hallmark of neurodegenerative disease. Demyelination is just another way of saying brain injury.

2. Mercury, MSG, and Zinc Deficiency

Mercury is a known neurotoxin that both inhibits brain cell growth and destroys healthy brain cells.[9] The developing brains of children in the womb are particularly vulnerable to mercury exposure through their mother.[10]

During pregnancy, mothers should be especially careful to avoid exposure to mercury because the level of mercury in a fetus's blood can be 70 percent higher than in the mother's.[11] The EPA reports that, in Americans,

> exposure to chemicals such as mercury, lead, arsenic, and pesticides can have negative effects on brain development, leading to cognitive delay, attention-deficit hyperactivity disorder (ADHD), lower IQ, higher rates of anxiety and depression, behavior and learning disorders, reduced self-regulatory capacities, and shortened attention span. Currently, neurodevelopmental disorders affect 10 to 15 percent of children born annually, and rates of certain disorders have been increasing over the past 40 years. Not only can prenatal exposures to toxins increase the risk of neurodevelopmental disorders at birth, but they can also lead to disorders later in childhood.[12]

Many researchers, including myself, believe that prenatal mercury exposure and/or postnatal exposure may be the most significant contributing factor for inhibited dopamine function.[13]

Some children are influenced by mercury more than others due to their chronic exposure to MSG (monosodium glutamate). MSG, a common ingredient in thousands of packaged processed foods, makes the brain even more vulnerable to the dangers of mercury.[14] In the presence of "excitotoxins" like MSG, mercury in the brain increases brain cell death.[15] MSG also significantly lowers the activities of glutathione and other antioxidants that would normally neutralize many of the negative effects of mercury.[16]

The US government's Agency for Toxic Substances and Disease Registry ranks mercury third in its list of the most toxic substances on the planet, behind arsenic and lead. Nonetheless, it continues to be dumped into our waterways and soil, spilled into our atmosphere, and consumed in our food and water.

Mercury exposure can be limited, but it is impossible to eliminate entirely because it is in the air we breathe and the water we drink. **Fortunately there are natural solutions to help the body eliminate mercury and minimize its dangers,** which we'll explore in the next chapter.

Major contributors to emissions of mercury are car exhaust, coal-fired power plants, dental amalgam fillings, tattoos, hospitals with medical-waste incinerators, and even common flu vaccines.

Gradually the government is recognizing the toxic effects of mercury and other heavy metals used in medical procedures. For example, California dentists are required by law to warn patients of the health risks from mercury fillings.[17]

But mercury is most commonly found in fish because of bioaccumulation from our polluted oceans. Mercury is ingested by smaller fish that are in turn ingested by larger fish. Each time a larger fish consumes a smaller fish their levels of mercury increase. Thus, the largest fish contain the highest amounts of toxic mercury.

Mercury is also found in nonorganic foods, which are exposed to fungicides. Trace amounts of mercury are even found in high fructose corn syrup, the most common sweetener today in soft drinks and packaged snacks.[18]

Boys are more vulnerable than girls to mercury toxicity in the first two years of life owing to higher testosterone levels, which can decrease the availability of zinc. Dietary zinc is essential for maintaining the metabolic processes necessary for mercury elimination.[19] Zinc deficiency has been directly linked to the development of ADHD.[20]

During the first two years, a boy's testosterone levels are as high as a grown man's. Then, after the age of two, testosterone levels dramatically drop until puberty. To make testosterone, his body uses the mineral zinc. Zinc is also used in the brain to detoxify mercury. During the first two years, with less zinc available in the brain, boys are more vulnerable to mercury exposure, which then gives rise to the many expressions of inhibited dopamine function.

ADHD, autism, and dementia are very different expressions of inhibited dopamine function, but they share a common denominator: they can be triggered by heavy metals like mercury.[21]

To a certain degree, **the brain is designed to filter out mercury unless its defenses are weakened by food additives like MSG or by zinc deficiency.** Unfortunately, MSG is approved by the FDA. MSG is not just in Chinese food; it is added to thousands of packaged foods. Manufacturers are not required to put MSG on the label; instead, they can simply say "natural flavors" or "hydrolyzed vegetable protein" (HVP). What is more tragic is that many baby formulas commonly use MSG.

3. Sugar

Excess consumption of soft drinks, bread, cookies, chips, ice cream, cakes, pudding, and the like elevates blood sugar levels. **High blood sugar levels cause injury to the brain**, contributing to low dopamine function by damaging brain neurons and creating chronic inflammation throughout the brain.[22]

High blood sugar levels in mothers during pregnancy can overstimulate a developing baby's brain, causing a decrease in dopamine receptor sites. This downregulation of dopamine receptors has been linked to ADHD.[23, 24] Mothers in the future will be instructed to avoid high-carb junk foods just as mothers today are told to avoid alcohol and smoking.

In addition, the high insulin levels that result from high blood sugar levels inhibit glutathione production, making the developing baby's brain more vulnerable to injury by toxic metals like lead, mercury, and aluminum.[25, 26] Pregnant mothers should particularly avoid lipsticks and other cosmetics that are known to contain both lead and aluminum.

Toxic metals are linked to a variety of mental disorders. Lead poisoning in the brain is directly linked to violence and criminal behavior,[27] high mercury levels in the brain are linked to ADHD and autism, and high aluminum levels in the brain are linked to Alzheimer's disease and dementia.[28, 29, 30]

Multiple research studies link sugar consumption to the symptoms of ADHD.[31] They postulate that sugar acutely increases dopamine, which over time leads to a reduction in dopamine receptors. This downregulation of dopamine receptors causes ADHD or inhibited dopamine function. Children with ADHD then ingest more sugar in an attempt to compensate for their inhibited dopamine function.

Note: Not all sugars are the same. **The best sugars are in either raw uncooked honey or in whole fruit.** For optimal dopamine function, eating lots of fruit salads for meals or snacks, separated from proteins and fats, will help restore normal brain function. In addition, the skin covering apples, pears, grapes, and other fruits, when organic, are covered with the most powerful and life-sustaining probiotics.

Sometimes raw fruits cause stomach distress but this is because they contain beneficial bacteria that are killing off nonbeneficial bacteria. If stomach distress occurs, cut back your fruit intake initially but then gradually increase. Raw fruits (but not fruit juices), which contain plenty of fiber, good bacteria, and antioxidants, are one of the best treatments for a healthy gut and brain.

4. Unfermented Soy and Pasteurized Dairy

Inhibited dopamine function can be caused by consuming unfermented soy, found in products like soy protein and soy milk. Soy products contain a high concentration of phytates, which leads to poor digestion.[32] In addition, the pasteurization of milk promotes an allergic response in the intestines, which in turn inhibits the utilization of beneficial milk proteins.[33] Inhibited digestion prevents the production of metabolic enzymes and amino acids necessary for healthy dopamine production and function.

Baby formulas often include either soy protein or pasteurized dairy protein. And most fast-food hamburgers are supplemented with indigestible soy products.

It's important to note that *fermented* soy and *raw* dairy products do not inhibit digestion to nearly the same extent. Examples of fermented soy include tempeh, miso, soy sauce, and the common Japanese breakfast food *natto*. Undenatured dairy proteins, which are not overprocessed with high heat, can also be very beneficial.

5. A Sedentary Lifestyle

The sedentary lifestyle of children sitting in school all day and then returning home to sit while doing their homework, watching TV, or playing video games prevents the lymphatic circulation needed to detoxify the brain of heavy metals, chemicals, and toxins in our air, water, and food. This increased toxicity causes brain inflammation and even infection.

Lack of exercise also prevents brain cell growth and limits the blood circulation needed to heal brain infections. Physical movement is necessary for brain development and the production of dopamine and other neurotransmitters in the brain.

To avoid the feelings of boredom associated with this low production of dopamine, instead of seeking out the exercise that would produce more, children tend to seek out forms of passive stimulation like TV and other forms of digital stimulation. This passive stimulation feels good, but it does not support brain development and growth.

6. Chronic Stress

Chronic psychological stress, like the kind induced by excessive punishment, loss, disapproval, violation, or threat, raises stress hormones, which in turn cause brain injury. Various forms of childhood or adult trauma can raise your baseline production of stress hormones, which in turn sustains higher blood sugar levels, causing injury and inflammation in the brain.

In addition, **chronic stress inhibits the production of glutathione, your body's master molecule for healing the brain.** We previously explored how low glutathione was always linked to inhibited dopamine function.

The injury to the brain, caused by stress, is unprecedented today because sugar products are so widely consumed. As mentioned before, high blood sugar levels cause injury in the brain. High blood sugar amplifies the negative effects of stress.

High stress levels during pregnancy or childbirth combined with high blood sugar levels can definitely contribute to ADHD or other symptoms of low dopamine function in children.

7. Stimulant Drugs and ADHD Medications

A myriad of brain scan research has proved that excessive dopamine stimulation from street drugs like cocaine, crack, heroin, and methamphetamines change and injure the brain.[34] Similar changes take place in the brain from prescribed stimulant drugs for ADD and ADHD.[35, 36, 37, 38]

Most parents are unaware of the similarity of ADHD drugs to illegal street drugs like cocaine and methamphetamines. **Ritalin, a commonly prescribed ADHD drug, and cocaine act in the brain through the same pathways.** Adderall, which is slightly different, acts in the brain in a way similar to methamphetamines or crystal meth. The abuse of street drugs and binge drinking of alcohol happens less today in universities because students now have access to legally prescribed ADHD drugs. Fifty to sixty percent of college kids take Ritalin or Adderall.[39]

The use of ADHD stimulant drugs is also considered by many to be a gateway drug that increases the potential of teens to move on to more serious illegal drugs. **Between 30 and 50 percent of adolescents in drug rehab centers have used Ritalin.[40]**

Stimulant drugs can have a big effect on the brain from a single exposure. A new study at UC San Francisco's Ernest Gallo Clinic and Research Center has revealed that cocaine may rewire the brain and drastically affect decision-making after just one use. This change makes the search for extra stimulation override other healthier priorities.[41]

A report published in 2005 by neurologist George A. Ricaurte and his team at Johns Hopkins School of Medicine is even more "damning" (as the researchers themselves put it) to ADHD meds. Ricaurte's group trained baboons and squirrel monkeys to self-administer an oral formulation of amphetamine similar to Adderall. "Two to four weeks later the researchers detected evidence of amphetamine-induced brain damage, encountering lower levels of dopamine and fewer dopamine transporters on nerve endings in the striatum."[42]

In addition to lowering levels of dopamine production, which in turn increases the brain's dependence on high dopamine stimulation, **stimulant drugs directly damage dopamine-producing brain cells.** In 2006

Steven Berman and other researchers found that ADHD drugs caused damage to the dopamine-producing neurons in the brain along with a host of side effects, including hyperactivity, depression, delayed growth, cognitive impairment, sleep disorders, and addiction.[43] According to William Carlezon of Harvard University, **ADHD medication damages the nucleus accumbens in the developing brain, leading to a loss of drive in adulthood.**[44] This research was confirmed by research at Brown University, University of Michigan, University of Pittsburgh, University of South Carolina, and universities in Holland, Sweden, Italy, and the Netherlands.[45]

Each study found damage to the nucleus accumbens, even when low doses were given for a short time. The nucleus accumbens regulates the production of feel-good brain chemicals like dopamine and serotonin, and accordingly is important for motivation, focus, pleasure, interest, and even falling in love.

Injury to this area of the brain is not only associated with addictive cravings and behaviors but also with ADHD. From this evidence-based perspective, addictions are simply one of the ways a person seeks to temporarily reduce or eliminate the symptoms of ADHD.

While these particular researchers confirmed the damage to the brain from stimulant drugs to be permanent, they have not yet studied the effects of natural solutions, as other researchers have, to assist the brain in healing this condition.

Please note, however: Parents who choose to prevent the brain injury caused by ADHD medications through natural solutions alone should always consult a health care professional who is already familiar with natural solutions. **One should never suddenly go off a stimulant drug.** Most holistic doctors will suggest reducing the dosage over time while simultaneously fully applying the various natural solutions.

8. Video Games

Suggesting that an immensely profitable product like video games are harmful in some manner is bound to be controversial. The *Wall Street Journal* reports, "A growing body of research suggests that 'gaming' improves creativity, decision-making and perception, improved hand-eye coordination and improved vision for discerning gray tones."[46] People who play video games can make decisions 25 percent faster. A popular TED talk also reinforces the many benefits of violent video games.[47]

While this all sounds amazing, anyone who takes a stimulant drug like cocaine or speed will also experience improved memory, increased creativity, and faster decision-making abilities. **Even playing violent video games is touted as therapeutic because, just like Ritalin and Adderall, it briefly increases dopamine levels.** High dopamine stimulation can temporarily improve ADHD symptoms, but as we have already discussed, it also creates long-term brain injury.

Video games have also been shown to increase creativity. But so do stimulant drugs! It is common knowledge that many creative writers, composers, and entertainers have a history of depending on drugs or alcohol for stimulation and motivation. Just because drugs help in one area doesn't mean they are not doing damage in another. And as the hundreds of creative people who eventually went through rehab now know, you can be just as creative without stimulant drugs.

Playing a video game improves hand-eye coordination, but so does throwing a ball. As with any activity, practice makes perfect. When it comes to extensive gaming sessions, the benefits are there, but so are the side effects. There are much healthier ways to improve performance.

Video games change your brain, sometimes in positive ways, but so do reading, playing the piano, listening to music, and even navigating your car—without negative side effects. Whatever we do directly changes the structure of our brains, sometimes for the better and sometimes for the worse.

Researchers found that the average London cab driver has an exceptionally large hippocampus, a part of the brain related to memory.[48] It turns out that the process of learning to navigate the streets of London actually increases hippocampus size. (When London cab drivers retire, their brains shrink back again, confirming the common saying "use it or lose it.")

Research confirms that video games, like other challenging activities, certainly create positive changes in the brain. But these studies overlook the real danger of video games. As with any fun activity, moderate use of video games—thirty minutes a day, or an occasional hour—is not a problem. **But excessive use is like taking a stimulant drug, and causes gradual brain injury.**

Violent video games can be even more destructive to the brain because, with the perception of increased risk and danger, much higher levels of dopamine are stimulated, and this, in turn, causes the brain to require higher dopamine stimulation to produce feel-good brain chemicals. This means that normal dopamine stimulation becomes flat, boring, unpleasant, and less interesting.

Using brain scans, researchers at Indiana University found that playing violent video games alters brain function in healthy young men after just a week of play, depressing activity among regions associated with emotional control.[49] Other studies have found an association between the dopamine high of compulsive gaming and becoming more sedentary, overweight, introverted, and prone to depression.[50]

To understand this dark side of video games, let's review what we have learned about ADHD and drugs. A stimulant drug or high dopamine–stimulating experience floods the brain with higher-than-normal levels of dopamine. This overstimulation causes dopamine receptor sites to close up or, in technical terms, downregulate. This means the brain now needs higher dopamine stimulation to increase focus, motivation, interest, or pleasure.

But even putting aside the downregulation of dopamine receptors, the higher than normal dopamine stimulation from video games or stimulant drugs has other negative side effects. With high dopamine stimulation, blood flow is increased to the "nucleus accumbens" or pleasure center in the middle of the brain. At the same time, blood flow decreases to the prefrontal cortex.[51] Activity in the prefrontal cortex is associated with decision-making and control over impulses. In other words, **while extended time on a video game increases our ability to play the game, it decreases our control over automatic impulses.**[52] (To a lesser degree, high dopamine stimulators like watching TV, listening to loud music, and junk food have a similar effect.)

A recent brain-imaging study by researchers at Stanford's school of medicine suggests that boys are more vulnerable than girls to video game addiction. Up to 90 percent of American youth play video games and as many as 31 percent (more than 5 million kids) may be addicted. But **boys are three times more likely than girls to be addicted to video games.**[53]

The neural circuitry that mediates the desire to play video games is similar to that observed to mediate substance dependence.[54] With excessive stimulation, the pleasure center in the brain becomes desensitized and less affected by normal stimulation. This causes the number one symptom of ADHD: boredom in response to normal stimulation and the increased need to escape boredom through increased stimulation.

In practical terms, this is why the opportunity to play a video game—or watch TV or eat a dessert—becomes more important to the child than the normal stimulation of doing what it takes to earn the approval of a parent or teacher. In addition, **the decreased activity of the prefrontal cortex inhibits the ability to sustain focus even on what we ourselves think is most important.** Consider how many times we make a New Year's resolution to eat less junk food and lose weight but don't follow through.

9. Induced Labor

Evidence shows that induced birthing procedures using synthetic oxytocin (trademark Pitocin) have doubled the risk of ADHD. In a study of three hundred children whose mothers received Pitocin at birth to induce labor, 67.1 percent of the children were diagnosed with ADHD.[55] Although induced labor is not the direct cause of autism, it does appear to be related; a study in North Carolina reported that women whose labor was induced were 16 percent more likely to have a child later diagnosed with autism.[56]

While inducing labor can and does save lives, it is overused to make the birthing process more convenient for doctors and hospitals. A quarter of mothers in the United States receive Pitocin during labor, and in some hospitals that figure is closer to 90 percent.[57]

With healthy dopamine function and hormonal balance, mothers are able to produce an abundance of their own oxytocin to induce natural birth.[58] Research reveals that the healthy production of neurotransmitters is directly associated with the release of oxytocin.[59] By learning to naturally increase oxytocin levels, there is no need to resort to synthetic oxytocin to induce labor. (For more information on natural solutions to increase oxytocin, read my book *Beyond Mars and Venus*.)

10. Absent Parenting and Boundary Enforcement

Both the availability of parents and their own level of personal happiness reduces the risk of a child being diagnosed with ADHD. **Research shows that children born to depressed mothers are one and a half to two**

times more likely to have ADHD.[60] In addition, when fathers are not available for rough-and-tumble play, a boy's risk of ADHD increases.[61] In this context, the availability and participation of fathers is even more significant for boys because boys are more likely to initiate this play with their fathers and not their mothers.[62]

Just as the moderate feelings of risk and danger from playing video games increases dopamine, the risk and danger of rough-and-tumble play also produces dopamine.[63] The difference is that the dopamine stimulated from rough-and-tumble play increases bonding with the parent rather than the computer.[64, 65]

When parents are not available to set and then enforce boundaries, children lose motivation to please their parents. When parents are too permissive or overfocused on pleasing their child, it does not give the child the opportunity to generate the increased dopamine that results from earning parental approval through cooperative behaviors.

II. Pornography

A Dutch study in 2006 found that pornography had the highest addictive potential of all internet applications.[66] A study at Cambridge University found that the brains of people with pornography addiction exhibited the same kinds of activity as alcoholism or drug abuse.[67]

Online pornography and other impersonal sex can stimulate massive dopamine levels, and this intense increase of dopamine, like that from any addictive drug, changes the brain by reducing the number of dopamine receptors. This change in the brain results in the need for the increased dopamine stimulation that more internet porn can provide. As a result, **regular use of internet porn can lead to a blunting of interest in sex with a real partner and an increased desire for more porn.**[68]

Comparing the effects of masturbation to sexual intercourse with a real partner, other significant hormonal changes also occur. In both sexes, orgasm prompts an increase in the production of the hormone prolactin. Prolactin is associated with sexual satiety in both men and women. It is a natural "I'm done" signal. Studies reveal that the increase of prolactin after intercourse is 400 percent greater than the moderate increase after masturbation.[69] Since masturbation to internet porn fails to produce higher prolactin levels, the desire for more porn and more masturbation increases.

In addition, **boys are more vulnerable than girls to the effects of internet porn because evidence suggests that boys are more stimulated by visual sexual stimuli.**[70] While the debate about what is a healthy amount of masturbation is age-old, the research is clear: addiction to masturbating to internet porn decreases normal sexual function. In one study, healthy volunteers who masturbated to internet porn had significantly more erectile difficulties with intimate sexual partners than with sexually explicit material.[71] In practical terms, this means a boy's sexual interest and subsequent attraction and motivation to initiate and sustain relationships with real girls is diminished as his desire for internet porn or fantasy sex increases.

12. Antibiotics, GMOs, Pesticides, and Plastics

Antibiotics

Antibiotics kill dangerous bacteria in the gut, but they kill good bacteria as well. The absence of good bacteria allows a toxic fungus called candida to overpopulate the gut. Children who have taken lots of antibiotics (as well as those who were not breast-fed) have a higher risk of candida infestations.[72] Taking probiotics after the use of antibiotics is one way to help avoid this outcome.[73] Children with ADHD and autism almost always have different degrees of indigestion caused by an excess of candida.[74] Constipation, diarrhea, and other bowel conditions are directly related to ADHD.[75]

Excessive candida in the gut inhibits the healthy production of B vitamins and neurotransmitters necessary for normal brain performance. Without access to vitamin B12, the liver is unable to make glutathione, an essential antioxidant needed to protect the brain from cellular damage caused by high dopamine stimulation and other toxic influences.

GMOs, pesticides, and herbicides

The residue of pesticides and herbicides contained in nonorganic foods will also kill off beneficial bacteria in the gut and give rise to excessive candida and gut problems. Certain genetically modified organisms (GMOs) have the most destructive effects. These plants are genetically modified not to die when sprayed with toxic pesticides and herbicides.

Farmers use pesticides to kill insects that attack crops, while they use herbicides to kill invading weeds.

The most popular weed killer in the world is Roundup. It contains glyphosate, which is the most powerful herbicide ever created. Nearly all the corn, soy, and cotton now grown in the United States is treated with glyphosate. GMO foods treated with glyphosate, like corn and soy, are contained in most processed snack foods. When you see "high-fructose corn syrup" on the label, think glyphosate.

Glyphosate is currently legal because it does not kill human cells, but studies have confirmed that glyphosate alters and destroys beneficial intestinal bacteria.[76]

In addition, when we eat meat from animals fed with GMO corn, soy, or alfalfa, which are laden with glyphosate, we are slowly destroying many of the good bacteria in our intestines.

Common unlabeled GMO foods in the grocery store include corn, corn syrup, beets, sugar, yellow squash, zucchini, papaya, pineapple, and Canola oil. In addition, many packaged foods and breads contain GMO additives or have been produced with GMOs. When you shop, there are still many non-GMO options. **If foods are certified organic, then they are not only pesticide free but also non-GMO.**

Studies also reveal that the residue of glyphosate in GMO foods inhibits the utilization of the amino acids phenylalanine, tryptophan, and tyrosine.[77] Phenylalanine is necessary to make tyrosine, which in turn makes dopamine—meaning that we can directly link the consumption of GMO foods to inhibited dopamine function and ADHD. But that's not the only link between these amino acids and ADHD symptoms. The inhibition of tyrosine is linked to weight gain, low metabolism, and inability to focus.

Tryptophan is necessary to make vitamin B3, which balances cholesterol, increases energy production, and is necessary for blood circulation to the brain. B3 deficiency has been directly linked to ADHD symptoms.[78] Tryptophan is also needed to make the calming brain chemical serotonin. Deficiency of serotonin is directly linked to higher stress levels, anxiety, and depression.

But one of the biggest problems caused by GMO foods treated with glyphosate is brain injury. Every second, the body's metabolism produces thousands of harmful free radicals. Our brains' natural defense against this free radical damage, as we've discussed, is glutathione. **Glyphosate impairs the transport of sulfate that the liver needs to make** glutathione.[79] Moreover, glyphosates inhibit the functioning of glutathione, as well as the production of key hormones and vitamin D.[80] Vitamin D production and utilization is essential for over two thousand genes and is a key player in brain development and healthy dopamine function.

Children with ADHD also have hormonal imbalances, which can be directly caused by exposure to synthetic chemicals. **In 2003 scientists discovered that the popular pesticide endosulfan blocks the action of testosterone, which in turn disrupts and delays the process of puberty in boys.**[81] Healthy dopamine function and motivation, particularly in boys, is directly related to testosterone. Although it did not look at the rates of ADHD, a 2007 study by the California Department of Public Health found that women who lived near farm fields sprayed with endosulfan during the first eight weeks of pregnancy were several times more likely to give birth to children with autism.

As of July 2010 the Environmental Protection Agency initiated action to gradually end its use in United States by July 31, 2016. After twenty years and many lawsuits, the EPA reported that endosulfan was being discontinued "because it can pose unacceptable health risks to farmworkers and wildlife and can persist in the environment." But while it is now no longer used in the United States, it is still used in many countries around the world from which Americans import food.

Another pesticide, atrazine, the most common herbicide used in the United States, is now banned in Europe. US farmers use about twenty-seven thousand tons of atrazine to protect corn and other crops from weeds, and in the process contaminate the rain, groundwater, rivers, and streams with the runoff and drift from crop dusting. Studies from University of California, Berkley, have shown that even minute amounts of atrazine in the water can have shocking consequences. At eight sites tested, from Iowa to Utah, researchers found that 92 percent of male frogs had abnormal testicles and extra female ovaries; exposure to atrazine at just twenty-five parts *per billion* was enough to produce a tenfold decrease in blood testosterone levels compared to normal male frogs.[82] And as we've seen, low testosterone in males inhibits normal dopamine function in the brain.

Plastics

Another major hormone disruptor for both boys and girls are two ingredients commonly found in certain plastics. In the last decade, scientists have discovered that plastic bottles, pacifiers, and baby bottles, as well as a host of soft drink plastic bottles, contain high levels of two toxins, phthalates and BPA. In 2005 a team of researchers at University of Cincinnati published research showing that phthalates, which leach out of plastics during use, irreversibly disrupt brain development in laboratory animals.[83]

In 2004 neuroscientists identified a crucial link between hormone disruptors and ADHD, as well.[84] When young laboratory animals were exposed to a variety of hormone disruptors, including phthalates, their brains were damaged. These laboratory animals became quite "hyper" and couldn't slow down.

Also, owing to the increasing exposure to these hormone disruptors in plastics, girls are showing signs of puberty a couple of years early and boys are being delayed by a couple of years.[85] The EPA also reports that "studies in laboratory animals suggest that fetuses exposed to phthalates, chemicals used in plastics, can have multiple health issues as adults, including infertility, issues with genitalia development, and sperm production problems."[86]

The Food and Drug Administration banned BPA from baby bottles and "sippy cups" in July 2012 because of concerns that the chemical could interfere with childhood development,[87] but BPA is still widely found in consumer packaging and is used as a lining in aluminum cans to protect them from corrosion. The chemical is also still found in plastics such as bottles, Tupperware, tableware, and food storage containers.

Because of growing public awareness of the dangers of plastic, many companies now label their plastic as "BPA free." Unfortunately, this simply means they replaced BPA with other kinds of plastic. Scientists at Georgetown University and the University of Texas claim these **new BPA-free plastics release chemicals that cause more hormone disruption than the old BPA-containing products.**[88]

13. Gluten Intolerance and Other Food Sensitivities

The guts of one-third of Americans are so compromised that they cannot tolerate gluten, a protein substance that is particularly high in bread.[89]

Although genetically modified wheat is not yet commercially available, the fast-rising yeast used to make bread is. **This fast-rising yeast causes bread to have higher gluten levels, making it harder to digest, and this indigestion causes inflammation in the brain.**[90]

By giving up gluten products, many people have reduced or eliminated ADHD symptoms.[91] In fact, a multitude of studies have shown that for many adults and children food sensitivities are a major cause of ADHD.[92, 93] Common culprits that can cause food allergies are gluten, unfermented soy products (soy milk and tofu), pasteurized dairy products, GMO foods, corn, high-fructose corn syrup, sugar, eggs, food dyes, preservatives, and artificial sweeteners. **Food allergies and sensitivities cause gut inflammation, which in turn leads to inflammation in the brain and ADHD.**

A double-blind study published in the *Lancet*, one of the world's oldest and best-known general medical journals, revealed the unmistakable link between what we eat and children's ADHD symptoms. Researchers recruited one hundred children with ADHD, and placed fifty of them on a restricted diet, consisting mainly of rice, meat, vegetables, pears, and water, with some children getting a few other foods. The other fifty, the control group, received their normal diet. **At the end of five weeks, 64 percent of the children on the restricted diet had significant improvement in their ADHD symptoms**, while none of the control group had improvements.[94] This study dramatically reveals the not-so-obvious connection between what we feed our children and the way they behave.

14. Toxicity

Neurotoxins are substances that interact with nerve cells in the brain and throughout the body by overstimulating nerves to death or interrupting their communication process. **Neurotoxins are particularly dangerous when we don't have enough glutathione or minerals that protect the brain.** This explains why some people are more influenced by neurotoxins than others: some people have more glutathione and minerals in their system than others.

Increasing levels of toxicity in the air we breathe, the water we drink, and the food we eat (nearly all processed and packaged foods include known neurotoxins) not only causes excessive damage in the brain but actively depletes the body of glutathione. The impact of this environmental stress on our bodies contributes to the brain injury that gives rise to ADHD.[95]

Below are the most common neurotoxins we encounter in daily life:

1. artificial sweeteners like aspartame and sucralose[96, 97]
2. MSG or hydrolyzed anything[98]
3. soy protein (fermented soy is OK)[99]
4. aluminum (common in drinking water and over-the-counter antacids)[100]
5. mercury (common in fish products and silver fillings)[101]
6. fluoride (commonly added to our water supply and, of course, toothpaste; fluoride's toxicity is why the warning labels on fluoridated toothpaste say "Do Not Swallow"[102])
7. yeast extract (commonly found in canned foods)[103]

We are bombarded with these neurotoxins every day, and our brain's health is dependent on our body's ability to neutralize their harmful effects as well as cleanse them from the body. However, **children are more vulnerable to these neurotoxins because their brains are still developing.**[104]

In addition to common neurotoxins, scientists have identified 201 common industrial chemicals as likely culprits contributing to ADHD and other mental disorders.[105] "The bottom line is you only get one chance to develop a brain," said Philippe Grandjean, lead author of the study, in an interview with WebMD. "We have to protect children against chemical pollution because damage to a developing brain is irreversible."[106]

Studies from Columbia Center for Children's Environmental Health in New York City show that the air we breathe, which is filled with ambient toxins spewed by vehicles, pesticides, and chemicals found in common household products, are all immediately detectable in the bloodstream. Their research suggests that **moms are passing on these toxic chemicals to their babies,** as scientists also find these toxins in the umbilical cord of babies once they are born.[107]

These reports, however, do not take into consideration how adept a mother's body can be at neutralizing the effects of toxicity. Healthy levels of glutathione during pregnancy are key. As mentioned before, **women who take Tylenol during pregnancy, which suppresses glutathione, have a much higher risk of giving birth to children with** autism, ADHD, behavior problems, poor language and motor skills, and communication difficulties.[108]

Our main hope in protecting ourselves from environmental toxins is to minimize exposure while also helping the body to detoxify. Detoxification is best achieved by occasional fasting and special supplements to sustain healthy glutathione levels.

Children should not fast because their bodies are still growing, but they can have special days to help the body detoxify by avoiding any processed or packaged foods and drinking lots of lemon water and three to five meals of bone broth soup that has been cooked for at least eight hours. The best bone broth recipes, easily found online, use bones from grass-fed beef and add lots of sulfurous vegetables like cauliflower, kale, broccoli, cabbage, bok choy, parsley, onions, brussels sprouts, green beans, sweet potato, spinach, and peas. This soup is rich in sulfur and other minerals the body needs for manufacturing glutathione in order to detoxify.

15. Nutritional Deficiencies

Over the past one hundred years, farming practices using synthetic fertilizers have depleted the soil of vitamins and minerals, which are necessary to stimulate the production of brain chemicals. For example, comparing the mineral content of today's food to food sixty years ago, there has been an 80 percent drop in calcium and iron. When comparing the vitamin content, most fruits and vegetables have had a drop of 75 percent in vitamin A and 50 percent in vitamin C.[109]

This common mineral and vitamin deficiency means that, **to get the same nutrition you would have gotten in the past, you must eat more food.** You would have to eat eight oranges today to get the same amount of vitamin A that your grandparents would have gotten from one. These missing vitamins and minerals are all needed to protect the brain from injury and to promote healthy dopamine function.

Foods that are genetically modified (GMOs) are often worse. One published study concluded that **non-GMO corn is twenty times richer in nutrition than GMO corn**.[110] In addition, GMO corn contains a number of toxic elements not found in organic corn, like chlorides, formaldehyde, and glyphosate, in harmful quantifies.[111]

Deficiency in another mineral, iodine, is also linked to brain injury. **The World Health Organization reports that iodine deficiency is one** of the main causes of impaired cognitive development in children.[112] The **thyroid gland** uses iodine not only to stimulate the metabolism but to detoxify the blood and protect the brain from injury. **The common use of chlorine in our water, potassium bromate in our bread yeast, and fluoride in our water gradually depletes iodine in the body.** According to the US National Research Council, "several lines of information indicate an effect of fluoride exposure on thyroid function."[113]

Because children with inhibited dopamine function seek out high dopamine stimulation, this increased dopamine production can also inhibit thyroid function, which then results in the same negative side effects as iodine deficiency. To make thyroid hormones, **the thyroid gland** combines iodine and the amino acid tyrosine. Tyrosine is also used by the brain to make more dopamine. When high levels of dopamine are produced because a child with ADHD is dependent on higher dopamine stimulation for pleasure, interest, focus, and motivation, it can deplete the body of the tyrosine required by the thyroid glands to regulate the metabolism as well as detoxify the body. We will explore in the next chapter natural solutions to ensure your child gets enough iodine as well as the amino acid tyrosine.

16. Brain Concussion or Mild Traumatic Brain Injury

Studies from the University of California, San Diego, show that children who have a history of concussion are more likely to develop ADHD and have difficulty controlling their moods.[114] ADHD or inhibited dopamine function can be directly triggered by a concussion, physical injury, a shock to the head, or a shock to the base of the spine.

Owing to recent lawsuits against the NFL, the long-term effects of concussions are finally coming into the light of public awareness. Four thousand former football players have filed lawsuits. Later in life, **older athletes who suffered from concussions while playing football report symptoms similar to Parkinson's as well as memory loss and ADHD.**[115] In addition, the army is now faced with over five hundred thousand soldiers returning from battle with mild traumatic brain injury, or TBI. "Mild TBI" is the new medical term to describe concussion.

TBI is the signature wound of the wars in Iraq and Afghanistan. Vets frequently suffer from this brain damage after exposure to improvised explosive devices (IEDs), a regular occurrence for troops traveling the roads in war zones like Iraq and Afghanistan. This has caused not only the classic symptoms of ADHD but also depression, anxiety, and dramatically high rates of suicide.

In November 2007, I was warmly invited to speak at a special conference for American military leaders about the need for relationship skills for returning soldiers. During that top secret conference, they were primarily discussing this new problem the military was facing: mild traumatic brain injury. It was reported that merely standing in a building or home two football fields away from an IED explosion could cause traumatic brain injury. This was a new problem, and they were looking for answers. They were also developing tests to diagnose TBI because one of its symptoms is **not knowing you have it**. Even to this day, the military has no specific healing policy for this condition other than suppressing the symptoms with medications.[116]

This lack of awareness regarding the symptoms of concussion or TBI is not confined to the military. **Most parents of children with TBI are unaware that their children may have sustained a concussion on the playground or that they are developing symptoms of ADHD,** since you can have a concussion and not black out.

Another problem with TBI is that while sometimes the symptoms show up right away, at other times they don't. When symptoms develop later, a patient may not make the connection to the earlier head injury. This is especially true when symptoms develop days or months later.

Typical symptoms of TBI are headache and a variety of other symptoms that directly correspond to many of the different symptoms of ADHD. They include

1. difficulty concentrating and slower reaction times (ADHD distracted type),
2. nausea and difficulty with bright lights and sounds (ADHD sensitive type),
3. irritability and restlessness (ADHD impulsive type), and
4. insomnia or sleeping more (ADHD compulsive type).

Because of these symptoms, after a concussion or accident, students may suffer a drop-off in their schoolwork and grades while adults' work performance may suffer. Unless corrected, these symptoms can not only last a lifetime but even get worse. Researchers at the University of

California, San Diego, found that after a concussion about 10 percent of kids had a full depressive disorder six months later.[117] Yet sometimes within hours after a brain injury, a child who's never been depressed before suddenly becomes depressed and suicidal.[118]

Addressing the Cause to Heal the Brain

The next chapter will explore a host of alternative solutions, which help to actually heal the brain by addressing the one cause, inhibited dopamine function, that gives rise to the many and varied symptoms of ADHD.

As we have seen, there are many contributing factors to inhibited dopamine function. When the many contributing factors of inhibited dopamine function have been recognized and eliminated or mitigated and we are aware of the many different expressions of ADHD, natural solutions *can* work. And just as there are many contributing factors to cause some degree of inhibited dopamine function in your son, there are many different natural solutions that may work for him, too.

CHAPTER 31

Natural Solutions to Restore Dopamine Function

Although the media doesn't talk about them and your doctor probably doesn't know about them, researchers have discovered an abundance of natural solutions for increasing brain performance. These natural solutions do not cure disease but rather awaken and support the body and brain in restoring normal dopamine function.

For example, in his bestselling book *Grain Brain*, Dr. David Perlmutter reports that **some children diagnosed with ADHD immediately improved by simply taking high doses of vitamin D3 and K2 and then following a gluten-free diet.** In his work with Parkinson's patients—Parkinson's is a more extreme version of inhibited dopamine function—he found that between 80 and 90 percent of his patients improved dramatically by increasing glutathione levels in the body.

Besides detox protocols like fasting with bone soup, **one way of dramatically increasing glutathione production is drinking undenatured whey protein, which comes from unpasteurized milk.** (Pasteurized milk, which has been processed with high heat, loses its potency to stimulate the production of glutathione and does not restore normal dopamine function.[1, 2]) This undenatured dairy protein, while not pasteurized, is still bacteria free. Drinking it is a safe, natural, and evidence-based way of addressing dopamine function issues.[3, 4]

Natural solutions work, but that doesn't mean that every solution is going to work for every child. Going off bread to reduce gut inflammation or drinking a super shake with undenatured whey will work for some, but not for everyone. These solutions, along with eating healthy organic foods and eliminating processed junk foods, will certainly help most children with ADHD, but they will not always be enough. The child who has gut issues—and many children with ADHD do—will require more than bone soup or undenatured whey protein shakes because they will not be able to fully digest their meals, no matter how healthy or organic their diet is. It may take some experimentation before finding the solution that will work for your children.

Skyler's Story

Skyler was diagnosed with ADHD and autistic spectrum disorder when he was four years old. By first eliminating processed foods, GMOs, soy, gluten, and pasteurized dairy, within days his behavior improved.

At the same time, his parents began giving him a variety of vitamin and mineral supplements as well as Bravo yogurt, which is made at home from milk, colostrum, and forty-two different probiotics. These probiotics are known to support the gut in making a molecule called GcMAF (Gc protein-derived macrophage activating factor). This important protein is normally produced by a healthy gut. GcMAF, along with other cofactors, activates vitamin D, which in turn supports hundreds of functions and helps to heal the body and brain.[5] Vitamin D, which is produced when you spend time in the sun, can only work if the gut is also working to make GcMAF.[6]

Every other day, Skyler also took a one-hour hot Epsom salt bath (starting at 98 degrees Fahrenheit and gradually adding more hot water so that the water temperature was around 103 degrees Fahrenheit for the last twenty minutes). This protocol generated heat-shock proteins, which last 48 hours. Heat-shock proteins are normally produced when you have a fever. **They have a miraculous ability to protect brain neurons while also supporting their regeneration and growth.**[7, 8]

During the next several months Skyler showed steady improvement. After three months he would listen when spoken to, and he could speak in full sentences and maintain eye contact. His sleep improved and his mood shifted from irritated and easily agitated to smiling and happy. On evaluation, he was no longer diagnosed with ADHD or autism spectrum disorder.

Skyler's brain challenge had started in his gut. As a baby he had ear infections. The use of antibiotics had destroyed many of the beneficial bacteria in his gut. By temporarily eliminating the most difficult foods for him to digest, inflammation in the gut was minimized. At the same time, by implanting his gut with missing probiotics, fermented with colostrum, he was able to restore healthy gut function. (Colostrum is the special milk produced by mothers in the first three days after giving birth to support babies' immune systems.)

To support optimal brain function, each day Skyler drank a predigested superfood shake with undenatured dairy proteins. To make the proteins easy to digest, the undenatured milk powder was first mixed with water and digestive enzymes and then set out for thirty to forty minutes. During this time, the dairy proteins were automatically broken down into peptides, which were then predigested and ready to use by his brain. Even though his digestion was compromised, because the proteins were predigested, his body and brain could immediately utilize them.

Skyler's transformation is not unusual. While speaking at an autism conference in 2015, I had the opportunity to listen to another speaker, Dr. Jeff Bradstreet, who discussed a similar protocol using Bravo yogurt GcMAF for autism spectrum disorder. **He reported that his treatment reversed autism in over seven hundred children out of three thousand in only three months.** While only 25 percent of the children experienced such a dramatic reversal, almost all were at least helped.

The dietary changes, hot baths, supplements, and homemade probiotic yogurt with colostrum that helped Skyler are just a few examples of the many natural solutions we will explore in this chapter. With this new insight, healing the brain doesn't have to be hard; you can do it for yourself and your children. Unlike drugs and medications, these natural solutions have no negative side effects.

For some children, to immediately heal the symptoms of ADHD it is enough to take bread out of their diet and get plenty of sunshine. But most children, like Skyler, need specific therapies along with extra supplements, herbs, vitamins, or superfoods.

The Long-Term Benefits of Natural Solutions

Nurturing a boy with ADHD is daunting for parents, and so the convenience of taking a stimulant drug can be very tempting. Unfortunately, as we have previously pointed out, these stimulant drugs have short-term benefits with long-term side effects.

Natural solutions—including more physical exercise, singing, dancing, art, drama, or sports, along with different therapies like counseling, chiropractic treatments, hot water therapy, infrared saunas, cryogenics, and homeopathy—work in both the short and long term. Especially when supported with dietary changes and specific nutritional supplements, **their effectiveness goes well beyond what any stimulant drug could ever provide.**

My primary purpose in listing the many proven solutions for ADHD below is to reinforce the validity of different natural solutions (though I will also share the solutions that I have personally seen to work most effectively). With so many well-tested options, going drug-free in your approach to supporting your son's brain health is finally a real choice.

With this new insight into the many causes of low dopamine function and so many different potential solutions, you will be able to find the best solution for your son. And in my experience, when you find the right solution, or collection of solutions, for your son, he will experience improvement within days.

Increased Exercise Can Reverse Symptoms of ADHD

One of the most obvious contributing factors that cause ADHD in children is lack of exercise. **The early stages of brain development are particularly dependent on physical exercise, rough-and-tumble play, and bodily movement.**[9] The brain needs regular, challenging, and varied physical movement to develop the ability to sustain healthy and appropriate focus. Without it, many children with ADHD simply cannot focus in school and often don't listen to their parents at home.

Brain plasticity is a term describing the brain's ability to adapt and change in response to our environment, and it's one of the most exciting new fields of brain research. Brain scans in children have revealed that the brain actually changes its structure in reaction to various stimulation or lack of stimulation. **Challenging physical exercise and new movements of the body are proven to create the most dramatic and positive changes in the brain.**[10]

Physical activity and movement exercise stimulate testosterone, which in turn stimulates the production of dopamine in the brain, and because boys are more dependent on testosterone than girls for healthy functioning, this means they are also more dependent on physical activity. When a child is tired, restless, or spaced out in a classroom, even a short recess for some physical activity can boost dopamine to awaken interest and motivation to listen and learn.

Up until the last two decades, brain scientists thought the brain stopped developing after the first few years of life. They believed brain connections were all formed during an early critical period and if a particular area was injured or undeveloped, those nerve cells could not form new connections or regenerate. New brain plasticity research has overturned this mistaken old view. **At all stages of life, the brain has the potential to regenerate and reorganize itself to compensate for injuries or inflammation caused by toxins and nutritional deficiencies.**[11] Dr. Anat Baniel, a psychologist and bestselling author of *Kids Beyond Limits*, explains, "The greatest potential for transformation, though often difficult to grasp, is not in trying to make children do what they can't, but in finding ways to help each child's brain differentiate and spontaneously discover how to go beyond his or her limitations."[12]

Brain plasticity is very real. For example, research reveals significant changes in the brain from merely practicing a new song on the piano. From repeating specific and new hand movements for about two hours over a period of five days, significant brain growth occurred.[13] **Brain scans have revealed that kids who play musical instruments have significantly more gray matter volume in the brain.**[14] And this new research into brain plasticity confirms that physical movement is one of the most powerful brain stimulators and helps develop a child's brain.

Grades Go Up with Supervised Physical Exercise

Other research has demonstrated that with increased supervised exercise at school, grades go up and behavior dramatically improves. **In Urban Dove Charter School, school administrators collected the lowest-performing students from other schools and helped them become**

high-achieving students through the use of physical activity.[15] During the first three hours of the day, the curriculum included specific supervised physical exercise and competitive sports. The children were also mentored later in the day between academic classes by their gym coaches, with whom they had formed a bond.

The results were miraculous: 98 percent of the children graduated from high school and 90 percent went on to college. Before intervention, not one of the children had been expected to graduate from high school or attend college.

The success of this program does not mean that every child just needs more exercise, nor does it mean that the absence of exercise is the primary cause of ADHD. But it does show that our children, particularly those with learning challenges, have tremendous untapped potential that can be tapped by more physical activity. As part of a holistic approach, combined with other nondrug solutions, a more moderate exercise program than the program used at Urban Dove may be equally effective.

Art Class Improves Brain Function

Art therapy has been shown to help students with ADHD reduce impulsive behaviors, enhance interpersonal behavior, and improve study skills and classroom performance.[16] Reading, writing, and math primarily require left-brain activity. **For all children, using art to increase activity on the right side of the brain has shown to increase grades and improve behavior.**[17]

Bestselling author Brian Mayne has assisted over a hundred thousand children improve brain performance by activating the whole of their brains through the combined use of words and pictures, a process he calls "Goal Mapping." By setting goals using the left brain, and then using the right brain by drawing colored pictures of what achieving those goals would look like, both children and adults experienced dramatic and positive changes.[18]

Because of my own ADHD, while writing my first book thirty years ago, *What You Feel You Can Heal*, I would get stuck focusing on one idea and had difficulty flowing from one topic to another. I overcame this tendency by writing for a page and then taking time to draw a cartoon summarizing the idea I was writing about. Drawing a picture required that I shift from my left-brain activity to use my right brain. This shift allowed me to use my whole brain and to better develop my ability to express my ideas and write books.

Unfortunately, without this vital insight about brain development, most schools in the United States have eliminated art classes for right-brain stimulation (as well as gym class for exercise). Instead, they focus primarily on left-brain activities like reading, writing, and math. Providing both left- and right-brain activities can stimulate whole brain development.

Homeopathy and Bodywork Can Heal Concussions

When ADHD or inhibited dopamine function is caused by concussion, physical injury, a shock to the head, or a shock to the base of the spine, behavior therapies are not always enough. Homeopathy and various forms of bodywork like chiropractic treatments, craniosacral therapy, cryotherapy (cold air treatment), or hot water hydrotherapy can make the difference.

Specific homeopathic remedies can awaken your body's ability to heal the brain. Homeopathy is a form of medicine approved by the FDA that does not use drugs. In simple terms, homeopathic remedies turn on your body's healing genes.

The US medical establishment often attack and attempt to discredit homeopathy on the grounds that Western science cannot determine how it works. In spite of tremendous opposition, it continues to be approved by the FDA because it has worked in many cases when drugs have not.[19]

There are now more than 150 scientific studies of homeopathy that fulfill strict evidence criteria and have been published in highly regarded medical journals. Many of these studies have shown favorable results for homeopathy when compared with a placebo or conventional medicine.[20, 21, 22, 23] **Two of homeopathy's great benefits are that it is inexpensive, and when it works, it has no side effects.**

One of its drawbacks is that, like any medical treatment, it does not always work. There are also many studies that suggest it does not work or that its effectiveness is limited to the placebo effect.

Dr. Garry Gordon, who has used homeopathy for over fifty years, is on the Board of Homeopathic Medical Examiners in Arizona and, in addition to being an MD, was awarded a degree as a doctor of homeopathic medicine (HMD). He is also the cofounder of the American College for the Advancement in Medicine, which now trains thousands of doctors each year around the world in the fundamentals of integrative medicine.

He explained to me that homeopathy has been used for over 235 years but that because of modern changes in our lifestyle **"homeopathic remedies are not as effective as they used to be."** Even over the last fifty years their effectiveness has lessened.

Homeopathy doesn't always work for three reasons:

1. The wrong remedy is used.
2. The modern diet is deficient in the necessary minerals and vitamins for the activated genes to do their job.
3. High stimulation from coffee, sugar, stimulant drugs, or video games tends to interfere with its effectiveness.

Homeopathy was most effective before the invention of stimulant drugs and junk food. Patients at that time were instructed to avoid the high stimulation of coffee for the treatments to work. For homeopathic remedies to be as effective today, one needs to abstain from today's hyperstimulation and take extra vitamin and mineral supplements.

To heal a concussion, decreasing hyperstimulation and getting extra vitamin and mineral support is the first step. Homeopathy is the second. Yet turning on your healing genes with homeopathy may still not be enough. When a physical shock to the body causes damage, a physical resetting of the body may also be required. The most obvious example of this is a broken bone. For a broken bone to heal straight, it must be reset. Chiropractic bodywork and craniosacral therapy can physically reset your brain's connection to the rest of the body.

Like homeopathy, chiropractic therapy is often discredited and attacked by the American medical establishment. But gradually science is catching up with what millions of patients around the world have discovered. Every month new studies reveal its effectiveness.[24] Even insurance plans are beginning to cover chiropractic treatments along with other effective nondrug treatments, like acupuncture.

A shock to the body can block the natural flow of cerebrospinal fluid that connects the brain and body through the many vertebrae of the spine. When this flow is restored, through minimizing nerve irritation, releasing tension in the spinal cord via chiropractic or craniosacral therapy, the brain can more effectively restore healthy dopamine function. Indeed, restoring this flow restores all aspects of health.

> *Worms will not eat living wood where the vital sap is flowing; rust will not hinder the opening of a gate when the hinges are used each day. Movement gives health and life. Stagnation brings disease and death.*
>
> —Proverb in traditional Chinese medicine

One of my readers, an Olympic medalist, shared with me that after many falls while skating freestyle she eventually developed symptoms of depression, anxiety, and ADHD. In her case chiropractic care and my nutritional suggestions were helpful but not enough to rid her of her symptoms. However, after following a six-week homeopathic brain function treatment (which I have also personally benefited from) developed by Dr. Salar Farahmand, a world-renowned researcher and practitioner in the field of homeopathic therapy, most of her symptoms went away.[25] She repeated the program again, and all her symptoms were gone. It was truly a miracle.

Teaching workshops at a variety of conferences around the world, I frequently hear miraculous testimonials about the benefits of chiropractic care. Anyone who has ever had a rib out of joint knows the immediate relief after visiting a chiropractor. You can take all the pain pills in the world, but the pain will continue until the rib is physically put back in place. Sometimes all it takes is a single adjustment.

When I was fourteen, after my second major concussion, ten treatments with my chiropractor took away my terrible headaches. Later in life, as a result of more concussions, I developed chronic neck tension. Using the Anat Baniel Method (ABM) of NeuroMovement, originally developed by Dr. Moshé Feldenkrais and then later advanced by Dr. Baniel, I was able to release my neck tension.

As Dr. Baniel explains, "The moment we pay attention to our movement, the brain resumes growing at a very rapid rate."[26] The Anat Baniel Method looks like a kind of bodywork, but it is really an innovative form of brainwork. **By moving the body slowly in new and specific ways, the traumatized brain is activated and can actually learn to heal itself.** In many cases I have witnessed children with severe brain injuries from birth begin to speak and walk in just a few treatments. (You can see it for yourself at Dr. Baniel's website, AnatBanielMethod.com.)

In the past, the standard medical procedure for concussion was only to monitor the person who had experienced it to see if something else, something treatable, showed up. It was assumed that "the brain will recover at its own pace within 7 to 10 days."[27]

This oversight is finally being corrected. The army now recognizes that soldiers with mild traumatic brain injury or TBI can be directly affected for three to six months, if not longer, as is now being recognized with football players. Unfortunately, their solution still assumes that the brain will recover at its own pace.

While modern medicine has no remedies, homeopathy has over twenty FDA-approved remedies. One of the best-designed double-blind studies for alternative medicine has demonstrated homeopathy's effectiveness in treating concussions.[28]

The Emotional Freedom Technique (EFT), which uses talk therapy along with stimulating specific pressure points on the body, has also shown tremendous benefits for soldiers with TBI and PTSD. The EFT reduces anxiety and stress by identifying negative thought patterns and painful emotions while tapping a specific series of acupuncture points. **In one study, 90 percent of soldiers practicing EFT no longer met the criteria for clinical PTSD**, compared with only 4 percent of the control group.[29] This same tool has been helpful for children, teens, and adults with ADHD.

Even today, the standard medical treatment for both concussion and mild traumatic brain injury is merely physical and mental rest. For physical rest, patients are encouraged to stop playing sports and disengage from active duty until they are free of symptoms. For mental rest, they are asked to refrain from reading, looking at a computer screen, or doing homework.

It is appalling that the only nondrug remedy modern medicine has for a concussion and the brain injury that results is simply to rest and avoid stimulation for six months. While this rest creates the opportunity for healing, it is natural solutions like homeopathy, chiropractic care, craniosacral therapy, the Anat Baniel Method, and the Emotional Freedom Technique, along with extra nutrition, that can deliver the results.

Hot Water Therapy

Hot water therapy combines hydrotherapy, the use of mineral waters, along with hyperthermia, the use of heat, to induce a low fever in the brain. Hot water therapy for healing the brain originates in Germany, a country well known for respecting the healing power of spa treatments. Even today, German health insurance gives heart disease patients a choice: they can receive drugs for heart disease or take a two-week trip to a German spa for hydrotherapy.[30] Both have been proved to help, but unlike the drugs, the spa has no negative side effects.

In my experience, this ancient German hot water therapy—"the cure when nothing else worked," according to a hundred-year-old text called the *Science of Vitality*, by E.H. Ruddock, MD—is one of the most powerful therapies available to heal the brain. It is relatively unknown in America, but it has been used for hundreds of years in German spas.

Because one can easily self-administer the treatment at home, there is not enough profit for the business of health care to support peer-reviewed scientific research.

In my Mars Venus Wellness center, we used hot water therapy extensively for ten years. (After ten years, I closed the spa because parents could do the special treatments at home and didn't need to travel to northern California.) When combined with extra nutrition, it has produced tremendous benefits for nearly every health challenge.

Recently, in 2013, there was a clinical study of forty children with autism.[31] **Researchers found just one thirty-minute bath, at 102 degrees Fahrenheit, helped soothe the symptoms of autism and made the children more sociable.** It improved their ability to communicate and made them less prone to repeating the same action over and over. Unfortunately, they did not continue the therapy to produce long-term benefits.

What is most significant in this study is that these changes did not occur when the bath was only a few degrees cooler at 98 degrees Fahrenheit. **A hot bath worked while a warm bath did not.** Based on my experience, in working with hundreds of adults and children over the last fifteen years, this study shows only a fraction of what can be done with a bath treatment if it is done consistently every other day for three months.

Hot water therapy involves taking a bath for an hour, lying down on your back with your face above water but with the rest of your head underwater. While maintaining this position, the water temperature is gradually increased over the course of an hour, beginning at approximately 98 degrees Fahrenheit for the first twenty minutes, and then increased to approximately 101 degrees Fahrenheit for the next twenty minutes, then to around 103 degrees Fahrenheit for a final twenty minutes. This protocol is repeated every other day for three months.

Make sure the last twenty minutes are at 103 degrees Fahrenheit. This final water temperature generates a low fever in the brain to activate healing molecules, called heat-shock proteins, which are now known to protect and repair brain neurons. **This induced low fever in the brain also increases glutathione production, which is already low in boys with ADHD,** and the heat-shock proteins released help repair dopamine function. During a fever, more immune factors are released to heal the brain as well.[32] The application of heat-shock proteins is a newly emerging therapy for healing diabetes, obesity, dementia, and even reducing tumors.[33, 34]

This hot water therapy is completely safe for all ages and stages of life. However, hot water therapy is not recommended if you have a history of high blood pressure or multiple sclerosis.

With supervision, hot water therapy can be done at home in a bathtub. Just add between six and twelve pounds of Epsom salt to the water. It is fine to occasionally sit up when it gets a little boring or if you wish to drink some cold water. If your bathtub is not long enough, then simply bend your knees. Keeping the head partially submerged is what allows the temperature of the brain to increase, but even if your son just sits up in the bathtub, it still helps a lot. Parents who brought their autistic children to my wellness spa noticed tremendous—and lasting—improvement in their children after only a few days of water therapy treatment, and most of the children who benefited just sat up in the hot mineral water spas.

Even without hot water therapy, fevers from sickness are very beneficial for the brain. **For many years, mothers of autistic children have reported that their children's symptoms of autism disappeared during a fever, only to reappear after the fever was over.**[35] More than 80 percent of children in another study of thirty children with autism spectrum disorders showed improvement in behavior during temperature elevations.[36] But the symptoms come back because the infection has not been fully healed.

Doing hot water therapy every other day gives your immune system the support it needs to finally rid the brain of the chronic infection and inflammation that is associated with all mental challenges from ADHD to autism. After just two weeks following this procedure, along with mineral and protein supplements, many of my clients have reported tremendous clarity, calm, and focus.

Many boys resist lying in a bath for a full hour because they become too bored. One remedy to overcome this resistance is to read to them or have them listen to a book on tape while they sit up in the tub. They should, however, avoid the high stimulation of listening to loud music or watching videos. **With low stimulation, the brain can heal much more efficiently.**

Another alternative is listening to special low stimulation classical music. Researchers at Advanced Brain Technologies have a "Listening Program" that simultaneously stimulates and relaxes the brain to reorganize the brain and restore normal dopamine function.[37] This program works even without the hot water treatment, but they can work even better combined.

With hot water therapy, it is always good at first to have children start the therapy sitting up. Then, after a few sessions, as they become accustomed to sitting for an hour, if possible introduce the idea of lying back in the water. Even if your child is not willing at first to lie back with their head partially underwater to keep the heat in, or remain in the tub for a full hour at all, there is still a tremendous benefit from simply sitting in the bathtub for a half hour. When done at night before bed, hot water therapy can also help sleep.

There are many effective variations of water therapy. Even taking a cold shower every day after your normal shower will increase glutathione production in the liver. **After taking a cold shower or bath, your body reacts by producing an internal fever to warm up.** It is common practice in Scandinavian countries to first heat up in a sauna and then for a few minutes lie in the snow. Alternating hot and cold also stimulates beneficial heat-shock proteins. Scandinavian clubs of men and women who regularly swim in the cold waters of the North Atlantic Ocean during winter are known for their vitality, brain health, and longevity.[38]

The same heat-shock proteins can also be generated in a twenty-minute session of applying intense cold to the head. This new treatment is called cryogenics. It is still a new treatment but is becoming more available at wellness centers around the world.

Young Tibetan monks generate an internal fever that leads to heat-shock proteins by practicing meditation while sitting outside in the snow in sub-zero temperatures wearing little more than a loincloth. They are able to generate enough body heat to melt the snow around them. However, as they say on TV, "Keep in mind these feats are performed by trained professionals and should not be practiced at home."

Infrared saunas are also very helpful for detoxification and the results are similar to hot water therapy. At my wellness center, to maximize the benefits of hot water therapy, following the bath treatment we would sit in a far-infrared sauna for twenty to thirty minutes and then finish with cold showers. Infrared saunas have proved to be much more efficient than traditional higher-heat saunas. Even young autistic children enjoyed sitting in them.

The far-infrared sauna has a threefold benefit, with or without hot water therapy:

1. Increased sweating helps detoxify the body of harmful mercury and other heavy metals. This is particularly helpful when a child or adult has deficiencies in glutathione.
2. An induced mild fever stimulates heat-shock proteins to restore neuron health and healthy dopamine function.
3. Increased circulation provides more nutrients to the brain.

Another therapy that provides similar support, developed by Japanese researchers studying the many benefits of heat-shock proteins, is lying on a BioMat. This special mat combines far-infrared heat with amethyst crystals to raise the body temperature, inducing a low fever.[39]

Both infrared companies and hot tub companies warn parents of exposing children to high temperatures. **There is, however, no research showing any dangers for children at high temperatures.** But because there is also no research showing it *is* safe, they are protecting themselves from lawsuits. These companies are simply not aware of the studies showing the benefits of hot water therapy not just for adults but children as well.[40] Hot water is safe for children, but they should always be supervised to ensure the top temperature remains around 103 degrees Fahrenheit.[41]

Elimination Diets Can Reverse ADHD

Both food allergies and indigestion trigger inflammation in the brain, which directly inhibits brain performance and often results in different degrees of ADHD.[42] Almost 90 percent of children with autism and ADHD have some degree of chronic colitis (the medical term for gut inflammation).[43] Because of this direct relationship between digestion and food allergies and ADHD, by eliminating certain foods, dramatic improvements have been observed.

The most well-known elimination diet, proved to reverse ADHD 50 percent of the time, is the Feingold elimination diet.[44] The Feingold diet gets great results by eliminating foods with artificial colors, artificial flavors, several preservatives, synthetic sweeteners, and salicylate (aspirin-like) foods. (The FDA lists over thirty-three double-blind clinical trials demonstrating that artificial food colors are related to ADHD and other related childhood problem behaviors.[45]) The bad news is that, in the Feingold diet, many of the foods found in the supermarket are taboo. The good news is that there are safe, natural versions available for nearly all problem foods. After eliminating all potentially problematic foods (see Feingold.org for the list) for four days, you can reintroduce each individually to see if it causes problems.

Other elimination diets include testing for specific food allergies and sensitivities that may be contributing to ADHD. **The most common foods to be tested are the foods we most commonly eat:**

1. wheat bread (and other gluten products)
2. sugar (and all sugar substitutes, natural or artificial)
3. corn (particularly GMO)
4. dairy (pasteurized)
5. soy (GMO and unfermented)

By eliminating these foods, along with processed foods containing artificial food colorings and additives, for many children the symptoms of ADHD quickly go away.[46] As with the Feingold diet, after removing all of these foods for four days, you can begin to test each one to see if the symptoms return. If symptoms return with a particular food, then it must be eliminated for some time, if not indefinitely. In some cases, after abstaining from a particular food for six months it can be reintroduced in moderation without triggering symptoms.

A more restrictive elimination diet for healing more challenging gut inflammation is the GAPS diet. The **GAPS diet** focuses on removing foods that are difficult to digest and damaging to gut flora and replacing them with nutrient-dense foods to give the intestinal lining a chance to heal and seal. This diet can take a couple of years to heal the gut and restore healthy digestion, but it has been a lifesaver for thousands of people suffering from severe irritable bowel syndrome, Crohn's disease, and other intestinal challenges. Dr. Natasha Campbell-McBride, who developed the GAPS diet, also used it to cure her three-year-old son's autism.[47]

Improving Gut Health and Digestion with Probiotics

Healthy digestion is a big part of healing ADHD. A study of 742,939 children revealed that children with ADHD are significantly more likely to have constipation and diarrhea.[48] The reason gut health is so important for healthy dopamine function in the brain is that in order to convert amino acids into the protein peptides that are the precursors to making dopamine, children need to fully digest the protein they eat. **Without good digestion, the brain does not get the nourishment that it needs.** In an unhealthy gut, digestion is compromised.

In addition, when the gut is not healthy the walls of the intestines begin to leak undigested proteins into the bloodstream. Once in the bloodstream, these undigested particles trigger inflammatory diseases.

In my experience helping children to improve digestion and eliminate inflammation in the gut, it does not always require extreme dietary restrictions and limitations to see benefits right away.

An alternative approach to using extreme elimination diets is to directly support gut health and heal food allergies. If your son has taken antibiotics recently, your doctor has probably recommended that your son also go on a regimen of "probiotics" (another word for good bacteria) to restore the gut function and digestion.

One natural source of probiotics is fermented foods like yogurt and kefir drinks. Naturopaths have been recommending fermented foods for hundreds of years, and modern medicine is finally catching up; in the last ten years, doctors have begun to recognize the powerful benefits of probiotics for gut and brain health.[49] **The most exciting recent studies show how the probiotics in fermented foods directly support your digestion, which in turn supports brain function.**

For example, there is increasing evidence suggesting an interaction between the intestinal microbiota, the gut, and the central nervous system in what is recognized as the microbiome–gut–brain axis. Recent data on the probiotic *Lactobacillus rhamnosus* suggests that these microbes can modulate the production of brain chemicals and, therefore, may have beneficial effects in the treatment of ADHD, depression, and anxiety.[50]

Probiotics also protect the body from the many toxic influences and foods that inhibit gut, liver, and brain function, which in turn trigger a variety of ADHD symptoms. As we've seen, the most toxic foods are genetically modified soy and corn, processed wheat or gluten products, excessive sugar, and pasteurized milk (as opposed to raw milk, butter, yogurt, kefir, or undenatured dairy proteins, which are often well tolerated and beneficial). If meat and dairy products are not labeled organic, it means the animals were fed GMO soy and corn, and that makes their meat toxic as well.

A healthy body and digestive system can tolerate some degree of these toxic foods but they definitely interfere with the body's ability to heal itself. To restore normal dopamine function, it is best to avoid or at least minimize your exposure to these toxic elements while taking naturally produced probiotics like the ones that are particularly abundant in fermented foods.

Cutting-edge probiotic drinks and yogurts are now being designed with the objective of developing probiotic-based strategies for treating neurodegenerative disorders like ADHD. **The best probiotic I have found is Bravo Probiotic yogurt.** Bravo is particularly helpful for restoring gut function, and through it, dopamine function, because unlike most yogurts or kefir drinks, which contain two or three strains of probiotics, Bravo products contain forty-two different probiotic strains.[51] For those who don't want to make the yogurt at home, it can be ordered online or one can use the Bravo concentrated capsules. However, it is most effective when made fresh at home. Those who are dairy intolerant can use the nondairy Bravo Probiotic drink.

CHAPTER 32

Natural Supplements for Better Brain Performance

Along with improved digestion, with the help of a few natural supplements, increased focus and positive mood in many children can be witnessed in days. Taking supplements means you don't have to wait until your digestion is fully healed and restored to see improved dopamine function. **Natural supplements can immediately provide the nutrients your body needs but is not getting because digestion is compromised.**

In working with thousands of boys with ADHD, I have marveled at the power of natural supplements, minerals, and vitamins for reversing the many symptoms of ADHD and inhibited dopamine function. Most of these supplements have an abundance of scientific evidence to back up their effectiveness and are available at your local health store or online. I have listed below the supplements that I have seen work the best. At MarsVenus.com I provide a short video for each to discuss suggested protocols for using them.

Antioxidants

Pine Bark

One of the main challenges caused by inhibited dopamine function is lack of focus. **And one of the easiest and most effective solutions for increasing focus is a natural supplement called Pycnogenol.**

Pycnogenol is a natural extract of pine bark. It has been used for over sixty years as an all-natural remedy for inflammation of the joints. It contains something called oligomeric proanthocyanidins (OPCs), which are superantioxidants known to reduce inflammation both in the joints and in the brain. A cheaper alternative to Pycnogenol that is also rich in OPCs is grapeseed extract.

In a double-blind study, over a period of four weeks sixty-one children with ADHD took 50 mg a day of Pycnogenol. The results showed a significant reduction in hyperactivity and improved concentration. In the placebo group, no positive effects were found.[1]

Vitamins C and E

OPCs also help activate the antioxidant benefit of other antioxidants. **When combined with vitamin C and E, their effectiveness increases fiftyfold.** By reducing inflammation in the gut and brain, these antioxidants, especially taken together, help to heal the brain.

In another study, one group of children with ADHD were given stimulant drugs like Ritalin or Adderall and another group was given a combination of vitamin C and OPCs. The short-term benefits in both groups were the same—except the natural supplement group had no side effects.[2]

High-Antioxidant Multivitamins

Special multivitamins high in OPCs and other antioxidants have also proved to improve brain performance. Children attending Anthony Elementary School saw dramatic results through implementing a program called Eat, Exercise, and Excel. Students were not only educated about the importance of good diet and exercise, but also took two chewable multivitamins called Potential every day. This was not an ordinary multivitamin. Besides a wide range of vitamins it contained a unique blend of fruit and berry concentrates high in antioxidants like the OPCs listed above. In addition, it contained 500 mg of the amino acid L-taurine, which is known to stabilize levels of dopamine.[3]

Anthony Elementary had been the lowest-performing public school in the Midwest, and within a year it had become one of the best. The results were so miraculous that PBS made a documentary about its success.[4] The program has continued on for the last ten years.

These are some of the benefits reported during state testing in the first year that this particular multivitamin was included in this turnaround program:

- The school was #1 in the district in math.
- The school was #2 in the district for English.
- There was a thirteenfold improvement in physical fitness (forty kids met the Presidential Physical Fitness Test standards, compared to three in the previous year).
- There was a 95 percent reduction in referrals for antisocial behavior.
- There was an 80 percent reduction in out-of-school suspensions.
- There was a 97 percent reduction in suspensions for violence.
- Teachers reported less difficulty managing classrooms.
- There was an 80 percent reduction in teacher attrition.
- Absenteeism among teachers and students fell markedly.
- Volunteer and community partnership numbers increased.

Glutathione

The antioxidant most effective in addressing low dopamine function is one we've already discussed: glutathione. On YouTube you can visually witness the profound effects of natural supplementation for Parkinson's disease, which, as we've seen, is an extreme version of inhibited dopamine function. **Just one intravenous treatment of glutathione can dramatically reduce the symptoms of advanced Parkinson's disease.** To watch the video, search for Dr. David Perlmutter's Parkinson's-Glutathione Therapy on YouTube.[5]

While doctors can prescribe intravenous treatments of glutathione, the results are temporary. For long-term results and healing, it is better if your body makes its own. A daily drink of undenatured whey protein can assist the body in doing so.

Amino Acids

Amino acids are the precursors to making brain chemicals as well as antioxidants like glutathione. An abundance of amino acids allows the brain to be the most effective it can be at restoring normal dopamine function.

In one case study researchers confirmed that a monitored program of amino acid supplementation with over-the-counter supplements such as L-tyrosine, L-DOPA, 5-HTP, and L-cysteine, along with a multivitamin, could stop the progression of Parkinson's disease without side effects and in some cases even reverse the condition.[6] **A modified version of this program was found to completely reverse symptoms of ADHD, suggesting that the efficacy of this treatment protocol was potentially superior to that of prescription drugs.**[7]

Omega-3

In his best-selling book *Grain Brain*, Dr. Perlmutter (whose glutathione therapy videos are referenced above) reveals his protocol for correcting symptoms of ADHD: taking children off gluten products and giving them 300 mg a day of DHA omega-3.

Taking DHA omega-3 alone has also been shown to improve learning and memory and support cognitive health with aging.[8] Repeatedly, researchers have found that children with ADHD have low levels of omega-3 fatty acids.[9]

While omega-3 oils can help on their own, many studies indicate that they are even more effective when combined with vitamin C. A study in India demonstrated that supplementation with flax oil (rich in omega-3) and vitamin C provided significant improvement in children with ADHD.[10]

One of the challenges with flax oil, versus omega-3 supplements made from fish oil, is that flax oil can easily go rancid. If you choose a vegetarian source of omega-3, both sprouted flax and chia can be added to your morning superfood shake in place of taking an oil capsule. Flax and chia are not only rich in omega-3s but also help balance blood sugar and keep you regular. **Moreover, flax oil by Panaseeda is made in a unique process and does not go rancid.**

Some children with ADHD have not benefited from extra omega-3, likely because, owing to elevated stress levels, weight gain, or high insulin levels, they are unable to metabolize beneficial omega-3 fats. To counteract this, one or two grams of acetyl-L-carnitine, an amino acid required for the metabolism of fat, can be taken to assist the body in utilizing the omega-3 supplements.[11]

Phosphatidylserine

Various research studies reveal that supplementation with the natural ingredient phosphatidylserine (PS), commonly found in egg yolks, not only improves memory and mood but also reduces ADHD symptoms. In one study, seventy-eight elderly people with mild cognitive impairment were given either PS supplements or a placebo. At the end of six months, participants taking the supplement experienced a significant improvement in memory.[12]

Using PS combined with omega-3 supplements may also aid in the treatment of ADHD and mood in children. In a similar study to the one above, two hundred children with ADHD were assigned fifteen weeks of treatment with either supplements containing PS and omega-3 or a placebo. Study results revealed that participants taking the supplements had a significant improvement in mood and a reduction in ADHD behavior when compared to those given the placebo.[13]

In another study involving thirty-six kids ranging in age between four and fourteen, PS was shown to improve a greater spectrum of symptoms than commonly prescribed ADHD drugs. The children were randomly assigned to receive either 200 mg a day of PS or placebo for two months. **Those taking the PS had significant improvements in attention, hyperactivity, impulsive behaviors, and short-term auditory memory.**[14]

Vitamin B6 and Magnesium

Both vitamin B6 and magnesium are required for the brain to experience normal dopamine function. Most children with inhibited dopamine function are deficient in magnesium.

One study in 2006 of 40 children with clinical symptoms of ADHD demonstrated that a regimen of vitamin B6 (3 mg) and magnesium (30 mg) over a two-month period reduced hyperactivity aggression and improved school attention.[15]

In my experience, doses even higher than those recommended on most supplement bottles can produce even better results. As discussed before, Epsom salt hot baths, which are very high in magnesium, are also helpful.

Vitamin B12 and Folic Acid

Plenty of research has shown that vitamin B12 and folic acid are directly linked to healthy brain development. Pregnant mothers are commonly instructed to take a multivitamin that contains both B12 and folic acid, a synthetic form of vitamin B9.

Folate, the natural form of B9, is used by the body to make DNA and other genetic material. It supports adrenal function and hormone production, and helps calm the nervous system. It is essential for healthy brain growth and development and encourages normal nerve and proper brain functioning.

Vitamin B12 is needed for red cell production, oxygen utilization, and energy production. Like folate (B9) it is also needed for adrenal function, hormone production, and the development of normal nerve cells. To utilize B9 the body also requires vitamin B12.

Folate is found in leafy green vegetables, especially broccoli, asparagus, spinach, and turnip greens, and a wide variety of beans, especially lentils. Fresh, raw, organic versions of these foods are especially high in folate. B12, however, is almost exclusively found in animal tissues, particularly liver, eggs, and dairy products.

Children with ADHD commonly have deficiencies of B12 and B9. These vitamins are essential in lowering homocysteine, which in turn increases glutathione, which as we've seen promotes healthy brain function and helps restore normal dopamine function.

There are a variety of studies in which B12 and folic acid supplements did not improve ADHD. This may be because lithium is also required to transport B12 and folic acid into cells.[16] **Children with ADHD often have low lithium levels.** In my experience with children, B vitamins, when combined with low-dose lithium orotate (see page 383), make all the difference, and dopamine function is quickly restored.

Vitamin D: The Sunshine Vitamin

A large research study involving 1,331 children with ADHD and the same number of children without ADHD demonstrated that vitamin D deficiency was more prevalent in children with ADHD than the control group.[17]

In a study in New Zealand of eighty adults with ADHD who were substantially deficient in vitamin D, **supplementation with vitamin D helped to reduce symptoms of ADHD.**[18] In another study, in regions of the United States where opportunities to experience sunshine were greater, ADHD symptoms were less common. (Exposure to sunshine increases vitamin D levels.)[19]

Vitamin D plays a protective role in brain health by increasing an enzyme (transpeptidase-glutamyl) that enhances the formation of glutathione.[20] Vitamin D also regulates the production of tyrosine in the brain, which then converts into dopamine.[21] Unless the body is able to make enough tyrosine, the brain cannot make enough dopamine. Vitamin D supplementation, or at least plenty of sunshine, is an essential requirement to make the dopamine necessary to wake our brains and increase our motivation.

Iron Supplementation

Iron deficiency has been implicated as one of the possible causes of ADHD in children. In one study, twenty-three children with ADHD were given 80 mg of iron supplements a day for three months, and their ADHD symptoms improved. No change was found in the placebo group.[22]

Over forty studies have directly demonstrated that anemia caused by iron deficiency results in impaired dopamine production, which leads to impaired neural functioning and behavior development, lethargy, reduced cognitive performance, and abnormal sleep patterns.[23] And in 2004 a French study of children with ADHD demonstrated that 84 percent of children with ADHD had abnormally low iron levels. The children with the most severe iron deficiencies were also the ones who were most inattentive, impulsive, and hyperactive. [24]

Iron supplements should be taken cautiously because too much iron is toxic. For a safe and all-natural support, try a little molasses every day. Blackstrap organic molasses is high in iron and other minerals, and one tablespoon has only about one and a half teaspoons of sugar. It can be added to a super shake for breakfast.

Another safe form of iron support is Floradix. Unlike an iron pill, which may cause constipation, Floradix is an all-natural, plant-based supplement with 10 mg of iron, a safe amount for any child. It is made from fruits, carrots, spinach, kelp, and other iron-rich foods.

Zinc

The mineral zinc is required for the transport of dopamine in the brain; every neuron in the brain has a zinc receptor and depends on zinc for healthy brain function. And many studies in the United States report evidence of lower zinc tissue levels in children who have ADHD.[25]

A couple of studies have shown that zinc supplementation increases the efficiency of ADHD drugs like Ritalin or Concerta.[26] When zinc supplements are taken with Ritalin, a lower dose of the Ritalin is required for the same level of effectiveness. However, it has not yet been proved that zinc supplementation alone can improve ADHD symptoms, except in Middle Eastern countries with suspected widespread zinc deficiency. **In areas of the world where zinc levels are the lowest, supplements with zinc *have* reduced ADHD symptoms.**[27] And zinc supplementation in zinc-deficient ADHD patients has been shown to improve the functioning of dopamine, if not ADHD symptoms themselves.[28]

Boys are more vulnerable to low zinc levels than girls because boys produce more testosterone, which can use up a boy's zinc reserves. I have seen zinc supplementation dramatically lower boys' impulsiveness when combined with lithium orotate (see page 383).

In one animal study, lithium treatment alone increased dopamine, but not serotonin and acetylcholine. Serotonin helps to relax the brain and restore dopamine receptor function, and acetylcholine helps to improve memory. But **coadministrating zinc with lithium significantly improved short-term memory in addition to cognitive function generally.** With the addition of zinc to lithium treatment, the enzymes that make acetylcholine were increased along with both dopamine and serotonin.[29]

My Own Daily Regimen

My recommendation of applying natural solutions for normal dopamine function is not just based on what I have seen in my work with children with ADHD. My own life has changed. As a child, after a serious concussion, I developed ADHD symptoms that lasted throughout my life. Then, fifteen years ago, **when I turned fifty, I was diagnosed with early-stage Parkinson's.** Rather than take the conventional medical treatment for Parkinson's, which is commonly known to only slow down the progression of this disease, I researched natural solutions and completely eliminated my symptoms. I was surprised to discover that my ADHD symptoms then disappeared as well.

My whole life, I had experienced many of the symptoms of inhibited dopamine function. I always waited to the last minute to do things and was easily distracted and disorganized. When I read books, it was a struggle and tiring. But rather than recognize those things as symptoms of ADHD or inhibited dopamine function, I just accepted that they were simply my normal state of being. **Once my dopamine function was restored, suddenly reading became easier, and in all areas of my life I was more relaxed, energized, and organized.**

I was already getting plenty of exercise, so by making a few changes in my breakfast I was able to restore normal dopamine function. Rather than having cereal and toast for breakfast I shifted to making a special dopamine-boosting superfood shake and a few extra supplements. For me, the results were immediate.

This simple protocol, alongside other helpful therapies, has now helped thousands of children restore normal dopamine function. The many therapies we have explored—such as exercise, art, and singing—all work better to reduce the symptoms of ADHD with the addition of nutritional support. **Everything works better when a boy starts his day with the nutritional support his brain has been missing.**

I start my day with three things that together contain almost all the previous suggestions for taking supplements to restore normal brain function:

1. **A Super Cleanse detox drink.** I start every day with a lemon and water mixture to help detox the liver. This daily cleansing of the liver helps it make more glutathione to heal the brain.
2. **A Mars Venus superfood shake**. Next I make a superfood shake that primarily contains water, enzymes, and undenatured powdered dairy proteins (casein and whey).

For convenience, I use the Mars Venus superfood shake mix I formulated with both undenatured whey and casein proteins, enzymes, all the B vitamins, omega-3 from chia and flax seeds, and phosphatidylserine. It is flavored with chocolate, which is also a dopamine producer, and sweetened with only a couple of teaspoons of glucose, just enough to stimulate nutrient absorption but not enough to spike blood sugar levels.[30]

Once water is added, I shake it up and then let it sit out to incubate for thirty minutes. During this time, the proteins are converted to protein peptides, which easily provide the amino acids the brain requires to immediately produce dopamine production in the brain as well as glutathione in the liver. After it has incubated, I add four ounces of Bravo yogurt or nondairy Bravo and shake it up again before drinking it.

3. **A few supplements**. While the shake is incubating, with plain chlorine-free water I take the following supplements:

- **Mars Venus Super Minerals** (2 capsules)
- **Potential multivitamins**, which contain vitamins and the OCPs discussed before[31] (2 tablets)
- **NADH co-enzyme1**, a superior form of vitamin B3 that generates energy in the brain and body without caffeine stimulation (two 20 mg lozenges)
- **L-tyrosine**, the precursor for dopamine (two 500 mg capsules)
- **5-HTP**, the precursor for serotonin (one 100 mg capsule)

For more information about these supplements, go to the health food store at MarsVenus.com. For each supplement I present a ten-minute video explaining its many benefits as well as how to use it.

Why Minerals Are Important

Of all the supplements I recommend above, minerals bonded to oratic acid like magnesium orotate have had the greatest and most immediate benefit for ADHD. **Every function in the brain and body requires**

mineral support, after which the minerals are discarded. For example, over three hundred different body functions depend on magnesium, from regular bowel movements to relaxing muscles to burning fat. And once it is used, it is used up and we must consume more.

We can get minerals from our foods, but we can't make or recycle them. We are dependent on our food supply to get the minerals we need. Since modern farming practices and methods of processing fast foods have rendered our food mineral deficient, we need some form of mineral supplementation.

Without enough minerals, your brain cannot do what it is designed to do. Minerals are cofactors for the production and utilization of brain chemicals. Fueling a car is the perfect example of the importance of minerals. Even if your car has no problems at all, if it is missing the fuel, it will not run. In a similar way, your brain could have no problems at all, but if you have a mineral depletion, it just stops working the way it is designed to.

For some children, mineral deficiency shows up as extreme mood swings commonly diagnosed as bipolar disorder. When your car has more horsepower, it runs out of fuel faster. Likewise, if you have a genius brain, you need more fuel, because a genius brain runs faster and has more activity to fuel. Given that, it then makes sense that in a study of more than seven hundred thousand students, those who scored top grades in school were four times more likely to be diagnosed with bipolar disorder than those with average grades.[32] **As Aristotle once claimed, "There is no great genius without a mixture of madness."**

Minerals work together with glutathione to ensure normal dopamine function. The alkalizing minerals magnesium, calcium, potassium, zinc, and lithium are most important for optimal brain function; they work together with vitamin D, omega-3, and vitamin K (organic butter and greens) to relax the brain while also restoring normal dopamine function.

Of these minerals, lithium is the most powerful for children with inhibited dopamine function. It directly protects brain cells from toxic stress, produces the hormone oxytocin (the "cuddle hormone") to improve social skills; protects the brain from excitotoxins like MSG; prevents brain shrinkage; protects the liver from damage; protects brain neurons from heavy metals like mercury, lead, aluminum, and cadmium; regenerates damaged brain cells; and even increases the production of brain cells.[33, 34, 35, 36, 37]

Lithium is used up whenever high levels of dopamine are stimulated through stress, anger, crying, soft drinks, dessert, chips, video games, stimulant drugs, and the like.[38] If high levels of dopamine are stimulated too often, lithium becomes depleted.

Lithium supplementation is so powerful that it is prescribed for a wide range of mental illnesses. An opinion article in the *New York Times* from **one psychiatrist and professor even suggested that everyone could benefit from low-dose lithium to reduce stress.**[39]

The big problem with lithium and other mineral supplementation is that most mineral supplements do not, and cannot, deliver minerals across the blood-brain barrier. When minerals are abundant in our food they are able to cross the protective barrier that filters the blood entering the brain. Only special mineral supplements can deliver minerals across the blood-brain barrier.

Dr. Hans Nieper, a famous alternative medicine practitioner who specialized in mineral transport systems to treat cancer, MS, and other serious diseases, discovered a way to effectively and efficiently deliver minerals to the brain. He developed a transport system that bonded minerals to orotic acid, a substance that appears in high quantities in mother's milk and whey protein. Unlike common mineral supplements, which are bonded to carbonate, citrate, phosphate, ascorbate, chloride, and other similar compounds, **minerals bonded to orotic acid are freely transported across the blood-brain barrier.** In thousands of children, I have witnessed these mineral orotates (which are all contained in the Mars Venus Super Minerals) improve brain function within days when combined with omega-3 fats and the B-vitamin NADH coenzyme1. They are super minerals for super brain function.

Lithium Orotate: The Misunderstood Mineral

One of Dr. Nieper's many discoveries was a new form of the mineral lithium. He found that lithium orotate, combined with good nutrition, could treat depression, migraine headaches, and bipolar disorder without any side effects. I have found it to be equally effective in healing ADHD. But **combined with other mineral orotates, its daily use can lower stress and support positive moods for everyone.**

In my experience, low-dose lithium orotate is the most important supplement for children with ADHD. For the last fifteen years I have been the most outspoken promoter of lithium orotate and over the last five years, more and more doctors have become aware of it and recommend it.

Lithium is a natural mineral; it is not a drug. Indigenous people around the world have flocked to various hot springs high in sulfur or lithium for healing for thousands of years. Native Americans have a five-thousand-year tradition of visiting Lithia Springs in Georgia to heal a multitude of illnesses. **The popular lemon-lime flavored soft drink 7 Up originally contained lithium citrate when it was launched in 1929, and continued to contain lithium until 1950**, when it was hijacked by the drug companies.

Lithium orotate is best known for healing depression, but it is also an essential mineral for healing ADHD. It helps to heal and activate injured dopamine receptor sites in the brain. Even after damaged dopamine neurons in the brain are healed, continued use of lithium orotate supports optimal brain function. Some doctors have reported success using low-dose lithium orotate to slow the progression of Alzheimer's disease.[40]

Despite its current limited use in medicine, most doctors have no idea that low-dose lithium orotate is completely safe for adults and children and sold over the counter. It does not have side effects, only benefits. But there is little public awareness of lithium orotate because it is one of the cheapest supplements to buy and therefore is not publicly marketed. Because it is completely natural, it can't be patented.

The other reason you may not have heard of lithium orotate is the bad reputation of its cousin, lithium carbonate, a less effective form of lithium that doctors have been prescribing to treat depression and bipolar disorder for the last fifty years. The use of lithium carbonate, but not lithium orotate, comes with a variety of negative side effects, including weight gain and fatigue. Lithium carbonate is only toxic because to be effective it must be prescribed in much higher doses than lithium orotate.

Doctors are particularly concerned about how much lithium a person is taking because the doses they prescribe for lithium carbonate are very high and toxic, often a hundred times greater than the recommended dose of lithium orotate. Thanks to the widespread medical use of toxic lithium carbonate, most people misunderstand lithium as a dangerous drug for mental illness. They are afraid to take it because of this confusion. As a result, most health food stores do not carry it.

The main difference between lithium carbonate and lithium orotate is that, for lithium carbonate to cross the blood-brain barrier,

toxic doses are required; lithium orotate easily crosses the blood-brain barrier even at low doses. This is a big difference. Lithium carbonate relieves the symptoms of depression and anxiety, but at the price of a healthy metabolism. Lithium orotate is effective at low doses and is non-toxic. But, as discussed before, it is most effective when combined with zinc, calcium, magnesium, and potassium.

Every beneficial mineral can become toxic when too much is taken. Too much potassium will cause a heart attack. Too much magnesium will cause diarrhea. Too much salt will cause water retention and heart disease. Too much copper will cause allergies. Too much calcium will cause arthritis. Too much selenium will cause nerve damage. And too much lithium will lower your metabolism and cause kidney problems.

Today, many holistic doctors are switching from prescribing toxic doses of lithium carbonate to nontoxic, low-dose lithium orotate. Combined with other mineral orotates and supplements, lithium orotate can successfully and safely treat depression, bipolar disorder, and ADHD.

Unlike antidepressants, which only suppress symptoms of depression, or stimulant drugs that only provide symptomatic relief for ADHD, mineral orotates support the natural process of emotional healing. For example, when we are faced with a depressing loss, the grieving process is important. Taking lithium orotate does not suppress our feelings of loss; instead, it lowers our stress and facilitates the healing of painful emotions by sustaining the production of healthy brain neurotransmitters. **During times of depression or increased stress, slightly higher doses of lithium orotate are required because your lithium is used up more quickly.**

It is easy to regulate your own dose of lithium orotate because the results are immediate, and no more than five or six small capsules a day are ever necessary. For adults, the effective dose of lithium orotate is between one and six capsules a day. For children, it is half that dose, one to three capsules a day. Each capsule contains only 4.5 to 4.8 mg of lithium; the rest of the capsule is the orotate.

Within the one-to-three capsules a day range for children, there is no set amount; some boys need more and others need less. If this relatively low dose doesn't have the desired effect, then other supplements are required as well. **Generally speaking, for ADHD, one super-mineral capsule and one extra lithium orotate twice a day is ideal.** More is not better, and again, as with any mineral supplement, too much can be toxic. But when taken safely, lithium is the superstar in the lineup of natural solutions for ADHD.[41]

Over the past fifteen years I have consistently endorsed, promoted, and recommended the use of lithium orotate to thousands of readers, seminar participants, counseling clients, children with autism, and visitors to MarsVenus.com. There are over six hundred thousand views of my three YouTube videos on this subject. Thousands of people have given me positive feedback, and I have yet to hear of any negative side effects from taking lithium orotate, only success stories.

It's also the number one constant in my personal supplement program. I have taken a super-mineral supplement that includes lithium orotate almost every day for the last fifteen years. When I occasionally miss a few days, I notice my stress levels increasing.

Of course, lithium orotate works better for some people than others, depending on what other supplements they are taking. **For ADHD, anxiety, or depression, simply taking lithium orotate is not enough.** In conjunction with a healthy diet and other good supplements, however, it can make all the difference.

At first, many parents resist the idea of taking lithium orotate for themselves or giving it to their children. Sometimes they say, "I don't know, lithium is for crazy people." or "It is a dangerous pharmaceutical drug." And yes, lithium orotate is so effective that, when someone is "crazy," it can help them, too. But it also lowers stress levels, improves sleep, protects brain cells from toxic damage, promotes serotonin production, improves dopamine function, increases calm and focus, and even stimulates brain cell growth. **It is so effective it would be crazy to *not* take it.** It is not a drug but a vital mineral that everyone can benefit from. It should be used as commonly as calcium, magnesium, and vitamin C.

Mineral Support for Everyone

I've been recommending not just lithium orotate but mineral orotates generally for fifteen years, and for fifteen years I have received thousands of positive reports from adults, teens, and parents regarding the immediate "wow" they or their children feel after taking mineral orotates for a few days. Even if you have a perfect diet, high levels of stress in the brain, from ADHD or other causes, depletes our bodies' mineral reserves. **Mineral support can help everyone manage stress more effectively.**

After one rather large keynote presentation, I stood for five hours signing books and listening to the positive results readers had received from my relationship books. Yet over half the people in line primarily commented on how the mineral orotates I recommend in some of my books and at MarsVenus.com had helped them and their family.

As an author and leader in the field of good communication, parenting, and loving relationships, I recognize the importance of new relationships skills. But nutritional support, particularly mineral support, is just as important. In my daily counseling practice, my clients always report that taking these special minerals makes a huge difference in both their mood and energy levels—which in turn makes it much easier to create a loving, nurturing, and fulfilling relationship.

With a nutritious predigested superfood protein shake, mineral orotates, and a few supplements, I have personally assisted thousands of parents in helping their children feel better and stop the use of prescribed stimulant drugs for ADHD. **Not every child is able to stop taking drugs entirely on this regimen, but they always feel much better.** And parents report that, with these extra supplements, their children shift from being distracted, oppositional, and moody to becoming attentive, cooperative, and happier in a matter of days.

Healing the Brain

Healing the brain is a big and complex subject. I have written part VI of *The Boy Crisis* to help provide real choices. By understanding the various causes of inhibited dopamine function, the one brain condition that gives rise to ADHD, you have the insight necessary to determine the best natural solution for you and your family.

The good news about natural solutions is there are no negative side effects. The worst any solution can do is not work. If one doesn't work, you can try another. **While this is not always an easy journey, you now have the necessary insight to discover what will work for you.** Always remember, too, you are not alone on this journey.

Please keep us updated with your successes. Join me at MarsVenus .com for down-to-earth advice on life and love and to share your experiences with natural solutions. Your successes will inspire others to find the right solutions for them. May you and your family enjoy a lifetime of health, happiness, and lasting love.

Conclusion

It was December 7, 1941. For years, we had been in denial of the crisis that was Hitler and the Axis powers. With Pearl Harbor, our denial ended.

Transforming denial into a response meant sixteen million of our sons being willing to sacrifice their lives. Yet our sons stepped up. And our daughters and parents joined them.

The new enemy is not Hitler. It is dad deprivation. It is not the Axis powers. It is a "purpose void." It is not a need for your son to sacrifice his life but to find a purpose for his life.

How do we get our sons to step up to a crisis for which there is no Pearl Harbor? A crisis that is more internal than external?

Whether our sons step up depends on how they are brought up. In the past, boys learned "I exist, therefore I serve." Today, many boys learn "I exist, therefore I deserve."

Being needed to serve creates a sense of purpose. Being served creates a sense of entitlement. Most parents know this intellectually, but our own need to be needed seduces us into serving our son rather than teaching him to serve. Which contributes to our sons' purpose void.

Once our sons value serving over being served, they are more likely to step up when we both alert them to a crisis and help them discover their role in the mission to end that crisis—such as the crisis of dad deprivation and the mission to be a great dad, and therefore an inspiration to others to be the same.

Boys who become a failure to launch are most frequently devoid of the two Ps: purpose and postponed gratification. Boys devoid of the two Ps are often also devoid of the equal checks and balances of the other two

Ps: two parents. When your son is dad enriched, he not only avoids the crisis of being dad deprived but is inspired with the mission to become a great dad.

Your Mission: Guiding Your Son to Discover His Mission

Becoming a great dad is not a mission for every son. Your mission is to guide your son to discover *his* mission. No piece of cake, because there's no precedent. Our fathers did not learn to discover their mission; they learned to fulfill a mission someone else discovered. The "discoverer" was the need to survive. His mission was provider-protector.

Your dad had two options: be the provider-protector or be a loser. Which didn't allow for questions like, "What creates the glint in my eye?" He learned to be a human doing first, and a human being second. Or not at all. Which often led him to withdraw from loving himself, and ultimately from the family he loved. To him feeling that his life insurance policy is more valuable than his life.

Your mission to help your son discover his mission begins with helping him to discover himself as a human being first, and then helping him find a way of being a human doing—of making a living—that supports him as a human being.

This reversal of his grandpa's sequence will ensure your son realizes that:

- the road to high pay is often a toll road—a road that takes a toll on him as a human being;
- the process that it takes for him to be successful at work often conflicts with what it takes for him to be successful in love; and
- if he follows his bliss it's the money he'll miss—unless he has the discipline of postponed gratification to, for example, work the extra hours it takes to be a successful artist, writer, actor, or whatever is his bliss.

Your role is to help him discover the discipline and inspiration to become a successful human doing *and* human being—to discover where his unique road to success at work and success in love find each other.

We have looked at what it takes to do this—for example, how to structure family dinner nights to help your son discover himself as a human being by encouraging him to reconsider what it takes to be a truly powerful man. The old definition of male "power": feeling obligated to earn money someone else spends while he dies sooner. The new definition of male power: discovering the work-life harmony that is most in accord with his unique self while not abandoning his commitments to others.

While your mission includes teaching your son how to listen, it also includes preparing your son to neither feel diminished in his energy nor fearful of voicing his perspectives by being shamed into thinking that *because he is born male* he is the only sex to experience privilege and power and should therefore keep his mouth shut.

Nevertheless, help him acknowledge inherent privilege where it exists. Yes, if he is born in a developed country, he has privilege. Privilege that includes first world problems (e.g., "Whole Foods ran out of my kombucha"). And that privilege includes his sister.

If you are raising him in a home with a middle-class or higher income, he has class privilege (e.g., "Can I use the new car to take Bonnie to a play tonight?"). And that privilege includes his sister.

If your son is Caucasian, he is much freer of racial discrimination. And that privilege includes his sister.

Yet if your daughter is brilliant and is motivated to be a CEO or a US president, she clearly sees a world with fewer role models for her than for her brother. And that may feel to her like male privilege. So help your son acknowledge that.

If your son loves children, and is motivated to be a full-time dad, as 49 percent of dads are (revealed only when the Pew Research Center cared enough to ask), he clearly sees a world with fewer role models for him than for his sister. And that may feel to him like . . . well, like what? Actually, the society hasn't really given him a word, or phrase, or pejorative accusation (e.g., "female privilege") to help him even articulate the barriers he feels to becoming a full-time dad. If he breaks his internal or external silence, he will face a discrimination parallel to that experienced by women who broke ranks with their expected role.

And also help your son see that his heritage as a male included an expectation of being disposable. An expectation that survives in law as male-only draft registration. An expectation he may experience as parental pride or peer group respect should he risk his body in football or war. And an expectation that is reinforced by social pressure, as in how women fall in love with officers and gentlemen, not privates and pacifists, and even early feminists giving out white feathers as symbols of cowardice in public venues such as at church to any man who did not risk his life in World War I.

That is, help your son understand that being male means calling it an honor to serve with his life so that his wife and children would live, and live better and freer, even as they put flowers on his grave. Discuss with your son whether this is male privilege and power, or male expectations, male pressure, male responsibility, and male obligation—sold to him via the social bribes of parental pride, female love, and the adulation of everyone should he become the one in a million to become a hero and still survive.

Help your son see that just being male does not make him an oppressor. That the obligations of traditional men built virtually every home and office, and every infrastructure of public sanitation and transportation that allows us to live almost twice as long today as we did in 1900. Both sexes made a myriad of sacrifices in life in the hope that their children would have to make fewer sacrifices in theirs. Both sexes served each other. Both sexes were and are in the same family boat.

Did men make more money? Yes. Did that empower men? Yes. And no. We have seen that your son is likely to be *less* healthy both physically and psychologically the more money he makes as the family's breadwinner.

Discuss with your son whether he feels this expectation on him to earn more is a form of discrimination against him as a male. If this feels too controversial to be asked, then that is exactly why it needs to be. Remember, boys prefer going where others fear to tread.

But your son, like each family member, must listen as well as be heard. And the training ground for this new mission is not the battlefield; it is the dinner table. The trainer is not a sergeant; it is a dad and mom. The training is not to risk his life; it is to resist the sirens of social bribes that sing to him to risk his life. It is not to be on constant alert for sounds of a nearby enemy; it is to be on constant alert for the sounds of social bribes that linger within himself.

The Solution to a Problem Created by a Solution

The evidence of the boy crisis among all sixty-three of the largest developed nations makes it clear that the problem is not you as a parent or teacher.

Ironically, the problem started with a solution: the solution to ensuring our survival. Enough economic luxury for a nation to be labeled "developed" led to more freedom to divorce, which led to millions of boys being raised with either no father involvement, minimal father involvement, or conditional father involvement.

Unlike a boy who loses his father in war and idolizes him as a hero, divorce does not leave a boy idolizing his dad as a hero. Although a boy whose father is a warrior sees his father lose his life, he feels inspired with a sense of purpose. A boy who envisions being a dad, but sees less of his dad after a divorce, sees in his future a "purpose void."

The freedom to divorce, in combination with the freedom to have children without being married, together create an unacknowledged worldwide gap: the gap between the dad-deprived boy and the dad-enriched boy.

The Boy Crisis makes it apparent why the gap between being dad deprived and dad enriched will become the single biggest predictor of the gap between boys who are economically poor and boys who are economically rich. And between boys who are emotionally impoverished and emotionally enriched.

Fortunately, there is a solution. That solution has two pillars: First, knowing that men who are the sole breadwinners have the poorest psychological health and the poorest physical health among men—and that both their psychological and physical health are the poorest during the years they earn the most. And, of course, sole-breadwinner dads feel the most pressure to earn the most. Second, knowing that women who share the financial burden feel psychologically *healthier.*

In brief, one solution is sharing the caring. And if there is a divorce, we have seen the four "must-dos" to secure the continuation of sharing the caring, and witnessed why these must-dos are a prerequisite to children doing as well as they would in an intact family.

Because your son's genes are half his biological dad's, and because he sees his dad reflected in himself every time he looks in a mirror, nothing can fully substitute for his biological dad. Yet we have seen how we can most effectively employ the energies of stepdads, grandparents, coaches, and organizations like My Brother's Keeper and the scouts to cumulatively help bridge the gap between boys who are dad deprived and boys who are dad enriched.

"The Love Dilemma": Altering the Natural Mindset

Virtually every couple faces a "love dilemma": While falling in love is biologically natural, sustaining love is biologically unnatural. When our partner airs her or his perspective, we often take it as criticism, and the Achilles' heel of human beings is our inability to handle personal criticism from a loved one without becoming defensive.

Love alone doesn't solve the problem, because the more deeply we love, the more vulnerable to criticism we feel; defensiveness is a mask of vulnerability. Soon we are "walking on eggshells," and the love fades.

Is the solution to make divorces harder? No. The solution is to make marriages better.

While children benefit enormously from the stability of biological parents who are married, those benefits are reduced significantly if their parents, while legally married, are psychologically divorced. Or in a minimum-security-prison marriage.

The Boy Crisis posits that divorces have less to do with money, sex, or children, and more with how we communicate about money, sex, or children. For our children not to fear marriage, then, they need to see that their parents have learned how to sustain love. Learning how to sustain love creates the single greatest opportunity for the most radical solution to the boy crisis. Since handling defensiveness requires an alteration of our natural response, I have introduced the Altered Mindsets method of couples' communication. Since sustaining love requires both art and discipline, I introduce the art and discipline of sustaining love.[1]

Whether via Altered Mindsets or other methods, new empathic communication skills need to be part of every elementary school's core curriculum. Caveat: Schools that train our kids need to simultaneously train their parents. Why? If our children learn empathic communication at school but witness defensive put-downs at home, they lose respect for their parents because they now know a better way. Without the school training both kids and parents simultaneously, the family can be under-mined. Then one more solution will have become yet another problem.

One of the ways your son can be a leader in this single biggest "battle of the boy crisis" is to become a teacher of boys—a teacher who under-stands that boys respond best when they are pushed and stretched. As comes naturally via competition. Think communications competitions. With communications trophies. Or caring competitions, with boys shar-ing what they learned while caring for their younger sibling or grandpar-ent. Or "debate" teams in which the winners are the ones best able to articulate the perspective of their "opponents." Then it's his emotional intelligence that makes him a hero.

In brief, the future offers your son the mission to be a pioneer of a new heroic intelligence—one that leads with emotional and health intelligence.

Extending Gender Liberation to Dads

For your son to have an opportunity to envision fathering as a new sense of purpose equal to the one your daughter now has to envision being an executive as her sense of purpose, perhaps the most important discovery your son can make is not in outer space but in his inner space: his "dad brain." Your son knowing that he has a "dad brain" that is a biologically natural part of him—that if he becomes a hands-on dad, he activates a nest of neurons that are otherwise dormant—expands his permission to see fathering as a natural gift of manhood.

That said, every involved dad needs to know the three Cs of fathering: consistency, consistency, consistency. Pick-and-choose fathering—here today, gone tomorrow; promises today, forgotten tomorrow—leaves your son feeling abandoned, untrusting, and cynical.

Applying gender liberation to dads is as much of a minefield as the integration of women into men's traditional roles. It surprises most dads when they discover that 93 percent of moms agree there is a father-absence crisis in America today.[2] Just as many women experience subtle discrimination at work that makes them skeptical that men are in favor of equality, so many dads experience subtle discrimination toward their fathering that makes them skeptical that women are in favor of equality.

Workplaces that valued the differences many women brought to work rather than expecting women to just adapt to the traditional male work style, were rewarded with women who felt valued for contributing in the way they could contribute best. Similarly, dads are far more inspired to be involved when they are valued for fathering in the way a father tends to father: by doing, exploring, playfully teasing, encouraging physical risk-taking while being trusted as a safety net, bonding through play, coaching, roughhousing, and using the leverage of the father-child bond to enforce boundaries. When mom gatekeeps dad into fathering in the way *she* feels a father should father, dad feels like a devalued babysitter. Feeling unwanted, he tends to withdraw, neglect his children, increase his time at work, or even seek another woman he feels *will* value him.

The Boy Crisis gives a dad the info he needs to communicate to a mom exactly how his style of fathering facilitates children's growth, even as he values the mom's own style. It asks moms and dads to view their tension over parenting style as being useful to their children in the same way that checks and balances are useful in governing a nation. Valuing our checks and balances also facilitates our next evolutionary step: valuing the unique contributions of those of our sons who would be dads. Or extending gender liberation to dads.

Your Son's Weakness as His Facade of Strength

We have seen how your son's weakness is his facade of strength. New research continually surprises me with the many facets of our sons' vulnerabilities.

First, while children with father loss have, by the age of nine, a 14 percent reduction in life expectancy as predicted by their shorter telomeres,[3] the life expectancy loss is even 40 percent greater for boys than for girls.[4]

Second, your son is more likely than your daughter to be depressed after a relationship breakup. At first I thought, "Really?" Turns out our "tough" sons are more like "rough, tough cream puffs." Closet romantics. But you knew that all along.

Third, your son is far more likely than your daughter to do poorly in a single-mother family, especially in families of divorce.

Fourth, your son is likely to fare worse than your daughter when moving to a new neighborhood—even to a "better" neighborhood. Boys are more vulnerable both when they lose old friendships, and because their less developed social skills leave them more challenged in creating new ones.

Fifth, boys who feel hurt by dad deprivation are more likely to be prey not only to recruitment by ISIS, gangs, and neo-Nazi and alt-right groups, but also to sexual abuse by authority figures.

Repeatedly, we are distracted from boys' vulnerability by our need to clean up the damage they do by either hurting themselves (drinking, drugs, gangs) or hurting us (ISIS-related terrorism, gang killings, school shootings). But by missing the vulnerability of those who strike terror in our hearts, we repeat the cycle: boys who hurt hurt us.

Our blindness has been magnified by the false assumption that our sons manifest depression the way our daughters do. This is what motivated me to develop an early-warning detection system for your son: the Warren Farrell Male Depression/Suicide Inventory.

Heroic intelligence has focused on developing a facade of strength more by building strength (e.g., muscle-building) than preventing its loss (e.g., routine check-ups, healthy eating, meditation, yoga). When a boy has a problem, such as ADHD, we tend to resort to a "quick fix" designed to immediately restore the facade of strength while neglecting the underlying weakness that created the problem. This evolves from an unconscious history: the faster our sons were battle ready, the more likely everyone else survived. Today we have the luxury to attend to your son's underlying problems. John Gray does just that: his focus on prevention and natural remedies integrates health intelligence to address one of the most ubiquitous manifestations of the boy crisis: ADHD.

From Cultural Shrug to Cultural Mission: A Gender Liberation Movement

To create a cultural shift from the boy crisis as a worldwide cultural shrug to the boy crisis as a worldwide cultural mission requires confronting the "Boy Crisis paradox": our attachment to our sons and our detachment from our sons.

The attachment is obvious. The detachment was necessary. Since our survival depended on preparing our sons to risk their survival, we couldn't afford to cuddle or coddle them. This both prepared our sons to detach from their own feelings and unconsciously prepared us to psychologically detach enough to cope should we lose them.

The unconscious fear we need to confront is that, if we guide our sons to clear away the fog of social bribes that blurs their ability to discover their unique selves, there will be no one to protect us. Fortunately, some of our sons will still find purpose in being the soldiers, firefighters, and the first responders we need, just as some of our daughters now do. But then your son's choice as a human doing will be in sync with his choice as a human being, as it is more likely to already be with your daughter (who is not subjected to the social bribes of being considered more feminine the more she risks her life). Your son's gift to us—risking his life to protect us—will be a choice, not the result of being too weak to resist social bribes.

The degree to which our sons become as free to be who they wish to be as our daughters are is the degree to which we will have taken a huge step—from women's liberation to gender liberation. This requires not a women's movement blaming men, nor a men's movement blaming women, but a gender liberation movement freeing both sexes from the rigid roles of the past toward more flexible roles for our future. It will require a cultural shift that leads with the understanding that both sexes are in the same family boat. That when only one sex wins, both sexes lose.

Family Dinner Night: The Five Essentials

The Boy Crisis exposes the enormous vulnerability of boys, and why your son may sequester that vulnerability behind the mask of masculinity. In raising your son, you face a Gordian knot: preparing him to "be a man" yet allowing him to be the open, curious, sensitive boy that you know is beneath his mask.

Woven throughout The Boy Crisis are references to one of the best ways to untangle that Gordian knot—family dinner night (FDN). Family dinner nights allow your son to experience the emotional safety it takes to access his vulnerabilities and express them. This helps him retain his open, curious, sensitive self. Yet as he learns to be both emotionally balanced and secure enough to speak his truth while hearing the truth of others, he is preparing to be the best of men.

When it comes to emotions, few boys are good self-starters. But if someone else provides a starting point, *and he feels he won't be judged for his input*, then he'll share what rings true and false, and his own story will unfold.

However, **a family dinner night can become a family dinner nightmare.** Here are the five essentials that can both prevent that nightmare and allow your family to make talking together your path to flourishing together:

1. **Timing.** Your family dining together every night is ideal, but for this more-structured FDN, once to twice a week is optimal. Schedule the same night or nights each week. Each dinner should last between one hour and ninety minutes. Prior to the end of each dinner, review your schedules for the following week to see if the FDN evening needs to be shifted. Doing an *occasional* FDN without a particular family member is okay.

2. **No electronics or TV.** Once the rule is made clear, electronics brought to the table are taken away for the rest of the evening.

3. **Rotation of moderator, range of topics.** Each family dinner night there is a new moderator, who announces the topic of the night. Topics may range from ones for which the moderator wishes input ("Should I take a job that requires me to travel on weekends?"), to ones more broadly relevant to the family's life ("Is college necessary?" "What should be the consequence of not doing an assigned chore?" "Should the kids share the cooking?"), to dilemmas at school ("Is it better to do a variety of sports, or specialize in one?" "What should I do about a kid in school that no one likes but I think is lonely?"). They can also, occasionally, be more theoretical ("Do you believe in God?" "What should be our immigration policy?").

4. **Check-ins, then discussion without taboos.** Before discussing, the moderator conducts a timed check-in of a max of three minutes per person. If someone has a serious problem, that takes priority for the night. If not, the next thirty minutes are divided among family members, who each share their perspectives on that night's topic. No interruptions. Each person is timed. After the formal time allotments, conversation can be less structured.

   Make no topic taboo at dinner. Boys love to be challenged; they'd rather only half-understand a conversation than be bored. And getting your daughter comfortable with controversy will support her to articulate her perspectives with less inhibition, too.

5. **Everyone's story, no one's judgment.** In my workshops on couples' communication, I ask couples to look at these four pictures.

Source: Illustration by Thomas Fuchs, originally printed in the *New York Times*

These four illustrations are the way illustrator Thomas Fuchs imagined that Mario Cuomo, the former governor of New York, would be depicted by, clockwise from top left, Warhol, Picasso, Mondrian, and Robert Crumb. **Each family member's story—even of the same**

**person or event at the same moment—will often appear as differ-
ent as these pictures.**

There will be times when someone in the family is clearly not
accurate. Imagine someone says, "The sun rotates around the earth."
Each family member's job is first to listen fully—without dismissive
body language or words—before explaining why you feel the earth
rotates around the sun. And to remember, as Carl Sagan put it in
Cosmos, "Ptolemy's Earth-centered universe held sway for 1500 years,
a reminder that intellectual capacity is no guarantee against being
dead wrong."

In brief, use *The Boy Crisis* along with family dinner nights as a conversation starter—boys open up best when someone else kicks the ball
into play and doesn't judge the way they kick.

> To kick-start an FDN, read aloud the questions in the FDN boxes along with
> the analyses preceding them on pages 55, 72, 183, 193, 218, and 242.

The Boy Crisis List: The Benefits of Dad, and the Dangers of Dad Deprivation*

W hen I did the research for my 2001 book *Father and Child Reunion*, I interspersed throughout the book ways children either benefited from father involvement, or were damaged by dad deprivation. In interviews after its publication, when I was asked how many benefits there were, I estimated twenty-five. I received many requests for a list.

So *The Boy Crisis* includes a list of fifty-five areas incorporating more than seventy specific benefits of dad involvement or dangers of dad deprivation.

This list is only of outcomes. The text of *The Boy Crisis* gives you the causes, solutions, and the optimal amount of father involvement under various conditions. For example, if children cannot live with both parents together, then only children that have about equal time with both parents are "about as well off as those in which the parents remained married."[1, 2, 3, 4]

---

* The documentation for each benefit can be found throughout part IV of *The Boy Crisis*, and a documented version of this list is at boycrisis.org.

The text of *The Boy Crisis* is also the place to discover how a fully involved dad develops a "dad brain" as he activates a nest of neurons that are otherwise dormant.[5] Or to discover the range of benefits *to* a dad of being a fully involved dad.[6]

The following list, then, is limited to headline-type summaries of the more than seventy benefits to children of a fully involved dad, and the dangers of dad deprivation.

1. Children with father loss have, by the age of nine, a 14 percent reduction in telomere length—the most reliable predictors of **life expectancy**. In addition, the telomere loss is 40 percent greater for boys than for girls.

2. A study of **ISIS** fighters concluded that almost all male and female fighters had in common "some type of an 'absent father' syndrome."

3. When children live with only their dads, the **parents** are only one-ninth as likely to have **conflict** as when children live with their moms.

4. The more frequently a father visits the hospital of an infant who is born prematurely, the more quickly the infant is released from the hospital and the better the infant's **social-personal development** and ability to **adapt**.

5. Students coming from father-present families score higher in **math and science** even when they come from *weaker* schools.

6. Father involvement is at least *five* times as important in preventing **drug use** than closeness to parent, parental rules, parent trust, strictness, or a child's gender, ethnicity, or social class.

7. A study of boys from *similar backgrounds* revealed that by the third grade, the boys with fathers present scored higher on every **achievement** test, and received higher **grades**.

8. Living in a home without a dad has a greater correlation with **suicide** among teenagers than any other factor.

9. Dads tend to enforce boundaries. Toddlers whose dads set limits and enforced boundaries as the children explored had better **social and emotional skills** twelve to eighteen months later.

10. The more interaction a boy has with his dad before six months of age, the higher his **mental competence**.

11. When dad has positive contact with children during the first two years, the children have fewer signs of unwanted and **uncontrolled behavior**.

12. Among preschool children admitted as **psychiatric patients** in two New Orleans hospitals, 80 percent came from homes without fathers. Similar percentages emerge among dad-deprived children in Canada, South Africa, and Finland, at ages from preschool through high school.
13. Worldwide, the amount of time a father spends with a child is one of the strongest predictors of the child's ability to **empathize** as he gets older."
14. By first grade, boys and girls raised in families with fathers present had significantly higher **IQ** scores than those in families where fathers were absent.
15. The more contact children have with their dads growing up, the more easily they make open, receptive, and trusting contact with new people in their lives. And the more contact an infant has prior to six months of age, the greater the infant's ability to **trust**.
16. The more involved dad is, the greater a boy's increase in **verbal development**.
17. Father absence predicts the profile of *both* the **bully** and the **bullied**: poor self-esteem, poor grades, and poor social skills.
18. Teenagers whose dads and moms live separately but who have equal time with both parents were more easily able to make **friends** than children living in any other situation—even more than teenagers living with both parents together.
19. Equal father involvement after divorce predicts the best relationships with **stepparents,** and greater overall **family cohesion**.
20. When 172,000 children's well-being was measured, through a combination of how well they did **psychologically, socially, and with their physical health**, children with equally shared parenting did much better than those in sole parenting or primary-parent arrangements, and almost as well as those in an intact family.
21. Even within the first few months after separation, shared parent time results in **less sibling rivalry** and **fewer negative attitudes toward the parents**.
22. Children living with their married **biological father**—as opposed to a **stepdad**—did significantly better **academically**. They have fewer **discipline** problems, and were more likely to complete high school, attend college, and graduate from college.

23. Both boys and girls suffer after their parents divorce, but the greatest feelings of deprivation and **depressive behavior** were observed among boys.
24. Even when race, education, income, and other socioeconomic factors are equal, living without dad *doubled* a child's chance of **dropping out** of high school.
25. Adolescents with minimal or no father involvement account for 71 percent of high school dropouts. They are also more likely to skip school and, in addition to dropping out, be kicked out (**expelled**).
26. Boys who are dad deprived are more likely than their sisters to be *un*employed; in contrast, boys from two-parent homes are more likely than their sisters to be *employed*.
27. When dad-deprived boys are employed, they are **less likely to succeed** as professionals.
28. Children who were born poor and raised by both married parents had an 80 percent chance of **moving to the middle class or above**; conversely, children who were born into the middle class and raised without a married dad were almost four times as likely to end up considerably poorer.
29. In a study of more than twelve thousand **teenagers after divorce**, children living with single dads fared better than children living with single moms.
30. Younger children living with only their dads are only half to one-third as likely to have frequent **headaches** and **stomachaches** than those living with only their moms.
31. Boys who do not live with their dads become both more demanding and **coercive** toward their moms.
32. Single dads are less than one-third as likely as single moms to let younger kids get away with late or irregular **bedtimes**.
33. Only 15 percent of children living with only their dads had problems with concentration (e.g., **ADHD**), versus 30 percent living with only their moms. This is despite the fact that when children with developmental delays are under the age of one, dads are more than *fifteen* times as likely as moms to take those children into their care.
34. Five- to eleven-year-old children living with their dads are less than one-third as likely to go to the **hospital** compared to those living with only their moms.

35. When dads were in equally shared arrangements, both parents evaluated their children as happier with their **social network**. Both parents felt they were able to have a more positive impact on their children, and provide better housing, work arrangements, and economic and physical health.

36. Divorced dads are less than one-quarter as likely to **bad-mouth** moms in front of their children as divorced moms are to bad-mouth dads in front of their children.

37. Children living with their dads felt **positively about moms**; children living with moms were more likely to think negatively of dads.

38. When dads have primary care of children of divorce, the children are more than twice as likely to have **contact with the other parent**.

39. Roughhousing by dads helps regulate both male and female toddlers' **aggression**, but especially helps a boy toddler control his testosterone-induced aggression by imprinting his left-brain circuits.

40. Boys living with dads have better enforced boundaries, leading to better **impulse control** and fewer **discipline** problems.

41. Around 90 percent of **homeless and runaway** youths are from fatherless homes.

42. Children between ten and seventeen living without their biological dads were more likely to be **victims** of child abuse, major violence, sexual assault, and domestic violence.

43. Every 1 percent increase in fatherlessness in a neighborhood predicts a 3 percent increase in adolescent **violence**.

44. Among youths in **prisons**, 85 percent grew up in a fatherless home. Prisons are basically centers for dad-deprived young men.

45. Adolescents without their biological dads but who were raised in **stepfamilies** faced even higher incarceration rates than in single-mom families.

46. Among black boys, **hypertension** is reduced by 46 percent when dads are significantly involved.

47. Among children raised without dads and teen mothers, it is the boys who experience "alarmingly high levels of pathology": substance abuse and criminal activity. These problems remain far greater for boys into adulthood.

48. Dad deprivation increases the likelihood of **teenage motherhood**.

49. Even when controlling for socioeconomic variables, children whose only "dads" are **sperm donors** are

    a. twice as likely to have **problems with the law** before age twenty-five;

    b. more than 2.5 times as likely to struggle with **substance abuse**; and

    c. slightly more likely to experience problems with **depression** and **mental health**.

50. Absence of dad contributes to **violent crime** as much as absence of **income**.
51. Among criminals assessed as **raping out of anger** and rage, 80 percent came from father-absent homes.
52. Many of the lone **school shooters** were dad deprived.
53. Dad-deprived boys search for structure and respect in **gangs**.
54. Children age ten to seventeen living with their biological parents were significantly less likely to experience **sexual assault** or **child abuse** compared to peers living in both single-parent families and stepfamilies.
55. Children age ten to seventeen living with their biological parents were less likely to witness **violence in their families** compared to peers living in both single-parent families and stepfamilies.

Bibliography

Each of these books offers something special to supplement *The Boy Crisis*. As do each of the "Dad-Inspiring Movies" listed in part IV, in the chapter "The Best Parent Is Both Parents, *But . . .*"

Biddulph, Steve. *The New Manhood* (Mona Vale: Finch Publishing Sydney, 2013).

Brizendine, Louann. *The Male Brain* (New York: Three Rivers Press, 2010).

Farrell, Warren. *Why Men Are the Way They Are* (New York: Berkely Books, 1988).

Farrell, Warren. *The Myth of Male Power* (New York: Simon & Schuster, 1993).

Farrell, Warren. *Women Can't Hear What Men Don't Say* (New York: Berkley Books, 1999).

Farrell, Warren. *Father and Child Reunion* (New York: Tarcher/Putnam, 2001).

Friedan, Betty. *The Second Stage* (Cambridge: Harvard University Press, 1998).

Golden, Tom. *Helping Mothers Be Closer to Their Sons* (Gaithersburg: G.H. Publishing, 2016).

Gray, John. *Men Are from Mars, Women Are from Venus (*New York: Harper, 2012).

Gray, John. *Beyond Mars and Venus* (Dallas: BenBella Books, 2017).

Gurian, Michael. *The Wonder of Boys* (New York: Jeremy P. Tarcher, 2006).

Gurian, Michael. *Boys and Girls Learn Differently!* (San Francisco: Jossey-Bass, 2011).

Gurian, Michael. *Saving Our Sons* (Chandler: Gurian Institute, 2017).

James, Abigail Norfleet. *Teaching the Male Brain* (Thousand Oaks: Corwin Press, 2007).

Keen, Sam and Gifford Keen. *Prodigal Father, Wayward Son* (Studio City: Divine Arts, 2015).

Kindlon, Dan and Michael Thompson. *Raising Cain* (New York: Ballantine Books, 2000).

Kipnis, Aaron. *Angry Young Men* (San Francisco: Jossey-Bass, 1999).

Kruk, Edward. *The Equal Parent Presumption* (Quebec: McGill-Queen's University Press, 2013).

Louv, Richard. *Last Child in the Woods* (Chapel Hill: Algonquin Books, 2006).

McCann, Rex. *Fatherless Sons* (Auckland: HarperCollins, 1999).

Mitscherlich, Alexander. *Society without the Father* (Verlag: R. Piper & Co., 1963).

Nemko, Marty. *Cool Careers for Dummies* (Hoboken, N.J.: Wiley, 2007)

Pollack, William. *Real Boys* (New York: Owl Books, 1999).

Pruett, Kyle and Marsha Pruett. *Partnership Parenting* (Cambridge, Mass: De Capo Press, 2009).

Raeburn, Paul. *Do Fathers Matter?* (New York: Scientific American / Farrar, Straus and Giroux, 2014).

Real, Terrence. *I Don't Want to Talk About It* (New York: Scribner, 1999).

Reichert, Michael and Richard Hawley. *Reaching Boys Teaching Boys* (San Francisco: Jossey-Bass, 2010).

Rosin, Hannah. *The End of Men* (New York: Riverhead Books, 2012).

Sax, Leonard. *Boys Adrift* (New York: Basic Books, 2016).

Sax, Leonard. *Why Gender Matters* (New York: Harmony Books, 2017)

Sommers, Christina Hoff. *The War Against Boys* (New York: Simon & Schuster, 2000).

Thompson, Michael and Teresa Barker. *It's a Boy* (New York: Ballantine Books, 2009).

Tyre, Peg. *The Trouble with Boys* (New York: Three Rivers Press, 2008).

Verrier, Nancy Newton. *The Primal Wound* (Baltimore: Gateway Press, Inc., 1993).

Wiseman, Rosalind. *Masterminds & Wingmen* (New York: Harmony Books, 2013).

Zimbardo, Philip and Nikita Coulombe. *Man, Interrupted* (Newburyport: Conari Press, 2016).

Acknowledgments

From Warren:

The Boy Crisis was an eleven-year project, so there are many more people who contributed to it than names I will recall. I hope those I miss will be forgiving.

I could never, though, forget my wife, Liz, for her almost daily emails of research from which this book benefits, and more important, for working with me to continually deepen our love, thus helping me to write from a centered place.

I also appreciate Liz's patience as hours spent writing meant other income lost, yet her astute and dedicated management of her own PR firm allowed us to nevertheless live comfortably.

As this book has evolved, John Gray's and my weekly walks and talks have both informed the book and nurtured our friendship. I know that each family that benefits from his nontraditional approach to ADHD will also acknowledge him.

I thank Marc Gafni for partnering with John and me in a series of insightful conversations on what is happening with boys, as well as for introducing me to our agent, Frank Weimann, who found just the right publisher in Glenn Yeffeth of BenBella.

I knew I'd love working with Glenn as soon as I discovered that BenBella is named after his children, Ben and Bella. Glenn takes considerable personal interest in the *The Boy Crisis*, and made sure it received the attention of Leah Wilson, the most dedicated editor I have ever had. Leah's brilliant dissection of every paragraph for the possibility of greater clarity, or the addition of another perspective, has improved the book considerably. As did the deep dive into the accuracy of virtually every endnote by Miki Alexandra Caputo. If there is anything that fell through the cracks, it's because BenBella allows John and me the final say!

My ability to envision how to reverse the boy crisis even at the governmental level was enhanced by the contributions of the Coalition to Create a White House Council on Boys and Men. First, by the initial eighteen-month process of drawing up our multipartisan proposal as I worked with the diverse perspectives of Michael Gurian, Peter Moore, Leonard Sax, Marty Nemko, and others. Second, by the Boy Scouts, whose director of government relations, Willie Iles, introduced me to many officials in the Obama administration. Third, by John Mackey of Whole Foods, who funded our efforts to communicate the need for a council to many of the 2016 Republican presidential candidates. And finally, by the weekly coalition calls and contributions of Glenn Barker, Tom Golden, Phil Cook, Mark Sherman, Molly Olson, Jim Ellis, Jimmy Boyd, Dick Woods, and Sean Kullman.

Real-life experience from families and schools was added by my sister, Gail; numerous mothers of sons with whom John and I met; Vanessa Dahn, via her foster home children; and the many insightful comments about the text from Al Zuckerman of Writer's House, as well as Kacy Cuoto, Nikita Coulombe, Emilie Whitman Martin, Mel Ruiz, Tynan Burke, and Valerie Andrews.

From John:

I want to thank my wife, Bonnie Gray, for thirty years of her devoted love and support. I also want to thank our three daughters and their partners—Shannon and Jon, Juliet and Dan, and Lauren and Glade—and our adorable grandchildren, Sophia, Bo, Brady, and Makena. Without Bonnie's support I could not have written my part of this book and sustained a successful career, a loving family, and great health.

So many thanks go to the editors at BenBella that Warren has acknowledged, and especially to my office team. I want to thank Hallina Popko, my executive assistant; Jon Myers, my marketing director for MarsVenus.com; Marcy Wynne, director of customer service; Glad Truitt, director of video production for my online blogs and web design; and all of the Mars Venus Life Coaches around the world. Special thanks to my daughter Lauren Gray, creative director of MarsVenus.com, for her popular video blogs.

A big thanks goes to the many researchers in health and wellness who have made the ADHD chapters possible, and the parents who not only have trusted these ideas to improve their marriages, but have given their children the opportunity to restore normal brain function and begin developing and expressing their full potential for happiness, learning, and success.

About the Authors

Dr. Warren Farrell is the author of books published in seventeen languages. They include two award-winning international bestsellers: *Why Men Are the Way They Are* and *The Myth of Male Power*. Warren has been chosen by the *Financial Times* as one of the world's top 100 thought leaders.

PHOTO BY SAM MARTIN

Dr. Farrell is currently the chair of the Coalition to Create a White House Council on Boys and Men. He is the only man in the United States to have been elected three times to the board of the National Organization for Women (NOW) in New York City. He started more than 300 men and women's groups, including ones joined by men from John Lennon to John Gray. Dr. Farrell has appeared repeatedly on *Oprah*, *TODAY*, and *Good Morning America*, and been the subject of features on *20/20* and in *Forbes*, the *Wall Street Journal*, *People*, *Parade*, and the *New York Times*.

PHOTO BY GLADE TRUITT

Dr. John Gray is the author of *Men Are from Mars, Women Are from Venus*, which *USA Today* listed as number six among the most influential books of the last quarter century. In hardcover, it was the number-one best-selling nonfiction book of the nineties. John Gray's books are translated into approximately forty-five languages in more than one hundred countries.

Dr. Gray's more recent books include *Mars and Venus in the Bedroom, Why Mars and Venus Collide,* and *Work With Me* (with Barbara Annis). John has appeared repeatedly on *Oprah*, as well as on *The Dr. Oz Show, TODAY, CBS This Morning,* and *Good Morning America.* He has been profiled in *Time, Forbes, USA Today, TV Guide,* and *People.* He was also the subject of a three-hour special hosted by Barbara Walters.

Endnotes

CHAPTER 1: THE CRISIS OF OUR SONS' MENTAL HEALTH

1. Amy P. Cohen, Deborah Azrael, and Matthew Miller, "Rate of Mass Shootings Has Tripled Since 2011, Harvard Research Shows," *Mother Jones*, October 15, 2014, http://www.motherjones.com/politics/2014/10/mass-shootings-increasing-harvard-research.

2. Anne Case and Angus Deaton, "Rising Morbidity and Mortality in Midlife Among White Non-Hispanic Americans in the 21st Century," *Proceedings of the National Academy of Sciences* 112, no 49 (2015): 15078, doi:10.1073/pnas.1518393112.

3. Suicide Prevention Resource Center, "Rate of Suicide by Race/Ethnicity, United States 2000-2014," in "Racial and Ethnic Disparities" (summarized from WISQARS Fatal Injury Reports, 1999–2014), http://www.sprc.org/racial-ethnic-disparities.

4. Federal Bureau of Investigation, "Crime in the United States: 2011," Expanded Homicide Data Table 1, http://www.fbi.gov/about-us/cjis/ucr/crime-in-the-u.s/2011/crime-in-the-u.s.-2011/tables/expandedhomicide-data-table-1.

5. University of Chicago, "Becoming a Man," Crime Lab, 2012, https://crimelab.uchicago.edu/page/becoming-man-bam-sports-edition-findings.

6. Centers for Disease Control and Prevention (CDC), *Morbidity and Mortality Weekly Report* 58, no. 1 (2009); and Web-based Injury Statistics Query and Reporting System (WISQARS), 2010.

7. Centers for Disease Control and Prevention (CDC), *Morbidity and Mortality Weekly Report* 58, no. 1 (2009); and Web-based Injury Statistics Query and Reporting System (WISQARS), 2010.

8. In 1933, the rate of suicide for males between fifteen and twenty-four was 1.54 times higher than for females in the same age range. See Mortality Statistics 1933, US Department of Commerce, Bureau of the Census (Washington, DC: Government Printing Office, 1936). Credit to Jack Kammer.

9. American Foundation for Suicide Prevention, "Additional Facts About Suicide in the US," 2015. https://afsp.org/about-suicide/suicide-statistics/, accessed July 7, 2017.

10. Alan Zarembo, "Suicide Rate of Female Military Veterans Is Called 'Staggering,'" *Los Angeles Times*, June 8, 2015, http://latimes.com/nation/la-na-female-veteran-suicide-20150608-story.html. Female veterans commit 28.7 suicides for each 32.1 committed by male veterans.

11. Armen Keteyian, "Suicide Epidemic Among Veterans." CBS News, November 13, 2007. http://www.cbsnews.com/stories/2007/11/13/cbsnews_investigates/main3496471.shtml.

12. Jason Breslow, "New Report Slams 'Unprecedented' Growth in US Prisons," *Frontline*, PBS, May 1, 2014, http://www.pbs.org/wgbh/pages/frontline/criminal-justice/locked-up-in-america/new-report-slams-unprecedented-growth-in-us-prisons.

13. J. Schmitt and K. Warner, "Ex-offenders and the Labor Market" (report, Center for Economic and Policy Research, November 2010), 6, http://www.cepr.net/documents/publications/ex-offenders-2010-11.pdf.

14. Office of Justice Programs' Bureau of Justice Statistics, "Prisoners in 2013," https://www.bjs.gov/index.cfm?ty=pbdetail&iid=5109.

15. The APA report estimates that half of prisoners have mental health problems. See American Psychological Association, "Incarceration Nation," *Monitor on Psychology* 45, no. 9 (October 2014): 56, http://www.apa.org/monitor/2014/10/incarceration.aspx.

16. Breslow. "'Unprecedented' Growth in US Prisons."

17. Saki Knafo. "Prison-Industrial Complex? Maybe It's Time for a Schools-Industrial Complex," *Huffington Post*, August 31, 2013, http://www.huffingtonpost.com/2013/08/30/california-prisons-schools_n_3839190.html.

18. Knafo, "Prison-Industrial Complex?"

19. American Foundation for Suicide Prevention, "Suicide Statistics," http://afsp.org/about-suicide/suicide-statistics.

20. "Children's Mental Health: New Report," CDC, archived September 10, 2015, http://web.archive.org/web/20150910003950/http://www.cdc.gov/features/childrensmentalhealth.

CHAPTER 2: THE CRISIS OF OUR SONS' PHYSICAL HEALTH

1. Randolph Nesse conducted a study of premature deaths in twenty countries. An estimated 375,000 lives per year would be saved were men's risks equal to women's. See Betsy Mason, "Men Die Young—Even if Old", *New Scientist*, July 25, 2002, https://www.newscientist.com/article/dn2586-men-die-young-even-if-old.

2. "Being a Man 'Is Bad for Health,'" BBC News, July 24, 2002, http://news.bbc.co.uk/2/hi/health/2148573.stm. See also Mason, "Men Die Young."

3. Rémy Slama et al., "Epidemiology of Male Reproductive Function," *Revue d'Epidémiologie et de Santé Publique* [Review of epidemiology and public health] 52 (2004), 221–42; as cited in Leonard Sax, *Boys Adrift* (New York: Basic Books, 2007), 231.

4. S. Cabler et al., "Obesity: Modern Man's Fertility Nemesis," *Asian Journal of Andrology* 12, no. 4 (2010): 480–89.

5. Adapted from National Center for Health Statistics, CDC, *National Vital Statistics Reports* 64, no. 2 (2016): table B, p. 5.

6. AFL-CIO, *Death on the Job: The Toll of Neglect*, 2015. See http://www.aflcio.org/Issues/Job-Safety/Death-on-the-Job-Report

7. US Bureau of Labor Statistics, Current Population Survey, Census of Fatal Occupational Injuries, 2015. Data is 2014 preliminary data. See http://www.bls.gov/iif/oshwc/cfoi/cfch0013.pdf.

8. See Warren Farrell, "The Death Professions: My Body, Not My Choice," in *The Myth of Male Power* (New York: Simon & Schuster, 1993). An updated Kindle edition is available on Amazon.

9. AFL-CIO, *Death on the Job: The Toll of Neglect* (AFL-CIO, 2015), https://aflcio.org/sites/default/files/2017-03/DOTJ2015Finalnobug.pdf.

10. Allison Field et al,. "Prospective Associations of Concerns About Physique and the Development of Obesity, Binge Drinking, and Drug Use Among Adolescent Boys and Young Adult Men." *JAMA Pediatrics* 168, no. 1 (2014): 34–39, doi:10.1001/jamapediatrics.2013.2915.

11. Ashleigh May, CDC, "Obesity: United States, 1999–2010," *Morbidity and Mortality Weekly Report* 62, no. 3 (2013): table 2, http://www.cdc.gov/mmwr/preview/mmwrhtml/su6203a20.htm#Tab2.

12. William H. McMichael, "Most U.S. Youths Unfit to Serve, Data Show," *Army Times*, November 9, 2009.

13. Natalie Rahhal, *Daily Mail.com*, October 16, 2017. http://www.dailymail.co.uk/health/article-4985856/Americans-fat-fight-crime-war-fires.html.

14. "Still Too Fat to Fight," *Mission: Readiness*, 2012. http://missionreadiness.s3.amazonaws.com/wp-content/uploads/Still-Too-Fat-To-Fight-Report.pdf.

CHAPTER 3: THE CRISIS OF OUR SONS' ECONOMIC HEALTH

1. US Bureau of Labor Statistics, "Employed Persons by Detailed Occupation, Sex, Race, and Hispanic or Latino Ethnicity," Household Data, Annual Averages 2009, table 11, http://www.bls.gov/cps/cpsaat11.pdf.

2. Andrea Coombes, "Men Suffer Brunt of Job Losses in Recession," *Wall Street Journal*, July 16, 2009, https://www.wsj.com/articles/SB10001424052970203577304574272570149153010.

3. Heidi Hartmann, Elyse Shaw, and Elizabeth Pandya, "Women and Men in the Recovery: Where the Jobs Are" (briefing paper, Institute for Women's Policy Research, November 2013), 12, Institute for Women's Policy Research, https://iwpr.org/wp-content/uploads/wpallimport/files/iwpr-export/publications/Women%20and%20Men%20in%20the%20Recovery_Web%20Final2.pdf.

4. Jonathan Vanian, "In 10 Years, Artificial Intelligence Will Transform Trucking, Says Otto Exec," *Fortune*, March 27, 2017. http://fortune.com/2017/03/27/uber-otto-artificial-intelligence-truck-driving/.

5. M. Greenstone and A. Looney, "Trends" (report), Milken Institute, July 2011, p. 11, http://wwwassets1b.milkeninstitute.org/publications/review/2011_7assets/Publication/MIReview/PDF/08-16MR51.pdf (accessed June 8, 2014, October 26, 2017).

6. David Wessel, "Meet the Unemployable Man," *Wall Street Journal*, May 1, 2010, https://www.wsj.com/articles/SB10001424052748703322204575226003417489846.

7. Belinda Luscombe. "Workplace Salaries: At Last, Women on Top," *Time*, September 1, 2010, http://www.time.com/time/business/article/0,8599,2015274,00.html.

8. National Association of Realtors, "First-Time Buyers, Single Women Gain Traction in NAR's 2016 Buyer and Seller Survey," National Association of Realtors, October 31, 2016, http://www.realtor.org/news-releases/2016/10/first-time-buyers-single-women-gain-traction-in-nar-s-2016-buyer-and-seller-survey. Single women represented 17 percent of home purchases, single males 7 percent.

9. Jeffrey Gentry, "Who Pays for the First Date? Survey Says Men Should," *USA Today*, September 25, 2014; survey conducted by NerdWallet.com.

10. Gentry, "Who Pays for the First Date?"

11. David Mielach, "75 Percent of Women Say They Won't Date Unemployed Men," *Business News Daily*, June 26, 2012, http://www.businessnewsdaily.com/2753-dating-unemployed-men-women.html; a survey of 925 respondents conducted by It's Just Lunch, a dating service.

12. Mielach, " Women Won't Date Unemployed Men."

13. Augustine J. Kposowa, "Unemployment and Suicide: A Cohort Analysis of Social Factors Predicting Suicide in the U.S. National Longitudinal Mortality Study," *Psychological Medicine* 31, no. 1 (January 2001): 127–38. See also Kposowa, "Marital Status and Suicide in the National Longitudinal Mortality Study," *Journal of Epidemiology and Community Health* 54 (April 2000): 256. The figure is 9.94 higher in divorced men than in divorced women. The 9.94 figure was obtained from Dr. Kposowa using information from table 1 on p. 256. Personal correspondence with Warren Farrell, June 29, 2000.

14. Gentry, "Who Pays for the First Date?"

15. Gentry, "Who Pays for the First Date?"

CHAPTER 4: THE CRISIS OF OUR SONS' EDUCATION

1. OECD, "How Do Girls Compare to Boys in Mathematics Skills?" in *PISA 2009 at a Glance* (Paris, France: OECD, 2010) 22, doi:10.1787/9789264095298-en.

2. D. Salahu-Din, H. Persky, and J. Miller, *The Nation's Report Card: Writing 2007*, NCES 2008–468, National Center for Education Statistics (NCES), Institute of Education Sciences, U.S. Department of Education, (Washington, DC, and Chapel Hill, NC, 2008), table A-9. Average scores and achievement-level results in NAEP writing for eighth-grade public school students, by gender and state. 2007.

3. In 1980 only 14 percent of boys said they did not like school very much at all; by 2001 that figure had increased to 24 percent. See University of Michigan, Institute for Social Research, Monitoring the Future (study), 1980–2001; cited in NCES, "How Do You Feel About School?" *Trends in Educational Equity of Girls and Women: 2004*, fig. 13, p. 45.

4. NCES, "Number and Percentage of Students Who Were Suspended and Expelled from Public Elementary and Secondary Schools, by Sex and Race/Ethnicity: 2002, 2004, and 2006," in *Condition of Education 2009*, ed. Michael Planty, William J. Hussar, and Thomas D. Snyder (Washington, DC: NCES, June 2009), table A-28-1, p. 206.

5. C. Cornwell et al., "Non-cognitive Skills and the Gender Disparities in Test Scores and Teacher Assessments: Evidence from Primary School," *Journal of Human Resources* 48 (Winter 2013): 236–64.

6. Original chart developed by Thomas G. Mortenson, Senior Scholar, Pell Institute for the Study of Opportunity in Higher Education, Washington, DC. Digest of Education Statistics, 2016, Table 318.10, https://nces.ed.gov/programs/digest/d16/tables/dt16_318.10.asp.

7. Ana Swanson, "What Men and Women Wanted in a Spouse in 1939—and How Different It Is Today," *Wonkblog* (blog), *Washington Post*, April 19, 2016, https://www.washingtonpost.com/news/wonk/wp/2016/04/19/what-men-and-women-wanted-in-a-spouse-in-1939-and-how-different-it-is-today.

8. Peg Tyre, "The Trouble with Boys," *Newsweek*, January 29, 2006, http://www.newsweek.com/education-boys-falling-behind-girls-many-areas-108593.

9. Taro Fujimoto, "Vocational Schools on the Move," *Japan Today*, July 21, 2008. https://japantoday.com/category/features/executive-impact/vocational-schools-on-the-move.

10. Kazuhiro Ohshima of the Katayanagi Institute is actively recruiting foreign students. See Fujimoto, "Vocational Schools."

11. Kristi Klein and Sara Hodges, "Gender Differences, Motivation, and Empathic Accuracy: When It Pays to Understand," *Personality and Social Psychology Bulletin* 27, no. 6 (June 2001): 720–30.

12. See www.lifeafterhate.org.

13. Clayton Cook, et. al., "Predictors of Bullying and Victimization in Childhood and Adloscence: A Meta-analytic Investigation," *School Psychology Quarterly* 25, no.2. See http://www.apa.org/news/press/releases/2010/07/bully-victim.aspx.

14. Lester Holt. "Men Falling Behind Women," NBC News, March 5, 2011, http://www.nbc-news.com/id/41928806/ns/business-us_business/t/men-falling-behind-women.

15. Paul Stern, director, *Raising Cain: Boys in Focus* (documentary), PBS Films, 2006; see also Michael Gurian Michael and Arlette C. Ballew, *The Boys and Girls Learn Differently: Action Guide for Teachers* (Hoboken, NJ: John Wiley & Sons, 2003), 23.

CHAPTER 5: THE CRISIS OF OUR SONS WORLDWIDE

1. Finlay Young, "The Trouble with Men: Why Men are Killing Themselves," *Newsweek*, February 12, 2015, http://www.newsweek.com/2015/02/20/suicide-men-305913.html.

2. OECD, *The ABC of Gender Equality in Education: Aptitude, Behavior, Confidence*, PISA (Paris, France: OECD Publishing, 2015), 26, doi:10.1787/9789264229945-en.

3. Sarah Keenlyside, "Young, Free and *Shengnu*: China's Bridget Joneses," *Telegraph*, July 30, 2012, http://www.telegraph.co.uk/women/sex/9424628/Young-free-and-shengnu-Chinas-Bridget-Joneses.html.

4. "From Carnivores to Herbivores: How Men Are Defined in Japan." *Japan Today*, February 16, 2012, http://www.japantoday.com/category/lifestyle/view/from-carnivores-to-herbivores-how-men-are-defined-in-japan.

5. William Kremer and Claudia Hammond, "Hikikomori: Why Are So Many Japanese Men Refusing to Leave Their Rooms?" BBC News, July 5, 2013, http://www.bbc.com/news/magazine-23182523.

6. Massimiliano Mascherini, Lidia Salvatore, Anja Meierkord, and Jean-Marie Jungblut, *NEETs—Young People Not in Employment, Education or Training: Characteristics, Costs and Policy Responses in Europe*, Eurofound, (Luxembourg: Publications Office of the European Union, 2012), http://www.eurofound.europa.eu/sites/default/files/ef_files/pubdocs/2012/54/en/1/EF1254EN.pdf.

7. According to the OECD's *ABC of Gender Equality in Education: Aptitude, Behavior, Confidence* (p. 3), 14 percent of boys versus 9 percent of girls did not attain the PISA baseline proficiency in reading, math, or science.

8. "What's the Problem with School?" Understanding and Raising Boys, PBS Parents, accessed December 26, 2011, http://www.pbs.org/parents/raisingboys/school02.html.

9. OECD, *ABC of Gender Equality*, 32, 107.

10. World Health Organization, "Adult Risk Factors: Obesity, Blood Sugar, Blood Pressure Data by Country" (2013), accessed May 30, 2014, http://apps.who.int/gho/data/node.main.NCD56?lang=en.

11. John Crace, "Children Are Less Able Than They Used to Be," *Guardian*, January 24, 2006, https://www.theguardian.com/education/2006/jan/24/schools.uk; see also Leonard Sax' *Boys Adrift* (p. 65), which references the same study, "Thirty Years On: A Large Anti-Flynn Effect? The Piagetian Test Volume & Heaviness Norms, 1975–2003," by Michael Shayer, M. Ginsburg, and Coe in *British Journal of Educational Psychology* 77, no. 1 (March 2007): 25–41. Boys' IQs have dropped about 15 points (a full standard deviation) since the 1980s. Girls' have dropped about 7-8 points. In the 1970s boys' IQs were about seven to eight points higher than girls'.

12. William T. Dickens and James R. Flynn, *Psychological Review* 108, no. 2 (2001): 346–69.

13. Daniel Nettle, *Evolution and Human Behavior* 29, no. 6 (November 2008): 416–23, doi:10.1016/j.evolhumbehav.2008.06.002.

14. US Census Bureau, "Living Arrangements of Children under 18 Years/1 and Marital Status of Parents by Age, Sex, Race, and Hispanic Origin/2 and Selected Characteristics of the Child for all Children 2010," Current Population Survey, table C3. UK source: Office of National Statistics.

15. "Being a Man 'Is Bad for Health,'" BBC News, July 24, 2002, http://news.bbc.co.uk/2/hi/health/2148573.stm. See also Betsy Mason, "Men Die Young—Even if Old", *New Scientist*, July 25, 2002, https://www.newscientist.com/article/dn2586-men-die-young-even-if-old.

16. "World Health Statistics, 2017", World Health Organization, p. 92, http://apps.who.int/iris/bitstream/10665/255336/1/9789241565486-eng.pdf.

17. Institute for Health Metrics and Evaluation, "Global Burden of Disease, 2010," *Lancet,* December 2012, http://thelancet.com/gbd/2010; cited in Tony Dokoupil, "Why Suicide Has Become an Epidemic—And What We Can Do to Help," May 23, 2013, *Newsweek.* See http://www.newsweek.com/2013/05/22/why-suicide-has-become-epidemic-and-what-we-can-do-help-237434.html.

18. Deepika Bhardwaj, "Men: The Forgotten Gender." YouTube video, 19:00, posted by TEDx Talks, February 25, 2015, http://youtu.be/1_2gl7lz25E; for specific statistics on suicide rates, see National Crime Records Bureau, "Accidental Deaths & Suicides in India 2013," accessed November 2, 2015, http://ncrb.gov.in/adsi2013/ADSI-2013.pdf.

CHAPTER 6: WHY ARE WE SO BLIND TO THE BOY CRISIS?

1. There were 923 males and 40 females fatally shot by police in 2016. For the full tally, see www.washingtonpost.com/graphics/national/police-shootings-2016.

CHAPTER 8: THE PATH-TO-PURPOSE GENERATION GAP

1. Kozo Tanno et al., "Associations of *Ikigai* as a Positive Psychological Factor with All-Cause Mortality and Cause-Specific Mortality Among Middle-Aged and Elderly Japanese People," *Journal of Psychosomatic Research* 67, no. 1 (2009): 67–75, doi:10.1016/j.jpsychores.2008.10.018.

2. See Warren Farrell, *Why Men Earn More: The Startling Truth Behind the Pay Gap— and What Women Can Do About It,* (New York: AMACOM, 2005); see also Warren Farrell, "Why Men Earn More," presentation, MP3 audio file, WarrenFarrell.com, 2006, http://warrenfarrell.com/?product=why-men-earn-more.

3. Warren Farrell, "Your Dad's Sense of Purpose? You," YouTube Video, 6:31, posted by Warren Farrell, May 1, 2017, https://youtu.be/JOelM9ulgDQ.

4. Christine Rousselle, "DNC Email: Straight White Men Need Not Apply," *Townhall,* October 30, 2017.

5. Duncan McCargo, *Contemporary Japan,* 3rd ed. (New York: Palgrave Macmillan, 2012), 80.

6. McCargo, *Contemporary Japan,* 80.

7. See Warren Farrell, *The Myth of Male Power* (New York: Simon & Schuster, 1993; Kindle ed., New York: Berkley, 2001).

8. Dave Philipps, "In Unit Stalked by Suicide, Veterans Try to Save One Another," *New York Times,* September 19, 2015, http://www.nytimes.com/2015/09/20/us/marine-battalion-veterans-scarred-by-suicides-turn-to-one-another-for-help.html.

CHAPTER 9: THE "HERO PARADOX": VALUE YOURSELF BY NOT VALUING YOURSELF

1. The word *hero* derives from the Proto-Indo-European root **ser-*. In Ancient Greek, *hērōs* (ἥρως) had the connotation of "protector." The Latin infinitive for "to protect" is *servare*. From the same root family comes the word *servus*, meaning "slave," from which we get our verb "to serve." See Julius Pokorny, *Indogermanisches Etymologisches Wörterbuch* (Bern: Francke, 1959); or, for slightly easier reading, *The American Heritage Dictionary of the English Language* (New York: American Heritage and Houghton Mifflin, 1969), 1538.
2. T. Jean Marie Arseneau-Robar et al., "Female Monkeys Use Both the Carrot and the Stick to Promote Male Participation in Intergroup Fights," *Proceedings of the Royal Society B* 283, no. 1843 (2016): doi:10.1098/rspb.2016.1817.
3. Arseneau-Robar et al., "Female Monkeys."
4. Louann Brizendine, *The Male Brain*, (New York: Three Rivers Press, 2010), xvi and 43.
5. Three female first responders (out of 411) also died: Kathy Mazza; Yamel Merino, and Moira Smith.
6. Selective Service System, "Benefits and Penalties," https://www.sss.gov/Registration/Why-Register/Benefits-and-Penalties.
7. Selective Service System, "Benefits and Penalties," https://www.sss.gov/Registration/Why-Register/Benefits-and-Penalties.
8. Selective Service, "Benefits and Penalties."
9. Selective Service, "State-Commonwealth Legislation," https://www.sss.gov/Registration/State-Commonwealth-Legislation.

CHAPTER 10: WHY DO MORE MARRIAGES FAIL IN COUNTRIES THAT SUCCEED?

1. "Women More Likely to Initiate Divorce: Study," *Divorce Magazine.com*, January 29, 2016. Based on a study by the American Sociological Association of divorces in heterosexual relationships.
2. See Warren Farrell, *Women Can't Hear What Men Don't Say*, (New York: Putnam / Penguin, 1999).
3. Interview with Michael Gurian, June 25, 2017.
4. Emily Yoffe, "The Uncomfortable Truth About Campus Rape Policy," *The Atlantic*, September 6, 2017, https://www.theatlantic.com/education/archive/2017/09/the-uncomfortable-truth-about-campus-rape-policy/538974/.
5. "Superbowl Ad 2015: T-Mobile," *Wall Street Journal*, http://www.wsj.com/video/super-bowl-2015-t-mobile-ad/F40DB477-4DE7-4656-8811-DB96275C91C5.html.
6. Jasmeet Sidhu, "How to Buy a Daughter," Medical Examiner, *Slate*, September 14, 2012, http://www.slate.com/articles/health_and_science/medical_examiner/2012/09/

sex_selection_in_babies_through_pgd_americans_are_paying_to_have_daughters_rather_than_sons_.html.

7. Lori Oliwenstein, "African-American Babies and Boys Least Likely to Be Adopted, Study Shows," *Caltech*, April 20, 2010, https://www.caltech.edu/news/african-american-babies-and-boys-least-likely-be-adopted-study-shows-1610.

8. Lori Oliwenstein, "African-American Babies."

9. Lori Oliwenstein, "African-American Babies."

10. Jasmeet Sidhu, "How to Buy a Daughter."

CHAPTER II: HOW RAISING OUR SONS SUCCESSFULLY IN THE PAST DIFFERS FROM RAISING OUR SONS SUCCESSFULLY FOR THEIR FUTURE

1. John Gottman et al., "Predicting Marital Happiness and Stability from Newlywed Interactions," *Journal of Marriage and the Family* 60, no. 1 (February 1998): 5–22, doi:10.2307/353438.

2. E. Lynge, "Unemployment and Cancer: A Literature Review," *IARC Scientific Publications* (138) (1997): 343–51.

3. T. A. Blakely, S. C. D. Collings, and J. Atkinson, "Unemployment and Suicide. Evidence for a causal association?" *Journal of Epidemiology and Community Health* 57, no. 8 (2003): 594-600, doi:10.1136/jech.57.8.594.

4. Kerwin Kofi Charles and Melvin Stephens Jr., "Job Displacement, Disability, and Divorce," *Journal of Labor Economics* 22, no. 2 (April 2004): 489–522, doi:10.1086/381258.

5. Andrew Rosen, "5 Highest Paid High School Principals in America," Jobacle, January 28, 2013, http://www.jobacle.com/blog/5-highest-paid-high-school-principals-in-america.html.

6. "Girls Who Started Their Own Businesses!" *Seventeen*, September 4, 2012, http://www.seventeen.com/life/school/advice/g1808/girls-who-started-businesses/?slide=6.

7. Vicki Salemi, "Women Dominated Professions," Monster, March 8, 2017, https://www.monster.com/career-advice/article/professions-women.

8. Michael F. Steger, Bryan J. Dik, and Ryan D. Duffy, "Measuring Meaningful Work: The Work and Meaning Inventory (WAMI)", *Journal of Career Assessment* 20, no. 3 (August 2012): 322–37.

CHAPTER 12: RAISING A BALANCED SON IN AN OUT-OF-BALANCE WORLD

1. Centers for Disease Control and Prevention and SHAPE America—Society of Health and Physical Educators, *Strategies for Recess in Schools* (Atlanta, GA: Centers for Disease Control and Prevention, US Dept. of Health and Human Services, 2017),

https://www.cdc.gov/healthyschools/physicalactivity/pdf/2016_12_16_schoolre-cessstrategies_508.pdf.

2. Gonzalez-Bono, E., et al, "Testosterone, cortisol, and mood in a sports team competition," *Hormones and Behavior* 1999; 35 (1): 55-62.

3. Howard LeWine, M.D., "FDA warns about blood clot risk with testosterone products," *Harvard Health Publishing*, June 24, 2014.

4. Saul McLeod, "Maslow's Hierarchy of Needs," *Simply Psychology*, 2017, https://www.simplypsychology.org/maslow.html.

5. Marc Gafni, *Your Unique Self* (Tucson, AZ: Integral Publishers, 2011).

PART IV: DAD-DEPRIVED BOYS VERSUS DAD-ENRICHED BOYS

1. N. Glenn and B. D. Whitehead (2009), *MAMA SAYS: A National Survey of Mothers' Attitudes on Fathering*, conducted by the University of Texas Office of Survey Research, of 1,533 mothers. Retrieved June 29, 2017, from National Fatherhood Initiative: http://www.fatherhood.org/ mama-says-survey

CHAPTER 13: DAD-DEPRIVED BOYS

1. Colter Mitchell et. al., "Father Loss and Child Telomere Length," *Pediatrics* (July 2017): doi: 10.1542/peds.2016-3245.

2. Britt J. Heidinger et. al., "Telomere Length in Early Life Predicts Lifespan," *Proceedings of the National Academy of Sciences* 109, no. 5 (2012):1743–48, doi: 10.1073/pnas.1113306109.

3. Mitchell et. al., "Father Loss."

4. Mitchell et. al., "Father Loss."

5. Warren Farrell, *Father and Child Reunion*, (New York: Putnam/Penguin, 2001).

6. In addition to my *Father and Child Reunion*, see, for inspiration how even a divorced dad's involvement can be crucial: "Diane Lane: A Life in the Spotlight," YouTube video, 7:47, CBS Sunday Morning, May 7, 2017, http://youtu.be/tygUK6aAjXA.

7. David Autor et al., "Family Disadvantage and the Gender Gap in Behavioral and Educational Outcomes" (working paper no. 22267, National Bureau of Economic Research, May 2016), doi:10.3386/w22267. For many studies and reasons, see also Thomas B. Edsall, "The Increasing Significance of the Decline of Men," *New York Times*, March 16, 2017, https://www.nytimes.com/2017/03/16/opinion/the-increasing-significance-of-the-decline-of-men.html.

8. Allan N. Schore, "All Our Sons: The Developmental Neurobiology and Neuroendocrinology of Boys at Risk,", *Infant Mental Health Journal* 38, no. 1 (2017): 15–52, doi:10.1002/imhj.21616.

9. Tara Kangarlou, "Imprisoned IS Members Open Up to Lebanese Social Workers," *AL-Monitor*, March 10, 2015, http://www.al-monitor.com/pulse/originals/2015/03/terrorism-social-work-jihadist-profile-roumieh-prison.html.

10. Kangarlou, "Imprisoned IS Members."

11. Warren Farrell, "The Boy Crisis: A Sobering Look at the State of Our Boys," You-Tube video, 12:50, TEDx Talks, October 19, 2015, http://youtu.be/Qi1oN1icAYc.

12. Francis Ianni, *The Search for Structure* (New York: Free Press, 1989).

13. Duke Hefland, "Ex-Skinhead's Unlikely Alliance," *Los Angeles Times*, August 12, 1996, http://articles.latimes.com/1996-08-12/local/me-33587_1_tom-leyden.

14. Farrell, "The Boy Crisis" (TEDx talk).

15. Jeremy Borden and Todd C. Frankel, "Dylann Roof's Teenage Years Marked by Father's Bitter Divorce," *Washington Post*, June 22, 2015, https://www.washingtonpost.com/news/post-nation/wp/2015/06/22/dylann-roofs-teenage-years-marked-by-fathers-bitter-divorce.

16. Carmen Noevi Velez and Patricia Cohen, "Suicidal Behavior and Ideation in a Community Sample of Children: Maternal and Youth Reports," *Journal of the American Academy of Child and Adolescent Psychiatry* 273 (1988): 349–56.

17. W. Bradford Wilcox, "Sons of Divorce, School Shooters," *National Review*, December 16, 2013, http://web.archive.org/web/20150905172547/http://www.nationalreview.com/corner/366405/sons-divorce-school-shooters-w-bradford-wilcox.

18. Kangarlou, "Imprisoned IS Members."

19. Jessica Elgot, "Islamic State Recruits Are Young, Angry and Rebellious, but Are They Actually Religious?" *Huffington Post*, UK, August 22, 2014, http://www.huffingtonpost.co.uk/2014/08/21/isis-recruits-are-young-angry-and-rebellious-but-are-they-actually-religious_n_5697744.html.

20. Kris Wolfe, "How Absent Fathers May Be Contributing to ISIS Recruitment," goodguyswag, October 21, 2014, http://goodguyswag.com/how-absent-fathers-may-be-contributing-to-isis-recruitment.

21. www.germanvictims.com

22. History Place, "Hitler's Boy Soldiers," Hitler Youth, 1999, http://www.historyplace.com/worldwar2/hitleryouth/hj-boy-soldiers.htm.

23. History Place, "Hitler's Boy Soldiers."

24. History Place, "Hitler's Boy Soldiers."

25. Hefland, "Ex-Skinhead's Unlikely Alliance."

26. Jodi Rave, "Teen Suicides Series, Part 2," *Missoulian*, October 26, 2005, http://missoulian.com/jodirave/teen-suicides-series-part-recent-red-lake-suicides-continue-alarming/article_786ee2bf-46d2-52ed-9301-8321e40365e8.html.

27. Kay S. Hymowitz, "Boy Trouble," *City Journal*, Autumn 2013, http://www.city-journal.org/html/boy-trouble-13615.html.

28. Frank Furstenberg, *Destinies of the Disadvantaged: The Politics of Teen Childbearing* (New York: Russell Sage Foundation, 2007), 63.

29. Richard Sipe, *Secret World* (New York: Brunner-Routledge, 1990)

30. Allen J. Beck and David Cantor, "Sexual Victimization in Juvenile Facilities Reported by Youth, 2012," National Survey of Youth in Custody, 2012, US Department of Justice, June 6, 2013, http://www.propublica.org/documents/item/709100-svjfry12-emb-052813.

31. The neural network includes circuits that link emotional importance to experience (the amygdala, the ventral anterior cingulate cortex, the inferior frontal gyrus,

insular cortex, and the ventral tegmentum), as well as others that help us impute needs, intentions, or mental state to other people (the ventromedial prefrontal cortex, the superior temporal sulcus). See Eyal Abraham et al., "Father's Brain Is Sensitive to Childcare Experiences," *Proceedings of the National Academy of Sciences* 111, no. 27 (2014): 9792–97, doi:10.1073/pnas.1402569111.

32. Research reported in Brigid Schulte, "Don't Call them Mr. Mom: More Dads at Home with Kids Because They Want to Be," *Washington Post*, June 5, 2014, https://www.washingtonpost.com/news/parenting/wp/2014/06/05/dads-who-stay-home-because-they-want-to-has-increased-four-fold.

33. Abraham et al., "Father's Brain."

34. "Do Mothers Really Have Stronger Bonds with Their Children Than Fathers Do?" *The Conversation*, April 20, 2016, https://theconversation.com/do-mothers-really-have-stronger-bonds-with-their-children-than-fathers-do-57590.

35. Abraham et al., "Father's Brain."

36. Kyle Pruett is with the Yale School of Medicine's Child Study Center.

37. Mark Greene, "The Lack of Gentle Platonic Touch in Men's Lives Is a Killer," *Good Men Project*, November 4, 2013, http://goodmenproject.com/featured-content/megasahd-the-lack-of-gentle-platonic-touch-in-mens-lives-is-a-killer.

38. Farrell, *Father and Child Reunion*.

39. Kim Parker and Wendy Wang, "Modern Parenthood: Roles of Moms and Dads Converge as They Balance Work and Family" (report, Pew Research Social and Demographic Trends, Washington, DC, 2013), q. 44; based on fathers with children under eighteen.

40. Pew Research analysis of decennial census and American community survey, cited in Gretchen Livingston, "The Rise of Single Fathers: A Ninefold Increase Since 1960," Pew Research Center, July 2, 2013, http://www.pewsocialtrends.org/2013/07/02/the-rise-of-single-fathers.

41. Brigid Schulte, "Don't Call Them Mr. Mom: More Dads at Home with Kids Because They Want to Be," June 5, 2014. See reader feedback.

42. Credit for chart from Jordan Weissmann, "The Overhyped Rise of Stay-at-Home Dads," *The Atlantic*, September 3, 2013, https://www.theatlantic.com/business/archive/2013/09/the-overhyped-rise-of-stay-at-home-dads/279279/. His source was Census.gov, "Who's Minding the Kids? Child Care Arrangements," April 2013, https://www.census.gov/prod/2013pubs/p70-135.pdf.

43. Katrin Bennhold, "The Female Factor: Paternity Leave Law Helps to Redefine Masculinity in Sweden," *New York Times*, June 15, 2010, http://query.nytimes.com/gst/fullpage.html?res=9F0CE5DD1338F936A25755C0A9669D8B63.

44. Warren Farrell, *Why Men Earn More*.

45. Kimberly Amadeo, "War on Terror Facts, Costs and Timeline," *The Balance: U.S. Economy*, October 9, 2017, https://www.thebalance.com/war-on-terror-facts-costs-timeline-3306300.

46. David Blankenhorn [president of the Institute of American Values], cited in "Taxpayer Costs of Divorce and Unwed Childbearing," *dads &*

things (blog), June 28, 2008, http://blog.fathersforlife.org/2008/06/28/us-taxpayer-costs-of-divorce-and-unwed-childbearing.

47. "Teen Pregnancy Statistics," TeenHelp.com, accessed October 25, 2017, https://www.teenhelp.com/teen-pregnancy/teen-pregnancy-statistics.

48. Sara McLanahan and Gary Sandefur, *Growing Up with a Single Parent*, (Cambridge: Harvard University Press, 1997).

49. Elizabeth Marquardt et al., "My Daddy's Name is Donor," (report, Institute for American Values, New York, 2010), http://americanvalues.org/catalog/pdfs/Donor_FINAL.pdf.

50. Marquardt et al., "Daddy's Name is Donor."

51. Marquardt et al., "Daddy's Name is Donor."

CHAPTER 14: *WHY* ARE DADS SO IMPORTANT?

1. Steve Hartman, "Finding a Car to Connect a Son with His Father, a Fallen Soldier," CBS News, November 3, 2017, https://www.cbsnews.com/news/finding-a-car-to-connect-a-son-with-his-father-a-fallen-soldier.

2. Henry Biller, *Paternal Deprivation: Family, School, Sexuality, and Society* (Lexington, MA: Lexington Books, 1974).

3. N. Radin, "The Role of the Father in Cognitive, Academic, and Intellectual Development," in *The Role of the Father in Child Development*, ed. M. E. Lamb (New York: John Wiley & Sons, 1981), 379–427; N. Radin, "The Influence of Fathers on Their Sons and Daughters," *Social Work in Education* 8 (1986): 77–91; N. Radin and G. Russell, "Increased Paternal Participation and Childhood Outcomes," in *Fatherhood and Family Policy*, ed. M. E. Lamb and A. Sagi (Hillsdale, NJ: Lawrence Erlbaum, 1983), 191–218.

4. See H. S. Goldstein, "Fathers' Absence and Cognitive Development of 12- to 17-Year-Olds," *Psychological Reports* 51 (1982): 843–48. See also N. Radin, "Role of the Father"; N. Radin, "Influence of Fathers."

5. Sheila Fitzgerald Krein and A. Beller, "Educational Attainment of Children from Single-Parent Families: Differences by Exposure, Gender, and Race," *Demography* 25 (May 1988): 403–26.

6. Edward Kruk, "The Vital Importance of Paternal Presence in Children's Lives," *Psychology Today*, May 23, 2012, http://www.psychologytoday.com/blog/co-parenting-after-divorce/201205/father-absence-father-deficit-father-hunger.

7. David Autor et al., "Family Disadvantage and the Gender Gap in Behavioral and Educational Outcomes," (working paper no. 22267, National Bureau of Economic Research, May 2016), doi:10.3386/w22267. Specifically, "For young adults from married households, employment is higher among men than women at all parental income quintiles; for young adults from non-married households, male employment at age 30 is everywhere lower than among women."

8. Kruk, " Vital Importance of Paternal Presence."

9. Carmen Noevi Velez and Patricia Cohen, "Suicidal Behavior and Ideation in a Community Sample of Children: Maternal and Youth Reports," *Journal of the American Academy of Child and Adolescent Psychiatry* 273 (1988): 349–56.

10. The only factor more important than father involvement was the child's age. Robert H. Coombs and John Landsverk, "Parenting Styles and Substance Use During Childhood and Adolescence," Journal of Marriage and the Family 50 (May 1988): 479, table 4. The factors considered were age, sex, ethnicity, social class, closeness to parent, parent trust, parental rules, parent strictness, etc. Age accounted for about 17 percent of the variation in drug use among the youth in their sample; positive father sentiment (closeness) accounted for another 10 percent, and no other factor accounted for more than 2 percent.

11. US Department of Justice, "What Can the Federal Government Do to Decrease Crime and Revitalize Communities?" Panel Papers, Office of Justice Programs, National Institute of Justice, 1998, 11 https://www.ncjrs.gov/pdffiles/172210.pdf.

12. APA, "Who Is Likely to Become a Bully, Victim or Both?" EurekaAlert!, July 8, 2010, http://www.eurekalert.org/pub_releases/2010-07/apa-wil070810.php.

13. Heather A. Turner, "The Effect of Lifetime Victimization on the Mental Health of Children and Adolescents," *Social Science & Medicine* 62, no. 1 (January 2006): 13–27.

14. Study employed data from the National Longitudinal Study of Adolescent Health; see Chris Knoester and Dana L Haynie, "Community Context, Social Integration into Family, and Youth Violence," *Journal of Marriage and Family* 67, no. 3 (2005): 767–80, doi:10.1111/j.1741-3737.2005.00168.x.

15. Raymond A. Knight and Robert A. Prentky, "The Developmental Antecedents of Adult Adaptions of Rapist Sub-types," *Criminal Justice and Behavior* 14, no. 4 (1987): 413–14, doi:10.1177/0093854887014004001. Knight and Prentky labeled this type of rapist as one with "displaced anger."

16. Richard V. Reeves, "Saving Horatio Alger: Equality, Opportunity, and the American Dream," Brookings Institution, Brookings Essay, August 20, 2014. See video: http://www.brookings.edu/research/essays/2014/saving-horatio-alger.

17. After adjustment for family history of hypertension, obesity, age, employment, smoking, diabetes, etc. See Todd Neale, "Two-Parent Homes Foster Lower BP in Black Males," *MedPage Today*, December 2, 2013, http://www.medpagetoday.com/Cardiology/Hypertension/43212?xid=nl_mpt_DHE_2013-12-03.

18. Mary Main and Donna R. Weston, "The Quality of the Toddler's Relationship to Mother and to Father: Related to Conflict Behavior and the Readiness to Establish New Relationships," *Child Development* 52, no. 3 (1981): 932–40, doi:10.2307/1129097.

19. Richard Koestner, C. Franz, and J. Weinberger, "The Family Origins of Empathic Concern: A Twenty-Six-Year Longitudinal Study," *Journal of Personality and Social Psychology* 58, no. 4 (April 1990): 709–17.

20. See the discussion of empathy and its connection to fathers and life's happiness in Warren Farrell, *Father and Child Reunion* (New York: Putnam/Penguin, 2001), 30–31.

21. Samantha Nazione et al., "An Experimental Study of Medical Error Explanations," *Journal of Health Communication*, Vol 20, 2015, Issue 12, p. 1422.

22. David J. Deming, "The Growing Importance of Social Skills in the Labor Market" (working paper no. 21473, National Bureau of Economic Research, August 2015), doi:10.3386/w21473.

23. US Department of Justice, "What Can the Federal Government Do?"

24. Cynthia C. Harper and Sara S. McLanahan, "Father Absence and Youth Incarceration," *Journal of Research on Adolescence* 14, no. 3 (September 2004): 369–97, doi:10.1111/j.1532-7795.2004.00079.x.

25. Sonja B. Starr, "Estimating Gender Disparities in Federal Criminal Cases," *American Law and Economics Review* 17, no. 1 (2014): 127–59, doi:10.1093/aler/ahu010.

26. Starr, "Estimating Gender Disparities."

27. Daniel Beaty, "Def Poetry: Knock Knock," YouTube video, 2:34, posted by Poetical TV, March 15, 2010, http://youtu.be/9eYH0AFx6yI.

CHAPTER 15: REDISCOVERING DAD

1. Ron L. Deal, "Marriage, Family, and Stepfamily Statistics," SmartStepfamilies, April 2014, http://www.smartstepfamilies.com/view/statistics. The document seeks to answer these questions: Why are so many statistics on divorce and remarriage dated to the 1980s and 1990s? Why don't we have more recent data? The US government (Vital Statistics) no longer tracks the trends of marriage, divorce, remarriage, and stepfamilies as they did in the past. Around 1996 they changed the marriage and family information they seek from individuals, so many statistics cannot be updated. For example, marriage licenses no longer ask if one or both partners have been previously married. It seems this data is no longer of interest to the US government.

2. US Census Bureau, "Living Arrangements of Children under 18 Years/1 and Marital Status of Parents by Age, Sex, Race, and Hispanic Origin/2 and Selected Characteristics of the Child for All Children 2010," Current Population Survey, table C3.

3. Warren Farrell, *Father and Child Reunion* (New York: Putnam/Penguin, 2001)

4. William J. Doherty, Brian J. Willoughby, and Jason L. Wilde, "Is the Gender Gap in College Enrollment Influenced by Nonmarital Birth Rates and Father Absence?" *Family Relations* 65, no. 2 (2015): 263–74, doi:10.1111/fare.12157.

5. Sara McLanahan and Gary Sandefur, *Growing Up with a Single Parent* (Cambridge, MA: Harvard University Press, 1994), 41. The four national surveys are the National Longitudinal Survey of Youth, the Panel Study of Income Dynamics, the High School and Beyond Study, and the National Survey of Families and Households. The socioeconomic variables that were controlled included race, mother's education, father's education, income, number of siblings, place of residence, and other background differences (p. 12 and appendix B).

6. Sara McLanahan, Laura Tach, and Daniel Schneider, "The Causal Effects of Father Absence," *Annual Review of Sociology* 39 (2013): 399–427, doi:10.1146/

annurev-soc-071312-145704. McLanahan is from Princeton's Office of Population Research; Tach is from Cornell's Department of Policy Analysis; and Schneider is from the Department of Sociology at UC Berkeley.

7. Bryce J. Christensen, "America's Academic Dilemma: The Family and the Schools," *Family in America* 2, no. 6, (June 1988); cited in Nicholas Davidson, "Life Without Father: America's Greatest Social Catastrophe," *Policy Review* (Winter 1990): 41.

8. Douglas A. Smith and G. Roger Jarjoura, "Social Structure and Criminal Victimization," *Journal of Research in Crime and Delinquency* 25, no. 1 (February 1988): 27–52.

9. Frank F. Furstenberg Jr. and Kathleen Mullan Harris, "When and Why Fathers Matter: Impacts of Father Involvement on the Children of Adolescent Mothers," in *Young Unwed Fathers: Changing Roles and Emerging Policies*, ed. Robert I. Lerman and Theodora J. Ooms (Philadelphia: Temple University Press, 1993), 127 and 130. The sample size of all children in this portion of the study was 253. Among the sons of inner-city teenage mothers, 15 percent had had a baby by age nineteen; none who had a close relationship with their biological father did.

10. Marianne Bertrand and Jessica Pan, "The Trouble with Boys: Social Influences and the Gender Gap in Disruptive Behavior," *American Economic Journal: Applied Economics, American Economic Association* 5, no. 1 (January 2013): 32–64.

11. J. Waldfogel, T. Craigie, and J. Brooks-Gunn, "Fragile Families and Child Wellbeing," *Future of Children* 20 (2010): 87–112. In the United States two-thirds of couples having children when they live together leave each other by the time the child reaches ten. See also Pamela Smock and Fiona Rose Greenland, "Diversity in Pathways to Parenthood: Patterns, Implications, and Emerging Research Directions," *Journal of Marriage and Family* 72, no. 3: 576–93.

12. Colter Mitchell et al., "Father Loss and Child Telomere Length," *Pediatrics* (July 2017): doi: 10.1542/peds.2016-3245.

13. Jason De Parle and Sabrina Vavernise, "For Women Under 30, Most Births Occur Outside Marriage," *New York Times*, February 17, 2012, http://www.nytimes.com/2012/02/18/us/for-women-under-30-most-births-occur-outside-marriage.html. Almost two-thirds of children in the United States are born to mothers under thirty.

14. Graph reconstructed from Jason De Parle and Sabrina Vavernise, "For Women Under 30, Most Births Occur Outside Marriage."

15. W. Bradford Wilcox, "Marriage Makes Our Children Richer—Here's Why," *Atlantic*, October 29, 2013, http://www.theatlantic.com/business/archive/2013/10/marriage-makes-our-children-richer-heres-why/280930.

16. See Child Trends, "New Brief Shows Nonmarital Childbearing Is Increasingly Common in United States," December 16, 2011, retrieved from http://archive.constant-contact.com/fs008/1101701160827/archive/1108965696926.html.

17. The Moynihan Report was published originally as *The Negro Family: The Case For National Action* in 1965.

18. See Sara McLanahan and Christopher Jecks, "Was Moynihan Right?" *Education Next* 15, no. 2 (Spring 2015): http://educationnext.org/was-moynihan-right.

19. Credit for chart from Sara McLanahan and Christopher Jecks, "Was Moynihan Right?" *Education Next* 15, no. 2 (Spring 2015). Their source is the National Center for Health Statistics, National Vital Statistics System, http://educationnext.org/was-moynihan-right.

20. Sara McLanahan and Christopher Jecks, "Was Moynihan Right?" *Education Next* 15, no. 2 (Spring 2015). Their source is the National Center for Health Statistics, National Vital Statistics System, http://educationnext.org/was-moynihan-right. See fig. 2.

21. George A. Akerlof and Janet L. Yellen, "An Analysis of Out-of-Wedlock Births in the U.S.", Brookings Institution, report, August 1, 1996, https://www.brookings.edu/research/an-analysis-of-out-of-wedlock-births-in-the-united-states.

22. Akerlof and Yellen, "Analysis of Out-of-Wedlock Births."

23. De Parle and Vavernise, "Women Under 30."

24. Richard Warshak, "Social Science and Parenting Plans for Young Children: A Consensus Report," *Psychology, Public Policy, and Law* 20 (February 2014): doi:10.1037/law0000005. For a popular summary, http://www.warshak.com/store/cr53.html.

25. Folate consumption prevents miscarriages and birth defects among human mothers. McGill University epigenetic researchers tested folate consumption among fathers and found that the father's diet *before conception* may be as important as the mother's in the health of their offspring. The study was done on mice, which share all but ten of humans' four thousand genes. R. Lambrot et al., "Low Paternal Dietary Folate Alters the Mouse Sperm Epigenome and Is Associated with Negative Pregnancy Outcomes," *Nature Communications* 4 (2013): article no. 2889, doi:10.1038/ncomms3889.

26. Rachel Levy-Shiff et al., "Fathers' Hospital Visits to their Preterm Infants as a Predictor of Father-Infant Relationship and Infant Development," *Pediatrics* 86, no. 2 (1990): 291–92. The authors are from Bar-Ilan University and Kaplan Hospital in Israel.

27. Frank A. Pedersen, Judith L. Rubenstein, and Leon J. Yarrow, "Infant Development in Father-Absent Families," *Journal of Genetic Psychology* 135 (September 1979): 55–57, doi:10.1080/00221325.1979.10533416.

28. Martin Deutsch and Bert Brown, "Social Influences in Negro-White Intelligence Differences," *Journal of Social Issues* 20, no. 2 (1964): 29.

29. Pedersen, Rubenstein, and Yarrow, "Infant Development," 55–57.

30. Kristin Berg Nordahl, "Early Father-Child Interaction in a Father-Friendly Context," (PhD thesis, Faculty of Psychology, University of Bergen, Norway, 2014). Nordahl is from the Norwegian Centre for Child Behavioural Development, Oslo.

31. Allan N. Schore, "All Our Sons: The Developmental Neurobiology and Neuroendocrinology of Boys at Risk," *Infant Mental Health Journal* 38, no. 1 (January/February 2017): 15–52, doi:10.1002/imhj.21616.

32. R. Dalton et al., "Psychiatric Hospitalization of Pre-school Children: Admission Factors and Discharge Implications," *Journal of the American Academy of Child and Adolescent Psychiatry* 26, no. 3 (May 1987): 308–12.

33. H. S. Merskey and G. T. Swart, "Family Background and Physical Health of Adolescents Admitted to an In-Patient Psychiatric Unit, I: Principal Caregivers," *Canadian Journal of Psychiatry* 34, no. 2 (1989): 79–83.

34. Nicholas Davidson, "Life Without Father: America's Greatest Social Catastrophe," *Policy Review* 51 (Winter, 1990): 42.

35. Zahn-Waxler, E. A. Shirtcliff, and K. Marceau, "Disorders of Childhood and Adolescence: Gender and Psychopathology," *Annual Review of Clinical Psychology* 4 (2008): 275–303, doi:10.1146/annurev.clinpsy.3.022806.091358.

36. Nobel laureate James Heckman, "Heckman Study: High Quality Early Childhood Education Provides Salient Benefits to Low-Income Children and Mothers," University of Chicago, Department of Economics, April 24, 2017, https://economics.uchicago.edu/blog/heckman-study-high-quality-early-childhood-education-provides-salient-benefits-low-income.

37. Schore, "All Our Sons."

38. Ed Tronick, *The Neurobehavioral and Social-Emotional Development of Infants and Children* (New York: W. W. Norton, 2007), 340 and 345.

39. Claire Cain Miller, "How Child Care Enriches Mothers, and Especially the Sons They Raise," *New York Times*, April 20, 2017, https://www.nytimes.com/2017/04/20/upshot/how-child-care-enriches-mothers-and-especially-the-sons-they-raise.html.

40. Heckman, "Heckman Study."

41. Credit to Chandler Arnold for gathering some of the research in this section, "Children of Stepfamilies: A Snapshot" (paper, Center for Law and Social Policy, November 1998), https://www.clasp.org/sites/default/files/public/resources-and-publications/archive/0028.pdf.

42. E. Mavis Hetherington and Kathleen M. Jodl, "Stepfamilies as Settings for Child Development," in *Stepfamilies: Who Benefits? Who Does Not?*, ed. Alan Booth and Judy Dunn, (Hillsdale, NJ: Lawrence Erlbaum, 1994).

43. Mary Parke, "Are Married Parents Really Better for Children? What Research Says About the Effects of Family Structure on Child Well-Being" (brief, Couples and Married Research and Policy, Center for Law and Social Policy, Washington, DC, May 2003), http://files.eric.ed.gov/fulltext/ED476114.pdf.

44. S. C. Risch, K. M. Jodi, and J. S. Eccles, "Role of the Father-Adolescent Relationship in Shaping Adolescents' Attitudes," *Journal of Marriage and the Family* 66, no. 1 (2004): 46-58.

45. Hetherington and Jodl, "Stepfamilies as Settings for Child Development."

46. Dr. E. Mavis Hetherington, principal researcher of the Virginia Longitudinal Study of Divorce and Remarriage and coauthor with John Kelly of *For Better or For Worse: Divorce Reconsidered* (New York, W. W. Norton, 2003). Dr. Hetherington gives the divorce rate for stepcouples as "50 percent higher in remarriages with stepchildren" (p. 178). Specifically, then, the divorce rate is 65–70 percent. The Virginia Longitudinal Study does not consist of a nationally representative sample but is a broader representation of stepfamilies in the United States than other previous research.

47. D. R. Morrison et al., eds., *Parent-Child Relations and Investments of Parental Time in Children* (Washington, DC: Child Trends, 1994).

48. Paul Glick, "Remarriage: Some Recent Changes and Variations," *Journal of Family Issues* 1, no. 4 (1980): 455–78.

49. Kathryn Harker Tillman, "Family Structure Pathways and Academic Disadvantage Among Adolescents in Stepfamilies," *Sociological Inquiry* 77, no. 3 (2007): 383–424, doi:10.1111/j.1475-682X.2007.00198.x.

50. Nan Marie Astone and Sara S. McLanahan, "Family Structure, Residential Mobility, and School Dropout: A Research Note," *Demography* 31, no. 4 (November 1994): 575–83.

51. Heather A. Turner, "The Effect of Lifetime Victimization on the Mental Health of Children and Adolescents," *Social Science & Medicine* 62, no. 1 (January 2006): 13–27.

52. Cynthia C. Harper and Sara S. McLanahan, "Father Absence and Youth Incarceration," *Journal of Research on Adolescence* 14, no. 3 (September 2004): 369–97, doi:10.1111/j.1532-7795.2004.00079.x.

53. Jimi Adams and Ryan Light, "Scientific Consensus, the Law, and Same Sex Parenting Outcomes," *Social Science Research* 53 (September 2015): 300–310, doi:10.1016/j.ssresearch.2015.06.008.

54. Mark Regnerus, "How Different Are the Adult Children of Parents Who Have Same-Sex Relationships? Findings from the New Family Structures Study," *Social Science Research* 41, no. 4 (July 2012): 752–70, http://www.sciencedirect.com/science/article/pii/S0049089X12000610; Loren Marks, "Same-Sex Parenting and Children's Outcomes: A Closer Examination of the American Psychological Association's Brief on Lesbian and Gay Parenting," *Social Science Research* 41, no. 4 (July 2012): 735–51, http://www.sciencedirect.com/science/article/pii/S0049089X12000580.

55. See Jeannette Lofas's interview with Larry Bilotta of Relationship Revelation Radio, Stepfamily Foundation, July 15, 2015, http://www.stepfamily.org/blog/dr-lofas-interview-on-same-sex-couples-and-remarriage.

56. Elizabeth Marquardt et al., "My Daddy's Name is Donor," (report, Institute for American Values, New York, 2010), http://americanvalues.org/catalog/pdfs/Donor_FINAL.pdf.

CHAPTER 16: WHAT DADS DO DIFFERENTLY

1. Richard Fletcher, University of Newcastle, Australia, and others, as cited in Sue Shellenbarger, "Roughhousing Lessons from Dad: Fathers Teach Risk-Taking, Boundary-Setting; Learning From 'Sock Wrestling,'" *Wall Street Journal*, June 11, 2014, http://online.wsj.com/news/article_email/rough-housing-lessons-from-dad-1402444262-lMyQjAxMTA0MDEwMTExNDEy W.j

2. Mogens Nygaard Christoffersen, "An Investigation of Fathers with 3 – 5-Year-Old Children" (paper presented at the Social Research-Institute, Ministerratskonferenz,

Stockholm, Sweden, April 27–28, 1995), chart 2, "Parents Living Alone with 3- to 5-Year-Old Children."

3. Mary Jo Coiro, Nicholas Zill, and Barbara Bloom, "Health of Our Nation's Children," US Department of Health and Human Services, National Center for Health Statistics, Centers for Disease Control and Prevention, *Vital and Health Statistics*, series 10, no. 191, December 1994. The National Health Interview Survey is based on a US Census Bureau sample of over 122,000 individuals, including over 17,000 children (table 16, p. 49). Nine percent of children with only biological fathers have late or irregular bedtimes; 33 percent of children with only biological mothers had late or irregular bedtimes.

4. Christoffersen, " Investigation of Fathers," chart 3.

5. University of Chicago, "Becoming a Man," Crime Lab, 2012, https://crimelab.uchicago.edu/page/becoming-man-bam-sports-edition-findings.

6. Richard Koestner, C. Franz, and J. Weinberger, "The Family Origins of Empathic Concern: A Twenty-Six-Year Longitudinal Study," *Journal of Personality and Social Psychology* 58, no. 4 (April 1990): 709–17.

7. D. A. Luepnitz, *Child Custody* (Lexington, MA: D. C. Heath, 1982); cited in Richard A. Warshak, "Father Custody and Child Development: A Review and Analysis of Psychological Research," *Behavioral Sciences and the Law* 4, no.2 (1986): 192.

8. Christoffersen, "Investigation of Fathers," chart 2.

9. Coiro, Zill, and Bloom, "Health of Our Nation's Children," table 13, p. 43.

10. Warren Farrell, *Father and Child Reunion* (NY: Putnam/Penguin, 2001).

11. "Saddest Boy Ever," excerpted from *The Jenny Jones Show*, "Boot Camp My Pre-teen" (1998), YouTube video, 0:38, posted by Patrick, December 10, 2011, http://youtu.be/gVXXDtWtHDY.

12. "Saddest Boy Ever."

13. D. A. Luepnitz, *Child Custody*, 112–25.

14. E. M. Hetherington, "Divorce: A Child's Perspective," *American Psychologist* 34, no. 10 (1979): 831–58.

15. Richard A. Warshak, "Father Custody and Child Development: A Review and Analysis of Psychological Research," *Behavioral Sciences & the Law* 4, no. 2 (1986): 190.

16. John Simmons, "IBM Says No to Home Work," *Wall Street Journal*, May 19, 2017, p. A1.

17. Daniel Paquette, University of Montreal, cited in in Sue Shellenbarger, "Roughhousing Lessons from Dad."

18. Shellenbarger, "Roughhousing Lessons from Dad."

19. Shellenbarger, "Roughhousing Lessons from Dad."

20. Shellenbarger, "Roughhousing Lessons from Dad."

21. Nadya Pancsofar and Lynne Vernon-Feagans, "Mother and Father Language Input to Young Children: Contributions to Later Language Development," *Journal of Applied Developmental Psychology* 27, no. 6 (2006): 571–87, doi:10.1016/j.appdev.2006.08.003.

22. Fletcher, University of Newcastle, Australia, and others, as cited in Shellenbarger, "Roughhousing Lessons from Dad."

23. K. Alison Clarke-Stewart and Craig Hayward, "Advantages of Father Custody and Contact for the Psychological Well-Being of School-Age Children," *Journal of Applied Developmental Psychology* 17, no. 2 (April–June 1996): 239–70, doi:10.1016/S0193-3973(96)90027-1.

24. For more on girls' safety with bio dads—and usually, but not as certainly, with stepdads—see Warren Farrell, *Father and Child Reunion.*

25. Dacher Keltner, "In Defense of Teasing," *New York Times Magazine*, December 5, 2008. See http://www.nytimes.com/2008/12/07/magazine/07teasing-t.html.

26. Janet Reitman, "How the Death of a Muslim Recruit Revealed a Culture of Brutality in the Marines," *New York Times Magazine*, July 6, 2017, https://www.nytimes.com/2017/07/06/magazine/how-the-death-of-a-muslim-recruit-revealed-a-culture-of-brutality-in-the-marines.html.

27. Pew Research Center, "Women Call the Shots at Home; Public Mixed on Gender Roles in Jobs," Social & Demographic Trends, September 25, 2008, http://www.pewsocialtrends.org/2008/09/25/women-call-the-shots-at-home-public-mixed-on-gender-roles-in-jobs.

28. Marcus Hamilton, July 2014, copyright 2015 by North American Syndicate.

29. Pew Research Center, "Women Call the Shots at Home; Public Mixed on Gender Roles in Jobs."

CHAPTER 17: IN THE EVENT OF DIVORCE . . . THE FOUR "MUST-DOS"

1. Paul Amato and Joan Gilbreth, "Nonresident Fathers and Children's Wellbeing: A Meta-analysis," *Journal of Marriage and the Family* 61, no. 3 (1999): 557–73, doi:10.2307/353560.

2. Michael E. Lamb, "Divorce and Parenting," in *Encyclopedia of Applied Developmental Science*, ed. C. B. Fisher and R. M. Lerner (New York: Sage, 2004), 794–96; as cited in William V. Fabricius et al., "Custody and Parenting Time: Links to Family Relationships and Well-Being After Divorce," in *The Role of the Father in Child Development*, 5th ed., ed. Michael E. Lamb (Hoboken, NJ: John Wiley & Sons, 2010).

3. Robert Bauserman, "Child Adjustment in Joint-Custody Versus Sole-Custody Arrangements: A Meta-analytic Review," *Journal of Family Psychology* 16, no. 1 (2002): 91–102; as cited in Fabricius, "Custody and Parenting Time."

4. Bauserman, "Child Adjustment."

5. Richard A. Warshak, "Social Science and Parenting Plans for Young Children: A Consensus Report," *Psychology, Public Policy, and Law* 20, no. 1 (2014): 46–67, doi:10.1037/law0000005.

6. Michael E. Lamb, K. J. Sternberg, and R. A. Thompson, "The Effects of Divorce and Custody Arrangements on Children's Behavior, Development, and Adjustment," *Family and Conciliation Courts Review* 35, no. 4 (1997): 393–404; as cited in Fabricius, "Custody and Parenting Time."

7. B. Jablonska and L. Lindberg, "Risk Behaviours, Victimisation and Mental Distress Among Adolescents in Different Family Structures," *Social Psychiatry and Psychiatric Epidemiology* 42, no. 8 (August 2007): 656–63, doi:10.1007/s00127-007-0210-3. The study was of 12,582 fifteen year olds.

8. Emma Fransson et. al., "Why should they live more with one of us when they are children to us both?" *Children and Youth Services Review* 66 (July 2016): 154–60, doi:10.1016/j.childyouth.2016.05.011.

9. In the United States the term *joint custody* does not necessarily imply equal time, just a sharing of major decisions; in Sweden joint parental custody means an approximately 50-50 arrangement of time.

10. M. Bergström, B. Modin, et al., "Living in Two Homes: A Swedish National Survey of Wellbeing in 12 and 15 Year Olds with Joint Physical Custody," *BMC Public Health* 13 (September 2013): 868.

11. Malin Bergström, "Mental Health and Wellbeing in Children in Shared Parenting and Other Living Arrangements" (presentation, Center for Health Equity Studies, Sweden, October 2014), http://www.divorcecorp.com/wp-content/uploads/2014/11/Mental-Health-Wellbeing-in-Different-Living-Arrangements_Malin-Bergstrom.pdf.

12. Bergström et al., "Living in Two Homes."

13. E. M. Hetherington, M. Cox, and R. Cox, "Effects of Divorce on Parents and Children," in *Non-traditional Families*, ed. M. Lamb (Hillsdale, NJ: Lawrence Erlbaum, 1982), 233–88; Judith Wallerstein and Joan B. Kelly, *Surviving the Breakup* (NY: Basic Books, 1980); and John W. Santrock and Richard A. Warshak, "The Impact of Divorce in Father-Custody and Mother-Custody Homes: The Child's Perspective," in *Children and Divorce*, ed. L. A. Kurdek (San Francisco: Jossey-Bass, 1983).

14. Hetherington, Cox, and Cox, "Effects of Divorce"; Wallerstein and Kelly, *Surviving the Breakup*; and Santrock and Warshak, "Impact of Divorce."

15. Hetherington, Cox, and Cox, "Effects of Divorce"; Wallerstein and Kelly, *Surviving the Breakup*; and Santrock and Warshak, "Impact of Divorce."

16. D. A. Luepnitz, "Maternal, Paternal, and Joint Custody: A Study of Families After Divorce" (PhD dissertation, State University of New York, Buffalo, 1980).

17. Paula M. Raines, "Joint Custody and the Right to Travel: Legal and Psychological Implications," *Journal of Family Law* 24 (June 1986): 625–56.

18. E. G. Pojman, "Emotional Adjustment of Boys in Sole Custody and Joint Custody Compared with Adjustment of Boys in Happy and Unhappy Marriages" (PhD dissertation, California Graduate Institute, Los Angeles, 1982).

19. Jablonska and Lindberg, "Risk Behaviours," 656–63.

20. Margaret Crosbie-Burnett, "Impact of Joint vs. Sole Custody and Quality of Coparental Relationship on Adjustment of Adolescents in Remarried Families," *Behavioral Sciences & the Law* 9, no. 4 (Fall 1991): 439–49, doi:10.1002/bsl.2370090407.

21. E. B. Karp, "Children's Adjustment in Joint and Single Custody: An Empirical Study" (PhD dissertation, California School of Professional Psychology, Berkeley, CA, 1982).

22. Luepnitz, "Joint Custody."

23. Shirley M. H. Hanson, "Healthy Single Parent Families," *Family Relations* 35, no. 1 (1986): 131, doi:10.2307/584291.

24. Based on responses from moms in parenting workshops designed to sustain the progress their sons had made in Young Men's Ultimate Weekend, 2010–17. YMUW was founded by Mark Schillinger. Workshops conducted by Mark and his partner, Rochelle Newman.

25. Linda Nielsen, "Shared Physical Custody: Summary of 40 Studies on Outcomes for Children," *Journal of Divorce and Remarriage* 55, no. 8 (2014): 613–35, doi:10.108 0/10502556.2014.965578.

26. Malin Bergström et al., "Fifty Moves a Year: Is There an Association Between Joint Physical Custody and Psychosomatic Problems in Children?" *Journal of Epidemiology & Community Health* 69, no. 8 (April 2015): 769–74, doi:10.1136/ jech-2014-205058.

27. "Warren Farrell Speaks in Toronto: Transforming the Boys Crisis," YouTube video, 2:30:36, Canadian Association for Equality, November, 23, 2012, https://www.you-tube.com/watch?v=P6w1S8yrFz4.

28. Personal correspondence, January 11, 2013; the author's name has been changed and emphasis added.

29. Glynnis Walker, *Solomon's Children* (New York: Arbor House, 1986), 27 and 84–85.

30. K. Alison Clarke-Stewart and Craig Hayward, "Advantages of Father Custody and Contact for the Psychological Well-Being of School-Age Children," *Journal of Applied Developmental Psychology* 17, no. 2 (April–June 1996): 239–70, doi:10.1016/ S0193-3973(96)90027-1.

31. Mogens Nygaard Christoffersen, "An Investigation of Fathers with 3 – 5-Year-Old Children" (paper presented at the Social Research-Institute, Ministerratskonferenz, Stockholm, Sweden, April 27–28, 1995), chart 2, "Parents Living Alone with 3- to 5-Year-Old Children," chart 4, "Psychosomatic Symptoms and Select Background Situations of the Parents."

32. Christoffersen, "Investigation of Fathers."

33. See Richard A. Warshak, *Divorce Poison*, rev. ed., (New York: Harper Collins, 2010).

34. Sara McLanahan and Gary Sandefur, *Growing Up with a Single Parent*, (Cambridge: Harvard University Press, 1997).

35. P. A. Cowan, C. P. Cowan, and J. Barry, "Couples' Groups for Parents of Preschoolers: Ten-Year Outcomes of a Randomized Trial," *Journal of Family Psychology* 25, no. 2 (2011): 240–50, doi:10.1037/a0023003.

36. Marianne Bertrand and Jessica Pan, "The Trouble with Boys: Social Influences and the Gender Gap in Disruptive Behavior," *American Economic Journal: Applied Economics*, 5(1) (2013): 32–64, doi: 10.1257/app.5.1.32.

37. David Autor et al., "Family Disadvantage and the Gender Gap in Behavioral and Educational Outcomes" (working paper no. 22267, National Bureau of Economic Research, May 2016), doi:10.3386/w22267.

38. Jablonska and Lindberg, "Risk Behaviours," 656–63. The study involved 12,582 fifteen-year-olds.

39. Pew Research analysis of decennial census and American community survey, cited in Gretchen Livingston, "The Rise of Single Fathers: A Ninefold Increase Since 1960," Pew Research Center, July 2, 2013, http://www.pewsocialtrends.org/2013/07/02/the-rise-of-single-fathers.

40. Pew analysis of decennial census, cited in Livingston, "Rise of Single Fathers: A Ninefold Increase Since 1960."

41. John W. Santrock and Richard A. Warshak: "Father Custody and Social Development in Boys and Girls," *Journal of Social Issues* 35, no. 4 (Fall 1979): 112–25, doi:10.1111/j.1540-4560.1979.tb00816.x.

42. Kyle D. Pruett, "The Nurturing Male: A Longitudinal Study of Primary Nurturing Fathers," in *Fathers and Their Families*, ed. Stanley H. Cath, Alan Gurwitt, and Linda Gunsberg (Hillsdale, NJ: Analytic Press, 1989), 390. The study finding that 30 percent of children living with moms and 15 percent living with dads had concentration problems was of 1,200 children aged three to five.

43. Among children with their fathers, 3 percent felt victimized, compared to 10 percent of children with their mothers. Christoffersen, "Investigation of Fathers," chart 3. Translated by David Bedard. E-mail, March 12, 1997. Dr. Christoffersen is with the Social Research Institute in Denmark. The study is especially significant because it examined more than one-quarter of all the three- to five-year-old children in Denmark who lived with their biological fathers (600 out of 2,040). The study compared these children to a group of about 600 (out of 33,708) living with their biological mothers.

44. Pruett, "Nurturing Male," 390.

45. Pruett, "Nurturing Male," 390.

46. Pruett, "Nurturing Male," 390.

47. Jablonska and Lindberg, "Risk Behaviours," 656–63.

48. K. Alison Clarke-Stewart and Craig Hayward, "Advantages of Father Custody and Contact for the Psychological Well-Being of School-Age Children," *Journal of Applied Developmental Psychology* 17, no. 2 (April–June, 1996): 239–70, doi:10.1016/S0193-3973(96)90027-1.

49. Douglas B. Downey and Brian Powell, "Do Children in Single-Parent Households Fare Better Living with Same-Sex Parent?" *Journal of Marriage and the Family* 55, no. 1 (February 1993): 55–71, doi:10.2307/352959.

50. Psychological well-being was determined by tests of self-esteem, adjustment, mood, and lack of depression. Clarke-Stewart and Hayward, "Advantages of Father," 257–58 (including table 4).

51. Mary Jo Coiro, Nicholas Zill, and Barbara Bloom, "Health of Our Nation's Children," US Department of Health and Human Services, National Center for Health Statistics, Centers for Disease Control and Prevention, *Vital and Health Statistics*, series 10, no. 191, December 1994.

52. Richard A. Warshak, "Father Custody and Child Development: A Review and Analysis of Psychological Research," *Behavioral Sciences & the Law* 4, no. 2 (1986): 190.

53. Betty Friedan, *The Feminine Mystique* (New York: W.W. Norton, 1963).

54. Augustine J. Kposowa, "Marital Status and Suicide in the National Longitudinal Mortality Study," *Journal of Epidemiology and Community Health* 54, no. 4 (2000): 254–61, doi:10.1136/jech.54.4.254.

55. Michael Weitzman, David G. Rosenthal, and Ying-Hua Liu, "Paternal Depressive Symptoms and Child Behavioral or Emotional Problems in the United States," *Pediatrics* 128, no. 6 (November 2011): 1126–34, doi:10.1016/j.yped.2012.04.001.

CHAPTER 18: THE FATHER WARRIOR: WHY FATHERING WILL BE A NEW MALE SENSE OF PURPOSE

1. See Warren Farrell, *Why Men Earn More: The Startling Truth Behind the Pay Gap—and What Women Can Do About It* (New York: AMACOM, 2005); and also the US Census Bureau's Survey of Income and Program Participation, 2001 Panel, Wave 2. The exact median earnings for the women are $46,896; for the men, $39,996. Latest available data as of 2004.

2. See Farrell, *Why Men Earn More.*

3. See Farrell, *Why Men Earn More.*

4. Robert M. Sapolsky, *Behave* (New York: Penguin Press, 2017). See discussion of study of parole officers who offered parole 60 percent of the time after lunch, versus 0 percent of the time before lunch.

5. Michael Alison Chandler, "On This List of the 50 Best Places to Work for New Dads, Netflix Leads the Pack," *Washington Post*, May 2, 2017, https://www.washingtonpost.com/news/inspired-life/wp/2017/05/02/theres-a-new-best-places-to-work-list-this-time-its-for-dads.

CHAPTER 19: DAD: DISCRIMINATION AGAINST DADS

1. Brigid Schulte, "Don't Call them Mr. Mom: More Dads at Home with Kids Because They Want to Be," *Washington Post*, June 5, 2014, https://www.washingtonpost.com/news/parenting/wp/2014/06/05/dads-who-stay-home-because-they-want-to-has-increased-four-fold.

2. Hani Nouman, Guy Enosh, and Pnina Niselbaum-Atzur, "The Role of Parental Communication, Child's Wishes and Child's Gender in Social Workers' Custody Recommendations," *Children and Youth Services Review* 70 (November 2016): 302–8, doi:10.1016/j.childyouth.2016.09.034.

3. See also Paul Raeburn, *Do Fathers Matter?: What Science is Telling Us About the Parent We've Overlooked* (New York: Scientific American, 2014), p. 233, citing a National Organization for Women link to a website that lists as the number one *myth* that "a father's involvement is crucial for the well-being of a child."

4. Brianna Neese is open to developing ways of using *The Boy Crisis* to counter the boy crisis. You may contact her at chantebrie@gmail.com.

5. See Raeburn, *Do Fathers Matter?*

6. Kim Parker and Wendy Wang, "Modern Parenthood: Roles of Moms and Dads Converge as They Balance Work and Family" (report, Pew Research Social and Demographic Trends, Washington, DC, 2013), q. 44; based on fathers with children under eighteen.

7. Elaine Sorensen, Lilliana Sousa, and Simone G. Schaner, "Assessing Child Support Arrears in Nine Large States and the Nation," (report, Urban Institute, July 11, 2007), 11, https://www.urban.org/sites/default/files/publication/29736/1001242-Assessing-Child-Support-Arrears-in-Nine-Large-States-and-the-Nation.PDF.

8. Taylor Weatherby, "Woman's Ultrasound Goes Terribly Wrong in Hilarious Doritos Super Bowl Ad," Hollywood Life, February 7, 2016, http://hollywoodlife.com/2016/02/07/doritos-super-bowl-commercial-2016-superbowl-ad-video-ultrasound.

9. Weatherby, "Doritos Super Bowl Ad."

CHAPTER 20: THE BEST PARENT IS BOTH PARENTS, *BUT* . . .

1. Warren Farrell, "Couples' Communication," http://warrenfarrell.com/couples-communication.

2. Joan C. Williams, "Why Men Work So Many Hours," *Harvard Business Review*, May 29, 2013, https://hbr.org/2013/05/why-men-work-so-many-hours. These statistics are from special tabulations of data from the US Census Bureau's 2011 American Community Survey. Since 2011 the trend for moms of young children to be working outside the home has been reversing.

3. "The Best Parent is Both Parents" was the motto of the Children's Rights Council, and also the title of a book by its late director, David Levy. This section title honors his memory.

4. Michael Gurian, *Saving Our Sons* (Spokane, WA: Gurian Institute Press, 2017).

5. Families and Work Institute, http://familiesandwork.fgmmedia.com/.

6. Warren Farrell, *Why Men Earn More: The Startling Truth Behind the Pay Gap—and What Women Can Do About It* (New York: Putnam/Penguin, 2005).

7. Annie E. Casey Foundation, "Double Jeopardy: How Third Grade Reading Skills and Poverty Influence High School Graduation," 2011, http://www.aecf.org/resources/double-jeopardy/.

8. CBS News, "A Young Boy's Yardwork," *CBS Sunday Morning*, October 15, 2017, https://www.cbsnews.com/videos/a-young-boys-yardwork.

9. See www.aarp.org/experience-corps.

10. Tufts University study funded by the John Templeton Foundation, 2015. See "Tufts University Study Finds Boy Scouts Builds Positive Character," Scouting Newsroom, October 21, 2015, http://www.scoutingnewsroom.org/press-releases/tufts-university-study-finds-boy-scouts-builds-positive-character.

11. Boy Scouts of America, "Tufts University Study Finds Boy Scouts Builds Positive Character," Scouting Newsroom, October 21, 2015, http://www.scoutingnewsroom.org/press-releases/tufts-university-study-finds-boy-scouts-builds-positive-character.

12. See mankindproject.org.

13. See www.challengingteenagesons.com/Public/RightWayMethod/YoungMens UltimateWeekend.

14. Contact Brad Leslie at ymaw.com/contact.

15. Contact Cameron Withey at cameron@riteofpassagejourneys.org.

16. Nicholas Zill, "How Adopted Children Fare in Middle School," Institute for Family Studies, December 2, 2015, https://ifstudies.org/blog/how-adopted-children-fare-in-middle-school.

17. Steve Hartman, "Bachelor Detective Takes On Case of Two Pittsburgh Boys," CBS News, December 25, 2015, http://www.cbsnews.com/news/bachelor-detective-takes-on-case-of-two-pittsburgh-boys.

18. Nicholas Zill, "How Adopted Children Fare in Middle School," Institute for Family Studies, December 2, 2015, https://ifstudies.org/blog/how-adopted-children-fare-in-middle-school.

19. Interview with Dr. Vanessa Dahn, founder of Safe Landing, Colorado, September 13, 2016. Safe Landing is an alternative foster care home that prioritizes affection over medication, and emphasizes each of these characteristics.

20. Credit to Dan Gobunow, personal conversation, 2016.

CHAPTER 21: FROM "CULTURAL SHRUG" TO CULTURAL SHIFT

1. Executive Office of the President of the United States, "Economic Costs of Youth Disadvantage and High-Return Opportunities for Change," (final report, My Brother's Keeper, Washington, DC, July 2015), https://obamawhitehouse.archives.gov/sites/default/files/docs/mbk_report_final_update1.pdf.

2. Paul Amato and Joan Gilbreth. "Nonresident Fathers and Children's Wellbeing: A Meta-analysis," *Journal of Marriage and the Family* 61, no. 3 (1999): 557–73, doi:10.2307/353560.

3. In 2015 a stranger's cell phone video allowed the world to witness Officer Michael Slager murder unarmed Walter Scott. See Michael S. Schmidt and Matt Apuzzo, "South Carolina Officer Is Charged with Murder of Walter Scott," *New York Times*, April 7, 2015, http://www.nytimes.com/2015/04/08/us/south-carolina-officer-is-charged-with-murder-in-black-mans-death.html.

4. Associated Press, "A Look at Key Players in The Fatal Shooting of Black Man by White Officer in South Carolina," *Fox News*, April 9, 2015, http://www.foxnews.com/us/2015/04/09/look-at-key-players-in-fatal-shooting-black-man-by-white-officer-in-south.html.

5. Brief of Elizabeth G. Patterson and South Carolina Appleseed Legal Justice Center as Amici Curiae in Support of Petitioner, Michael D. Turner v. Rebecca L. Rogers, 131 S.Ct. 2507 (2011) (No. 10-10), http://www.americanbar.org/content/dam/aba/publishing/preview/publiced_preview_briefs_pdfs_2010_2011_10_10_PetitionerAmCuEPattersonandtheSCAppleseed.authcheckdam.pdf. Elizabeth G. Patterson

is the former director of the South Carolina Department of Social Services and a University of South Carolina law professor.

6. Brief of Patterson for Petitioner, Turner v. Rogers, 131 S.Ct. 2507 (2011) (No. 10-10).

7. Brief of Patterson for Petitioner, Turner v. Rogers, 131 S.Ct. 2507 (2011) (No. 10-10).

8. Kim Parker and Wendy Wang, "Modern Parenthood: Roles of Moms and Dads Converge as They Balance Work and Family" (report, Pew Research Social and Demographic Trends, Washington, DC, 2013), q. 44; based on fathers with children under eighteen.

9. "Federal Funding Comparison FY 2013 to FY 2016 Federal Funding," (summary table, US Department of Health and Human Services, 2015) http://www.ncsc.org/~/media/Files/PDF/Services%20and%20Experts/Government%20Relations/FY%20 2015%20and%20FY%202016%20Comparison%20for%20HHS-Feb17-15.

10. Phone Interview with First Things First director, Julie Baumgardner, April 8, 2016.

11. Phone Interview with First Things First director, Julie Baumgardner, April 8, 2016.

12. Steven L. Nock and Christopher J. Einolf, "The One Hundred Billion Dollar Man: The Annual Public Costs of Father Absence" (report, National Fatherhood Initiative, Germantown, MD, June 2008), 1–14, https://www.hud.gov/sites/documents/100_BILLION_DOLLAR_MAN.PDF. For a summary, see the executive summary on p. 3.

13. Nock and Einolf, "Hundred Billion Dollar Man," 1–14.

14. USDA. "WIC Participant and Program Characteristics 2014: Food Package Report," https://www.fns.usda.gov/wic/wic-participant-and-program-characteristics-2014 -food-package-report.

15. Christian Henrichson and Ruth Delaney, "The Price of Prisons: What Incarceration Costs Taxpayers" (report, Center on Sentencing and Corrections, Vera Institute of Justice, New York, updated July 2012), http://www.vera.org/sites/default/files/resources/downloads/price-of-prisons-updated-version-021914.pdf.

16. Henrichson and Delaney, "Price of Prisons."

17. Heather Zaveri et al., "Parents and Children Together: Design and Implementation of Responsible Fatherhood Programs" (OPRE Report 2015–76, US Department of Health and Human Services, Washington, DC, September 2015), http://www.acf.hhs. gov/sites/default/files/opre/pact_initial_rf_implementation_report_9_11_15_508b. pdf.

18. Steven Block et al., "A Mixed-Method Assessment of a Parenting program for Incarcerated Fathers," *Journal of Correctional Education* 65, no. 1 (2014): 50–67.

19. Dave Philipps, "Father's History Could Offer Insight into Mind of Las Vegas Gunman," *New York Times*, October 13, 2017, https://www.nytimes.com/2017/10/13/us/stephen-paddock-father-vegas.html.

20. Philipps, "Mind of Las Vegas Gunman."

21. Philipps, "Mind of Las Vegas Gunman."

22. Philipps, "Mind of Las Vegas Gunman."

23. Philipps, "Mind of Las Vegas Gunman."

24. Philipps, "Mind of Las Vegas Gunman."

25. Simon Chapman et al., "Association Between Gun Law Reforms and Intentional Firearm Deaths in Australia, 1979–2013," *JAMA* 316, no. 3 (July 2016): 291–9, doi:10.1001/jama.2016.8752.
26. Chapman et al., "Gun Law Reforms in Australia."
27. Fiona MacDonald, "Massive Study of Australia's Gun Laws Shows One Thing: They Work," *Science Alert*, June 23, 2016, http://www.sciencealert. com/20-year-review-of-australia-s-gun-laws-has-one-clear-finding-they-work.
28. Simon Chapman et al., "Gun Law Reforms in Australia."

CHAPTER 23: HEROIC INTELLIGENCE VERSUS HEALTH INTELLIGENCE

1. National Center for Health Statistics, CDC, *National Vital Statistics Reports* 64, no. 2 (2016): table B, "Number of Deaths, Percentage of Total Deaths, Death Rates, and Age-Adjusted Death Rates for 2013, Percentage Change in Age-Adjusted Death Rates in 2013 from 2012, and Ratio of Age-Adjusted Death Rates by Sex and by Race for the 15 Leading Causes of Death for the Total Population in 2013: United States," p. 5.
2. National Center for Health Statistics, *National Vital Statistics Reports* 64, no. 2 (2016): table B, p. 5.
3. E. Arias, B. L. Rostron, and B. Tejada-Vera, "United States life tables, 2005," *National Vital Statistics Reports* 58, no 10 (Hyattsville, MD: National Center for Health Statistics, 2010), table 12, "Estimated Life Expectancy at Birth in Years, by Race and Sex: Death-Registration States, 1900–1928, and United States, 1929–2000."
4. "World Health Statistics 2016: Monitoring health for the SDGs Annex B: Tables of Health Statistics by Country, WHO Region and Globally," World Health Organization, 2016.
5. "World Health Statistics 2016: Monitoring Health," WHO.
6. M. Planty et al., *The Condition of Education 2009* (report, NCES 2009-081, US Department of Education, Institute of Education Sciences, 2009), 118, http:// nces. ed.gov/pubs2009/2009081.pdf.
7. Planty et al., *Condition of Education 2009*, 118.
8. Nikita Coulombe, "Disney Sucks, but We're Also Hypocrites," *Medium*, May 17, 2017, https://medium.com/@NikitaCcoulombe/ disney-sucks-but-were-also-hypocrites-e5e1e184ce17.
9. Coulombe, "Disney Sucks."
10. Kenneth Wetcher, Art Barker, and P. Rex McCaughtry, *Save the Males: Why Men Are Mistreated, Misdiagnosed, and Misunderstood* (Summit, NJ: Psychiatric Institutes of America Press, 1991).
11. "Why Men Are Readmitted to Hospitals More than Women," *Stone Hearth News* (blog), April 18, 2012, http://web.archive.org/ web/20120430102049/http://www.stonehearthnewsletters.com:80/ why-men-are-readmitted-to-hospitals-more-than-women/health-care-costs-2.

12. "Why Men Are Readmitted."

13. Matt McGrath, "Men May Have Evolved Better 'Making Up' Skills," Science and Environment, BBC News, August 4, 2016, http://www.bbc.com/news/science-environment-36969103.

14. Peter Reuell, "Resolving Conflict: Men vs. Women," Harvard Gazette, August 8, 2016, http://news.harvard.edu/gazette/story/2016/08/resolving-conflict-men-vs-women.

15. Interview with Vanessa Dahn, September 13, 2016, referring to what she often heard from the biological parent (usually the mom) of children who eventually entered her foster home. Dr. Dahn is the founder of Safe Landing, an alternative foster care home in Colorado.

16. Charlotte England, "Doctors in Denmark Want to Stop Circumcision for Under-18s," *Independent*, December 7, 2016, http://www.independent.co.uk/news/world/europe/denmark-considering-banning-circumcision-for-children-under-18s-a7459291.html.

17. Maasai Association, "Maasai Ceremonies and Rituals: Circumcision," accessed December 17, 2016. http://www.maasai-association.org/ceremonies.html

18. Dan Bollinger and Robert S. Van Howe, "Alexithymia and Circumcision Trauma: A Preliminary Investigation," *International Journal of Men's Health* 10, no. 2 (Summer 2011): 184–195.

19. Bollinger and Van Howe, "Alexithymia and Circumcision Trauma," 184-195.

20. See Ronald Goldman, *Circumcision: The Hidden Trauma* (Boston: Vanguard Publications: 1997).

21. Jesse Mez et al., "Clinicopathological Evaluation of Chronic Traumatic Encephalopathy in Players of American Football," *JAMA* 318, no. 4 (July 2017): 360–70, doi:10.1001/jama.2017.8334.

22. Jesse Mez et al., "Traumatic Encephalopathy in Football."

23. Steven Reinberg, "High School Football Players Suffer More Symptoms After Concussion: Study," *Health Day*, May 2, 1016, https://consumer.healthday.com/cognitive-health-information-26/concussions-news-733/high-school-footballers-don-t-recover-as-quickly-from-concussions-as-college-players-710559.html.

24. Reinberg, "More Symptoms After Concussion."

25. Prevacus, "Statistics: Concussion Rate Doubled in Decade," Concussions 101, accessed November 2, 2017, http://prevacus.com/concussions-101/statistics.

26. Prevacus, "Statistics: Concussion Rate."

27. Caleb M. Alder et al., "MRI Evidence of Neuropathic Changes in Former College Football Players," *Clinical Journal of Sport Medicine* (October 17, 2016): doi:10.1097/JSM.0000000000000391.

28. David Armstrong, "Disqualified After Concussions, College Football Players Recruited Back onto the Field," *STAT*, January 8, 2016, https://www.statnews.com/2016/01/08/concussions-college-football-players.

29. National Center for Catastrophic Sport Injury Research; cited in Prevacus, "Statistics: Concussion Rate."

30. "Start Your Own NFL FLAG League." NFLFLAG. https://www.nflflag.com/pages/league-organizers/create-your-league?view=tabs

31. Nicholas D. Kristof, "A Veteran's Death, the Nation's Shame," *New York Times*, April 14, 2012, http://www.nytimes.com/2012/04/15/opinion/sunday/kristof-a-veterans-death-the-nations-shame.html.

32. Kristof, "Veteran's Death."

33. Thom Shanker and Richard A. Oppel Jr., "War's Elite Tough Guys, Hesitant to Seek Healing," *New York Times*, June 5, 2014, https://www.nytimes.com/2014/06/06/us/politics/wars-elite-tough-guys-hesitant-to-seek-healing.html.

CHAPTER 24: EMOTIONAL INTELLIGENCE AND MENTAL HEALTH

1. M. H. Meier et al., "The Role of Harsh Discipline in Explaining Sex Differences in Conduct Disorder: A Study of Opposite-Sex Twin Pairs," *Journal of Abnormal Child Psychology* 37, no. 5 (July 2009): 653–64.

2. B. Maughan et al., "Conduct Disorder and Oppositional Defiant Disorder in a National Sample: Developmental Epidemiology," *Journal of Child Psychology and Psychiatry* 45, no. 3 (2004): 609–21.

3. Bureau of the Census, "Population in Group Quarters by Type, Sex and Age, for the United States: 1990 and 2000" (unpublished tabulation, Census 2000, PHC-T-26, November 10, 2003), http://www2.census.gov/programs-surveys/decennial/2000/phc/phc-t-26/tab01.pdf.

4. Sarah Whittle et al., "Positive Parenting Predicts the Development of Adolescent Brain Structure: A Longitudinal Study," *Developmental Cognitive Neuroscience* 8 (April 2014): 7–17, doi:10.1016/j.dcn.2013.10.006.

5. Sarah Whittle et al., "Positive Parenting," 7–17.

6. K. Alison Clarke-Stewart and Craig Hayward, "Advantages of Father Custody and Contact for the Psychological Well-Being of School-Age Children," *Journal of Applied Developmental Psychology* 17, no. 2 (April–June 1996): 239–70, doi:10.1016/S0193-3973(96)90027-1.

7. Aaron S. Heller and B. J. Casey, "The Neurodynamics of Emotion: Delineating Typical and Atypical Emotional Processes During Adolescence," *Developmental Science* 19, no. 1 (2016): 3–18, doi:10.1111/desc.12373.

8. J. Van der Graaff et al, "Perspective Taking and Empathic Concern in Adolescence: Gender Differences in Developmental Changes," *Developmental Psychology* 50, no. 3 (20140: 881–88, doi:10.1037/a0034325.

9. Greg Welikson, "The Power of Connection: Enhancing Well-Being Through Brotherhood," *Rainbow* 143, no. 3 (Summer 2017): 18–21, http://www.deltataudeltaarchive.com/wp-content/uploads/2017/06/Rainbow_Summer2017.pdf.

10. Sarah Whittle, et al, "Positive parenting predicts the development of adolescent brain structure: a longitudinal study," *Developmental Cognitive Neuroscience*, Vol 8, April 2014, pp. 7-17.

11. Andrew M. Seaman, "Moving Out of Poverty Linked to Kids' Mental Health," Reuters, March 4, 2014, https://www.reuters.com/article/us-poverty-kids/moving-out-of-poverty-linked-to-kids-mental-health-idUSBREA2324J20140304; see also

http://media.jamanetwork.com/jama-report/girls-benefit-boys-suffer-when-their-families-move-from-high-poverty-areas-to-better-neighborhoods.

12. Seaman, "Moving Out of Poverty."

13. Tony Trueman, "Girls Achieve High Status in Criminal Street Gangs Because of Their People Skills, Research Shows," Science X, April 25, 2014, http://phys.org/news/2014-04-girls-high-status-criminal-street.html; based on Dr. Simon Harding's *The Street Casino: Survival in Violent Street Gangs* (Chicago: University of Chicago Press, 2014).

14. Trueman, "Girls Achieve High Status."

15. Trueman, "Girls Achieve High Status."

16. Interview with Vanessa Dahn, September 13, 2016.

17. Alejandra Matos, "In Missouri, Students Who Bully Could Be Charged with a Felony," *Washington Post*, January 6, 2017, https://www.washingtonpost.com/local/education/in-missouri-students-who-bully-could-be-charged-with-a-felony/2017/01/06/0e71f17e-d1e2-11e6-945a-76f69a399dd5_story.html.

18. Joshua Weller et al., "Preadolescent Decision-Making Competence Predicts Interpersonal Strengths and Difficulties," *Journal of Behavioral Decision Making* 28, no. 1 (2015): 76–88, doi:10.1002/bdm.1822.

19. See http://warrenfarrell.com/couples-communication.

20. Claire Vallotton et al, "Child Behavior Problems: Mothers' and Fathers' Mental Health Matters Today and Tomorrow," *Early Childhood Research Quarterly* 37 (4th Quarter 2016): 81–93, doi:10.1016/j.ecresq.2016.02.006.

21. Claire Vallotton et al, "Child Behavior Problems."

CHAPTER 25: REVERSING DEPRESSION, PREVENTING SUICIDE

1. Finlay Young, "Why Men Are Killing Themselves," *Newsweek*, February 12, 2015, http://www.newsweek.com/2015/02/20/suicide-men-305913.html.

2. Source for 2006 is the CDC's National Center for Injury Prevention and Control. For 1933, the Statistical Resources Branch of CDC's Division of Vital Statistics; cited in Jack Kammer, *Heroes of the Blue Sky Rebellion* (Halethorpe, MD: Healthy Village Press, 2009), 8.

3. Centers for Disease Control and Prevention (CDC), *Morbidity and Mortality Weekly Report* 58, no. 1 (2009); and Web-based Injury Statistics Query and Reporting System (WISQARS), 2010.

4. CDC, *Morbidity and Mortality Weekly Report*, 58, no. 1; and WISQARS, 2010.

5. Jed Diamond, "Women Seek Help, Men Die: New Findings on Depression and Suicide Will Save Millions of Lives," *Good Men Project*, November 11, 2013, https://goodmenproject.com/featured-content/kt-women-seek-help-men-die-new-findings-on-depression-and-suicide-will-save-millions-of-lives.

6. This is the GDP in the Eurozone's periphery countries. The rate is across all ages, which equates to over six thousand suicides in total over the period 2011–12. University of Portsmouth, "Male Suicide on Rise as Result of Austerity, Report

Suggests," *ScienceDaily*, October 16, 2015, http://www.sciencedaily.com/releases/2015/10/151006085437.htm.

7. Young, "Trouble with Men."

8. Hanna Rosin, "The Silicon Valley Suicides," *Atlantic*, December 2015, http://www.theatlantic.com/magazine/archive/2015/12/the-silicon-valley-suicides/413140.

9. Lisa A. Martin et al., "The Experience of Symptoms of Depression in Men vs Women," *JAMA Psychiatry* 70, no. 10 (2013): 1100–6.

10. Tanya M. Caldwell, Anthony F, Jorm, and Keith B. G. Dear, "Suicide and Mental Health in Rural, Remote and Metropolitan Areas in Australia," *Medical Journal of Australia* 181, suppl. 7 (2004): S10, https://www.mja.com.au/journal/2004/181/7/suicide-and-mental-health-rural-remote-and-metropolitan-areas-australia.

11. Gabrielle Glaseraug, "A Suicidologist's New Challenge: The George Washington Bridge," *New York Times*, August 19, 2016, http://www.nytimes.com/2016/08/21/nyregion/a-suicidologists-new-challenge-the-george-washington-bridge.html. The research advice is from Dr. Madelyn Gould.

12. Julie Scelfo, "Suicide on Campus and the Pressure of Perfection," *New York Times*, July 27, 2015, http://www.nytimes.com/2015/08/02/education/edlife/stress-social-media-and-suicide-on-campus.html.

13. Julie Scelfo, "Suicide on Campus and the Pressure of Perfection," *New York Times*, July 27, 2015. See https://www.nytimes.com/2015/08/02/education/edlife/stress-social-media-and-suicide-on-campus.html.

14. Personal correspondence in 2009 between Tom Golden, author of *The Way Men Heal* (G. H. Publishing, 2013), and Elizabeth Clarke, the NASW executive director at the time.

15. Joan Ryan, "Sorting Out Puzzle of Male Suicide," *San Francisco Chronicle*, January 26, 2006, http://www.sfgate.com/bayarea/article/Sorting-out-puzzle-of-male-suicide-2505891.php.

16. Zachary Kaminsky et al., "Epigenetic and Genetic Variation at SKA2 Predict Suicidal Behavior and Post-traumatic Stress Disorder," *Translational Psychiatry* 5 (August 2015): e627, doi:10.1038/tp.2015.105.

17. Henry Ford Health System, "Depression Care Program Eliminates Suicide," *ScienceDaily*, May 20, 2010, https://www.sciencedaily.com/releases/2010/05/100518170032.htm.

18. Henry Ford, "Depression Care."

19. Joanne Silberner, "What Happens If You Try to Prevent Every Single Suicide?" *Shots: Health News from NPR* (blog), NPR, November 2, 2015, http://www.npr.org/sections/health-shots/2015/11/02/452658644/what-happens-if-you-try-to-prevent-every-single-suicide.

20. See mankindproject.org and boystomen.org; see also Bill Kauth, *A Circle of Men* (Silverlight Publishing, 2015); and Warren Farrell, *The Liberated Man* (New York: Berkely, 1993).

21. See mensshed.org. Some nine hundred groups are in Australia, England, Ireland, Finland, and Greece.

22. Summary of Dr. Vanessa Dahn's written correspondence to me, November 19, 2016.

23. Janet Kemp and Robert Bossarte, "Suicide Data Report, 2012" (Department of Veterans Affairs, Mental Health Services, Suicide Prevention Program, 2012), p. 18, fig. 3, "Estimated Number of Veteran Suicides per Day by Year," https://www.va.gov/opa/docs/suicide-data-report-2012-final.pdf (accessed August 25, 2017); see also pp. 35–36.

24. Office of Public and Intergovernmental Affairs, "VA Conducts Nation's Largest Analysis of Veteran Suicide," Department of Veterans Affairs, July 7, 2016, http://www.va.gov/opa/pressrel/pressrelease.cfm?id=2801.

25. Legion Transitions Program, "A War in the Mind," YouTube video, 7:45, posted by Legion BC Yukon, June 28, 2012, http://youtu.be/QyGAggA0_t0.

26. Robert F. Worth, "Why Modern Warfare Destroys the Brain," June 10, 2016, *New York Times*, http://www.nytimes.com/2016/06/12/magazine/what-if-ptsd-is-more-physical-than-psychological.html.

27. Worth, "Modern Warfare."

28. Joe Klein, "The Power of Pitching In," *Time*, July 1, 2013.

29. Klein, "Power of Pitching In."

30. Credit to Nikita Coulombe for "top-down" thought, October 16, 2017.

31. Credit for standardized part transferability comment to Nikita Coulombe, September 28, 2017.

CHAPTER 26: HIDDEN HAZARDS TO YOUR SON'S HEALTH

1. E. Carlsen et al., "Evidence for Decreasing Quality of Semen During Past 50 Years," *BMJ* 305, no. 6854 (1992): 609–13.

2. Richard Sharpe et al., "Male Reproductive Health: Its Impacts in Relation to General Wellbeing and Low European Fertility Rates," *European Science Foundation*, September 2010.

3. Shirley S. Wang, "The Decline in Male Fertility," *Wall Street Journal*, July 15, 2013, https://www.wsj.com/articles/SB10001424127887323394504578607641775723354.

4. University of Guelph. "Parents, Especially Fathers, Play Key Role in Young Adults' Health." *ScienceDaily*, June 24, 2016, http://www.sciencedaily.com/releases/2016/06/160624140429.htm.

5. Stanton C. Honig, "Modifiable Lifestyle Issues and Male Reproductive Health," in "Advancing Men's Reproductive Health in the United States" (summary of scientific research, CDC, National Center for Chronic Diesease Prevention, September 13, 2010), 20–22, http://www.cdc.gov/reproductivehealth/ProductsPubs/PDFs/Male-Reproductive-Health.pdf.

6. Honig, S., MD, "Modifiable Lifestyle Issues," 20–22.

7. Agarwal A, et al, "Are men talking their reproductive health away?", *Asian Journal of Andrology*, 2015 May-Jun; 17(3): 433-4.

8. Leonard Sax, *Boys Adrift*, rev. ed. (New York: Basic Books, 2016), 132; citing Guillette Jr. et al, "Reduction in Penis Size and Plasma Testosterone Concentrations in

Juvenile Alligators Living in a Contaminated Environment," *General and Comparative Endocrinology* 101, no. 1 (1996): 32–42.

9. Sax, *Boys Adrift*, 130.

10. Sax, *Boys Adrift*, 128.

11. Laura Sessions Stepp, "Cupid's Broken Arrow," *Washington Post*, May 7, 2006.

12. "What Are the Key Statistics About Testicular Cancer?" American Cancer Society, last revised, January 6, 2017, http://www.cancer.org/cancer/testicularcancer/detailedguide/testicular-cancer-key-statistics.

13. Honig, "Modifiable Lifestyle Issues," 20–22.

14. Honig, "Modifiable Lifestyle Issues," 20–22.

15. David P. Barash and Judith Eve Lipton, *Gender Gap: The Biology of Male-Female Differences* (New York: Transaction Publishers, 2001).

16. L. D. Johnston et al., *Monitoring the Future: National Survey Results on Drug Use, 1975–2014* (monograph, 2014 overview, key findings on adolescent drug use, Institute for Social Research, University of Michigan, Ann Arbor), http://www.monitoringthefuture.org/pubs/monographs/mtf-overview2014.pdf.

17. See Gary Wilson, *Your Brain on Porn: Internet Pornography and the Emerging Science of Addiction*, (Commonwealth Publishing, 2014).

18. Andrew Tilghman, "Spooked by Obesity Trends, the U.S. Military Is Redefining Its Basic Fitness Standards," *Military Times*, August 7, 2016, http://web.archive.org/web/20160809064002/http://www.militarytimes.com/story/military/careers/2016/08/07/military-fitness-standards-body-fat/87748588/?from=global&sessionKey=&autologin=.

19. "Overweight and Obesity Rates for Adults by Gender, 2010," Henry J. Kaiser Family Foundation, retrieved April 29, 2014, http://kff.org/other/state-indicator/adult-overweightobesity-rate-by-gender.

20. C. L. Ogden et al. (2010, December). "Obesity and Socioeconomic Status in Adults: United States, 2005–2008" (NHCS Data Brief, no. 50, HHS, CDC, National Center for Health Statistics, December 2010), 1, http://www.cdc.gov/nchs/data/databriefs/db50.pdf.

21. Sonia Caprio et al., "Metabolic Impact of Obesity in Childhood," *Endocrinology and Metabolism Clinics of North America* 28, no. 4, (December 1999): 731–47, doi:10.1016/S0889-8529(05)70099-2.

22. "Affordable Care Act Rules on Expanding Access to Preventive Services for Women." See http://web.archive.org/web/20170121004223/https://www.hhs.gov/healthcare/facts-and-features/fact-sheets/aca-rules-on-expanding-access-to-preventive-services-for-women.

23. "Affordable Care Act Rules on Expanding Access to Preventive Services for Women," Fact Sheets, HHS, August 1, 2011, http://www.hhs.gov/healthcare/facts-and-features/fact-sheets/aca-rules-on-expanding-access-to-preventive-services-for-women.

24. "Affordable Care Act," HHS.

25. "Women's Preventive Services Guidelines," Human Resources and Services Administration, 2016," last reviewed October 2017, https://www.hrsa.gov/womens-guidelines-2016/index.html.

26. Scott Williams et al., "Survey of State Public Health Department Resources for Men and Boys: Identification of an Inadvertent and Remediatable Service and Health Disparity," *American Journal of Men's Health* 4 (2010): 344–52, doi:10.1177/1557988309356100.

27. "Putting Men's Health Care Disparities on the Map," Henry J. Kaiser Family Foundation, September 1, 2012, http://kff.org/disparities-policy/report/putting-mens-health-care-disparities-on-the.

28. Section 92.1 of the ACA states that discrimination is prohibited "on the basis of race, color, national origin, sex, age, or disability."

29. Anemona Hartocollis, "With Special Clinics, Hospitals Vie for Hesitant Patients: Men," *New York Times*, May 28, 2014, http://www.nytimes.com/2014/05/29/nyregion/with-special-clinics-hospitals-vie-for-hesitant-patients-men.html.

30. Hartocollis, "Special Clinics."

31. Hartocollis, "Special Clinics."

32. Ariana Eunjung Cha, "The Startling Rise in Oral Cancer in Men, and What It Says About Our Changing Sexual Habits," *Washington Post*, October 25, 2016, https://www.washingtonpost.com/news/to-your-health/wp/2016/10/25/the-startling-rise-in-oral-cancer-in-men-and-what-it-says-about-our-changing-sexual-habits.

33. Laurie McGinley, "Cancer Death Rate Has Dropped Again. But It's Still Higher for Men than Women," *Washington Post*, January 5, 2017. https://www.washingtonpost.com/news/to-your-health/wp/2017/01/05/cancer-death-rate-drops-25-percent-from-1991-peak-still-higher-for-men-than-women.

34. See www.menshealthnetwork.org.

35. See mankindproject.org.

36. Richard Bolles, *What Color is Your Parachute?* (New York: Penguin/Random House, 2017).

37. See M. S. Fiebert, "References Examining Assaults by Women on Their Spouses or Male Partners: An Updated Annotated Bibliography," *Sexuality & Culture* 18, no. 2 (June 2014): 405–67, doi:10.1007/s12119-013-9194-1. For an in-depth explanation of why domestic violence is a two-way street, and ways to prevent it, see Warren Farrell, *Women Can't Hear What Men Don't Say* (New York: Berkely, 1999).

38. "Office on Women's Health Report to the White House Council on Women and Girls" (memo from Department of Health and Human Services to White House Council on Women and Girls, November 2009), https://www.womenshealth.gov/publications/federal-report/hhs-cwg-report.pdf.

CHAPTER 27: FROM HURT PEOPLE HURTING PEOPLE TO HEALED PEOPLE HEALING PEOPLE

1. Diane Swanbrow, "Empathy: College Students Don't Have as Much as They Used To," *Michigan News*, May 27, 2010, http://ns.umich.edu/new/

releases/7724-empathy-college-students-don-t-have-as-much-as-they-used-to. The article presents Sara Konrath's meta-analysis of seventy-two studies of college students.

2. Jessica Alexander and Iben Sandahl, *The Danish Way of Parenting: What the Happiest People in the World Know About Raising Confident, Capable Kids* (New York: TarcherPerigee, 2016).

3. Interview with Christine Greenberg, Social Media Dir., Unified Caring, August 30, 2017. Essays at Unifiedcaring.org

4. "Warren Farrell's Couples' Communication Video-from-Workshop," YouTube video, 3:49, drwarrenfarrell, June 5, 2017, https://www.youtube.com/watch?v=SHtXyzKk6bQ.

5. Hilda L. Solis and Keith Hall, *Women in the Labor Force: A Databook* (report 1034, Bureau of Labor Statistics, US Department of Labor, December 2011), p. 78, table 25, "Wives Who Earn More than Their Husbands, 1987–2009." The study controlled for age, education, income, and hours worked; cited in Honor Whiteman, "Money on the Mind: Breadwinning Men Have Worse Mental, Physical Health," *Medical News Today*, August 19, 2016, http://www.medicalnewstoday.com/articles/312425.php.

6. Solis and Hall, *Women in the Labor Force*, p. 78, table 25.

7. Warren Farrell, *Why Men Earn More—and What Women Can Do About It* (New York: AMACOM, 2005)

8. See the webpage for their program at www.soberforever.net/jtprogram1.cfm.

9. Centers for Disease Control and Prevention and SHAPE America—Society of Health and Physical Educators. Strategies for Recess in Schools (Atlanta, GA: CDC, HHS, 2017), www.cdc.gov/healthyschools.

CHAPTER 28: THE NEW NEURAL CRISIS

1. Key findings to "Trends in the Parent-Report of Health Care Provider-Diagnosis and Medication Treatment for ADHD: United States, 2003–2011," Centers for Disease Control and Prevention (CDC), last updated September 7, 2017, https://www.cdc.gov/ncbddd/adhd/features/key-findings-adhd72013.html.

2. Alex Johnson, "Half of College Students Consider Suicide," NBC News, August 18, 2008, http://www.nbcnews.com/id/26272639/ns/health-mental_health/t/half-college-students-consider-suicide.

3. "Teen Suicide Statistics," TeenSuicide.us, accessed October 17, 2017, http://www.teensuicide.us/articles1.html.

4. "Data & Statistics," Autism Spectrum Disorder (ASD), CDC, last updated July 11, 2016, http://www.cdc.gov/ncbddd/autism/data.html.

5. Meredith Melnick, "Developmental Disabilities, Including Autism and ADHD, Are on the Rise," *Time*, May 23, 2011, http://healthland.time.com/2011/05/23/developmental-disabilities-including-autism-and-adhd-are-on-the-rise.

6. Marcus A. Winters and Jay P. Greene, "Leaving Boys Behind: Public High School Graduation Rates," Manhattan Institute, April 18, 2006, https://www.

manhattan-institute.org/html/leaving-boys-behind-public-high-school-gradua-tion-rates-5829.html.

7. Tamar Lewin, "At Colleges, Women Are Leaving Men in the Dust," *New York Times*, July 9, 2006, http://www.nytimes.com/2006/07/09/education/09college.html.

8. "Autism Prevalence Now 1 in 88 children, 1 in 54 boys," National Autism Association, accessed October 17, 2017, http://nationalautismassociation.org/autism-prevalence-now-1-in-88-children-1-in-54-boys.

9. "Facts About Autism," Autism Speaks, accessed October 17, 2017, https://www.autismspeaks.org/what-autism/facts-about-autism.

10. "Facts About ASD," ASD, CDC, last updated March 28, 2016, https://www.cdc.gov/ncbddd/autism/facts.html.

11. "Basic Information," Attention-Deficit / Hyperactivity Disorder (ADHD), CDC, last updated May 31, 2017, https://www.cdc.gov/ncbddd/adhd/facts.html.

12. Brenda Patoine, "What's the Real Deficit in Attention Deficit/Hyperactivity Disorder?" Dana Foundation, August 31, 2010, http://dana.org/News/Details.aspx?id=43498.

13. Larry Silver, "When It's Not Just ADHD," *ADDitude*, accessed October 17, 2017, http://www.additudemag.com/adhd/article/774.html

14. Darin D. Dougherty et al., "Dopamine Transporter Density in Patients with Attention Deficit Hyperactivity Disorder," *Lancet* 354 (December 1999): 2132–33, doi:10.1016/S0140-6736(99)04030-1.

15. Wendy Richardson, "The Link Between ADHD & Addiction," ADD and Addiction, accessed October 17, 2017, http://www.addandaddiction.com/?p=2014.

16. Bryon Adinoff, "Neurobiologic Processes in Drug Reward and Addiction," *Harvard Review of Psychiatry* 12, no. 6 (2004): 305–20, doi:10.1080/10673220490910844.

17. Roy A. Wise, "Dopamine and Reward: The Anhedonia Hypothesis 30 years on," *Neurotoxicity Research* 14, nos. 2–3 (2008): 169–83, doi:10.1007/BF03033808.

18. "Low Dopamine Levels: Symptoms & Adverse Reactions," *Mental Health Daily* (blog), accessed October 17, 2017, http://mentalhealthdaily.com/2015/04/02/low-dopamine-levels-symptoms-adverse-reactions.

19. Michael Y. Aksenov et al., "Cocaine-Mediated Enhancement of Tat Toxicity in Rat Hippocampal Cell Cultures: The Role of Oxidative Stress and D1 Dopamine Receptor," *NeuroToxicology* 27, no. 2 (2006): 217–28, doi:10.1016/j.neuro.2005.10.003.

20. Doron Merims and Nir Giladi, "Dopamine Dysregulation Syndrome, Addiction and Behavioral Changes in Parkinson's Disease," *Parkinsonism & Related Disorders* 14, no. 4 (2008): 273–80, doi:10.1016/j.parkreldis.2007.09.007.

21. Ellen Littman, "Never Enough? Why Your Brain Craves Stimulation," *ADDitude*, accessed October 17, 2017, http://www.additudemag.com/adhd/article/12324.html.

22. "Basic Information," ADHD, CDC, May 31, 2017.

23. Åse Dragland, "Risky Young Drivers Are Highly Emotional," *ScienceNordic*, April 6, 2014, http://sciencenordic.com/risky-young-drivers-are-highly-emotional.

24. "Brain Chemical Makes Us More Impulsive," Health, *Live Science*, June 29, 2010, http://www.livescience.com/6645-brain-chemical-impulsive.html.

25. Karen Hopkin, "Musical Chills Related to Brain Dopamine Release," *Scientific American*, January 9, 2010, transcript and audio, https://www.scientificamerican. com/podcast/episode/musical-chills-related-to-brain-dop-11-01-09.

26. Crystal A. Clark and Alain Dagher, "The Role of Dopamine in Risk Taking: A Specific Look at Parkinson's Disease and Gambling," *Frontiers in Behavioral Neuroscience* 8 (2014): 196, doi:10.3389/fnbeh.2014.00196.

27. Nicole M. Avena, Pedro Rada, and Bartley G. Hoebel, "Evidence for Sugar Addiction: Behavioral and Neurochemical Effects of Intermittent, Excessive Sugar Intake," *Neuroscience & Biobehavioral Reviews* 32, no. 1 (2008): 20–39, doi:10.1016/j. neubiorev.2007.04.019.

28. Pedro Rada, Nicola M. Avena, and Bartley G. Hoebel, "Daily Bingeing on Sugar Repeatedly Releases Dopamine in the Accumbens Shell," *Neuroscience* 134, no. 3 (2005): 737–44, doi:10.1016/j.neuroscience.2005.04.043.

29. Jens C. Pruessner et al. "Dopamine Release in Response to a Psychological Stress in Humans and Its Relationship to Early Life Maternal Care: A Positron Emission Tomography Study Using [^{11}C]Raclopride," *Journal of Neuroscience* 24, no. 11 (2004): 2825–31, doi:10.1523/JNEUROSCI.3422-03.2004.

30. Eugene Sheely, "The Winner Effect: How Success Affects Brain Chemistry," *Gamification* (blog), February 21, 2014, http://www.gamification.co/2014/02/21/ the-winner-effect.

31. Scott Edwards, "Love and the Brain," *On the Brain*, And the Brain, accessed October 17, 2017, http://neuro.hms.harvard.edu/harvard-mahoney-neuroscience-institute/ brain-newsletter/and-brain-series/love-and-brain.

32. Belle Beth Cooper, "Novelty and The Brain: Why New Things Make Us Feel So Good," Lifehacker, May 23, 2013, http://lifehacker.com/novelty-and-the-brain -why-new-things-make-us-feel-so-g-508983802

33. Jason Zweig, "Your Money and Your brain: Humankind Evolved to Seek Rewards and Avoid Risks but Not to Invest Wisely," CNNMoney, August 23, 2007, http:// money.cnn.com/2007/08/14/pf/zweig.moneymag/?postversion=2007082313.

34. M. J. Koepp, "Evidence for Striatal Dopamine Release During a Video Game," *Nature* 393 (1998): 266–68, doi:10.1038/30498.

35. Daniel Siegel, "Dopamine and Teenage Logic," *Atlantic*, January 24, 2014, https://www. theatlantic.com/health/archive/2014/01/dopamine-and-teenage-logic/282895.

36. David J. Linden, "Video Games Can Activate the Brain's Pleasure Circuits," *Psychology Today*, October 25, 2011, https://www.psychologytoday .com/blog/the-compass-pleasure/201110/video-games-can-activate-the-brains- pleasure-circuits-0.

37. Sheely, "Winner Effect."

38. Jules Standish, "Colours to Boost Your Mood! Don't Be Scared to Clash," *Daily Mail*, December 8, 2014, http://www.dailymail.co.uk/femail/article-2864623/Colours- boost-mood-Dont-scared-clash-scientists-brighter-clothes-make-happier.html.

39. Donald L. Hilton Jr., "Pornography Addiction: A Supranormal Stimulus Considered in the Context of Neuroplasticity," *Socioaffective Neuroscience & Psychology* 3 (2013): 20767: doi:10.3402/snp.v3i0.20767.

40. Luke Gilkerson, "Brain Chemicals and Porn Addiction: Science Shows How Porn Harms Us," *Covenant Eyes* (blog), February 3, 2014, http://www.covenanteyes.com/2014/02/03/brain-chemicals-and-porn-addiction.

41. Scicurious [Bethany Brookshire], "Stressed Out and Not Thinking Straight? Blame Dopamine Release in Your Prefrontal Cortex," *Neurotic Physiology* (blog), December 5, 2012, http://scicurious.scientopia.org/2012/12/05/stressed-out-and-not-thinking-straight-blame-the-dopamine-in-your-prefrontal-cortex.

42. Scicurious, "Stressed Out?"

43. Annemoon M. M. van Erp and Klaus A. Miczek, "Aggressive Behavior, Increased Accumbal Dopamine, and Decreased Cortical Serotonin in Rats," *Journal of Neuroscience* 20, no. 24 (2000): 9320–25, http://www.jneurosci.org/content/jneuro/20/24/9320.full.pdf.

44. Eliza Barclay, "Why Sugar Makes Us Feel So Good," *The Salt* (blog), NPR, January 16, 2014, http://www.npr.org/sections/thesalt/2014/01/15/262741403/why-sugar-makes-us-feel-so-good.

45. Marcello Solinas et al., "Caffeine Induces Dopamine and Glutamate Release in the Shell of the Nucleus Accumbens," *Journal of Neuroscience* 22, no. 15 (2002): 6321–24, https://pdfs.semanticscholar.org/0d8d/1cc8d5af8e80b44ed98cc59123cfe0dc760a.pdf.

46. David J. Linden, "Exercise, Pleasure and the Brain: Understanding the Biology of 'Runner's High,'" *Psychology Today*, April 21, 2011, https://www.psychologytoday.com/blog/the-compass-pleasure/201104/exercise-pleasure-and-the-brain.

47. Kara Gavin, "Pleasure and Pain: Study Shows Brain's "Pleasure Chemical" Is Involved in Response to Pain, Too," *University of Michigan News*, October 25, 2006, http://www.ns.umich.edu/new/releases/1003-pleasure-and-pain-study-shows-brains-q-pleasure-chemicalq-is-involved-in-response-to-pain-too.

48. Mary-Frances O'Connor et al., "Craving Love? Enduring Grief Activates Brain's Reward Center," *Neuroimage* 42, no. 2 (2008): 969–72, doi:10.1016/j.neuroimage.2008.04.256.

49. O'Connor, "Craving Love?"

50. Compound F, "PTSD: Rewards of Stress, the Rush of War, & Drug Abuse: Part 1," *Daily Kos* (blog), June 25, 2007, http://www.dailykos.com/story/2007/6/24/350260/-.

51. Dana Dovey, "Alcohol Addiction Affects Dopamine Levels in Brain, Making It Harder to Catch a Buzz, Easier to Relapse," *Medical Daily*, March 4, 2016, http://www.medicaldaily.com/alcohol-addiction-dopamine-levels-376577.

52. Jun Chen, Christophe Wersinger and Anita Sidhu, "Chronic Stimulation of D1 Dopamine Receptors in Human SK-N-MC Neuroblastoma Cells Induces Nitric-oxide Synthase Activation and Cytotoxicity," *Journal of Biological Chemistry* 278, no. 30 (2003): 28089–28100, doi:10.1074/jbc.M303094200.

53. Kris Gunnars, "How Sugar Hijacks Your Brain and Makes You Addicted," *Authority Nutrition* (blog), Healthline, January 26, 2013, https://authoritynutrition.com/how-sugar-makes-you-addicted.

54. Pamela Spann, "The Negative Effects of High-Stakes Testing" (course paper, Education Law and Policy, Loyola University, 2015), http://www.luc.edu/media/lucedu/law/centers/childlaw/childed/pdfs/2015studentpapers/Spann.pdf.

55. "Data & Statistics," ADHD, CDC, last updated October 12, 2017, https://www.cdc.gov/ncbddd/adhd/data.html.

56. Christ Woolston, "Kids, Soda, and Obesity," Health Day, last updated January 20, 2017, https://consumer.healthday.com/encyclopedia/food-and-nutrition-21/food-and-nutrition-news-316/kids-soda-and-obesity-644731.html.

57. Fran Kritz, "What You Don't Know Unless You've Been There: Heroin," Heroin, Addiction.com, August 5, 2015, https://www.addiction.com/12360/what-you-dont-know-unless-youve-been-there-heroin.

58. Compound F, "PTSD: Rewards of Stress".

59. Tony Cox, "Brain Maturity Extends Well Beyond Teen Years," interview with Sandra Aamodt, *Tell Me More*, October 10, 2011, transcript, Brain Candy, NPR, http://www.npr.org/templates/story/story.php?storyId=141164708.

60. Alan Schwarz and Sarah Cohen, "A.D.H.D. Seen in 11% of U.S. Children as Diagnoses Rise," Health, *New York Times*, March 31, 2013, http://www.nytimes.com/2013/04/01/health/more-diagnoses-of-hyperactivity-causing-concern.html.

61. L. Alan Sroufe, "Ritalin Gone Wrong," *New York Times*, January 28, 2012, http://www.nytimes.com/2012/01/29/opinion/sunday/childrens-add-drugs-dont-work-long-term.html.

62. Jason Yanofski, "The Dopamine Dilemma—Part II," *Innovations in Clinical Neuroscience* 8, no. 1 (2011): 47–53, https://www.ncbi.nlm.nih.gov/pmc/articles/PMC3036556.

63. T. E. Robinson and B. Kolb, "Structural Plasticity Associated with Exposure to Drugs of Abuse," *Neuropharmacology* 47, suppl. 1 (2004): 33–46, doi:10.1016/j.neuropharm.2004.06.025.

64. Peter W. Kalivas, Nora D. Volkow, and J. Seamans, "Unmanageable Motivation in Addiction: A Pathology in Prefrontal-Accumbens Glutamate Transmission," *Neuron* 45, no. 5 (2005): 647–50, doi:10.1016/j.neuron.2005.02.005.

65. Yong Li and Julie A. Kauer, "Repeated Exposure to Amphetamine Disrupts Dopaminergic Modulation of Excitatory Synaptic Plasticity and Neurotransmission in Nucleus Accumbens," *Synapse* 51, no. 1 (2003):1–10, doi:10.1002/syn.10270.

66. Jason Yanofski, "The Dopamine Dilemma—Part II," *Innovations in Clinical Neuroscience* 8, no. 1 (2011): 47–53, https://www.ncbi.nlm.nih.gov/pmc/articles/PMC3036556.

67. Gene-Jack Wang et al., "Long-Term Stimulant Treatment Affects Brain Dopamine Transporter Level in Patients with Attention Deficit Hyperactive Disorder," *PLOS ONE* 8, no. 5 (2013): e63023.

68. Sroufe, "Ritalin Gone Wrong."

69. Yanofski, "Dopamine Dilemma—Part II."

70. Preussner et al., "Dopamine Release."

71. Jim Schnabel, "Dopamine Linked to 'Anxious' Amygdalas," Dana Foundation, December 31, 2008, http://www.dana.org/News/Details.aspx?id=42898.

72. Albert-Ludwigs-Universität Freiburg, "Sensory Stimuli Control Dopamine in the Brain," *ScienceDaily*, January 13, 2017, https://www.sciencedaily.com/releases/2017/01/170113093358.htm.

73. D. J. Diehl and S. Gershon, "The Role of Dopamine in Mood Disorders," *Comprehensive Psychiatry* 33, no. 2 (1992): 115–20, doi:10.1016/0010-440X(92)90007-D.

74. Adam Hadhazy, "Fear Factor: Dopamine May Fuel Dread, Too," *Scientific American*, July 14, 2008, https://www.scientificamerican.com/article/fear-factor-dopamine.

75. Barclay, "Why Sugar Makes Us Feel So Good."

CHAPTER 30: THE MANY CAUSES OF ADHD

1. Zeyan Liew et al., "Acetaminophen Use During Pregnancy, Behavioral Problems, and Hyperkinetic Disorders," *JAMA Pediatrics* 168, no. 4 (2014): 313–20, doi:10.1001/jamapediatrics.2013.4914.

2. Susan Scutti, "Acetaminophen Use During Pregnancy May Increase Risk of Hyperactivity in Kids," CNN, August 15, 2016, http://www.cnn.com/2016/08/15/health/acetaminophen-pregnancy-kids-adhd.

3. T. Rousar, "Glutathione Reductase Is Inhibited by Acetaminophen-Glutathione Conjugate in Vitro," *Physiological Research* 59, no. 2 (2010): 225–32, pmid:19537930.

4. Paavo O. Airola, *How to Get Well* (Phoenix, AZ: Health Plus, 1980), 237.

5. Amanda Chan, "Fever Increases Immune System Defense, Study Shows," *Huffington Post*, November 4, 2011, http://www.huffingtonpost.com/2011/11/03/fever-immune-system-cells_n_1074445.html.

6. William Shaw, "Evidence that Increased Acetaminophen Use in Genetically Vulnerable Children Appears to Be a Major Cause of the Epidemics of Autism, Attention Deficit with Hyperactivity, and Asthma," *Journal of Restorative Medicine* 2, no. 1 (2013): 14–29, doi:10.14200/jrm.2013.2.0101.

7. Olivia Dean et al., "A Role for Glutathione in the Pathophysiology of Bipolar Disorder and Schizophrenia? Animal Models and Relevance to Clinical Practice," *Current Medicinal Chemistry* 16, no. 23 (2009): 2965–76, doi:10.2174/092986709788803060.

8. William M. Johnson, Amy Wilson-Delfosse, and John J. Mieyal, "Dysregulation of Glutathione Homeostasis in Neurodegenerative Diseases," *Nutrients* 4, no. 10 (2012):1399–440, doi:10.3390/nu4101399.

9. University of Calgary, "Mercury-University of Calgary Study" (2012) YouTube video, 2:14, posted by DrRyan French, April 29, 2012, https://www.youtube.com/watch?v=73XyJq9Z3-k.

10. S.K. Sagiv, S.W. Thurston, D. C. Bellinger, C. Amarasiriwardena & S.A. Korrick, "Prenatal exposure to mercury and fish consumption during pregnancy and ADHD-related behavior in children," Archives of Pediatrics & Adolescent Medicine, 2009, 166(12), 1123–1131.http://doi.org/10.1001/archpediatrics.2012.1286.

11. "Fish: Toxic for Mothers, Poisonous to Babies," People for the Ethical Treatment of Animals (PETA), 2014, https://www.peta.org/living/food/fish-toxic-mothers-poisonous-babies/.

12. "NIEHS/EPA Children's Environmental Health and Disease Prevention Research Centers. Protecting Children's Health Where They Live, Learn, and Play," Environmental Protection Agency (EPA), last updated October 19, 2017, https://www.epa.gov/sites/production/files/2017-10/documents/niehs_epa_childrens_centers_impact_report_2017_0.pdf.

13. "NIEHS/EPA Children's Environmental Health and Disease Prevention Research Centers. Protecting Children's Health Where They Live, Learn, and Play," Environmental Protection Agency (EPA), last updated October 19, 2017. https://www.epa.gov/sites/production/files/2017-10/documents/niehs_epa_childrens_centers_impact_report_2017_0.pdf.

14. J. Albrecht & E. Matyja. "Glutamate: A potential mediator of inorganic mercury neurotoxicity," *Metabolic Brain Disease*, Vol. 11, No. 2, June 1996, pp. 175-184.

15. Ewa Matyja, Jan Albrecht, "Ultrastructural evidence that mercuric chloride lowers the threshold for glutamate neurotoxicity in an organotypic culture of rat cerebellum," *Neuroscience Letters*, Volume 158, Issue 2, 1993, Pages 155-158, ISSN 0304-3940, https://doi.org/10.1016/0304-3940(93)90252-G.

16. K. Singh & P. Ahluwalia. "Studies on the Effect of Monosodium Glutamate [MSG] Administration on Some Antioxidant Enzymes in the Arterial Tissue of Adult Male Mice," *Journal of Nutritional Science and Vitaminology*, 49 (2), 145-148.

17. Charlie Brown, "California Dentist Forced to Disclose Health Risks of Mercury Fillings," Counsel for Consumers of Dental Choice Counsel for Consumers of Dental Choice, 2002. http://www.mercurypoisoned.com/california.html.

18. R. Dufault, R. Schnoll, W.J., Lukiw, B. LeBlanc, C. Cornett, L. Patrick, R. Crider, "Mercury exposure, nutritional deficiencies and metabolic disruptions may affect learning in children," Behavioral and Brain Functions: BBF, 2009, 5, 44. http://doi.org/10.1186/1744-9081-5-44.

19. R. Dufault, R. Schnoll, W.J. Lukiw, B. LeBlanc, C. Cornett, L. Patrick, R. Crider, "Mercury exposure, nutritional deficiencies and metabolic disruptions may affect learning in children."

20. Katarina Ćurković & Mario Ćurković & Josipa Radić & Dunja Degmečić. "The role of zinc in the treatment of hyperactivity disorder in children," Acta medica Croatica: časopis Hravatske akademije medicinskih znanosti, 2009, 63. 307-13. https://www.ncbi.nlm.nih.gov/pubmed/20034331.

21. Richard Horowitz, "Are ADHD and Dementia Preventable Diseases?" *Psychology Today*, December 28, 2013, http://www.psychologytoday.com/blog/why-can-t-i-get-better/201312/are-adhd-and-dementia-preventable-diseases.

22. A. Rovlias and S. Kotsou, "The Influence of Hyperglycemia on Neurological Outcome in Patients with Severe Head Injury," *Neurosurgery* 46, no. 2 (2000).

23. DOE/Brookhaven National Laboratory, "Deficits in Brain's Reward System Observed in ADHD Patients: Low Levels of Dopamine Markers May Underlie Symptoms," *ScienceDaily*, September 10, 2009, http://www.sciencedaily.com/releases/2009/09/090908193432.htm.

24. Rachel Reilly, "Food Addiction DOES Exist," *Daily Mail*, August 27, 2013, http://www.dailymail.co.uk/health/article-2402746/Food-addiction-DOES-ex.

25. Associated Press, "High Blood Sugar in Pregnancy Puts Baby at Risk," NBC News, June 22, 2007, http://www.nbcnews.com/id/19374297/ns/health-pregnancy.

26. Syed Ibrahim Rizvi and M. A. Zaid, "Intracellular Reduced Glutathione Content in Normal and Type 2 Diabetic Erythrocytes: Effect of Insulin and (-)Epicatechin," *Journal of Physiology and Pharmacology* 52, no. 3 (2001): 483–88, pmid:11596865.

27. Alex Knapp, "How Lead Caused America's Violent Crime Epidemic," *Forbes*, January 3, 2011, http://www.forbes.com/sites/alexknapp/2013/01/03/how-lead-caused-americas-violent-crime-epidemic.

28. Kelly FitzGerald, "Prenatal Mercury Intake Linked to ADHD," *Medical News Today*, October 9, 2012, http://www.medicalnewstoday.com/articles/251293.php.

29. Liz Bestic, "Is Aluminium Really a Silent Killer?" *Telegraph*, March 5, 2012, http://www.telegraph.co.uk/news/health/9119528/Is-aluminium-really-a-silent-killer.html.

30. H. Meiri, E. Banin, and M. Roll, "Aluminum Ingestion—Is It Related to Dementia?" *Reviews on Environmental Health* 9, no. 4 (1991): 191–205, pmid:1842454.

31. Richard Johnson et al., "Attention-Deficit/Hyperactivity Disorder: Is it Time to Reappraise the Role of Sugar Consumption?" *Postgraduate Medicine* 123, no. 5 (2011): 39–49, doi:10.3810/pgm.2011.09.2458.

32. R. F. Hurrell et al., "Soy Protein, Phytate, and Iron Absorption in Humans," *American Journal of Clinical Nutrition* 56, no. 3 (1992): 573–78, pmid:1503071.

33. F. Roth-Walter et al., "Pasteurization of Milk Proteins Promotes Allergic Sensitization," *Allergy* 63, no. 7 (2008): 882–90, doi:10.1111/j.1398-9995.2008.01673.x.

34. "Alcohol and Drug Abuse," Amen Clinics, accessed October 17, 2017, http://www.amenclinics.com/healthy-vs-unhealthy/alcohol-drug-abuse.

35. Genetic Science Learning Center, "Ritalin and Cocaine: The Connection and the Controversy," Learn.Genetics, University of Utah, August 30, 2013, http://learn.genetics.utah.edu/content/addiction/ritalin.

36. "Methylphenidate," Wikipedia, last modified October 18, 2017, http://en.wikipedia.org/wiki/Methylphenidate.

37. Rachel Rettner, "ADHD Drug May Spur Brain Changes, Study Suggests," Health, *Live Science*, May 15, 2013, http://www.livescience.com/32044-adhd-drug-treatment-brain-changes.html.

38. Deborah C. Mash et al., "Dopamine Transport Function is Elevated in Cocaine Users," *Journal of Neurochemistry* 81, no. 2 (2002): 292–300, doi:10.1046/j.1471-4159.2002.00820.x.

39. Katie Couric, correspondent, "Popping Pills a Popular Way to Boost Brain Power," *60 Minutes*, April 22, 2010, transcript, CBS News, https://www.cbsnews.com/news/popping-pills-a-popular-way-to-boost-brain-power.

40. "Ritalin Abuse: Statistics," summary of *Frontline: Medicating Kids*, directed by Marcela Gaviria (Boston: WGBH, 2001), http://www.pbs.org/wgbh/pages/frontline/shows/medicating/drugs/ritalinstats.html.

41. Robin Wilkey, "Cocaine Rewires Brain, Overrides Decision-Making After Just One Use, Says Study," *Huffington Post*, August 27, 2013, http://www.huffingtonpost.com.au/entry/cocaine-decision-making_n_3818400.

42. Edmund S. Higgins, "Do ADHD Drugs Take a Toll on the Brain?" *Scientific American*, July 2009, https://www.scientificamerican.com/article/do-adhd-drugs-take-a-toll.

43. Steven M. Berman et al., "Potential Adverse Effects of Amphetamine Treatment on Brain and Behavior: A Review," *Molecular Psychiatry* 14, no. 2 (2009): 123–42, doi:10.1038/mp.2008.90.

44. Sax, "Boys Adrift."

45. T. E. Robinson, "Structural plasticity associated with exposure to drugs of abuse," *Neuropharmacology* 47, suppl. 1 (2004): 33–46, doi:10.1016/j.neuropharm.2004.06.025; Kalivas, Volkow, and Seamans, "Unmanageable Motivation"; Shao-Pii Onn and Anthony A. Grace, "Amphetamine Withdrawal Alters Bistable States and Cellular Coupling in Rat Prefrontal Cortex and Nucleus Accumbens Neurons Recorded *in vivo*," *Journal of Neuroscience* 20, no. 6 (2000): 2332–45, http://www.jneurosci.org/content/20/6/2332; Li and Kauer, "Repeated Exposure to Amphetamine"; Rochellys Diaz Heijtz, Bryan Kolb, and Hans Forssberg, "Can a Therapeutic Dose of Amphetamine During Pre-adolescence Modify the Pattern of Synaptic Organization in the Brain?" *European Journal of Neuroscience* 18, no. 12 (2003): 3394–99, doi:10.1046/j.0953-816X.2003.03067.x; Gaetano Di Chiara et al., "Dopamine and Drug Addiction: The Nucleus Accumbens Shell Connection," *Neuropharmacology* 47, suppl. 1 (2004): 227–41, doi:10.1016/j.neuropharm.2004.06.032; Louk J. M. J. Vanderschuren et al., "A Single Exposure to Amphetamine Is Sufficient to Induce Long-Term Behavioral, Neuroendocrine, and Neurochemical Sensitization in Rats," *Journal of Neuroscience* 19, no. 21 (1999): 9579–86, http://www.jneurosci.org/content/19/21/9579.full.pdf.

46. Robert Lee Hotz, "When Gaming Is Good for You," *Wall Street Journal*, March 13, 2012, http://www.wsj.com/articles/SB10001424052970203458604577263273943183932.

47. Daphne Bavelier, "Your Brain on Video Games," (lecture, TEDxCHUV, Lausanne, France, June 2012), https://www.ted.com/talks/daphne_bavelier_your_brain_on_video_games.

48. "Taxi Drivers' Brains 'Grow' on the Job," BBC News, http://news.bbc.co.uk/2/hi/677048.stm

49. Fran Lowry, "Playing Violent Video Games Changes Brain Function," Medscape Medical News, November 29, 2011, https://www.medscape.com/viewarticle/754368.

50. John Lee, "Adult Video Gamers Are Heavier, More Introverted and More Likely Depressed," Choose Help, August 19, 2009, http://www.choosehelp.com/news/non-substance-addictions/adult-video-gamers-are-heavier-more-introverted-and-more-likely-depressed.html.

51. Goh Matsuda and Kazuo Hiraki, "Sustained Decrease in Oxygenated Hemoglobin During Video Games in the Dorsal Prefrontal Cortex: A NIRS Study of Children," *NeuroImage* 29, no. 3 (2006): 706–11, doi:10.1016/j.neuroimage.2005.08.019.

52. Doug Hyun Han et al., "Brain Activity and Desire for Internet Video Game Play," *Comprehensive Psychiatry* 52, no. 1 (2011): 88–95, doi:10.1016/j.comppsych.2010.04.004.

53. Michelle Brandt, "Video games activate reward regions of brain in men more than women, Stanford study finds," Stanford Medicine, February 4, 2008, https://med.

stanford.edu/news/all-news/2008/02/video-games-activate-reward-regions-of-brain-in-men-more-than-women-stanford-study-finds.html.

54. Hyun Han et al., "Brain Activity."

55. Lisa Kurth and Robert Haussmann, "Perinatal Pitocin as an Early ADHD Biomarker: Neurodevelopmental Risk?" *Journal of Attention Disorders* 15, no. 5 (2011): 423–31, doi:10.1177/1087054710397800.

56. Liz Szabo, "Brain Changes of Autism May Begin in the Womb," *USA Today*, August 12, 2013, http://www.usatoday.com/story/news/nation/2013/08/12/autism-labor-induction/2641391.

57. National Partnership for Women & Families, "What Are Some Factors Driving Use of Induced Labor in the United States?" data brief of Listening to Mothers III survey (May 2013), *Transforming Maternity Care* (blog), http://transform.childbirthconnection.org/reports/listeningtomothers/induction.

58. National Partnership for Women & Families, "The Role of Hormones in Childbirth," Childbirth Connection, accessed October 17, 2017, http://www.childbirthconnection.org/maternity-care/role-of-hormones/

59. Françoise Moos and Philippe Richard, "Excitatory Effect of Dopamine on Oxytocin and Vasopressin Reflex Releases in the Rat,"*Brain Research* 241, no. 2 (1982): 249–60, doi:10.1016/0006-8993(82)91061-7.

60. Diana Mahoney, "Maternal Depression Predicts ADHD in Kids," *Clinical Psychiatry News*, July 1, 2007, http://www.mdedge.com/clinicalpsychiatrynews/article/22771/pediatrics/maternal-depression-predicts-adhd-kids.

61. J. Panksepp. "Can PLAY Diminish ADHD and Facilitate the Construction of the Social Brain?" *Journal of the Canadian Academy of Child and Adolescent Psychiatry*, 2007; 16(2), 57–66.

62. Michael Murray, "Roughhousing with Dad Crucial for Development, say Researchers," ABC News, June 17, 2011, http://abcnews.go.com/Health/dads-roughhousing-children-crucial-early-development/story?id=13868801.

63. Crystal A. Clark and Alain Dagher, "The Role of Dopamine in Risk Taking: A Specific Look at Parkinson's Disease and Gambling," *Frontiers in Behavioral Neuroscience* 8 (2014): 196, doi:10.3389/fnbeh.2014.00196.

64. Northeastern University, "How Humans Bond: The Brain Chemistry Revealed," *ScienceDaily*, 17 February 2017, https://www.sciencedaily.com/releases/2017/02/170217160940.htm.

65. Emory Health Sciences, "How Dads Bond with Toddlers," *Neuroscience News*, February 17, 2017, http://neurosciencenews.com/oxytocin-dad-bonding-6127.

66. Gert-Jan Meerkerk, Regina J. J. M. van den Eijnden, and Henk Garretsen, "Predicting Compulsive Internet Use: It's All about Sex!" *CyberPsychology & Behavior* 9, no. 1 (2006): 95–103, doi:10.1089/cpb.2006.9.95.

67. YBOP, "Cambridge University Study: Internet Porn Addiction Mirrors Drug Addiction," Your Brain on Porn, July 10, 2014, http://yourbrainonporn.com/cambridge-university-brain-scans-find-porn-addiction.

68. YBOP, "Men: Does Frequent Ejaculation Cause a Hangover?" Your Brain on Porn, May 17, 2012, http://www.yourbrainonporn.com/node/941.

69. Stuart Brody and Tillmann H. C. Kruger, "The Post-orgasmic Prolactin Increase Following Intercourse Is Greater than Following Masturbation and Suggests Greater Satiety," *Biological Psychology* 71, no. 3 (2006): 312–15, doi:10.1016/j.biopsycho.2005.06.008.

70. Heather A. Rupp and Kim Wallen, "Sex Differences in Response to Visual Sexual Stimuli: A Review," *Archives of Sexual Behavior* 37, no. 2 (2008): 206–18, doi:10.1007/s10508-007-9217-9.

71. YBOP, "Cambridge University Study."

72. Amber J. Tresca, "Can Breastfeeding an Infant Help Protect Him from Developing IBD?" VeryWell, Dotdash, December 5, 2016, https://www.verywell.com/preventing-ibd-with-breastfeeding-1942673.

73. B.Y. Park, G. Wilson, J. Berger, M. Christman, B. Reina, A.P. Doan. "Is Internet Pornography Causing Sexual Dysfunctions? A Review with Clinical Reports," *Behavioral Sciences*, 2016, 6(3),17.

74. Kristen Michaelis, "New Research Confirms ADHD Caused by Food," Food Renegade, accessed October 17, 2017, http://www.foodrenegade.com/new-research-confirms-adhd-caused-by-food.

75. Connor McKeown et al., "Association of Constipation and Fecal Incontinence with Attention-Deficit/Hyperactivity Disorder," *Pediatrics* 132, no. 5 (2013): e1210–15, doi:10.1542/peds.2013-1580.

76. Gaia Health, "Glyophasphate: Chronic Disease Degeneration," *Gaia* (blog), April 26, 2013, archived February 19, 2014, http://web.archive.org/web/20140219112346/http://gaia-health.com/gaia-blog/2013-04-26/xxx-3/

77. Gaia Health, "Glyophosphate."

78. http://orthomolecular.org/resources/omns/v09n23.shtml.

79. Gaia Health, "Glyophosphate."

80. Anthony Samsel and Stephanie Seneff, "Glyphosate's Suppression of Cytochrome P450 Enzymes and Amino Acid Biosynthesis by the Gut Microbiome: Pathways to Modern Diseases," *Entropy* 15 (2013): 1416–63, doi:10.3390/e15041416.

81. Kate Ramsayer, "Slowing Puberty? Pesticide May Hinder Development in Boys," *ScienceNews*, December 10, 2003, https://www.sciencenews.org/article/slowing-puberty-pesticide-may-hinder-development-boys.

82. Tyrone B. Hayes et al., "Hermaphroditic, Demasculinized Frogs After Exposure to the Herbicide Atrazine at Low Ecologically Relevant Doses," *PNAS* 99, no. 8 (2002): 5476, doi:10.1073/pnas.082121499; Harvard University, "Feminization of Male Frogs in the Wild," *Nature*, October 31, 2002, doi:10.1038/news021028-7.

83. Elsevier, "Six Environmental Research Studies Reveal Critical Health Risks from Plastic," *ScienceDaily*, October 3, 2008, https://www.sciencedaily.com/releases/2008/10/081002172257.htm.

84. Yoshinori Masuo et al., "Motor Hyperactivity Caused by a Deficit in Dopaminergic Neurons and the Effects pf Endocrine Disruptors: A Study Inspired by the Physiological Roles of PACAP in the Brain," *Regulatory Peptides* 123, nos. 1–3 (2004): 225–34, doi:10.1016/j.regpep.2004.05.010.

85. I. Colón et al., "Identification of Phthalate Esters in the Serum of Young Puerto Rican Girls with Premature Breast Development," *Environmental Health Perspectives* 108, no. 9 (2000): 895–900, https://www.ncbi.nlm.nih.gov/pmc/articles/PMC2556932.

86. "Human Health: Early Life Exposures & Lifetime Health," Endocrine Disruptor Research, EPA, archived March 18, 2015, http://web.archive.org/web/20150318001656/http://www.epa.gov/research/endocrinedisruption/early-life-exp.htm.

87. Sabrina Tavernise, "F.D.A. Makes It Official: BPA Can't Be Used in Baby Bottles and Cups," *New York Times*, July 17, 2012, http://www.nytimes.com/2012/07/18/science/fda-bans-bpa-from-baby-bottles-and-sippy-cups.html.

88. Mina Kim and Molly Samuel, "Are BPA-Free Plastics Any Safer?" KQED Science, March 5, 2014, https://ww2.kqed.org/science/2014/03/05/are-bpa-free-plastics-any-safer.

89. Nancy Shute, "Gluten Goodbye: One-Third of Americans Say They're Trying to Shun It," *The Salt* (blog), NPR, March 9, 2013, http://www.npr.org/blogs/thesalt/2013/03/09/173840841/gluten-goodbye-one-third-of-americans-say-theyre-trying-to-shun-it.

90. http://www.motherjones.com/environment/2015/02/bread-gluten-rising-yeast-health-problem/.

91. Joseph Mercola, "Children with ADHD? Stop Feeding Them Gluten," Mercola, November 2, 2011, http://articles.mercola.com/sites/articles/archive/2011/11/02/gluten-contribute-to-adhd.aspx.

92. Serena Gordon, "Allergies, Asthma Show Links to ADHD," Health Day, August 22, 2013, https://consumer.healthday.com/respiratory-and-allergy-information-2/food-allergy-news-16/allergies-asthma-show-links-to-adhd-study-679471.html.

93. Courtney Hutchison, "ADHD from Allergy? Study Shows Benefit from Diet Changes," ABC News, February 4, 2011, http://abcnews.go.com/Health/Allergies/adhd-food-allergy-case-restricting-diet/story?id=12832958.

94. Hutchison, "ADHD from Allergy?"

95. Deborah C. Rice, "Parallels Between Attention Deficit Hyperactivity Disorder and Behavioral Deficits Produced by Neurotoxic Exposure in Monkeys," *Environmental Health Perspectives* 108, suppl. 3 (June 2000): 405–8, https://www.ncbi.nlm.nih.gov/pmc/articles/PMC1637819/pdf/envhper00312-0043.pdf.

96. Timothy J. Maher and Judith Wurtman, "Possible Neurologic Effects of Aspartame, a Widely Used Food Additive," *Environmental Health Perspectives* 75 (1987): 53–57, doi:10.2307/3430576.

97. J. P. Finn and G. H. Lord, "Neurotoxicity Studies on Sucralose and Its Hydrolysis Products with Special Reference to Histopathologic and Ultrastructure Changes," *Food and Chemical Toxicology* 38, suppl. 2 (2000): S7–17, doi:10.1016/S0278-6915(00)00024-7.

98. Clementina M. van Rijn, Enrico Marani, and Wop J. Rietveld, "The Neurotoxic Effect of Monosodium Glutamate (MSG) on the Retinal Ganglion Cells of the Albino Rat," *Histology and Histopathology* 1, no. 3 (1986): 291–5, pmid:2980121.

99. Brian Palmer, "Is Your Veggie Burger Killing You?" *Slate*, April 2010, http://www. slate.com/articles/news_and_politics/explainer/2010/04/is_your_veggie_burger_ killing_you.html.

100. J. G. Joshi, "Aluminum, a Neurotoxin Which Affects Diverse Metabolic Reactions," *Biofactors* 2, no. 3 (1990): 163–69, pmid:2198876.

101. Louis W. Chang, "Neurotoxic effects of mercury: A Review," *Environmental Research* 14, no. 3 (December 1977), 329–73, doi:10.1016/0013-9351(77)90044-5.

102. Nick Meyer, "Fluoride Officially Classified as a Neurotoxin in One of World's Most Prestigious Medical Journals," AltHealthWORKS, December 20, 2015, http:// althealthworks.com/2262/fluoride-officially-classified-as-a-neurotoxin-by-worlds- most-prestigious-medical-journal/.

103. Michael P. Byrne et al., "Fermentation, Purification, and Efficacy of a Recombinant Vaccine Candidate against Botulinum Neurotoxin Type F from *Pichia pastoris*," *Protein Expression and Purification* 18, no. 3 (2000): 327–37, doi:10.1006/ prep.2000.1200.

104. "Chlorine," Environmental Protection Agency (EPA), Publication No. 7782-50-5, last updated January 2000, https://www.epa.gov/sites/production/files/2016-09/ documents/chlorine.pdf.

105. Saundra Young, "Putting the next generation of brains in danger," CNN, February 17, 2014, http://www.cnn.com/2014/02/14/health/chemicals-children-brains/ index.html.

106. EHANS, "One Chance."

107. Stephanie Smith, "Toxic Chemicals Finding Their Way into the Womb," CNN, July 28, 2010, www.cnn.com/2010/HEALTH/06/01/backpack.cord.blood.

108. Jonathan Benson, "When Pregnant Women Take Tylenol, Their Children Are More Likely to Be Born with Autism," *Natural News*, December 1, 2013, http://www. naturalnews.com/043087_Tylenol_autism_pregnant_women.html.

109. Diane McLaren, "Do Fruits & Veggies Have Enough Nutrients Today," Healthy You Naturally, http://www.healthyyounaturally.com/edu/enough_nutrients.htm.

110. Mike Barrett, "Analysis Finds Monsanto's GM Corn Nutritionally Dead, Highly Toxic," Natural Society, April 28, 2013, http://naturalsociety.com/ analysis-monsanto-gm-corn-nutritionally-dead-toxic.

111. Susan Scutti, "Nutritional Value Of Corn: Does GMO Corn Contain The Same Nutrients?" *Medical Daily*, June 4, 2013, http://www.medicaldaily.com/ nutritional-value-corn-does-gmo-corn-contain-same-nutrients-246496.

112. "Micronutrient Deficiencies," Nutrition, World Health Organization, accessed October 18, 2017, http://www.who.int/nutrition/topics/idd/en.

113. Fluoride Action Network, overview of the National Research Council's 2006 report, accessed October 18, 2017, http://fluoridealert.org/researchers/nrc/findings.

114. "Teen concussions increase risk for depression," Health Behavior News Service, Center for Advancing Health, Science Daily, last updated January 9, 2014, www. sciencedaily.com/releases/2014/01/140109175502.htm.

115. Nordqvist, "Concussions."

116. Leo Doran, "Military Struggling with Traumatic Brain Injury Fallout," *InsideSources*, September 8, 2017, http://www.insidesources.com/military-traumatic-brain-injury-fallout.

117. Health Behavior News Service (HBNS), part of the Center for Advancing Health, "Teen Concussions Increase Risk for Depression," *ScienceDaily*, January 9, 2014, http://www.sciencedaily.com/releases/2014/01/140109175502.htm.

118. HBNS, "Teen Concussions."

CHAPTER 31: NATURAL SOLUTIONS TO RESTORE DOPAMINE FUNCTION

1. P. Mickie et al., "Oral Supplementation with Whey Proteins Increases Plasma Glutathione Levels of HIV-Infected Patients," *European Journal of Clinical Investigation* 31, no. 2 (2001): 171–78, doi:10.1046/j.1365-2362.2001.00781.x.

2. G. Bounous and P. Gold, "The Biological Activity of Undenatured Dietary Whey Proteins: Role of Glutathione," *Clinical & Investigative Medicine* 14, no. 4 (1991): 296–309, pmid:1782728.

3. P. Tosukhowong et al., "Biochemical and Clinical Effects of Whey Protein Supplementation in Parkinson's Disease: A Pilot Study," *Journal of the Neurological Sciences* 367 (2016): 162–70, doi:10.1016/j.jns.2016.05.056.

4. Andrew Weil, "A New Approach to Parkinson's?" Weil Lifestyle, March 10, 2009, https://www.drweil.com/health-wellness/body-mind-spirit/disease-disorders/a-new-approach-to-parkinsons.

5. Jacques Fernandez de Santos, "An Interview with Prof. Marco Ruggiero: Understanding the GI and Brain Microbiome and the Role of GcMAF in Harmonizing the Immune System with the Microbiome Populations," *Townsend Letter* (October 2016), http://www.townsendletter.com/Oct2016/ruggiero1016.html.

6. Dario Siniscalco et al., "The *in vitro* GcMAF Effects on Endocannabinoid System Transcriptionomics, Receptor Formation, and Cell Activity of Autism-Derived Macrophages," *Journal of Neuroinflammation* 11 (20140): 78, doi:10.1186/1742-2094-11-78.

7. http://www.springer.com/us/book/9781402082306.

8. M. A. Buccellato et al., "Heat Shock Protein Expression in Brain: A Protective Role Spanning Intrinsic Thermal Resistance and Defense Against Neurotropic Viruses," *Progress in Brain Research* 162 (2007): 395–415, doi:10.1016/S0079-6123(06)62019-0.

9. Jon Hamilton, "Scientists Say Child's Play Helps Build a Better Brain," *Morning Edition*, August 6, 2014, transcript, nprEd, NPR, http://www.npr.org/sections/ed/2014/08/06/336361277/scientists-say-childs-play-helps-build-a-better-brain.

10. Mara Betsch, "Brain Games and Exercise: A Drug-Free Treatment for ADHD?" *Health*, February 29, 2016, http://www.health.com/health/condition-article/0,,20252861,00.html.

11. Stephanie Liou, "Neuroplasticity," *HOPES* (blog), Huntington's Outreach Project for Education, at Stanford, June 26, 2010, https://www.stanford.edu/group/hopes/cgi-bin/wordpress/2010/06/neuroplasticity.

12. Anat Baniel, "More Help for Children with Special Needs," Anat Baniel Method, accessed October 18, 2017, http://www.anatbanielmethod.com/children/more-help-for-children-with-special-needs.

13. Baniel, "Movement Techniques."

14. Gwen Dewar, "Music and Intelligence," Parenting Science, accessed October 18, 2017, http://www.parentingscience.com/music-and-intelligence.html.

15. Urban Dove Charter School, "Full Proposal" (application to the New York State Education Department, Albany, September 2010), http://www.p12.nysed.gov/psc/documents/Full_App_Urban_Dove_CS_Sept_2010REDACT.pdf.

16. Cathy Malchiodi, "Art Therapy in Schools" (paper, International Art Therapy Organization & Art Therapy Alliance, 2010), archived March 16, 2012, http://web.archive.org/web/20120316131619/http://www.internationalarttherapy.org/SchoolArtTherapy.pdf.

17. Ellen Winner and Lois Hetland, "Does Studying the Arts Enhance Academic Achievement?" *Education Week*, November 1, 2000, http://www.edweek.org/ew/articles/2000/11/01/09winner.h20.html.

18. Brian Mayne, "Goal Mapping for Kids," Lift International, archived April 1, 2015, http://web.archive.org/web/20150401173509/http://www.liftinternational.com/goal-mapping/kids.html

19. Brauer Natural Medicine, "What Does Research Say About Homeopathic Medicines?" accessed October 18, 2017, https://www.brauer.com.au/what-does-research-say-about-homeopathic-medicines.

20. Wayne B. Jonas, Ted J. Kaptchuk, and Klaus Linde, "A Critical Overview of Homeopathy," *Annals in Internal Medicine* 138, no. 5 (2003): 393–99, doi:10.7326/0003-4819-138-5-200303040-00009.

21. Klaus Linde et al., "Are the Clinical Effects of Homoeopathy Placebo Effects? A Meta-analysis of Placebo-Controlled Trials," *Lancet* 350, no. 9081 (1997): 834–43, doi:10.1016/S0140-6736(97)02293-9.

22. Jos Kleijnen, Paul Knipschild, and Gerben ter Riet, "Clinical Trials of Homoeopathy," *British Medical Journal* 302 (1991): 316–23, https://www.ncbi.nlm.nih.gov/pmc/articles/PMC1668980/pdf/bmj00112-0022.pdf.

23. Dana Ullman, *Homeopathic Family Medicine: Evidence Based Nanopharmacology* (self-pub., Homeopathic Educational Services, 2005–), e-book.

24. See the American Chiropractic Association's webpage for news releases, www.acatoday.org/News-Publications/Newsroom/News-Releases.

25. Farzad Farahmand, "Homeopathic Wonders: In Memory of Dr. Salar Farahmand," Homeopathic Wonders, accessed October 18, 2017, http://www.homeopathicwonders.com/in-memory-of-dr-salar.

26. Anat Baniel, "Movement Techniques That Keep You Young," interview for the Future of Health Now 2012 (conference), San Francisco, CA, July 10, 2012; see also her book *Kids Beyond Limits* (New York: TarcherPerigee, 2012).

27. Benjamin Wedro, "Concussion," ed. Melissa Conrad Stöppler, MedicineNet, reviewed on November 6, 2015, http://www.medicinenet.com/brain_concussion/page4.htm.

28. Edward H. Chapman et al., "Homeopathic Treatment of Mild Traumatic Brain Injury: A Randomized, Double-Blind, Placebo-Controlled Clinical Trial," *Journal of Head Trauma Rehabilitation* 14, no. 6 (1999): 521–42, doi:10.1097/00001199-199912000-00002.

29. Dawson Church et al., "Psychological Trauma Symptom Improvement in Veterans Using Emotional Freedom Techniques: A Randomized Controlled Trial," *Journal of Nervous and Mental Disease* 201, no. 2 (2013): 153–60, doi:10.1097/NMD.0b013e31827f6351.

30. Chuck Emerson Media Services "Spas in Germany," How to Germany, accessed October 19, 2017, http://www.howtogermany.com/pages/spas.html.

31. Fiona Macrae, "A Hot Bath 'Helps Soothe the Symptoms of Autism and Makes Children More Sociable,'" *Daily Mail*, December 13, 2013, http://www.dailymail.co.uk/health/article-2522714/Autism-symptoms-soothed-hot-bath.html.

32. Antonio De Maio, "Heat Shock Proteins: Facts, Thoughts, and Dreams," *Shock* 11, no. 1 (1999): 1–12, doi:10.1097/00024382-199901000-00001.

33. Darren C. Henstridge, Martin Whitham, and Mark A. Febbraio, "Chaperoning to the Metabolic Party: The Emerging Therapeutic Role of Heat-Shock Proteins in Obesity and Type 2 Diabetes," *Molecular Metabolism* 3, no. 8 (2014): 781–93, doi:10.1016/j.molmet.2014.08.003.

34. Rui-Chun Lu et al., "Heat Shock Protein 70 in Alzheimer's Disease," *BioMed Research International* 2014 (2014): 435203, doi:10.1155/2014/43520.

35. Salynn Boyles, "Report: Fever Improves Autism Symptoms," WebMD, December 3, 2007, http://www.webmd.com/brain/autism/news/20071203/report-fever-improves-autism-symptoms.

36. Boyles, "Fever Improves Autism Symptoms."

37. See https://advancedbrain.com/the-listening-program-research.

38. Pirkko Huttunen, Leena Kokko, and Virpi Ylijukuri, "Winter Swimming Improves General Well-Being," *International Journal of Circumpolar Health* 63, no. 2 (2004): 140–44, doi:10.3402/ijch.v63i2.17700.

39. De Maio, "Heat Shocks Proteins."

40. Minna L. Hannuksela and Samer Ellahham, "Benefits and Risks of Sauna Bathing," *American Journal of Medicine* 110, no. 2 (2001): 118–26, doi:10.1016/S0002-9343(00)00671-9.

41. Rose Welton, "Children and Hot Tubs," Livestrong, last updated August 14, 2017, http://www.livestrong.com/article/271400-children-hot-tubs.

42. Courtney Hutchison, "ADHD from Allergy? Study Shows Benefit from Diet Changes," ABC News Medical Unit, February 4, 2011, http://abcnews.go.com/Health/Allergies/adhd-food-allergy-case-restricting-diet/story?id=12832958.

43. A. J. Wakefield et al., "Enterocolitis in Children with Developmental Disorders," *American Journal of Gastroenterology* 95 (2000): 2285–95, doi:10.1111/j.1572-0241.2000.03248.x.

44. For research on the topic, see www.feingold.org/Research/PDFstudies/list.html.

45. Thomas J. Sobotka, "ADHD in Childhood and Related Problem Behaviors," interim toxicology review memorandum, September 1, 2010, attachment 4, exhibit 1, FDA/

CFSAN March 30–31, 2011, Food Advisory Committee, http://www.fda.gov/downloads/AdvisoryCommittees/CommitteesMeetingMaterials/FoodAdvisoryCommittee/UCM248124.pdf.

46. Georgia Ede, "Food Sensitivities and ADHD," *Diagnosis: Diet* (blog), December 21, 2012, http://diagnosisdiet.com/food-sensitivities-and-adhd.

47. See www.gapsdiet.com.

48. Connor McKeown et al., "Association of Constipation and Fecal Incontinence with Attention-Deficit/Hyperactivity Disorder," *Pediatrics* 132, no. 5 (2013): e1210–15, doi:10.1542/peds.2013-1580.

49. Elizabeth C. Verna and Susan Lucak, "Use of Probiotics in Gastrointestinal Disorders: What to Recommend?" *Therapeutic Advances in Gastroenterology* 3, no. 5 (2010): 307–19, doi:10.1177/1756283X10373814.

50. Javier A. Bravo et al., "Ingestion of *Lactobacillus* Strain Regulates Emotional Behavior and Central GABA Receptor Expression in a Mouse via the Vagus Nerve," *PNAS* 108, no. 38 (2011): 16050–55, doi:10.1073/pnas.1102999108.

51. Alper Evrensel and Mehmet Emin Ceylan, "The Gut-Brain Axis: The Missing Link in Depression," *Clinical Psychopharmacology and Neuroscience* 13, no. 3 (2015): 239–44, doi:10.9758/cpn.2015.13.3.239.

CHAPTER 32: NATURAL SUPPLEMENTS FOR BETTER BRAIN PERFORMANCE

1. Jana Trebatická et al., "Treatment of ADHD with French Maritime Pine Bark Extract, Pycnogenol," *European Child & Adolescent Psychiatry* 15, no. 6 (2006): 329–35, doi:10.1007/s00787-006-0538-3.

2. Rachel Elizabeth, "OPC-3 Isotonix for ADHD," Livestrong, August 14, 2017, http://www.livestrong.com/article/525476-opc-3-isotonix-for-adhd.

3. Mia Ericson et al., "Taurine Elevates Dopamine Levels in the Rat Nucleus Accumbens; Antagonism by Strychnine," *European Journal of Neuroscience* 23, no. 12 (2006): 3225–29, doi:10.1111/j.1460-9568.2006.04868.x.

4. Center for the Improvement of Human Functioning International, "Eat, Exercise and Excel" (2004), YouTube video, 28:56, posted by Riordan Clinic, September 15, 2011, http://youtu.be/Jf4yJwAORfE.

5. David Perlmutter, "Parkinson's Glutathione Therapy," YouTube video, 2:55, posted by ProtandimAntiAging (LifeVantage), November 5, 2010, http://youtu.be/KWuOezgVHdI.

6. Marty Hinz, Alvin Stein, and Thomas Uncini, "Amino Acid Management of Parkinson's Disease: A Case Study," *International Journal of General Medicine* 4 (2011): 165–74, doi:10.2147/IJGM.S16621.

7. Marty Hinz et al., "Treatment of Attention Deficit Hyperactivity Disorder with Monoamine Amino Acid Precursors and Organic Cation Transporter Assay Interpretation," *Neuropsychiatric Disease and Treatment* 7 (2011): 31–38, doi:10.2147/NDT.S16270.

8. Lloyd A. Horrocks and Young K. Yeo, "Health Benefits of Docosahexaenoic Acid (DHA)," *Pharmacological Research* 40, no. 3 (1999): 211–25, http://citeseerx.ist.psu.edu/viewdoc/download?doi=10.1.1.334.6891&rep=rep1&type=pdf.

9. NewsTarget, "Fish Oils Treat ADHD Better than Prescription Drugs, Study Shows," *Natural News,* June 20, 2006, http://www.naturalnews.com/019432_fish_oil_nutrition.html.

10. Kalpana Joshi et al., "Supplementation with Flax Oil and Vitamin C Improves the Outcome of Attention Deficit Hyperactivity Disorder (ADHD)," *Prostaglandins, Leukotrienes and Essential Fatty Acids* 74 (2006): 17–21, doi:10.1016/j.plefa.2005.10.001.

11. ADHD Treatment Guide, "10 Ways Carnitine Can Help Treat ADHD," *ADHD Treatments* (blog), April 17, 2009, http://adhd-treatment-options.blogspot.com/2009/04/10-ways-carnitine-can-help-treat-adhd.html.

12. Yael Richter et al., "The Effect of Soybean-Derived Phosphatidylserine on Cognitive Performance in Elderly with Subjective Memory Complaints: A Pilot Study," *Clinical Interventions in Aging* 8 (2013): 557–63, doi:10.2147/CIA.S40348.

13. I. Manor et al., "The Effect of Phosphatidylserine Containing Omega3 Fatty-Acids on Attention-Deficit Hyperactivity Disorder Symptoms in Children: A Double-Blind Placebo-Controlled Trial, Followed by an Open-Label Extension," *European Psychiatry* 27, no. 5 (2012): 335–42, doi:10.1016/j.eurpsy.2011.05.004.

14. S. Hirayama et al., "The Effect of Phosphatidylserine Administration on Memory and Symptoms of Attention-Deficit Hyperactivity Disorder: A Randomised, Double-Blind, Placebo-Controlled Clinical Trial," *Journal of Human Nutrition and Dietetics* 27, suppl. 2 (2014): 284–91, doi:10.1111/jhn.12090.

15. M. Mousain-Bosc et al., "Improvement of Neurobehavioral Disorders in Children Supplemented with Magnesium-Vitamin B6: II. Pervasive Developmental Disorder-Autism," *Magnesium Research* 19, no. 1 (2006): 46–52, pmid:16846100.

16. Nancy Mullan, "MTHFR+ and Lithium," *Chronic Disease Recovery* (blog), April 30, 2013, https://chronicdiseaserecovery.wordpress.com/2013/04/30/mthfr-and-lithium.

17. Abdulbari Bener, Azhar O. Khattab, and Mohamad M. Al-Dabbagh, "Is High Prevalence of Vitamin D Deficiency Evidence for Autism Disorder?: In a Highly Endogamous Population," *Journal of Pediatric Neurosciences* 9, no. 3 (2014): 227–33, doi:10.4103/1817-1745.147574.

18. J. J. Rucklidge et al., "Moderators of Treatment Response in Adults with ADHD Treated with a Vitamin-Mineral Supplement," *Progress in Neuro-Psychopharmacology & Biological Psychiatry* 50 (April 2014):163–71, doi:10.1016/j.pnpbp.2013.12.014.

19. Martijn Arns et al., "Geographic Variation in the Prevalence of Attention-Deficit/Hyperactivity Disorder: The Sunny Perspective," *Biological Psychiatry* 74, no. 8 (2013): 585–90, doi:10.1016/j.biopsych.2013.02.010.

20. Mohammad Reza Sharif et al., "The Relationship Between Serum Vitamin D Level and Attention Deficit Hyperactivity Disorder," *Iranian Journal of Child Neurology* 9, no. 4 (Autumn 2015): 48–53, https://www.ncbi.nlm.nih.gov/pmc/articles/PMC4670977.

21. X. Cui et al., "Vitamin D Regulates Tyrosine Hydroxylase Expression: N-Cadherin a Possible Mediator," *Neuroscience* 304 (September 2015): 90–100, doi:10.1016/j.neuroscience.2015.07.048.

22. Eric Konofal, Michel Lecendreux, Juliette Deron, Martine Marchand, Samuele Cortese, Samuele Mohammed Zaïm, Marie Christine Mouren, Isabelle Arnulf, "Effects of Iron Supplementation on Attention Deficit Hyperactivity Disorder in Children," *Pediatric Neurology.* January 2008, 38. 20-6. doi:10.1016/j.pediatrneurol.2007.08.014.

23. Erica L. Unger et al., "Dopamine D_2 Receptor Expression Is Altered by Changes in Cellular Iron Levels in PC12 Cells and Rat Brain Tissue," *Journal of Nutrition* 138, no. 12 (2008): 2487–2494, doi:10.3945/jn.108.095224.

24. E. Konofal et al., "Iron Deficiency in Children with Attention-Deficit/Hyperactivity Disorder," *Archives of Pediatrics & Adolescent Medicine* 158, no. 12 (2004): 1113–15, doi:10.1001/archpedi.158.12.1113.

25. K. Dodig-Curković et al., "The Role of Zinc in the Treatment of Hyperactivity Disorder in Children," *Acta Medica Croatica* 63, no. 4 (2009), 307–13, pmid: 20034331.

26. L. Eugene Arnold, "Zinc for Attention-Deficit/Hyperactivity Disorder: Placebo-Controlled Double-Blind Pilot Trial Alone and Combined with Amphetamine," *Journal of Child and Adolescent Psychopharmacology* 21, no. 1 (February 2011): 1–19, doi:10.1089/cap.2010.0073.

27. L. Eugene Arnold and Robert A. Disilvestro, "Zinc in Attention-Deficit/Hyperactivity Disorder," *Journal of Child and Adolescent Psychopharmacology* 15, no. 4 (2005): 619–27, doi:10.1089/cap.2005.15.619.

28. Peter Lepping and Markus Huber, "Role of Zinc in the Pathogenesis of Attention-Deficit Hyperactivity Disorder," *CNS Drugs* 24, no. 9 (2010): 721–28, doi:10.2165/11537610-000000000-00000.

29. Punita Bhalla, Vijayta Dani Chadha, and D. K. Dhawan, "Effectiveness of Zinc in Modulating Lithium Induced Biochemical and Behavioral Changes in Rat Brain," *Cellular and Molecular Neurobiology* 27, no. 5 (2007): 595–607, doi:10.1007/s10571-007-9146-0.

30. Ewen Callaway, "Star Students, Beware Bipolar Disorder," *New Scientist*, February 3, 2010, https://www.newscientist.com/article/dn18462-star-students-beware-bipolar-disorder.

31. Jonathan V. Wright, "Lithium: The Misunderstood Mineral, Part 1," Tahoma Clinic, May 4, 2010, http://tahomaclinic.com/2010/05/lithium-the-misunderstood-mineral-part-1.

32. G. J. Moore, "Lithium-Induced Increase in Human Brain Grey Matter," *Lancet* 356, no. 9237 (2000): 1241–42, pmid:11072948.

33. Shu-Sen Cui et al., "Prevention of Cannabinoid Withdrawal Syndrome by Lithium: Involvement of Oxytocinergic Neuronal Activation," *Journal of Neuroscience* 21, no. 24 (2001): 9867–76, pmid:11739594.

34. Hashimoto R. et al., "Lithium Induces Brain-Derived NeuroTrophic Factor and Activates TrkB in Rodent Cortical Neurons," *Neuropharmacology* 43, no. 7 (December 2002): 1173–79, pmid: 12504924.

35. Alan E. Lewis, "Lithium: Under-appreciated Brain Nutrient & Protector," Pacific BioLogic, May 1, 2009, https://www.pacificbiologic.com/sites/default/files/Lithium%20article.pdf.

36. E. J. Scharman, "Methods Used to Decrease Lithium Absorption or Enhance Elimination," *Journal of Toxicology: Clinical Toxicology* 35, no. 6 (1997): 601–608, pmid: 9365427.

37. Anna Fels, "Should We All Take a Bit of Lithium?" *New York Times*, September 13, 2014, https://www.nytimes.com/2014/09/14/opinion/sunday/should-we-all-take-a-bit-of-lithium.html.

38. James Phelps, "Lithium for Alzheimer Prevention: What Are We Waiting For?" *Psychiatric Times*, October 7, 2016, http://www.psychiatrictimes.com/bipolar-disorder/lithium-alzheimer-prevention-what-are-we-waiting.

39. John Gray, "ADHD | ADD: Part 1—Understanding Attention Deficit Hyperactivity Disorder," *Mars Venus* (blog), Health Advice, November 28, 2012, http://www.marsvenus.com/blog/john-gray/adhd-add-part-1-understanding-attention-deficit-hyperactivity-disorder.

40. Available at www.marsvenus.com/p/super-foods-shake-for-men.

41. Available at www.marsvenus.com/p/super-minerals-for-men.

CONCLUSION

1. The Altered Mindsets method involves the creation of a "conflict-free zone" and resolving conflicts only during a two-hour "caring and sharing" time that begins with six mindsets that temporarily alter our biologically natural defensiveness and allow us to replace it with emotionally associating criticism with an opportunity to be more deeply loved. You can find an introduction to the method in my book *Women Can't Hear What Men Don't Say* (New York: Berkely, 1999) and updates to the method in my couples' workshops, see http://warrenfarrell.com/where-warren-will-be.

2. Norval Glenn and Barbara Dafoe Whitehead, "MAMA SAYS: A National Survey of Mothers' Attitudes on Fathering" (National Fatherhood Initiative, October 2009), http://www.fatherhood.org/mama-says-survey.

3. Colter Mitchell et al., "Father Loss and Child Telomere Length," *Pediatrics* (July, 2017): e20163245, doi:10.1542/peds.2016-3245.

4. Mitchell et al., "Father Loss."

APPENDIX B

1. Robert Bauserman, "Child Adjustment in Joint-Custody Versus Sole-Custody Arrangements: A Meta-analytic Review," Journal of Family Psychology 16, no. 1 (2002): 91–102; as cited in William V. Fabricius et al., "Custody and Parenting Time: Links to Family Relationships and Well-Being After Divorce," in The Role

of the Father in Child Development, 5th ed., ed. Michael E. Lamb (Hoboken, NJ: John Wiley & Sons, 2010).

2. E. G. Pojman, "Emotional Adjustment of Boys in Sole Custody and Joint Custody Compared with Adjustment of Boys in Happy and Unhappy Marriages" (PhD diss., California Graduate Institute, Los Angeles, 1982).

3. D. A. Luepnitz, "Maternal, Paternal, and Joint Custody: A Study of Families After Divorce" (doctoral dissertation, State University of New York at Buffalo, 1980).

4. B. Jablonska and L. Lindberg, "Risk Behaviours, Victimisation and Mental Distress Among Adolescents in Different Family Structures," *Social Psychiatry and Psychiatric Epidemiology* 42, no. 8 (August 2007): 656–63, doi:10.1007/s00127-007-0210-3.

5. The neural network includes circuits that link emotional importance to experience (the amygdala, the ventral anterior cingulate cortex, the inferior frontal gyrus, insular cortex, and the ventral tegmentum), as well as others that help us impute needs, intentions or mental state to other people (the ventromedial prefrontal cortex, the superior temporal sulcus). See Eyal Abraham et al., "Father's Brain Is Sensitive to Childcare Experiences," *Proceedings of the National Academy of Sciences* 111, no. 27 (2014): 9792–97, doi:10.1073/pnas.1402569111. Description of neural network from Melissa Healy, "Caring for a Baby Changes a Man's Brain, Study Shows," *Los Angeles Times*, May 28, 2014, http://beta.latimes.com/science/sciencenow/la-sci-sn-men-parenting-mom-brain-20140527-story.html.

6. Kyle D. Pruett, "The Nurturing Male: A Longitudinal Study of Primary Nurturing Fathers," in *Fathers and Their Families*, ed. Stanley H. Cath, Alan Gurwitt, and Linda Gunsberg (Hillsdale, NJ: Analytic Press, 1989), 390.

Index

Page numbers followed by *f* indicate illustrations or graphs; page numbers followed by *t* indicate tables; page numbers followed by *n* indicate endnotes.